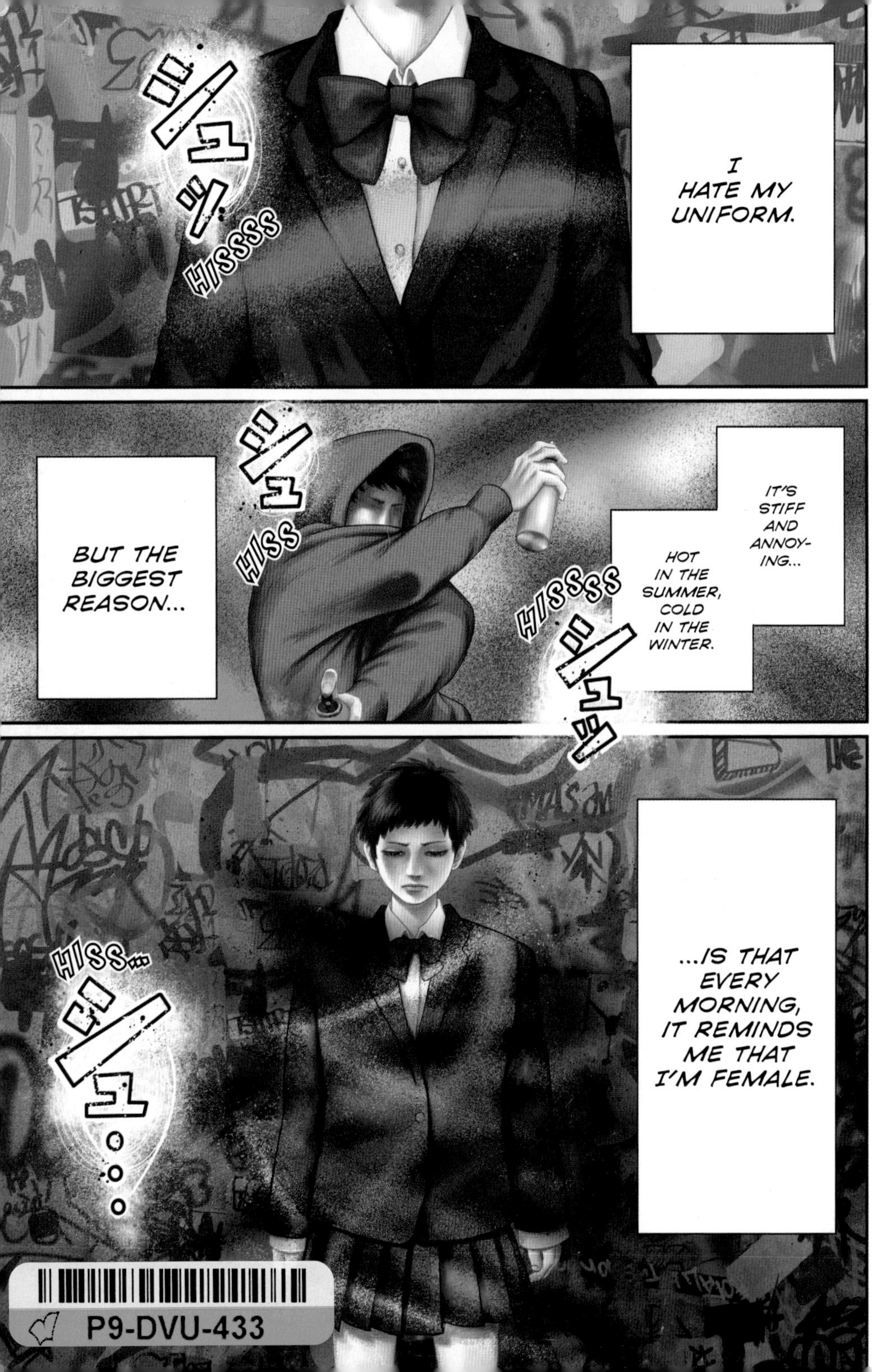
I HATE MY UNIFORM.
HISSSS
IT'S STIFF AND ANNOY-ING...
HOT IN THE SUMMER, COLD IN THE WINTER.
HISSSS
HISS
BUT THE BIGGEST REASON...
...IS THAT EVERY MORNING, IT REMINDS ME THAT I'M FEMALE.
HISS...

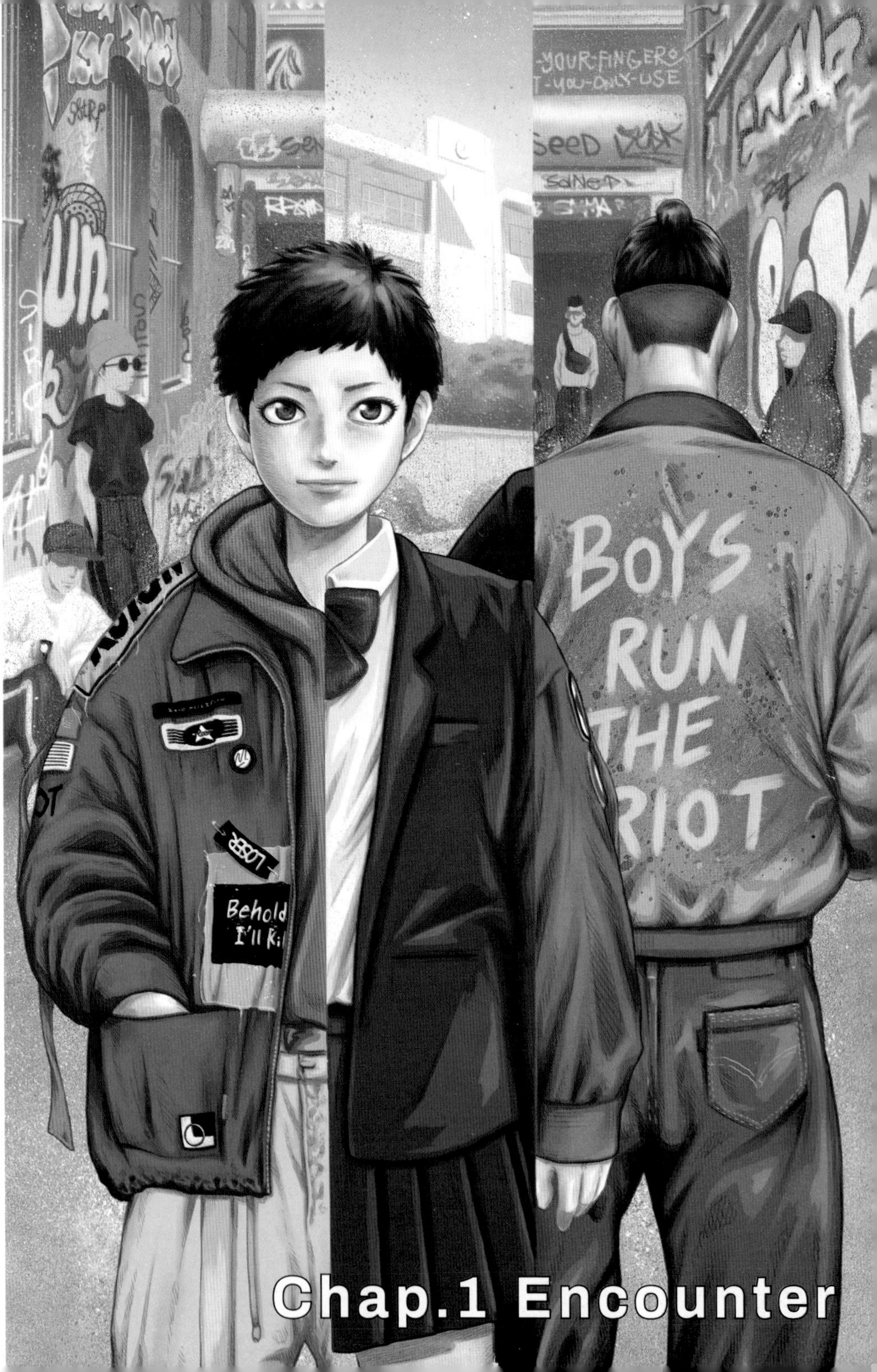
-YOUR-FINGERS
T-YOU-ONLY-USE
SEED
BOYS
RUN
THE
RIOT
LOSER
Behold
I'll Ki
Chap.1 Encounter

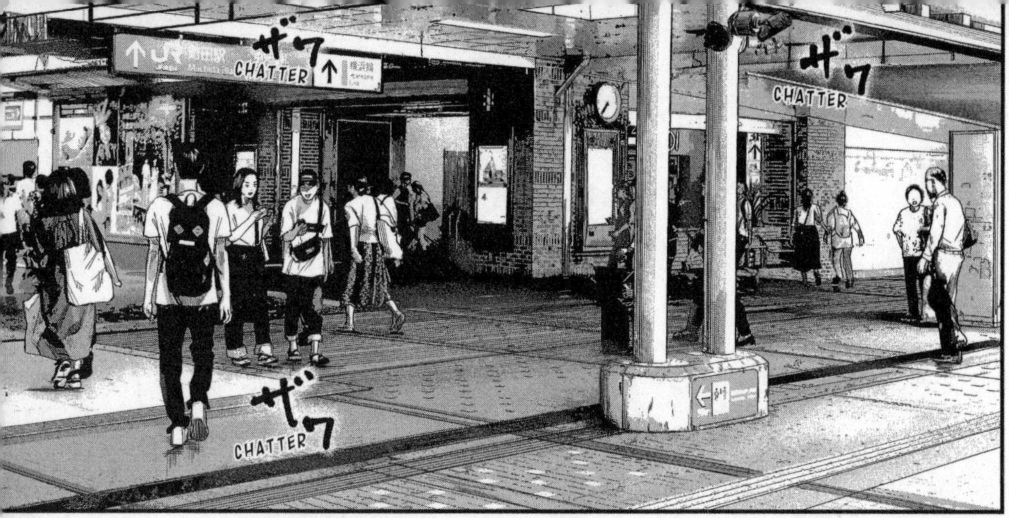
ザワ
CHATTER
ザワ
CHATTER
ザワ
CHATTER

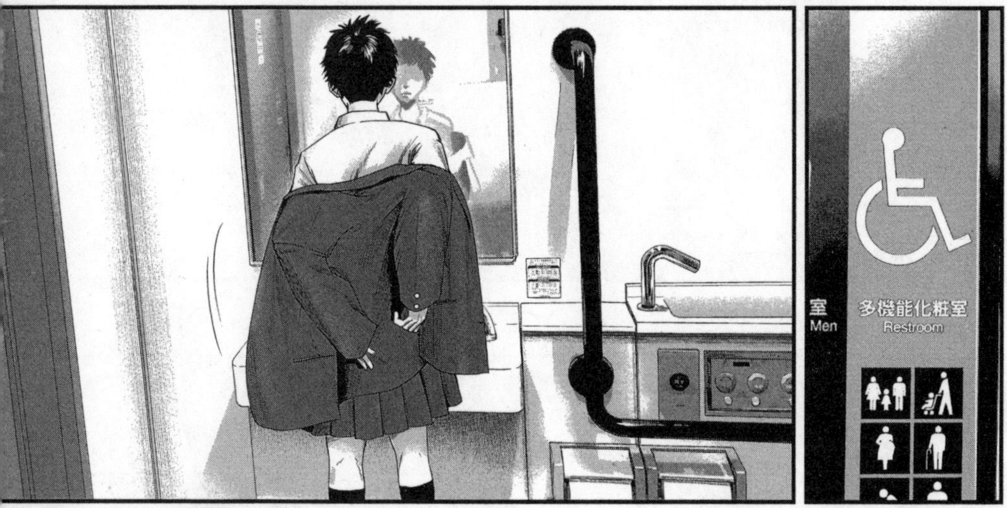
室
Men
多機能化粧室
Restroom

Editor's Note: Please bind responsibly! For more information, see page 226.

Sign: Accessible Restroom

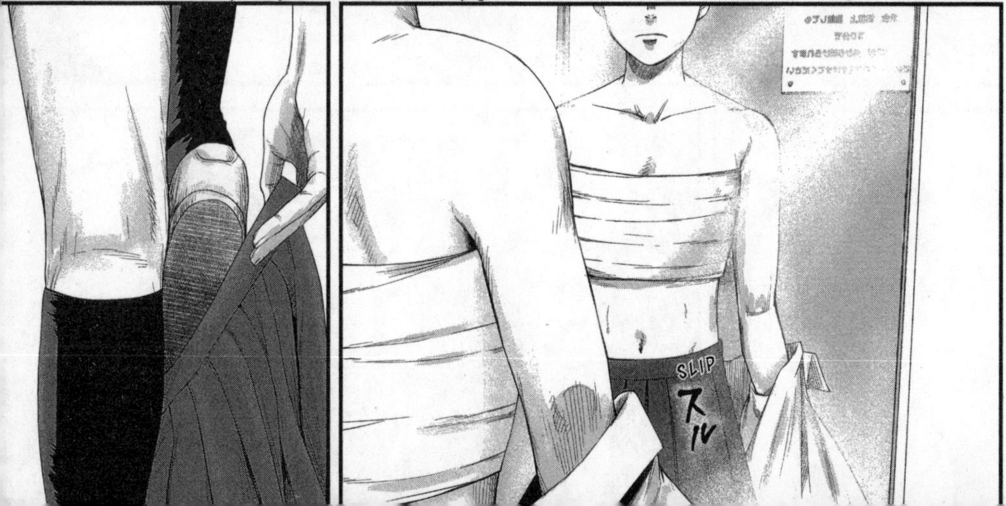
SLIP
スル

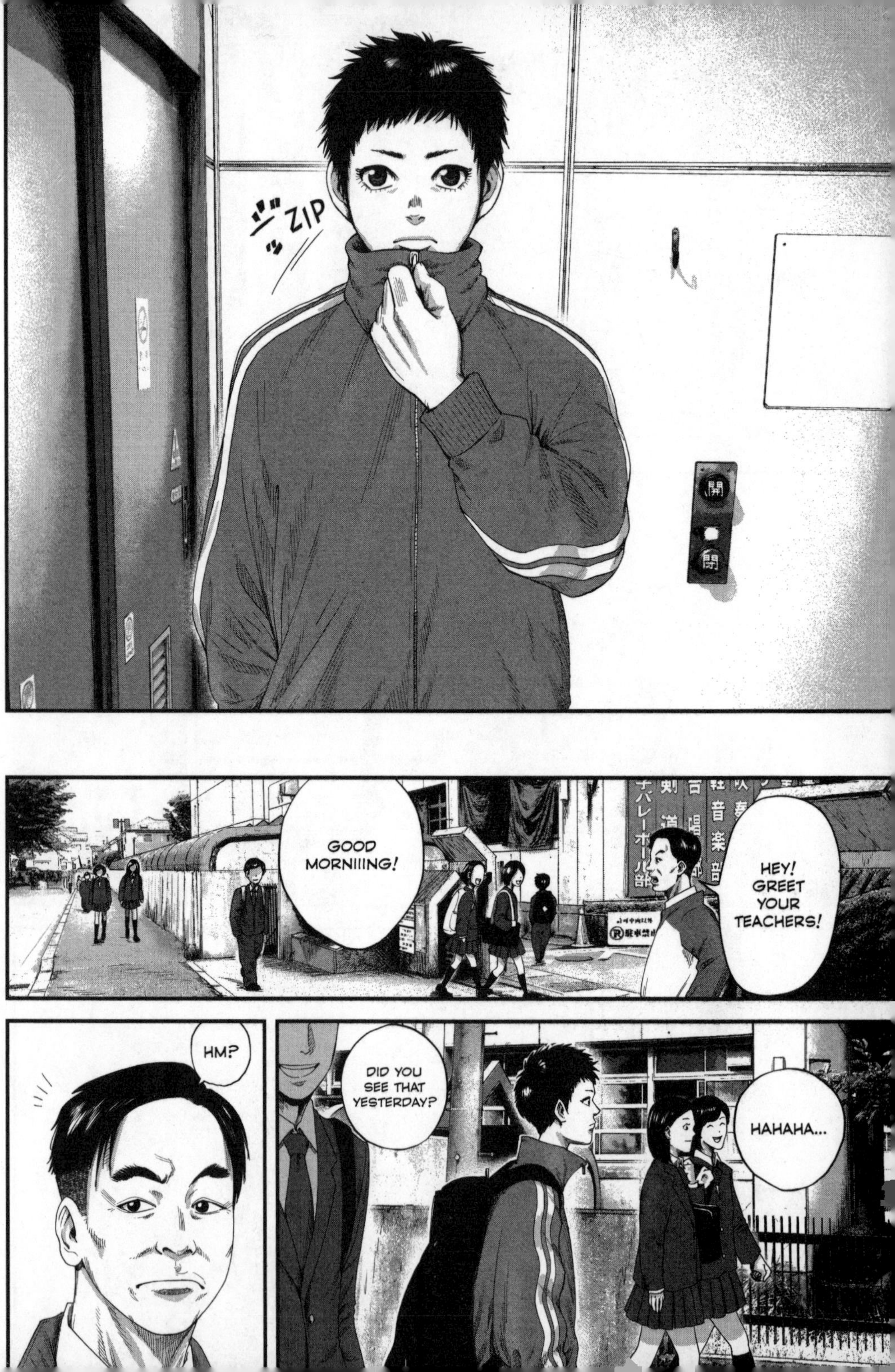
ZIP
HEY! GREET YOUR TEACHERS!
GOOD MORNIIIING!
HAHAHA...
DID YOU SEE THAT YESTERDAY?
HM?

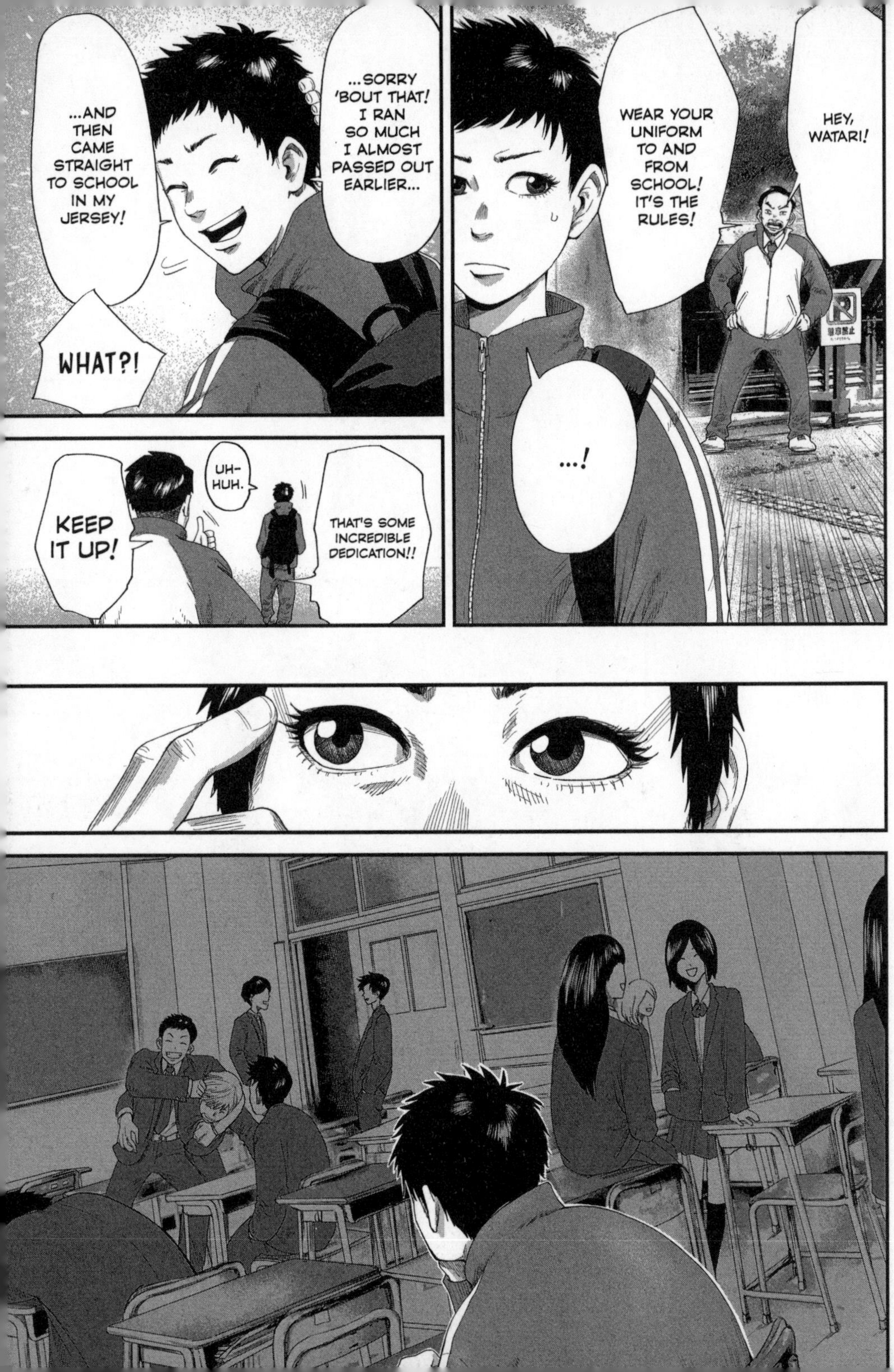
HEY, WATARI!
WEAR YOUR UNIFORM TO AND FROM SCHOOL! IT'S THE RULES!
...!
...SORRY 'BOUT THAT! I RAN SO MUCH I ALMOST PASSED OUT EARLIER...
...AND THEN CAME STRAIGHT TO SCHOOL IN MY JERSEY!
WHAT?!
THAT'S SOME INCREDIBLE DEDICATION!!
UH-HUH.
KEEP IT UP!

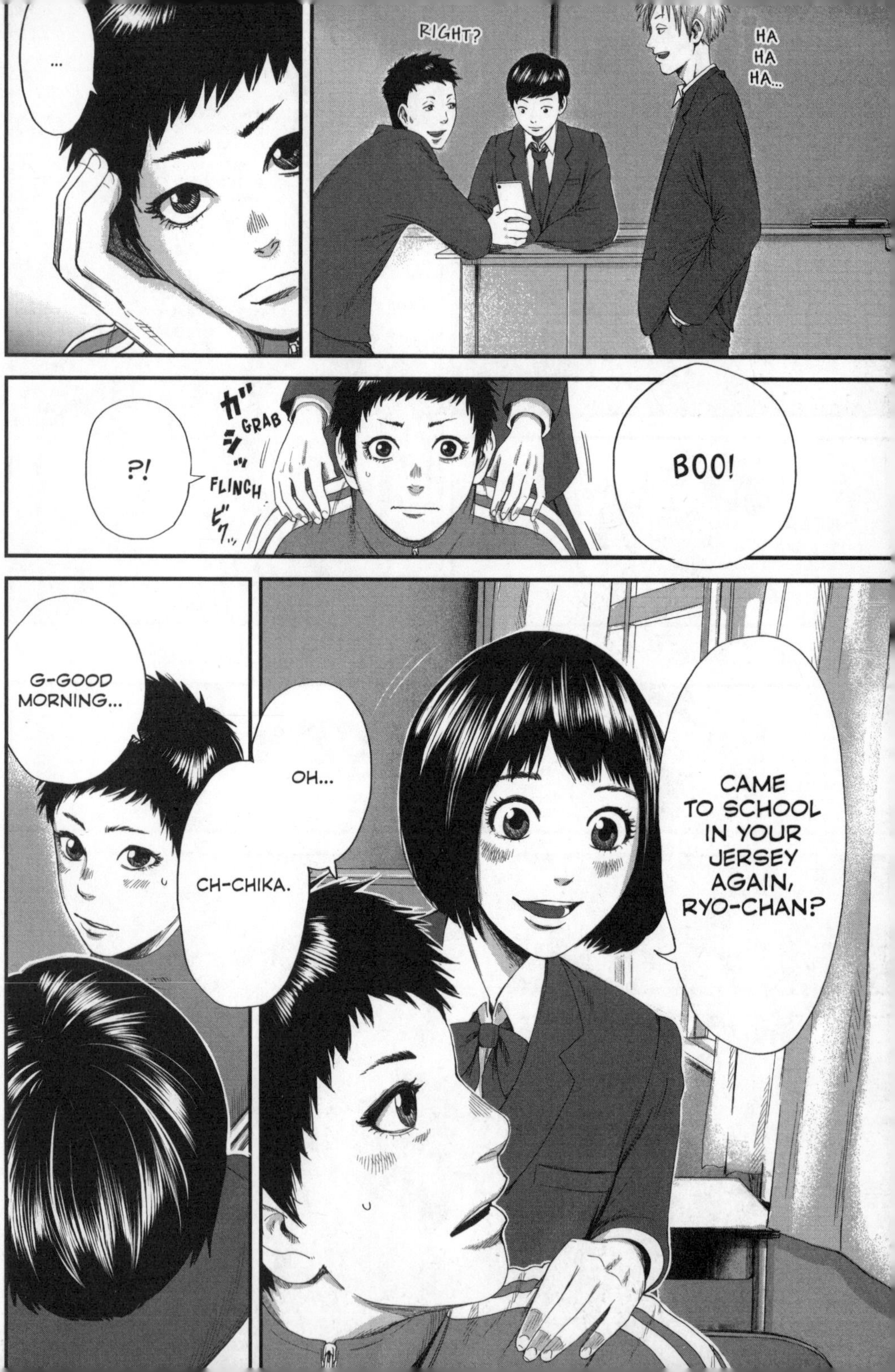
HA HA HA...
RIGHT?
...
BOO!
ガシッ GRAB
ビクッ FLINCH
?!
CAME TO SCHOOL IN YOUR JERSEY AGAIN, RYO-CHAN?
OH... CH-CHIKA.
G-GOOD MORNING...

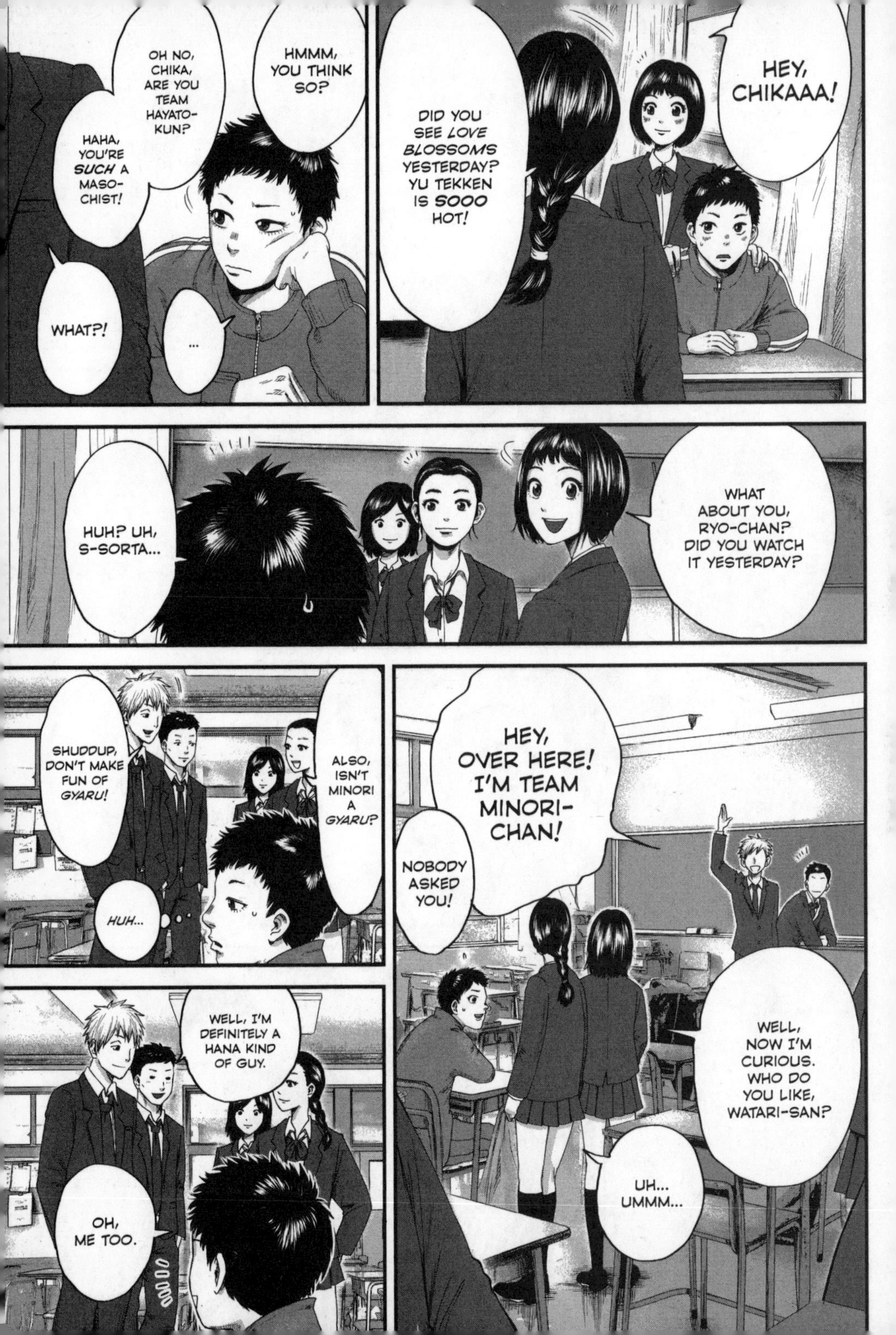
HEY, CHIKAAA!
DID YOU SEE *LOVE BLOSSOMS* YESTERDAY? YU TEKKEN IS *SOOO* HOT!
HMMM, YOU THINK SO?
OH NO, CHIKA, ARE YOU TEAM HAYATO-KUN?
HAHA, YOU'RE *SUCH* A MASO-CHIST!
...
WHAT?!
WHAT ABOUT YOU, RYO-CHAN? DID YOU WATCH IT YESTERDAY?
HUH? UH, S-SORTA...
HEY, OVER HERE! I'M TEAM MINORI-CHAN!
NOBODY ASKED YOU!
ALSO, ISN'T MINORI A *GYARU*?
SHUDDUP, DON'T MAKE FUN OF *GYARU*!
HUH...
WELL, I'M DEFINITELY A HANA KIND OF GUY.
OH, ME TOO.
WELL, NOW I'M CURIOUS. WHO DO YOU LIKE, WATARI-SAN?
UH... UMMM...

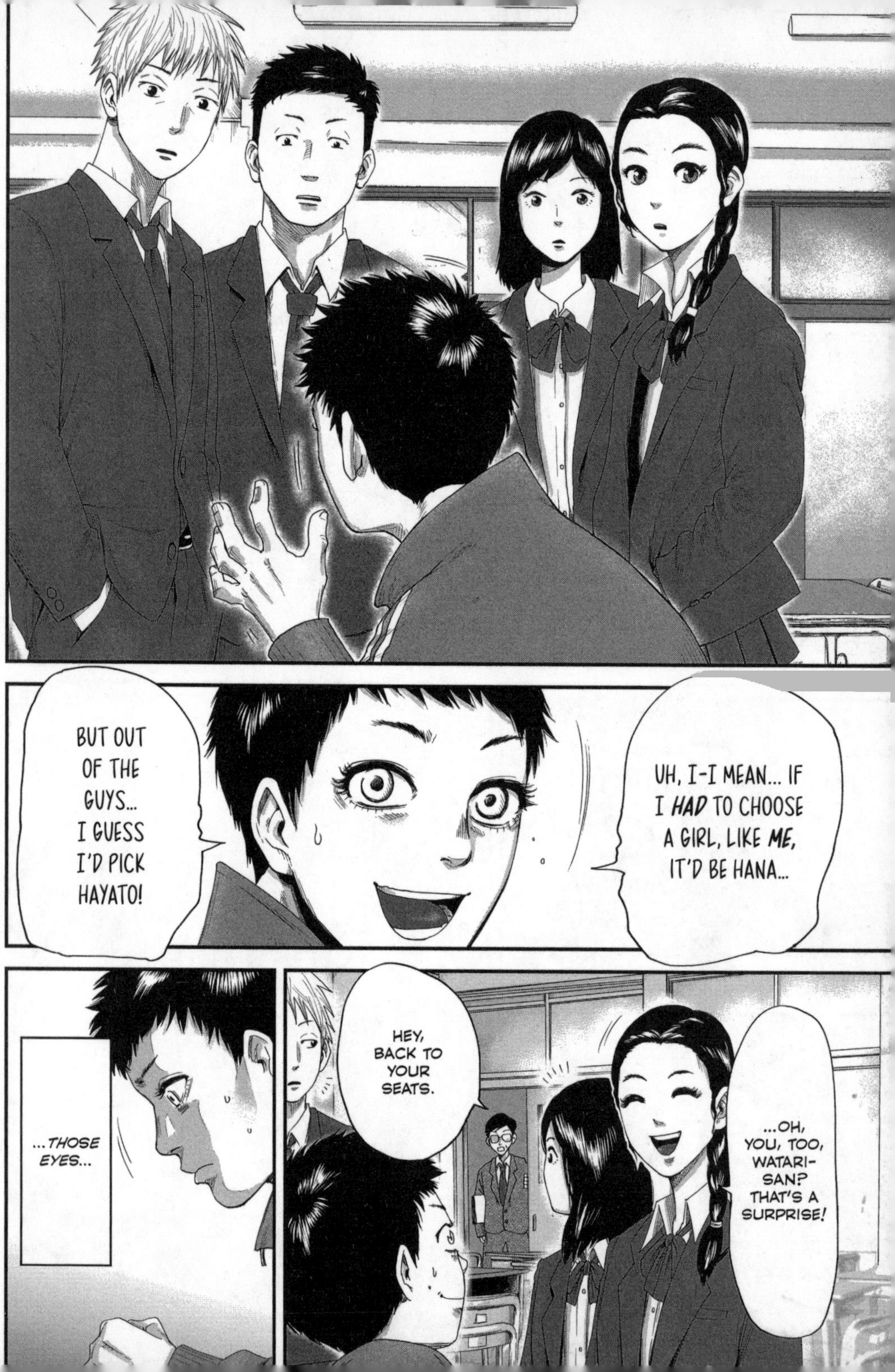
UH, I-I MEAN... IF I *HAD* TO CHOOSE A GIRL, LIKE *ME*, IT'D BE HANA...
BUT OUT OF THE GUYS... I GUESS I'D PICK HAYATO!
...OH, YOU, TOO, WATARI-SAN? THAT'S A SURPRISE!
HEY, BACK TO YOUR SEATS.
...*THOSE EYES...*

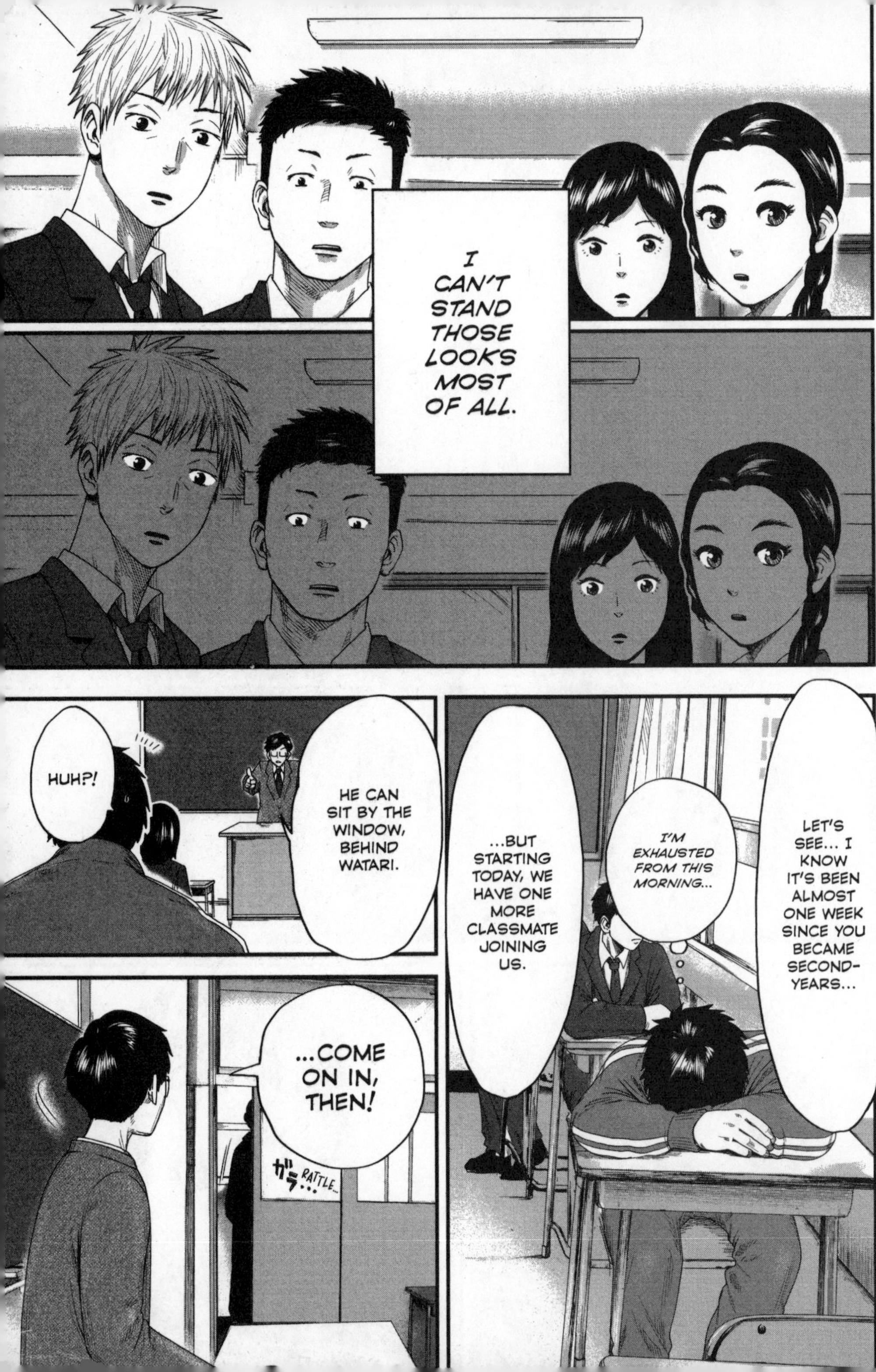
I CAN'T STAND THOSE LOOKS MOST OF ALL.
LET'S SEE... I KNOW IT'S BEEN ALMOST ONE WEEK SINCE YOU BECAME SECOND-YEARS...
I'M EXHAUSTED FROM THIS MORNING...
...BUT STARTING TODAY, WE HAVE ONE MORE CLASSMATE JOINING US.
HE CAN SIT BY THE WINDOW, BEHIND WATARI.
HUH?!
...COME ON IN, THEN!
ガラ RATTLE...

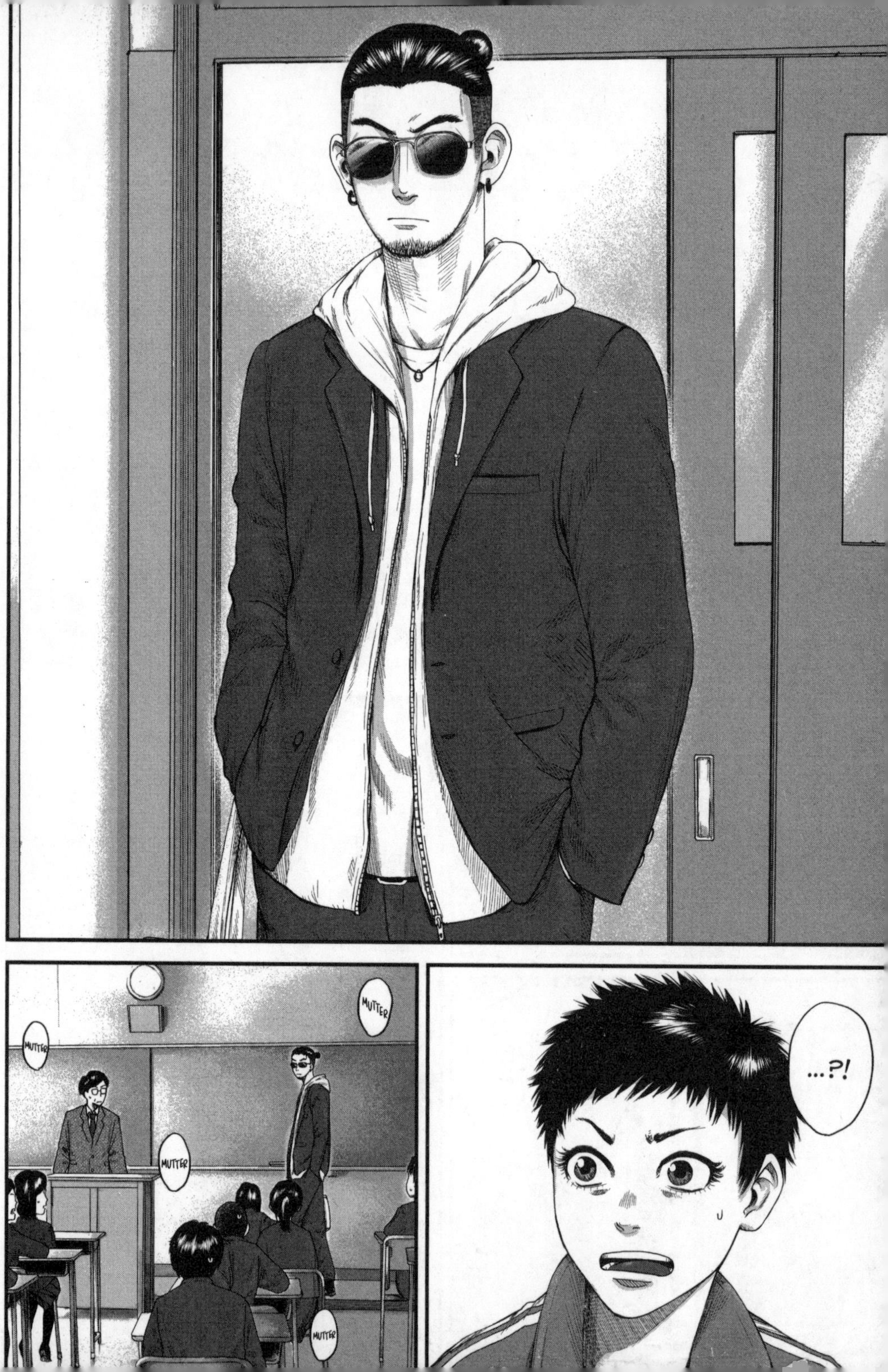
...?!
MUTTER
MUTTER
MUTTER
MUTTER

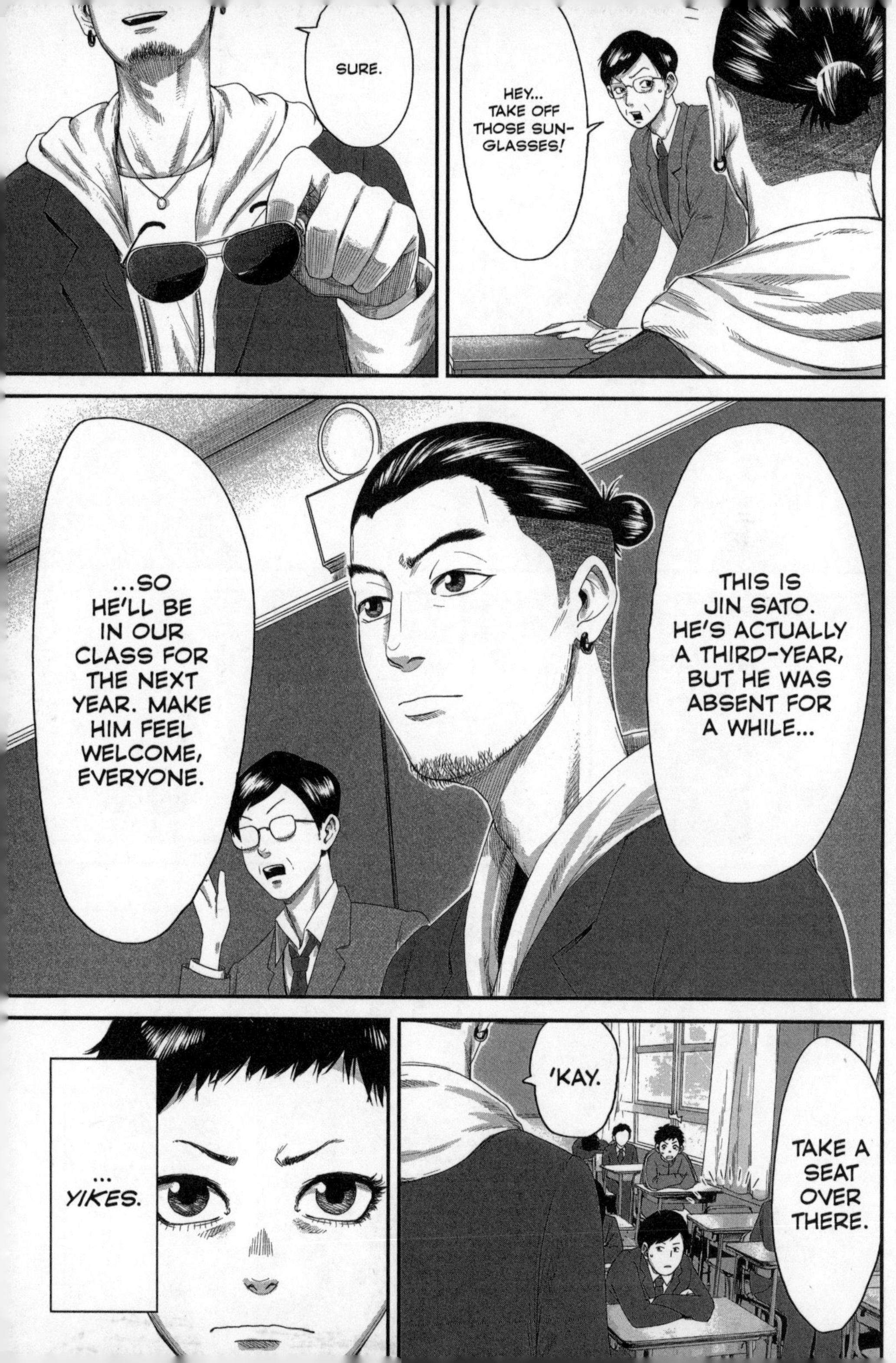
HEY... TAKE OFF THOSE SUN-GLASSES!
SURE.
THIS IS JIN SATO. HE'S ACTUALLY A THIRD-YEAR, BUT HE WAS ABSENT FOR A WHILE...
...SO HE'LL BE IN OUR CLASS FOR THE NEXT YEAR. MAKE HIM FEEL WELCOME, EVERYONE.
TAKE A SEAT OVER THERE.
'KAY.
... YIKES.

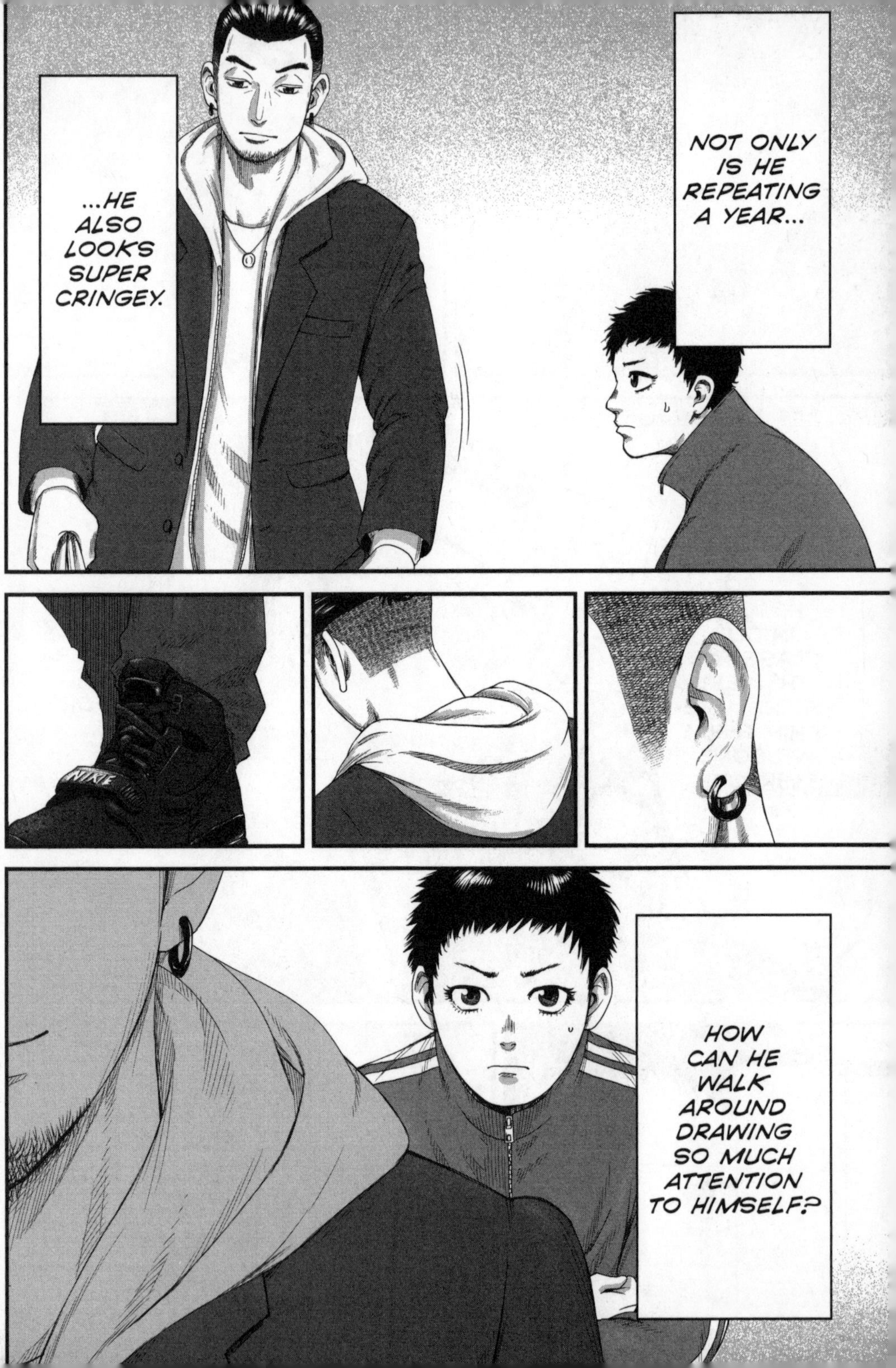
NOT ONLY IS HE REPEATING A YEAR...
...HE ALSO LOOKS SUPER CRINGEY.
NIKE
HOW CAN HE WALK AROUND DRAWING SO MUCH ATTENTION TO HIMSELF?

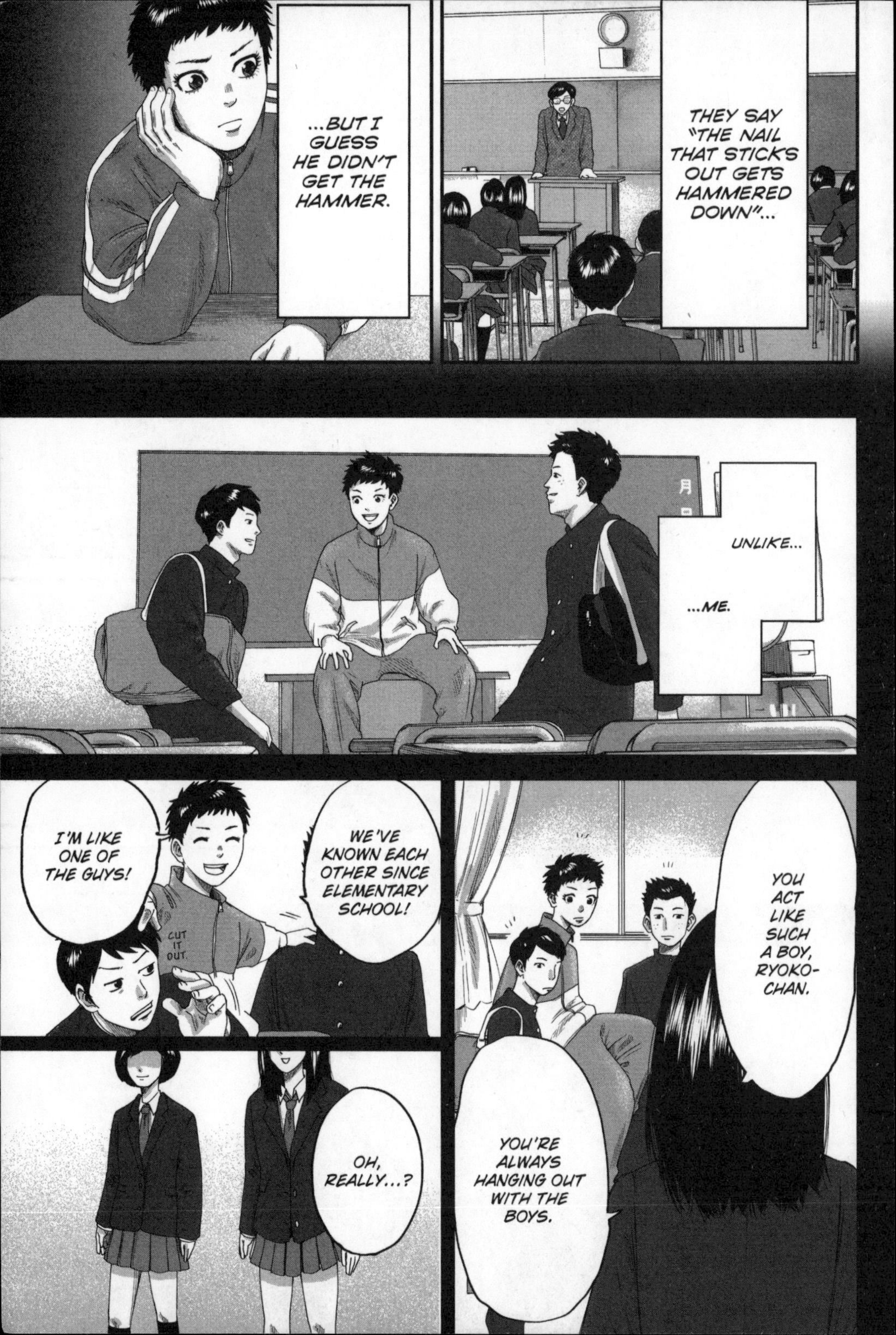
THEY SAY "THE NAIL THAT STICKS OUT GETS HAMMERED DOWN"...
...BUT I GUESS HE DIDN'T GET THE HAMMER.
UNLIKE...
...ME.
YOU ACT LIKE SUCH A BOY, RYOKO-CHAN.
YOU'RE ALWAYS HANGING OUT WITH THE BOYS.
WE'VE KNOWN EACH OTHER SINCE ELEMENTARY SCHOOL!
I'M LIKE ONE OF THE GUYS!
CUT IT OUT.
OH, REALLY...?

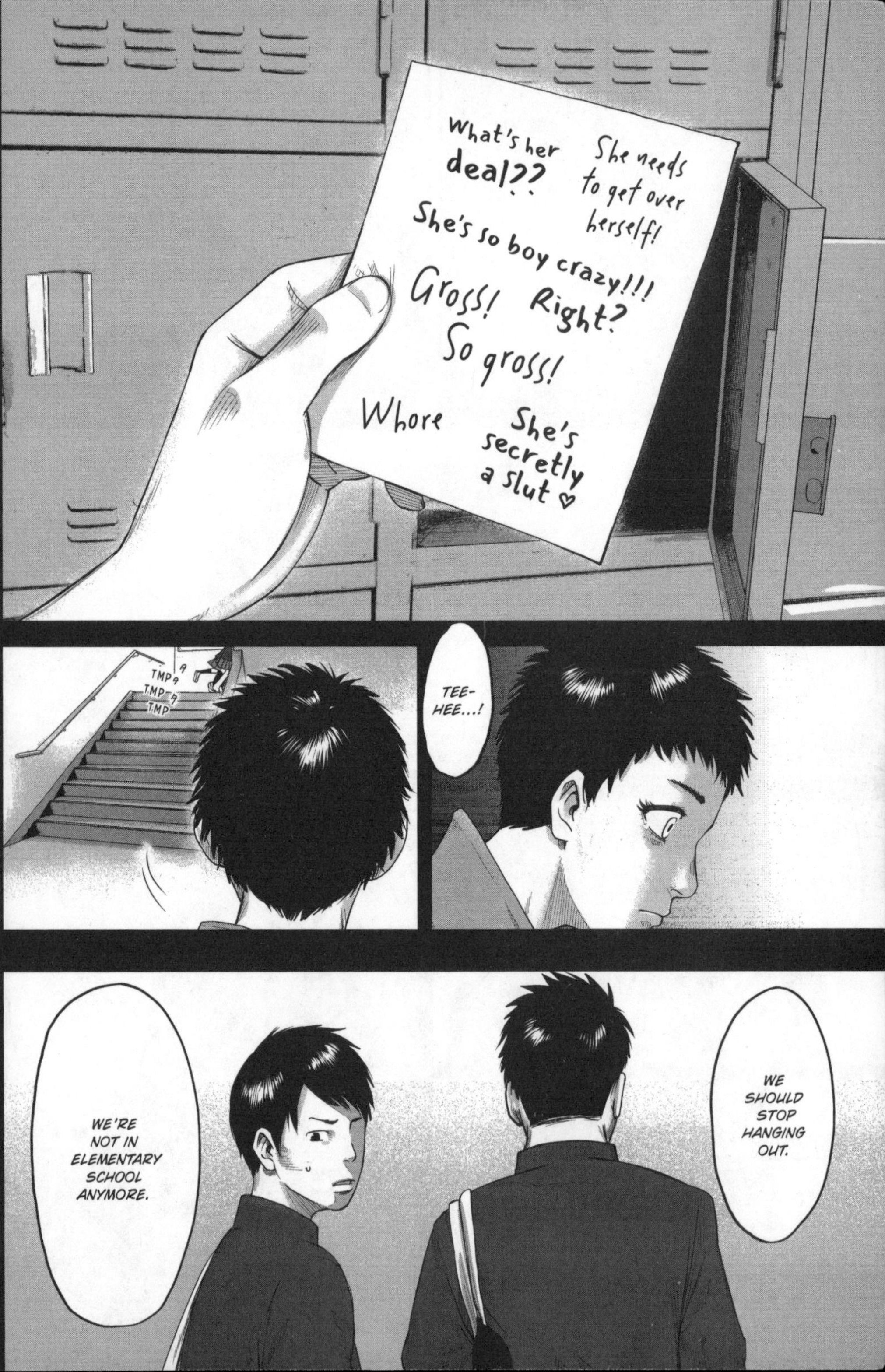

What's her deal??
She needs to get over herself!
She's so boy crazy!!!
Gross! Right?
So gross!
Whore
She's secretly a slut ♡
TEE-HEE...!
TMP TMP TMP
WE SHOULD STOP HANGING OUT.
WE'RE NOT IN ELEMENTARY SCHOOL ANYMORE.

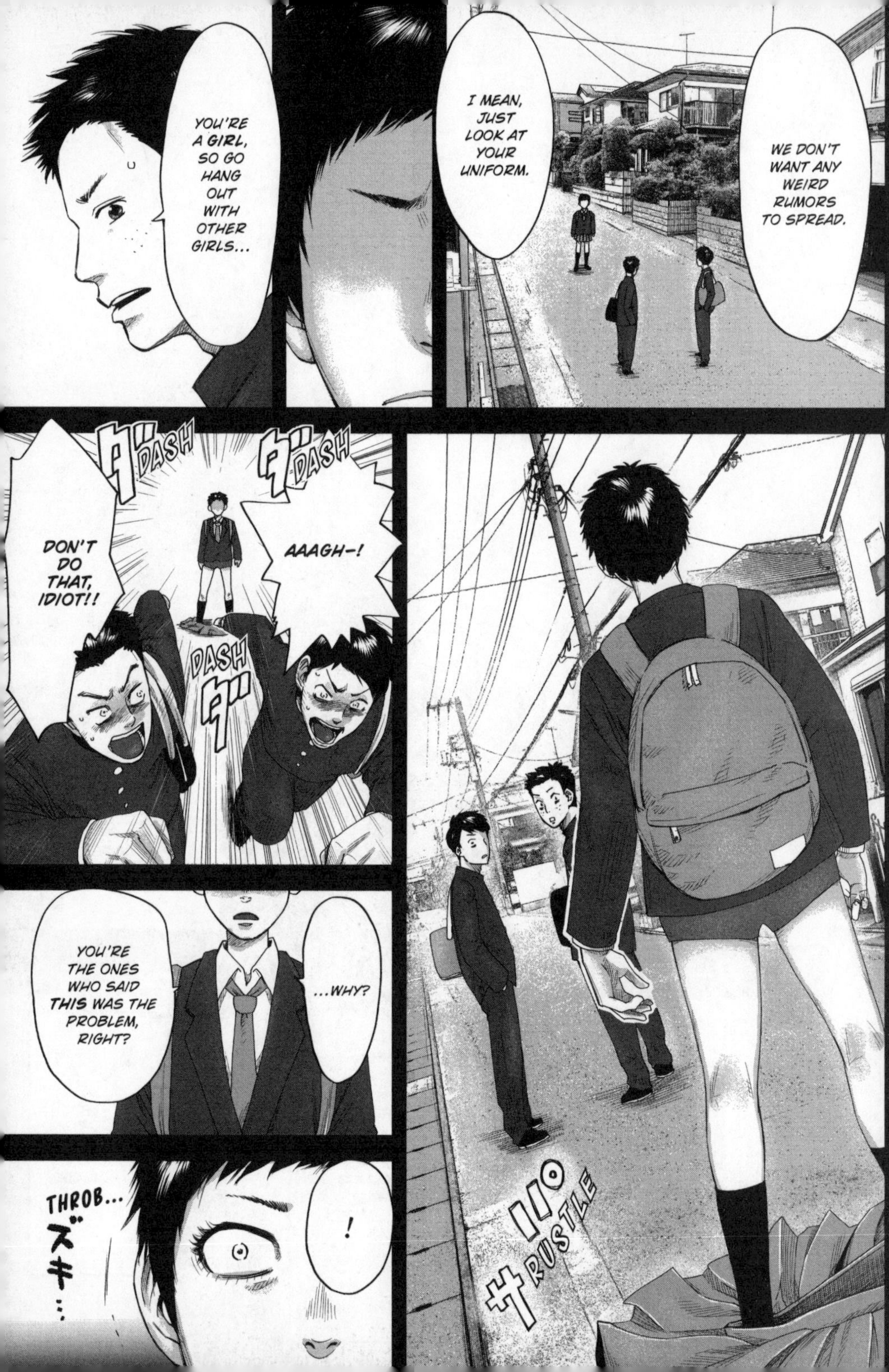
WE DON'T WANT ANY WEIRD RUMORS TO SPREAD.
I MEAN, JUST LOOK AT YOUR UNIFORM.
YOU'RE A GIRL, SO GO HANG OUT WITH OTHER GIRLS...
サッ RUSTLE
ダッ DASH
ダッ DASH
AAAGH-!
DON'T DO THAT, IDIOT!!
ダッ DASH
...WHY?
YOU'RE THE ONES WHO SAID THIS WAS THE PROBLEM, RIGHT?
!
THROB...
ズキ...

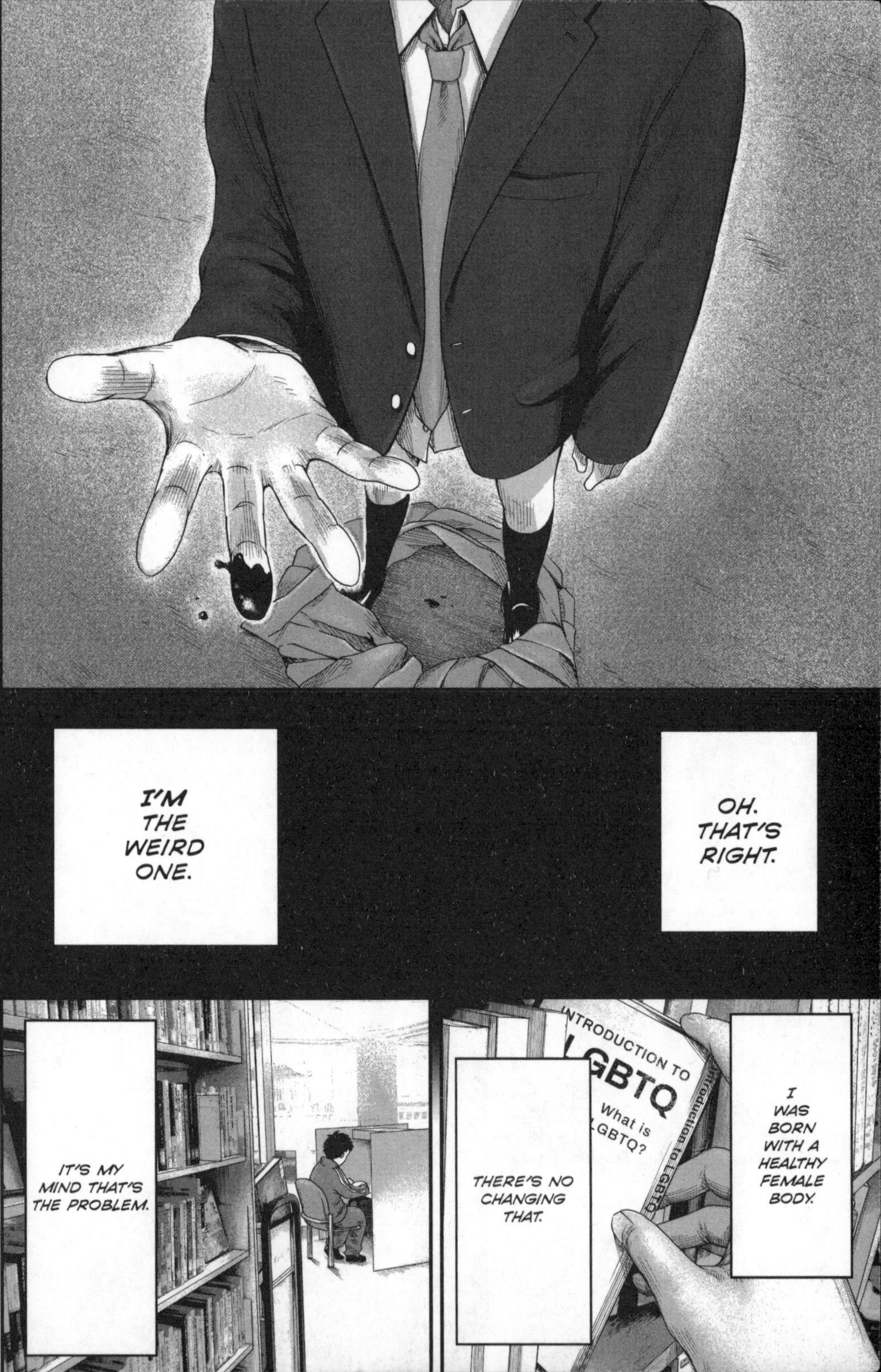
OH. THAT'S RIGHT.
I'M THE WEIRD ONE.
I WAS BORN WITH A HEALTHY FEMALE BODY.
INTRODUCTION TO LGBTQ
What is LGBTQ?
THERE'S NO CHANGING THAT.
IT'S MY MIND THAT'S THE PROBLEM.

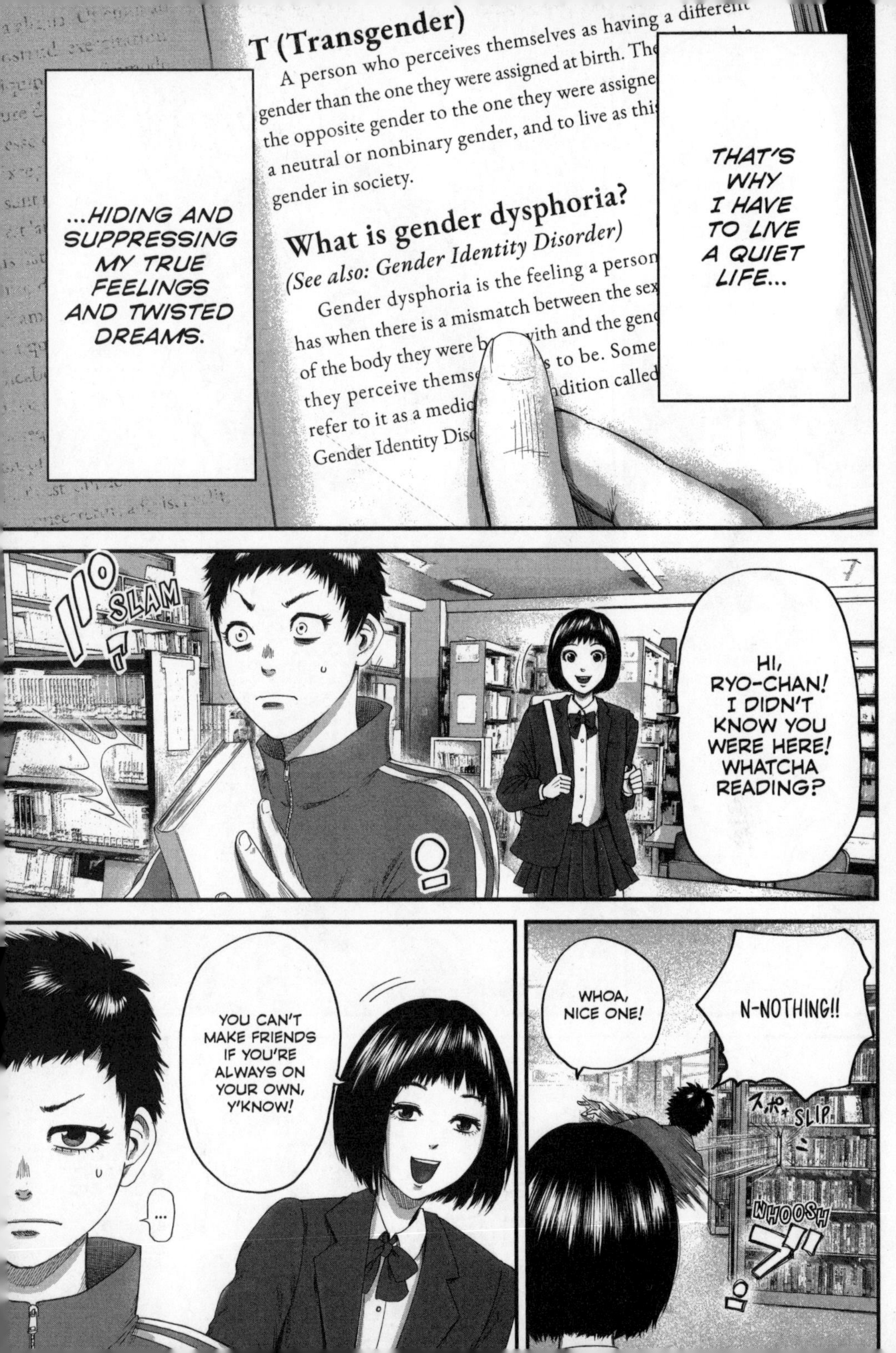
T (Transgender)
A person who perceives themselves as having a different
gender than the one they were assigned at birth. The
the opposite gender to the one they were assigne
a neutral or nonbinary gender, and to live as thi
gender in society.
What is gender dysphoria?
(See also: Gender Identity Disorder)
Gender dysphoria is the feeling a person
has when there is a mismatch between the sex
of the body they were b with and the gend
they perceive themse s to be. Some
refer to it as a medic ndition called
Gender Identity Disc
THAT'S WHY I HAVE TO LIVE A QUIET LIFE...
...HIDING AND SUPPRESSING MY TRUE FEELINGS AND TWISTED DREAMS.
SLAM
HI, RYO-CHAN! I DIDN'T KNOW YOU WERE HERE! WHATCHA READING?
N-NOTHING!!
SLIP
WHOOSH
WHOA, NICE ONE!
YOU CAN'T MAKE FRIENDS IF YOU'RE ALWAYS ON YOUR OWN, Y'KNOW!
...

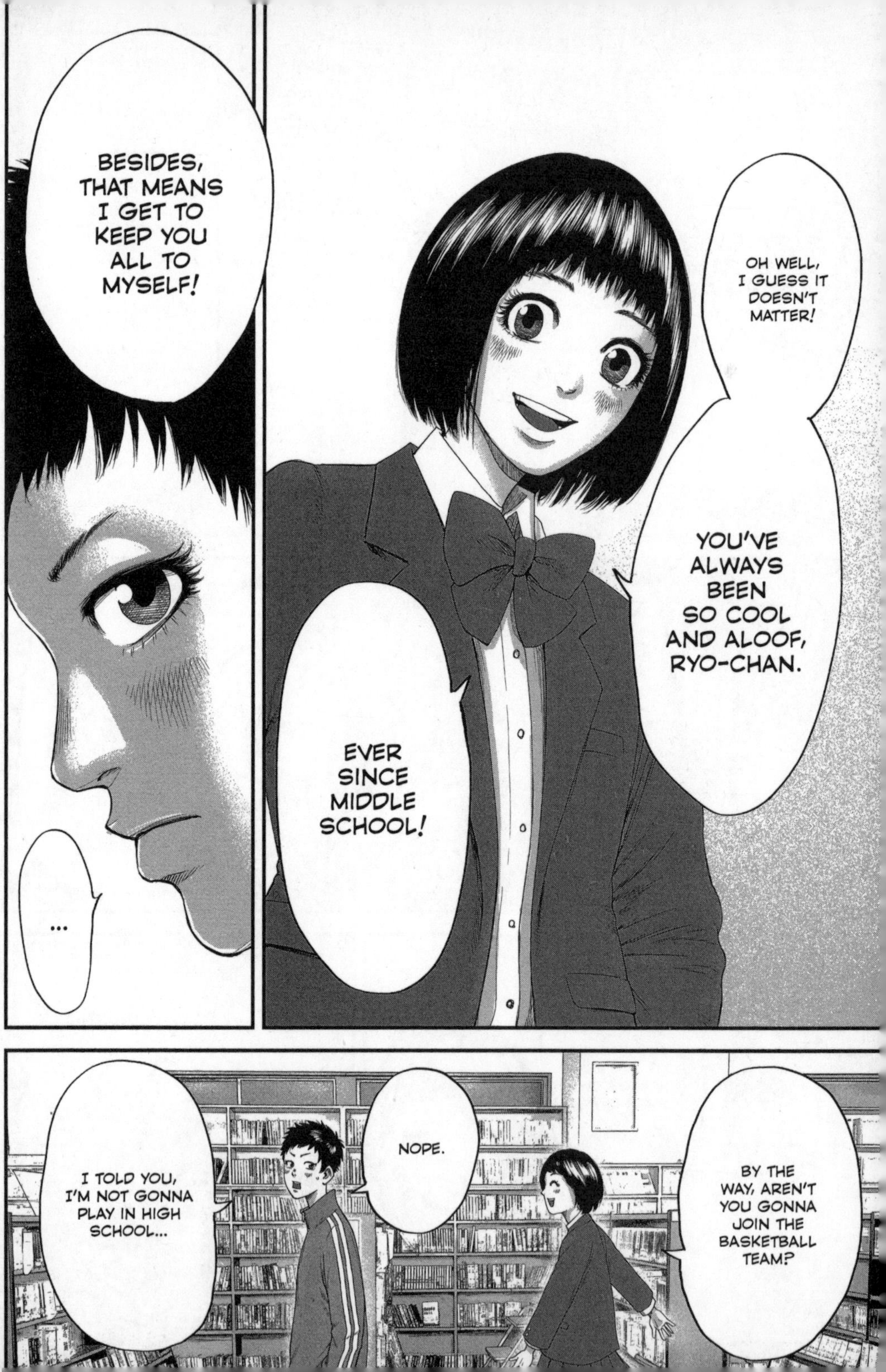
OH WELL, I GUESS IT DOESN'T MATTER!
YOU'VE ALWAYS BEEN SO COOL AND ALOOF, RYO-CHAN.
EVER SINCE MIDDLE SCHOOL!
BESIDES, THAT MEANS I GET TO KEEP YOU ALL TO MYSELF!
...
BY THE WAY, AREN'T YOU GONNA JOIN THE BASKETBALL TEAM?
NOPE.
I TOLD YOU, I'M NOT GONNA PLAY IN HIGH SCHOOL...

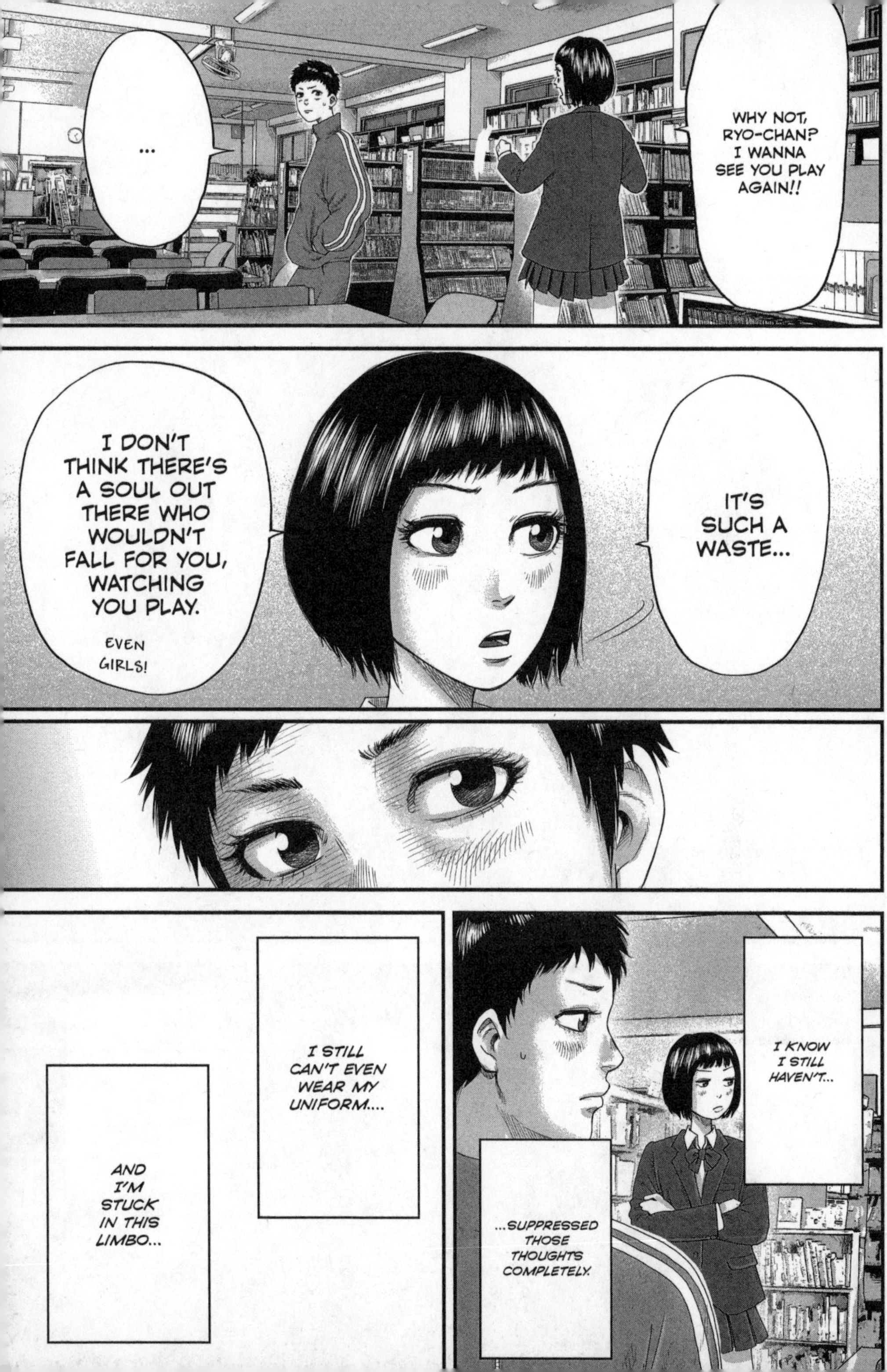
WHY NOT, RYO-CHAN? I WANNA SEE YOU PLAY AGAIN!!
...
IT'S SUCH A WASTE...
I DON'T THINK THERE'S A SOUL OUT THERE WHO WOULDN'T FALL FOR YOU, WATCHING YOU PLAY.
EVEN GIRLS!
I KNOW I STILL HAVEN'T...
...SUPPRESSED THOSE THOUGHTS COMPLETELY.
I STILL CAN'T EVEN WEAR MY UNIFORM....
AND I'M STUCK IN THIS LIMBO...

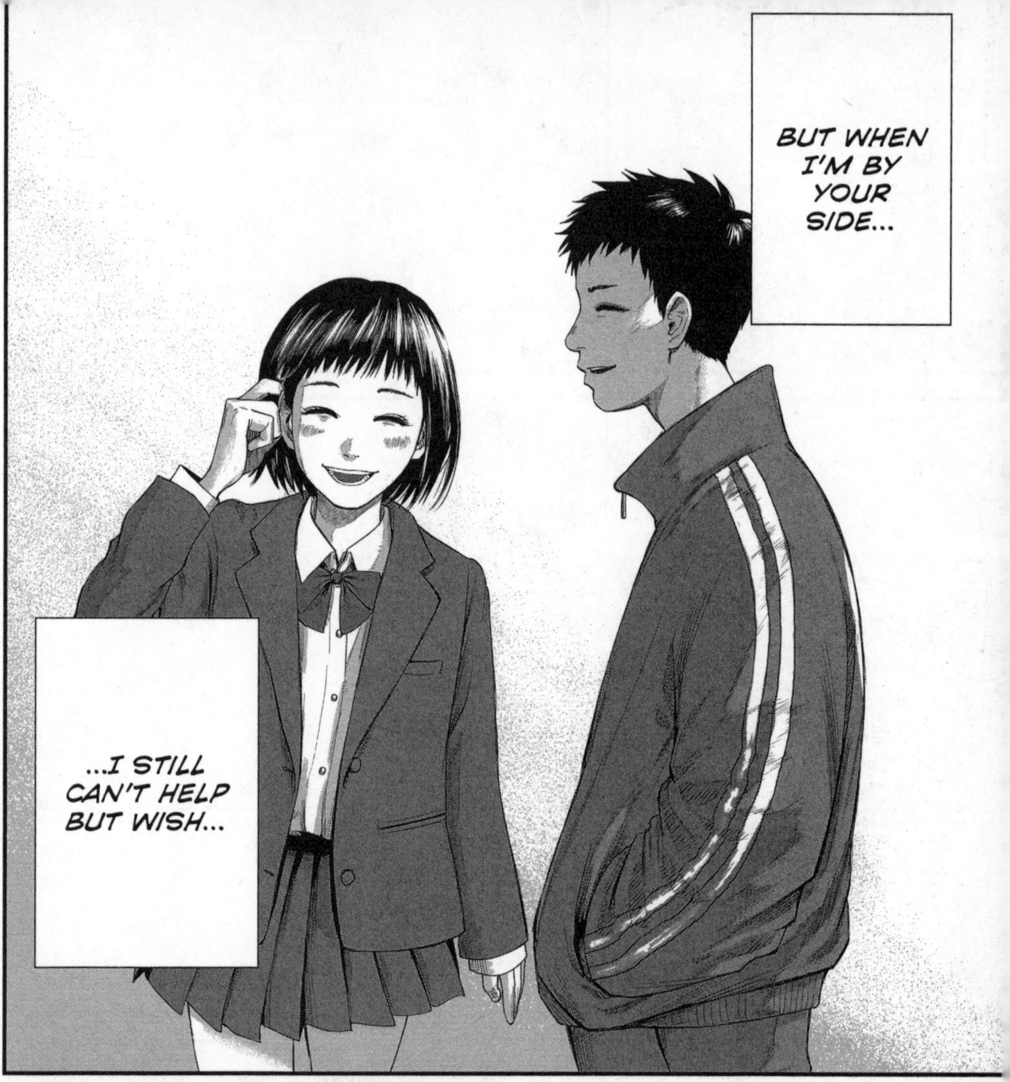
BUT WHEN I'M BY YOUR SIDE...
...I STILL CAN'T HELP BUT WISH...
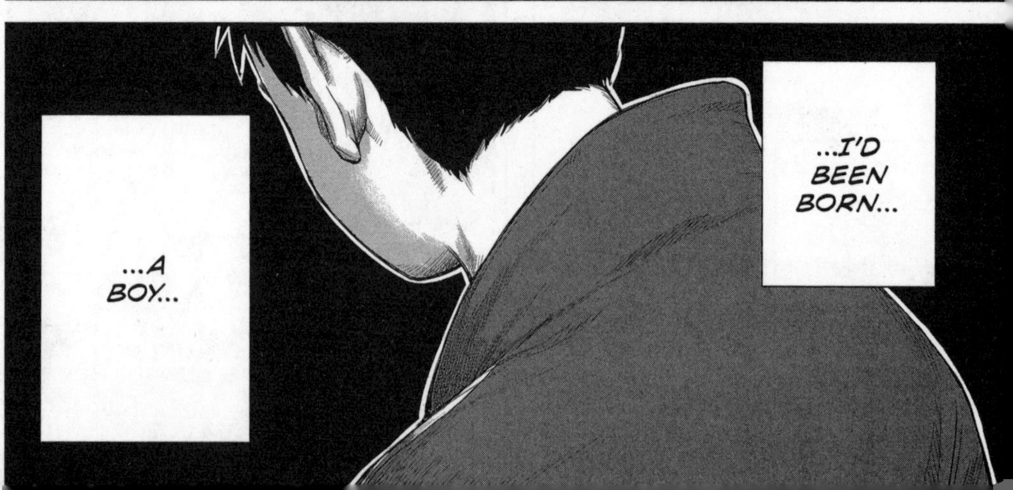
...I'D BEEN BORN...
...A BOY...

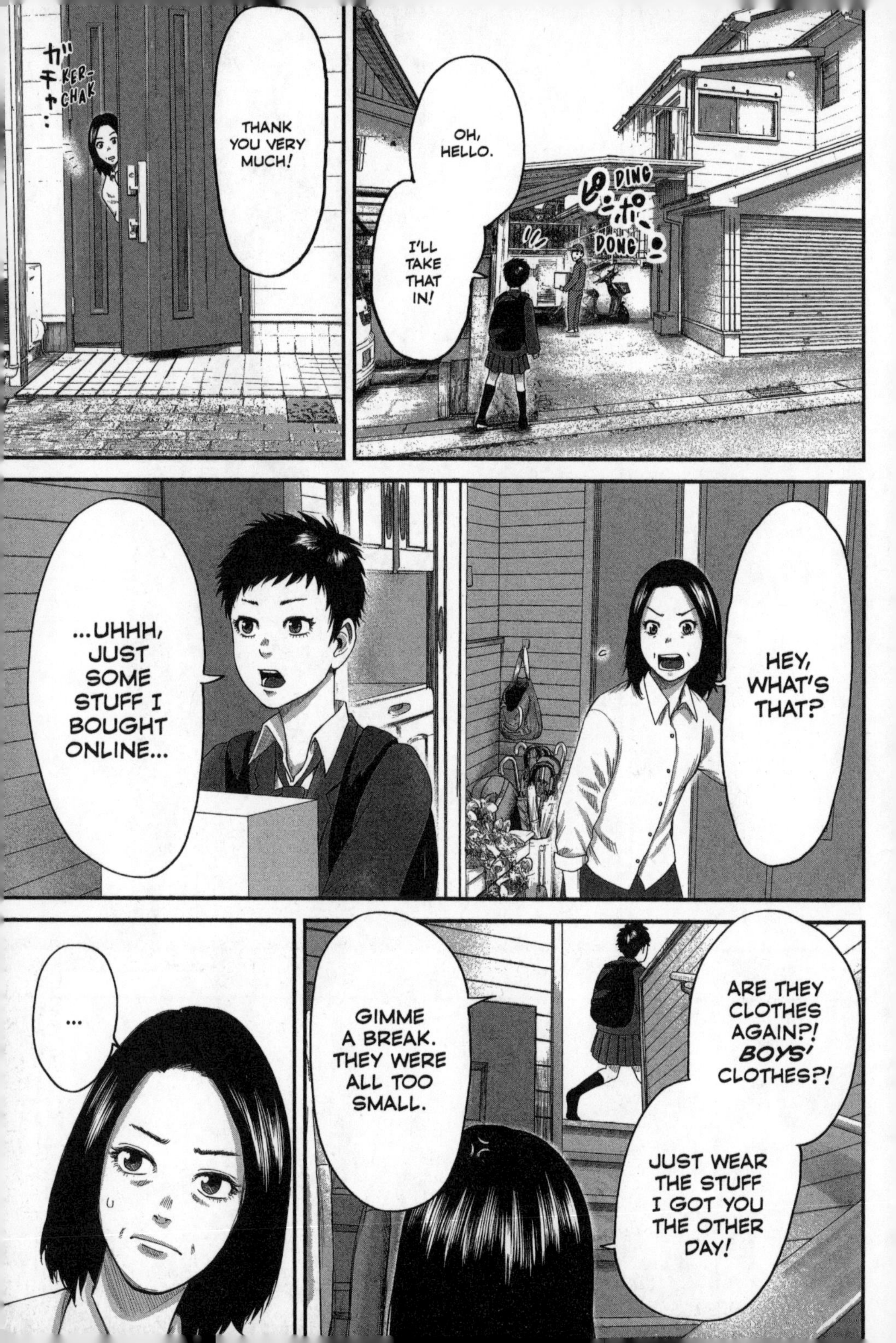
DING DONG
OH, HELLO.
I'LL TAKE THAT IN!
KER-CHAK
THANK YOU VERY MUCH!
HEY, WHAT'S THAT?
...UHHH, JUST SOME STUFF I BOUGHT ONLINE...
ARE THEY CLOTHES AGAIN?! *BOYS'* CLOTHES?!
JUST WEAR THE STUFF I GOT YOU THE OTHER DAY!
GIMME A BREAK. THEY WERE ALL TOO SMALL.
...

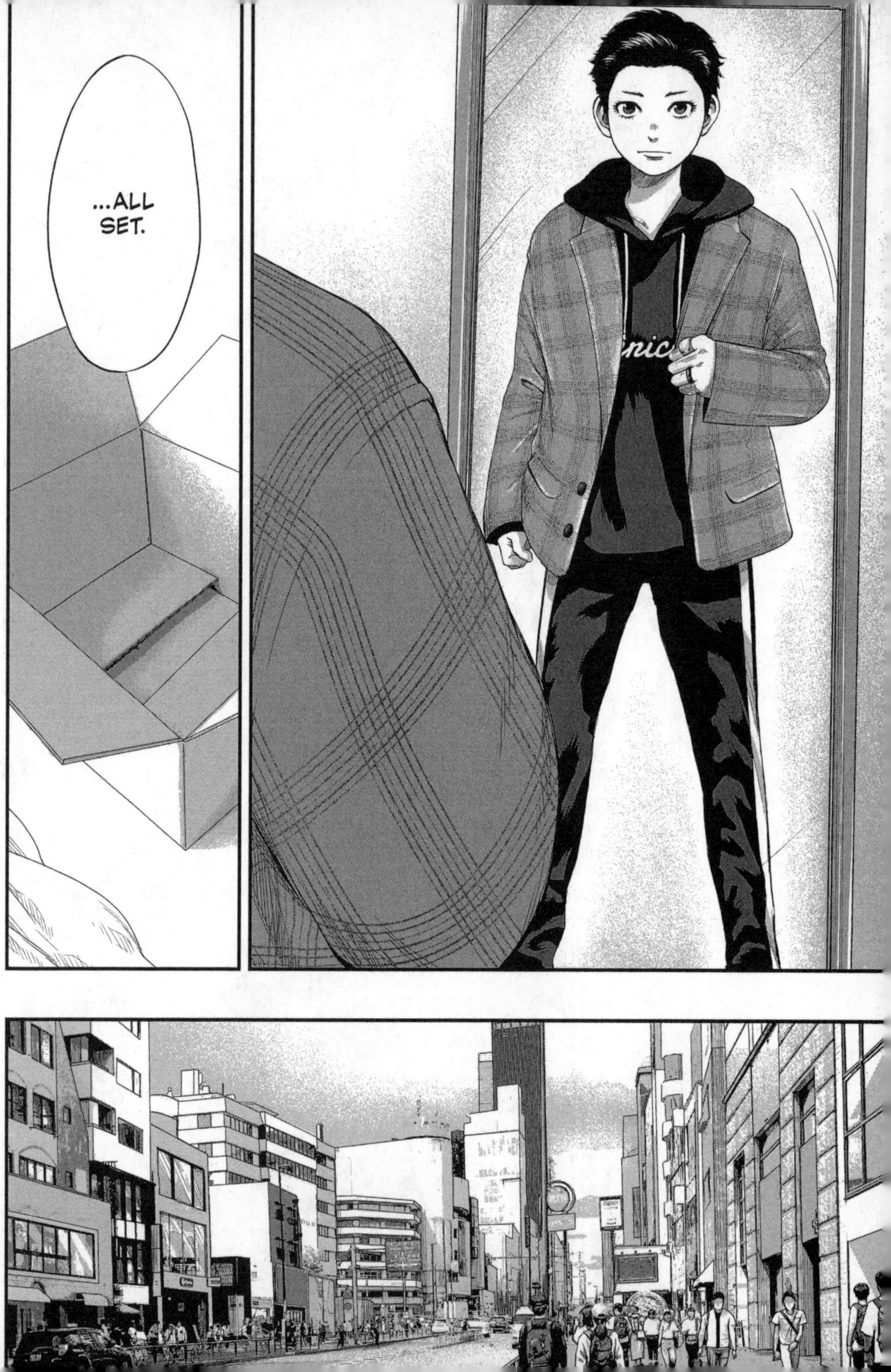
...ALL SET.

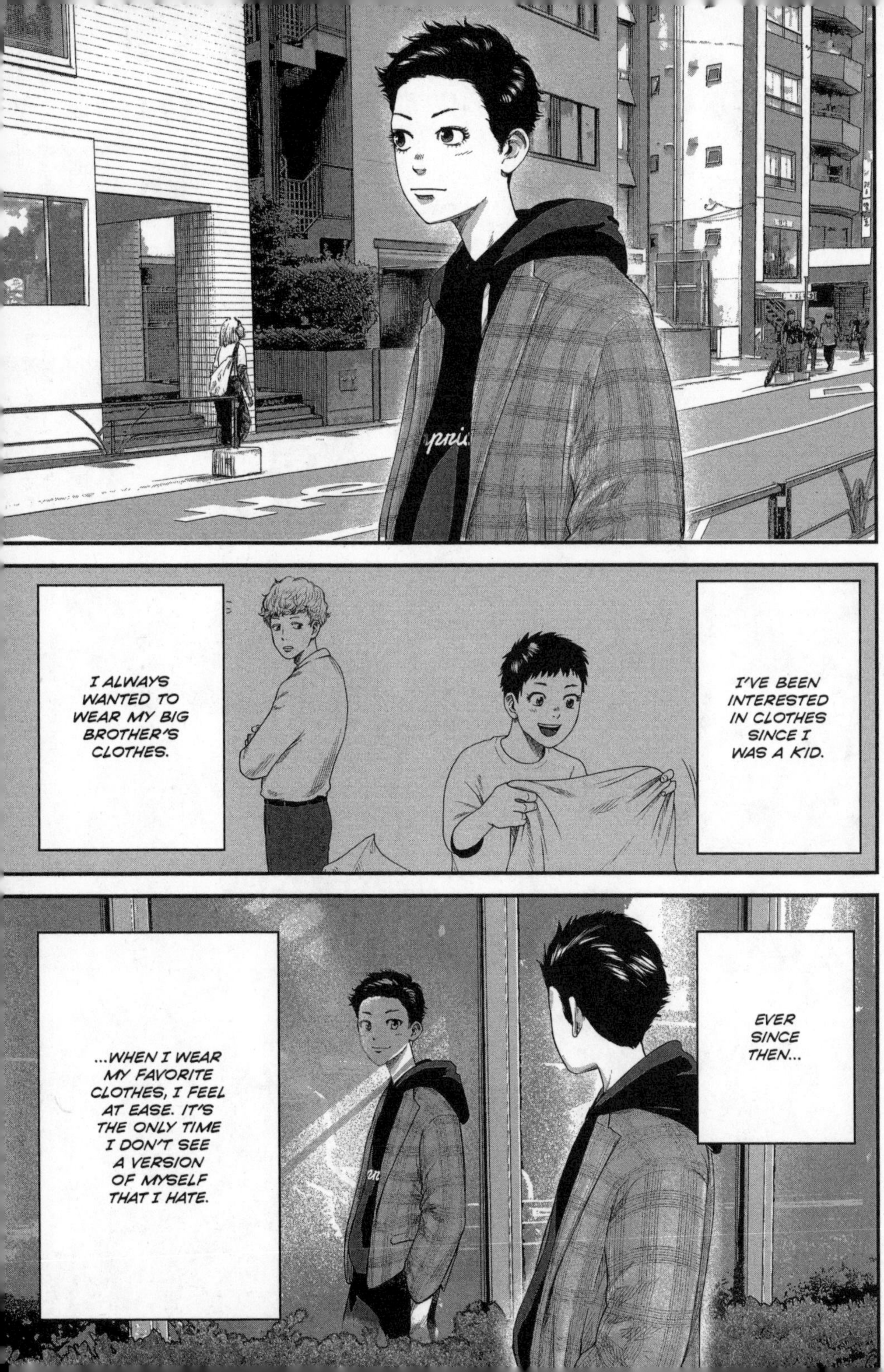
I'VE BEEN INTERESTED IN CLOTHES SINCE I WAS A KID.
I ALWAYS WANTED TO WEAR MY BIG BROTHER'S CLOTHES.
EVER SINCE THEN...
...WHEN I WEAR MY FAVORITE CLOTHES, I FEEL AT EASE. IT'S THE ONLY TIME I DON'T SEE A VERSION OF MYSELF THAT I HATE.

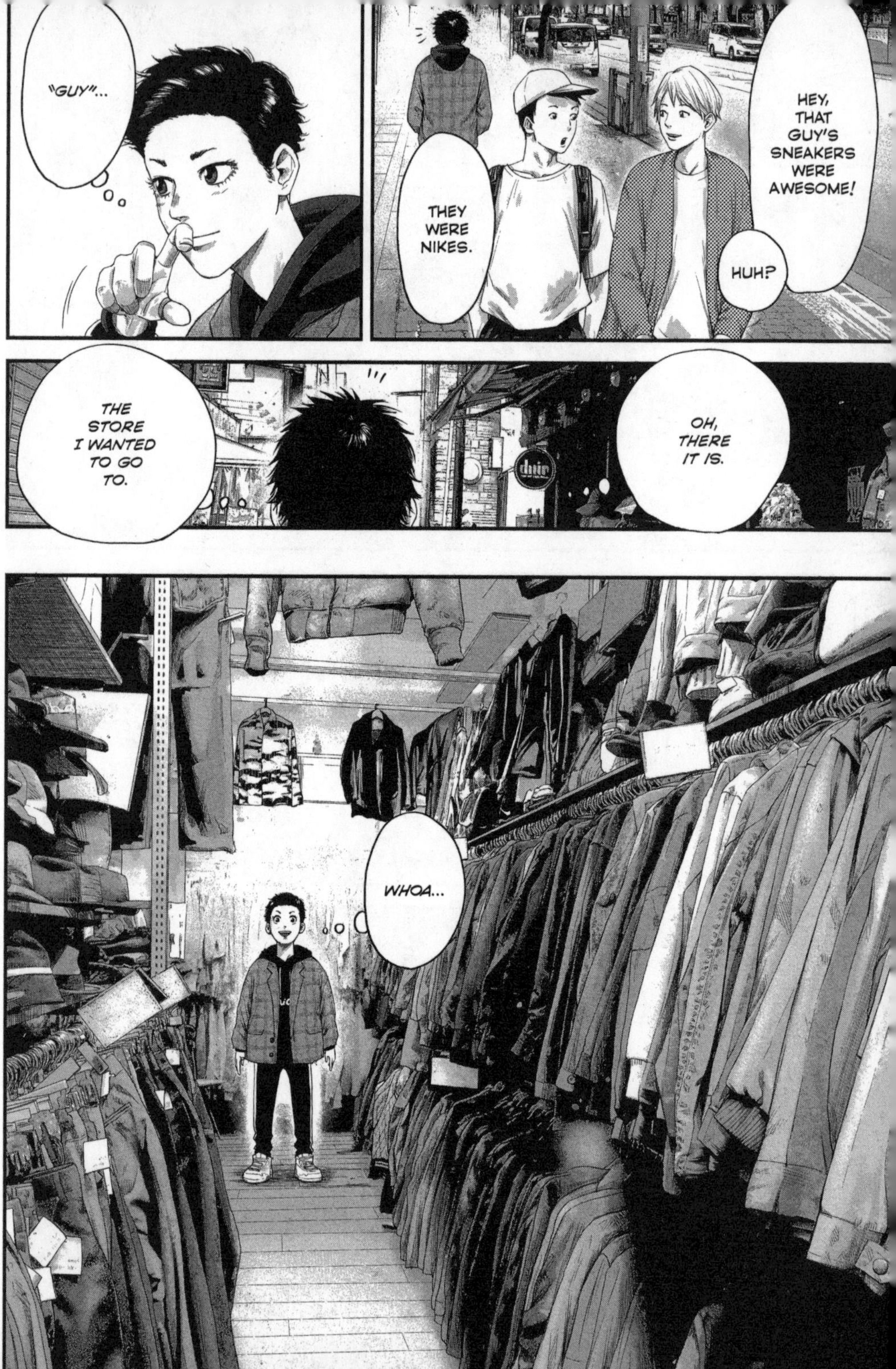
HEY, THAT GUY'S SNEAKERS WERE AWESOME!
HUH?
THEY WERE NIKES.
"GUY"...
OH, THERE IT IS.
THE STORE I WANTED TO GO TO.
WHOA...

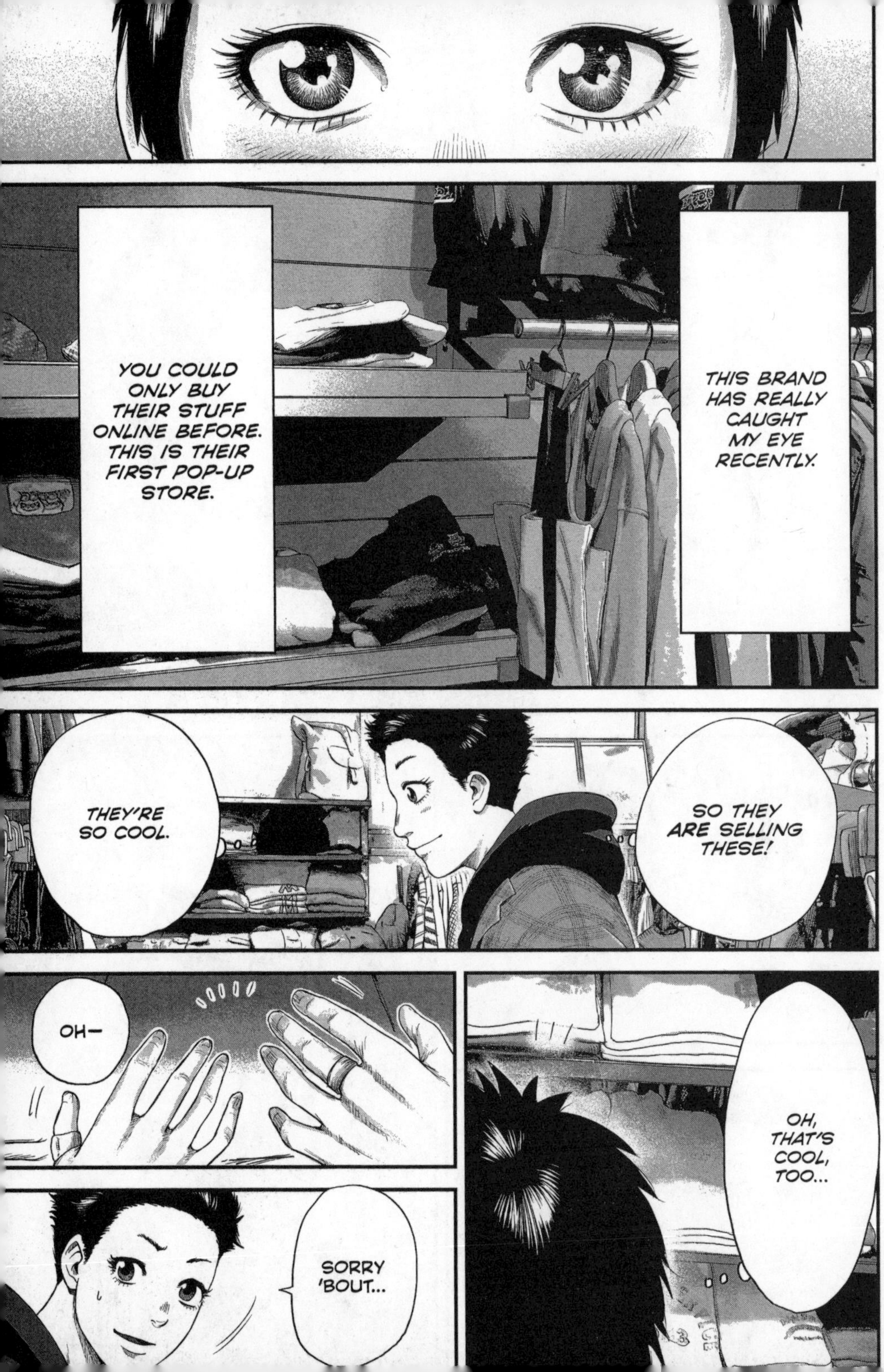
THIS BRAND HAS REALLY CAUGHT MY EYE RECENTLY.
YOU COULD ONLY BUY THEIR STUFF ONLINE BEFORE. THIS IS THEIR FIRST POP-UP STORE.
SO THEY ARE SELLING THESE!
THEY'RE SO COOL.
OH, THAT'S COOL, TOO...
OH—
SORRY 'BOUT...

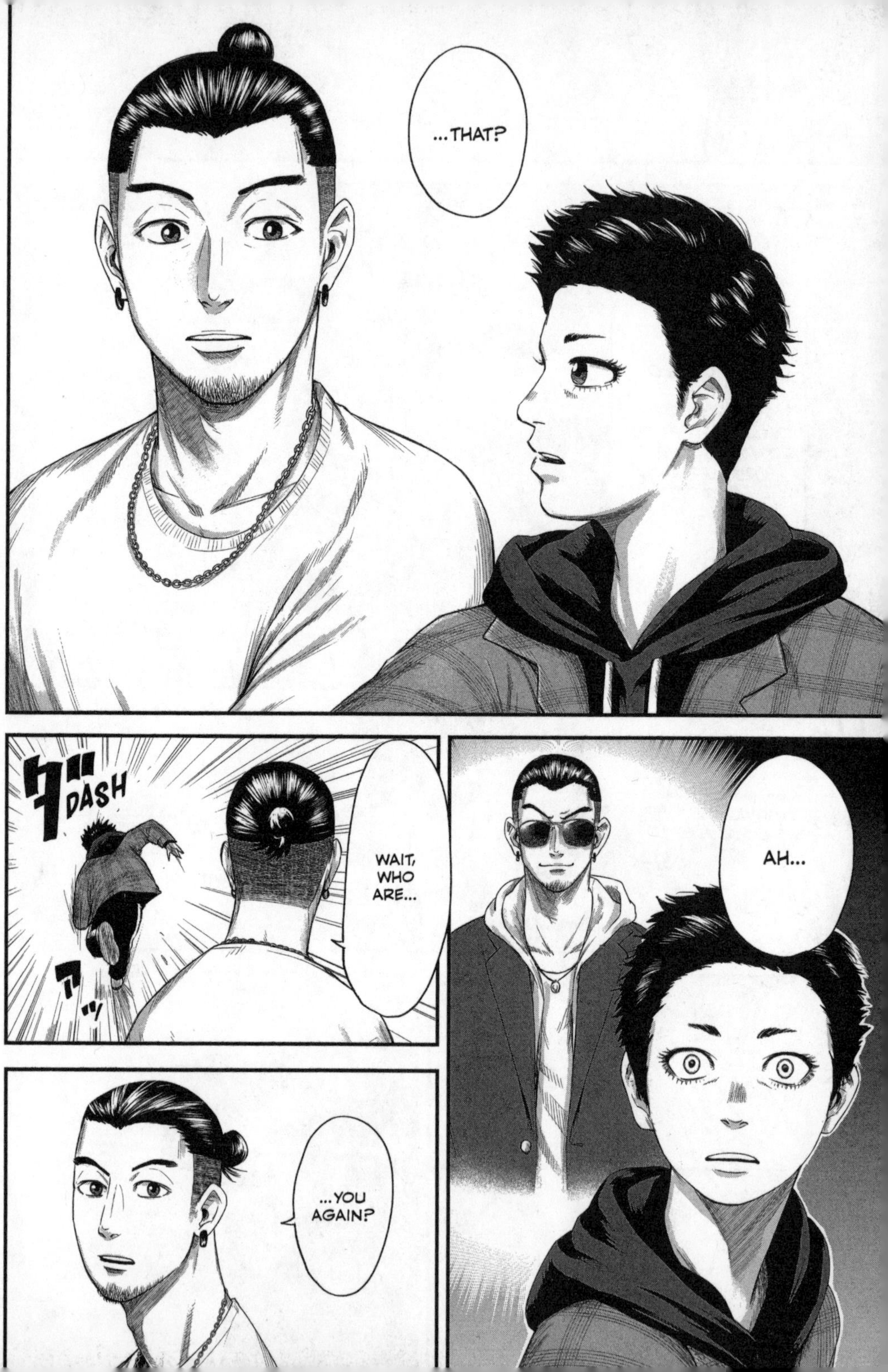
...THAT?
AH...
DASH
WAIT, WHO ARE...
...YOU AGAIN?

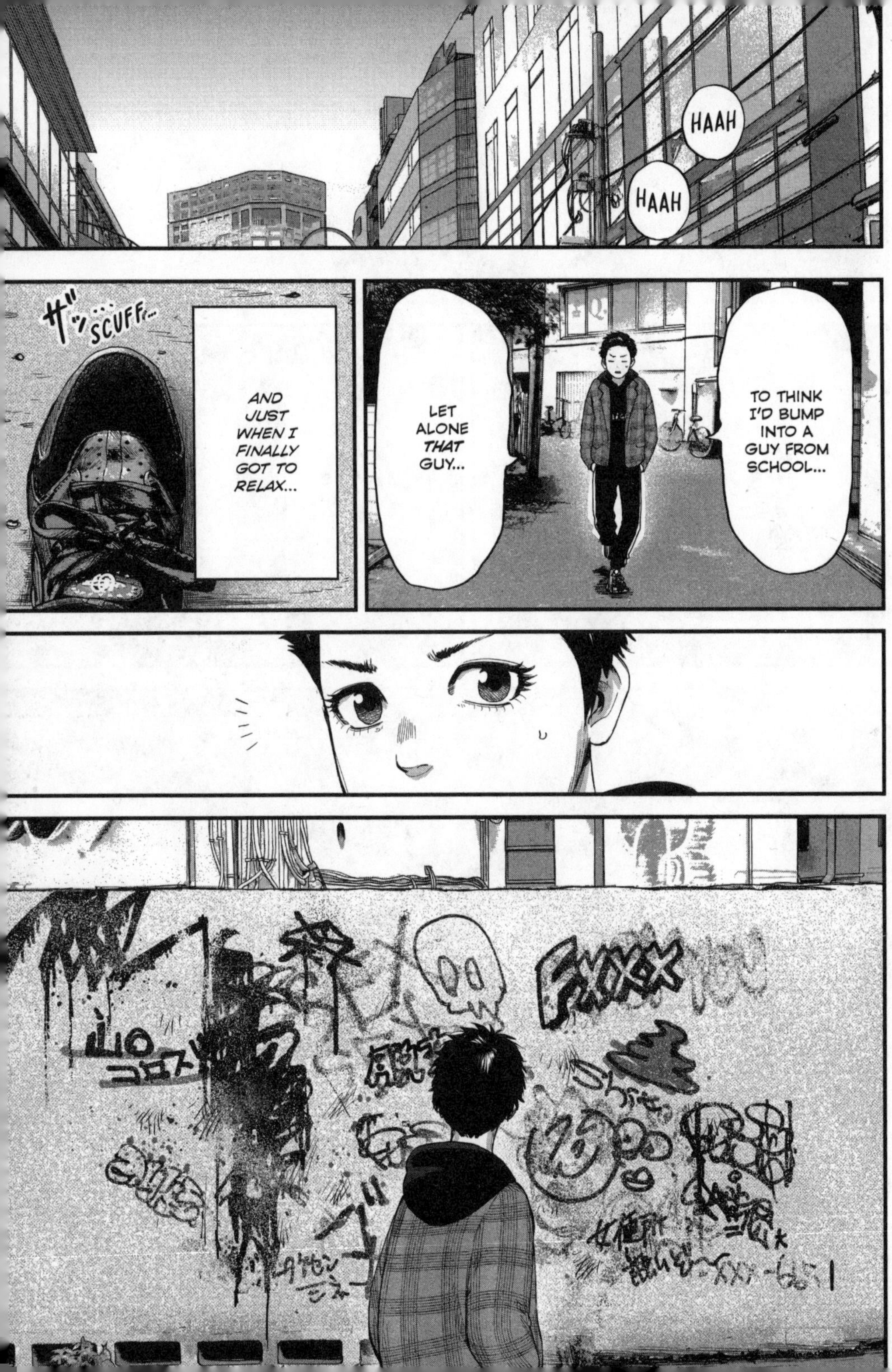
HAAH
HAAH
TO THINK I'D BUMP INTO A GUY FROM SCHOOL...
LET ALONE *THAT* GUY...
ザッ… SCUFF...
AND JUST WHEN I FINALLY GOT TO RELAX...

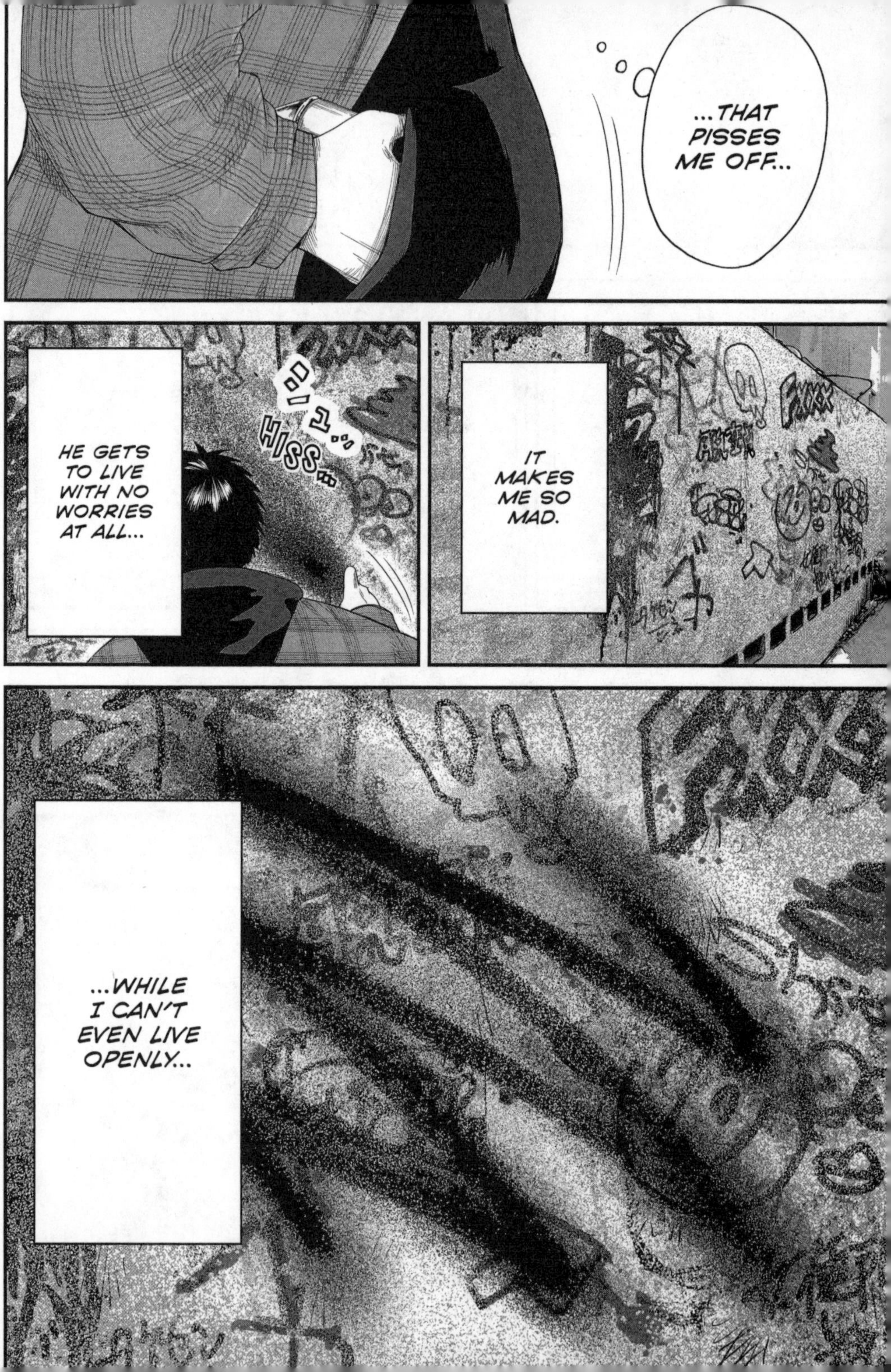
...THAT PISSES ME OFF...
IT MAKES ME SO MAD.
HISS...
HE GETS TO LIVE WITH NO WORRIES AT ALL...
...WHILE I CAN'T EVEN LIVE OPENLY...

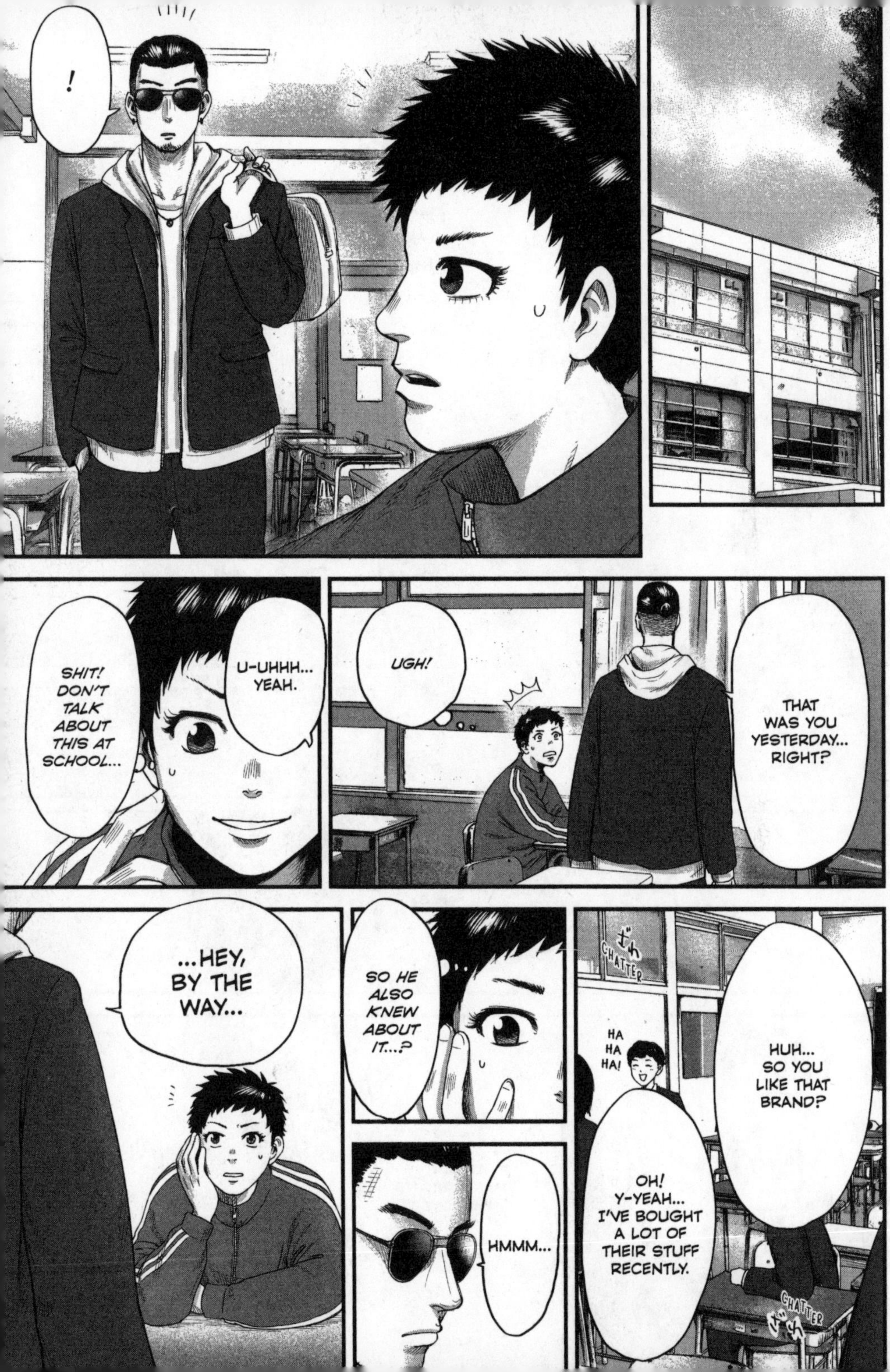
!
THAT WAS YOU YESTERDAY... RIGHT?
UGH!
U-UHHH... YEAH.
SHIT! DON'T TALK ABOUT THIS AT SCHOOL...
HUH... SO YOU LIKE THAT BRAND?
CHATTER
HA HA HA!
OH! Y-YEAH... I'VE BOUGHT A LOT OF THEIR STUFF RECENTLY.
CHATTER
SO HE ALSO KNEW ABOUT IT...?
HMMM...
...HEY, BY THE WAY...

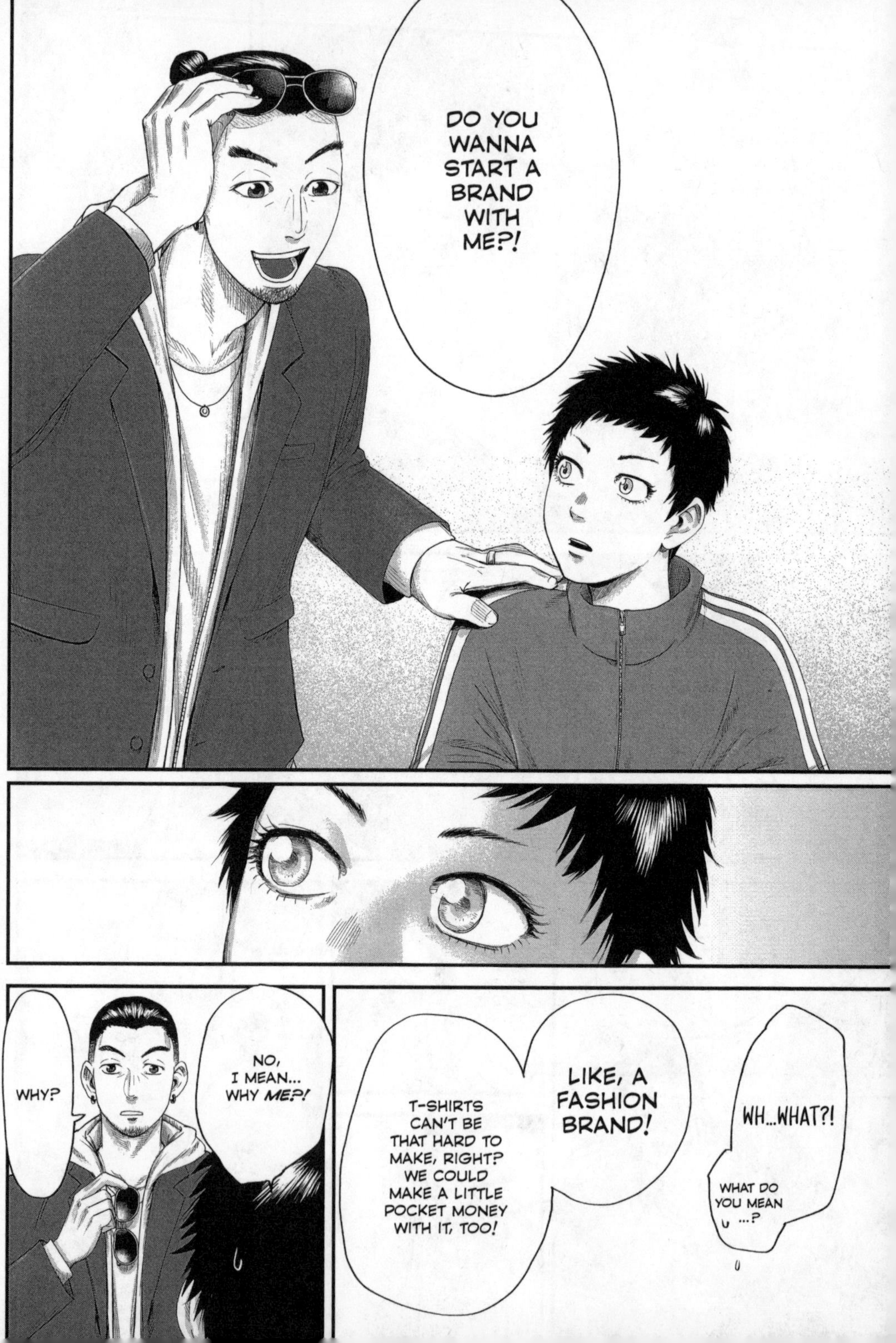
DO YOU WANNA START A BRAND WITH ME?!
WH...WHAT?!
WHAT DO YOU MEAN ...?
LIKE, A FASHION BRAND!
T-SHIRTS CAN'T BE THAT HARD TO MAKE, RIGHT? WE COULD MAKE A LITTLE POCKET MONEY WITH IT, TOO!
NO, I MEAN... WHY *ME?!*
WHY?

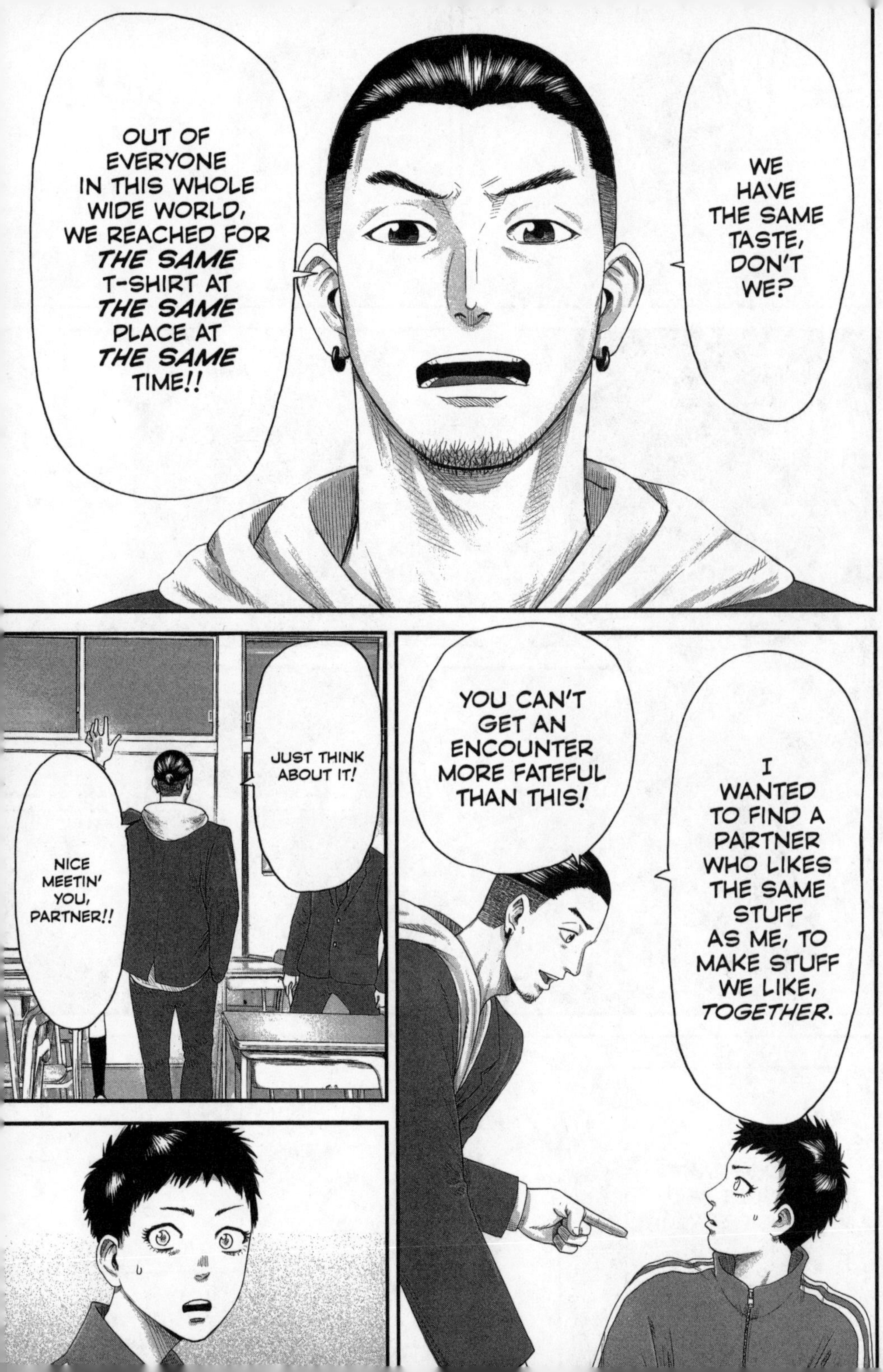
WE HAVE THE SAME TASTE, DON'T WE?
OUT OF EVERYONE IN THIS WHOLE WIDE WORLD, WE REACHED FOR *THE SAME* T-SHIRT AT *THE SAME* PLACE AT *THE SAME* TIME!!
I WANTED TO FIND A PARTNER WHO LIKES THE SAME STUFF AS ME, TO MAKE STUFF WE LIKE, *TOGETHER*.
YOU CAN'T GET AN ENCOUNTER MORE FATEFUL THAN THIS!
JUST THINK ABOUT IT!
NICE MEETIN' YOU, PARTNER!!

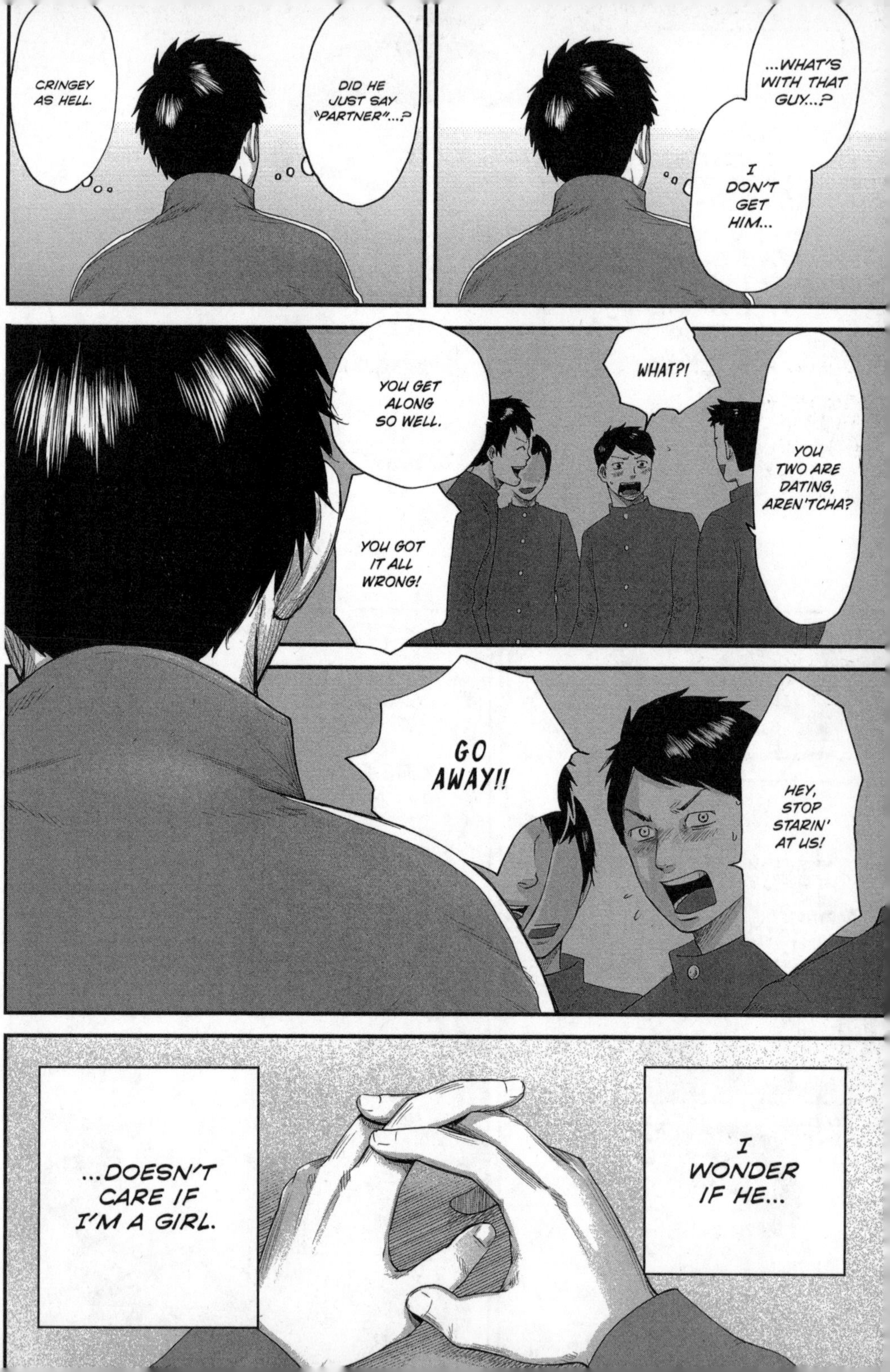
...WHAT'S WITH THAT GUY...?
I DON'T GET HIM...
DID HE JUST SAY "PARTNER"...?
CRINGEY AS HELL.
YOU TWO ARE DATING, AREN'TCHA?
WHAT?!
YOU GET ALONG SO WELL.
YOU GOT IT ALL WRONG!
HEY, STOP STARIN' AT US!
GO AWAY!!
I WONDER IF HE...
...DOESN'T CARE IF I'M A GIRL.

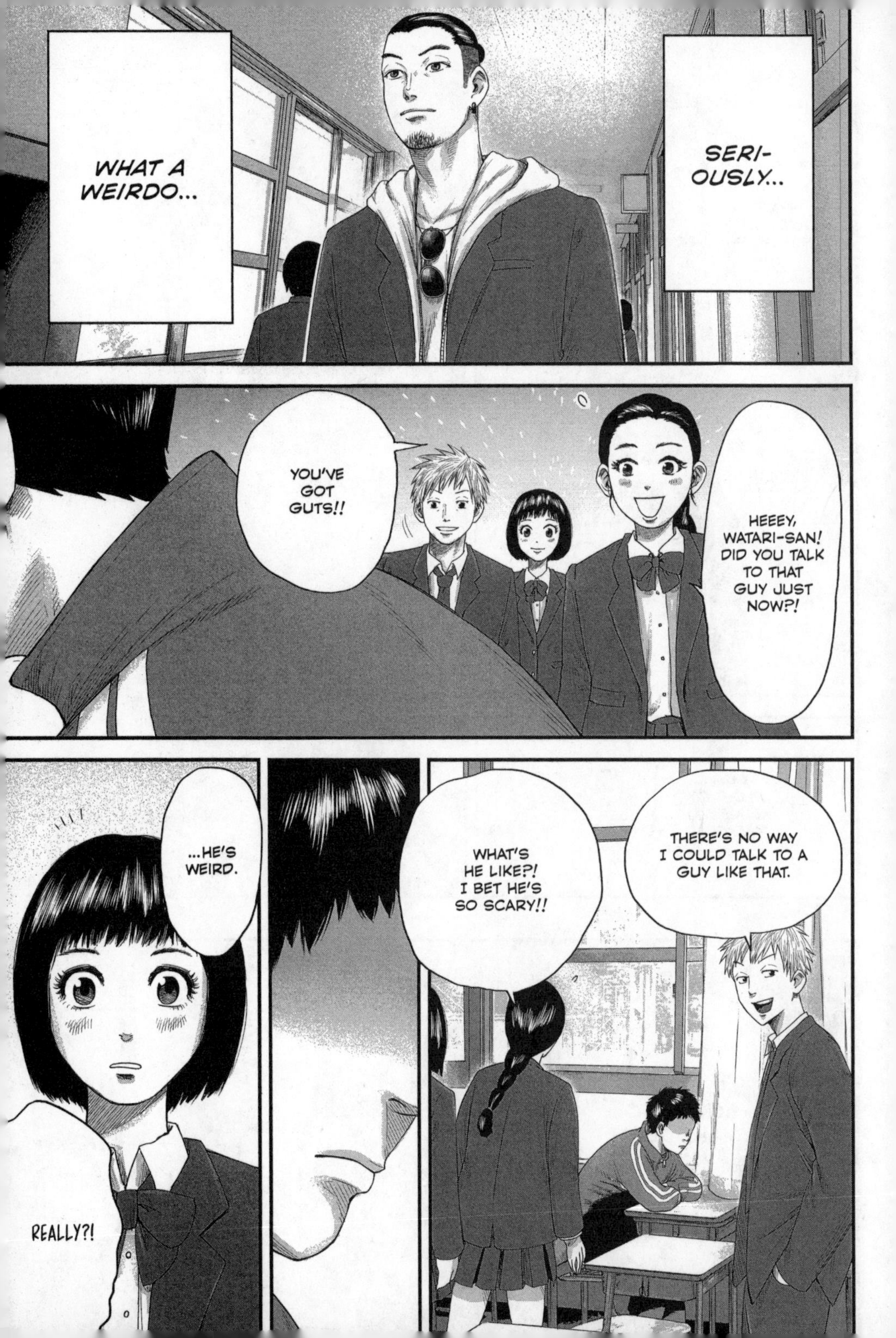
SERI-OUSLY...
WHAT A WEIRDO...
HEEEY, WATARI-SAN! DID YOU TALK TO THAT GUY JUST NOW?!
YOU'VE GOT GUTS!!
THERE'S NO WAY I COULD TALK TO A GUY LIKE THAT.
WHAT'S HE LIKE?! I BET HE'S SO SCARY!!
...HE'S WEIRD.
REALLY?!

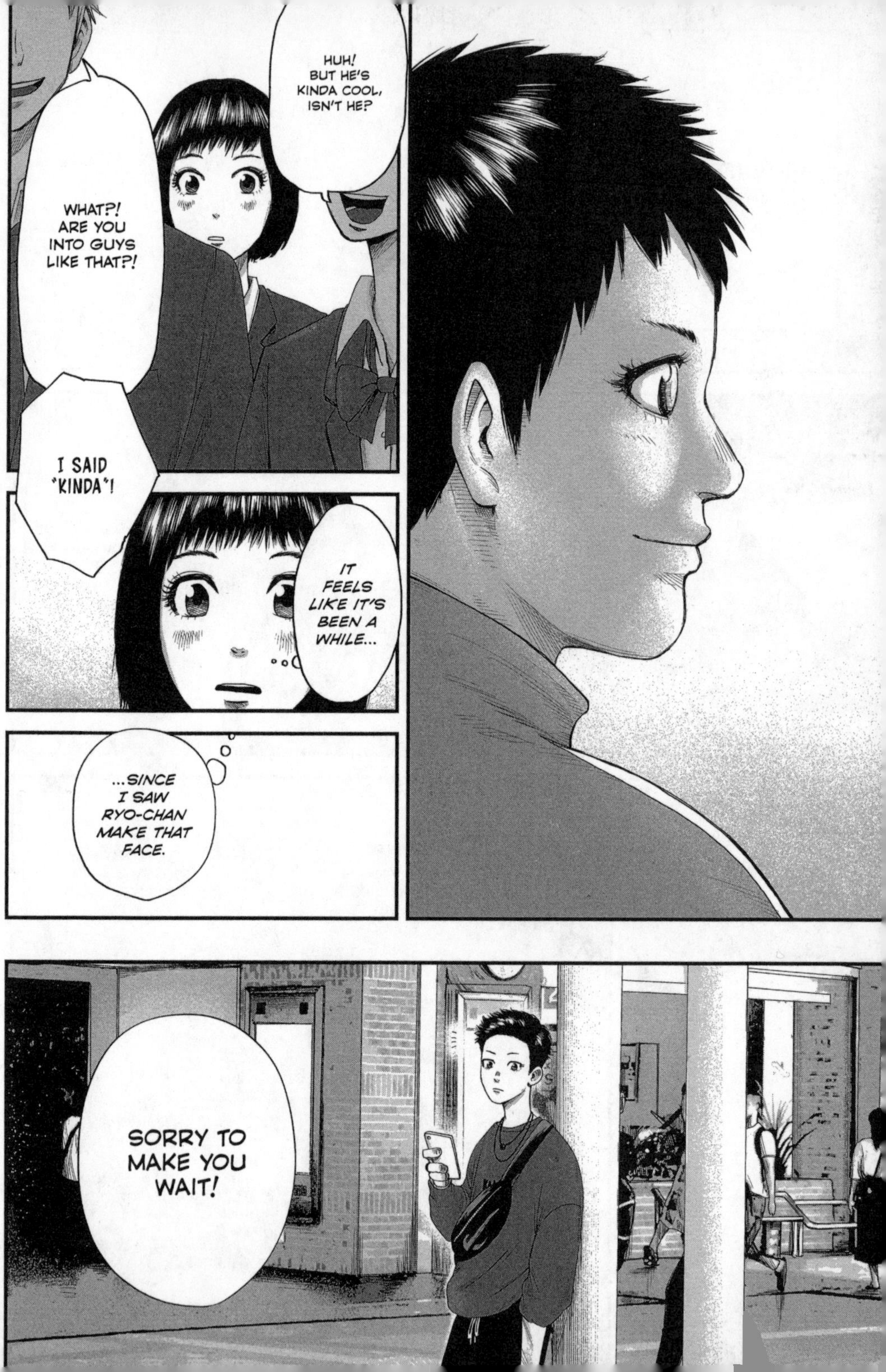
HUH! BUT HE'S KINDA COOL, ISN'T HE?
WHAT?! ARE YOU INTO GUYS LIKE THAT?!
I SAID "KINDA"!
IT FEELS LIKE IT'S BEEN A WHILE...
...SINCE I SAW RYO-CHAN MAKE THAT FACE.
SORRY TO MAKE YOU WAIT!

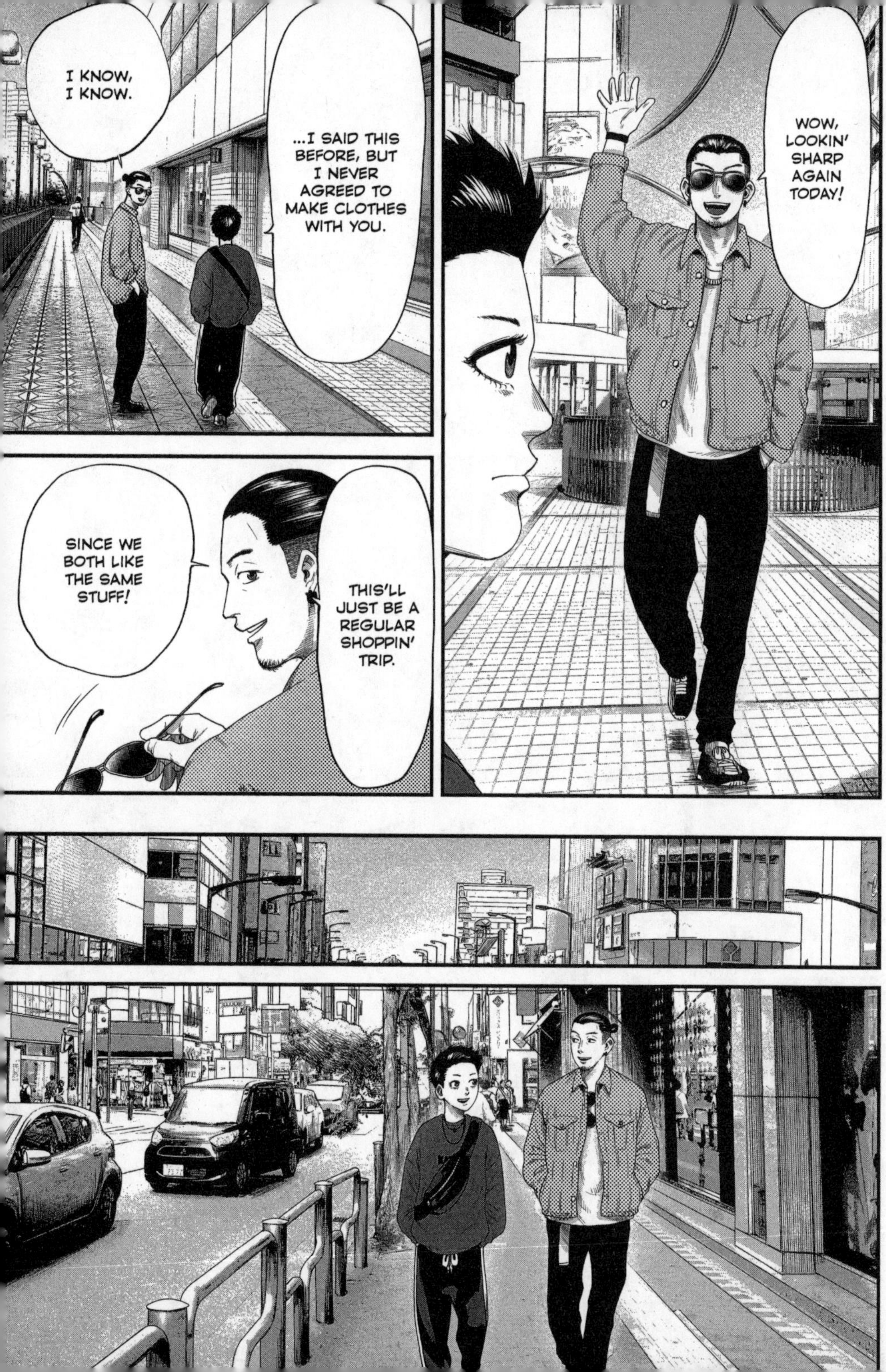
WOW, LOOKIN' SHARP AGAIN TODAY!
...I SAID THIS BEFORE, BUT I NEVER AGREED TO MAKE CLOTHES WITH YOU.
I KNOW, I KNOW.
THIS'LL JUST BE A REGULAR SHOPPIN' TRIP.
SINCE WE BOTH LIKE THE SAME STUFF!

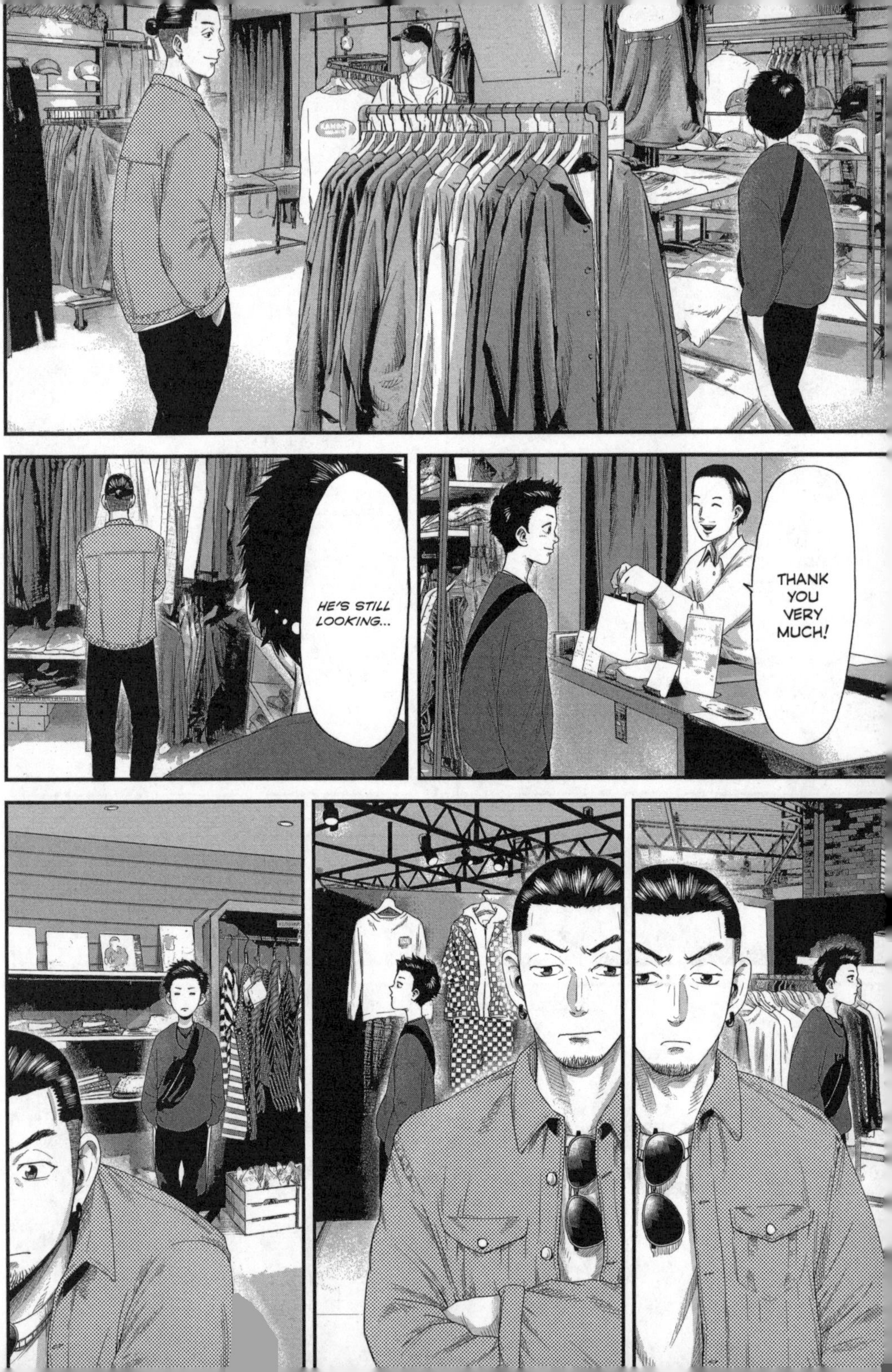
THANK YOU VERY MUCH!
HE'S STILL LOOKING...

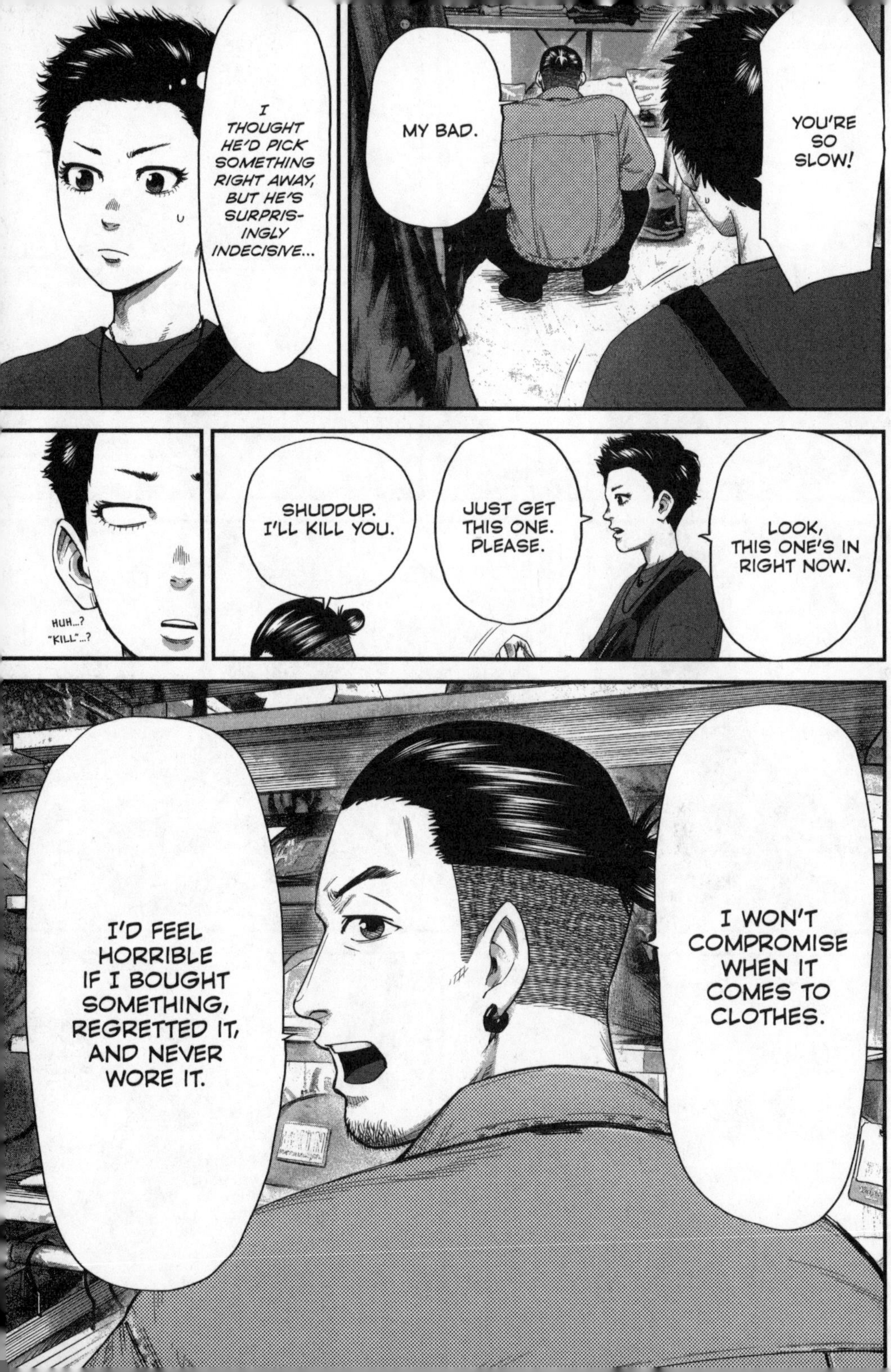
YOU'RE SO SLOW!
MY BAD.
I THOUGHT HE'D PICK SOMETHING RIGHT AWAY, BUT HE'S SURPRISINGLY INDECISIVE...
LOOK, THIS ONE'S IN RIGHT NOW.
JUST GET THIS ONE. PLEASE.
SHUDDUP. I'LL KILL YOU.
HUH...? "KILL"...?
I WON'T COMPROMISE WHEN IT COMES TO CLOTHES.
I'D FEEL HORRIBLE IF I BOUGHT SOMETHING, REGRETTED IT, AND NEVER WORE IT.

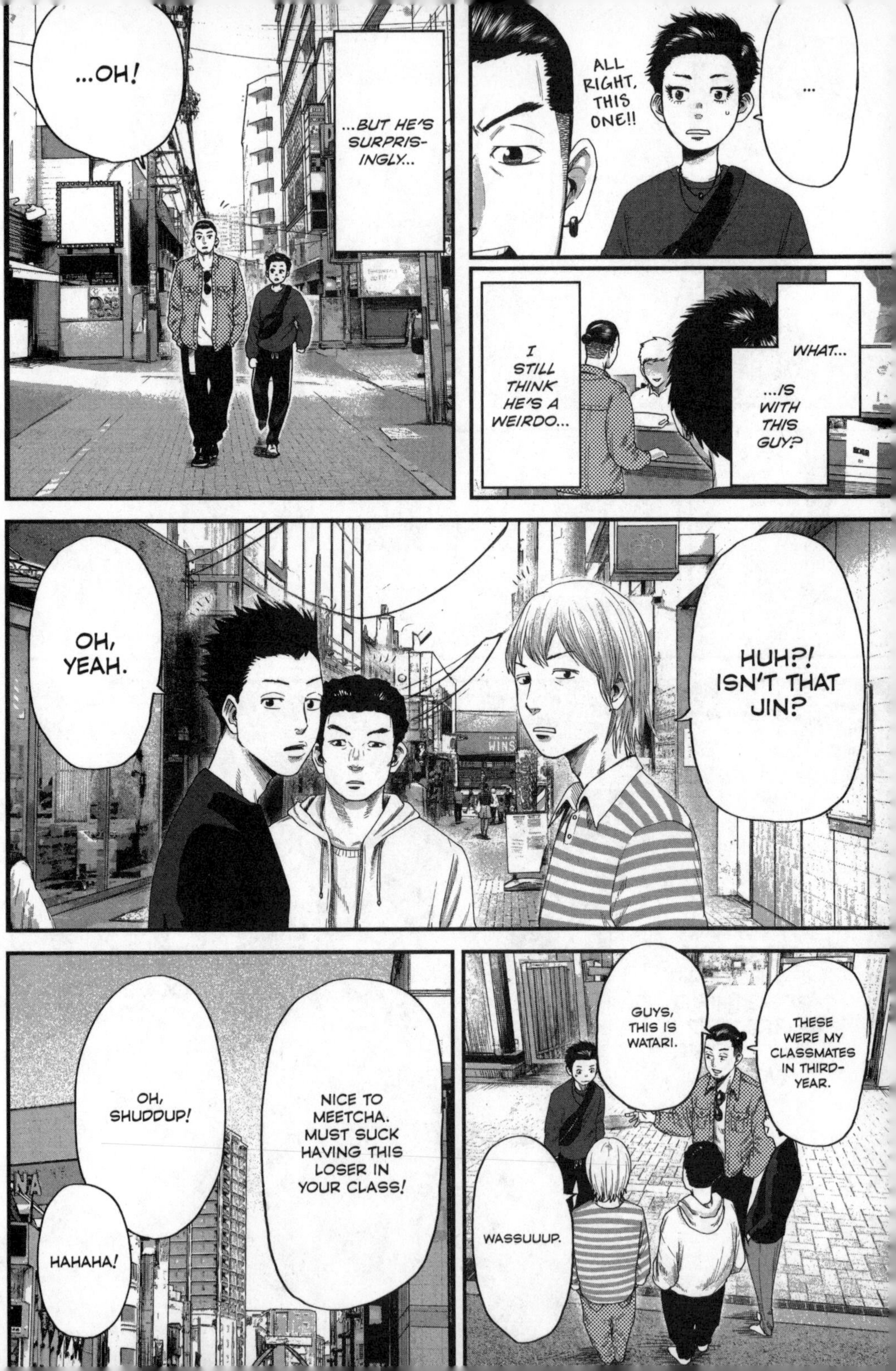
...
ALL RIGHT, THIS ONE!!
WHAT...
...IS WITH THIS GUY?
I STILL THINK HE'S A WEIRDO...
...BUT HE'S SURPRIS-INGLY...
...OH!
HUH?! ISN'T THAT JIN?
OH, YEAH.
THESE WERE MY CLASSMATES IN THIRD-YEAR.
GUYS, THIS IS WATARI.
WASSUUUP.
NICE TO MEETCHA. MUST SUCK HAVING THIS LOSER IN YOUR CLASS!
OH, SHUDDUP!
HAHAHA!

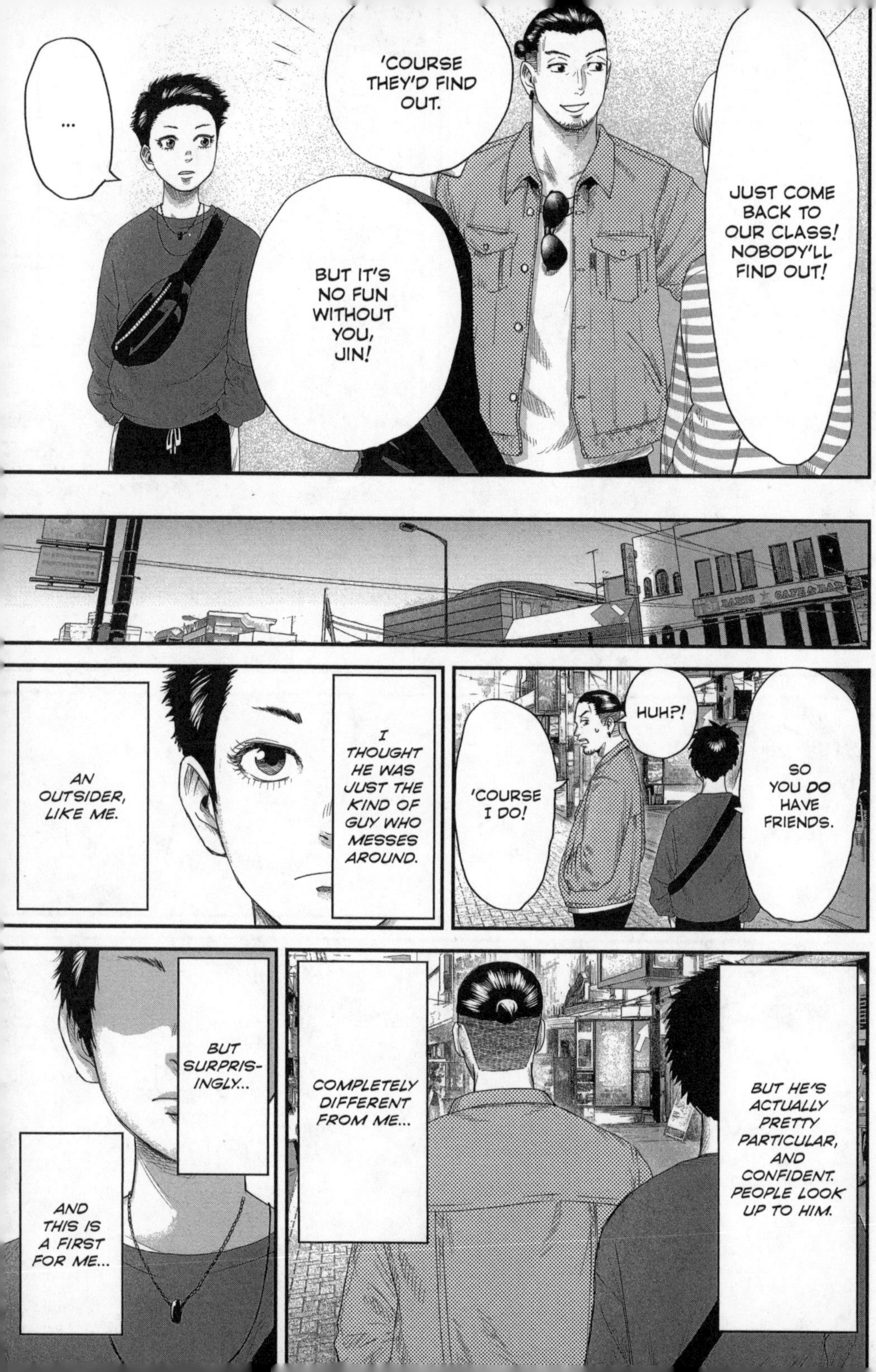
JUST COME BACK TO OUR CLASS! NOBODY'LL FIND OUT!
'COURSE THEY'D FIND OUT.
BUT IT'S NO FUN WITHOUT YOU, JIN!
...
SO YOU DO HAVE FRIENDS.
HUH?!
'COURSE I DO!
I THOUGHT HE WAS JUST THE KIND OF GUY WHO MESSES AROUND.
AN OUTSIDER, LIKE ME.
BUT HE'S ACTUALLY PRETTY PARTICULAR, AND CONFIDENT. PEOPLE LOOK UP TO HIM.
COMPLETELY DIFFERENT FROM ME...
BUT SURPRIS-INGLY...
AND THIS IS A FIRST FOR ME...

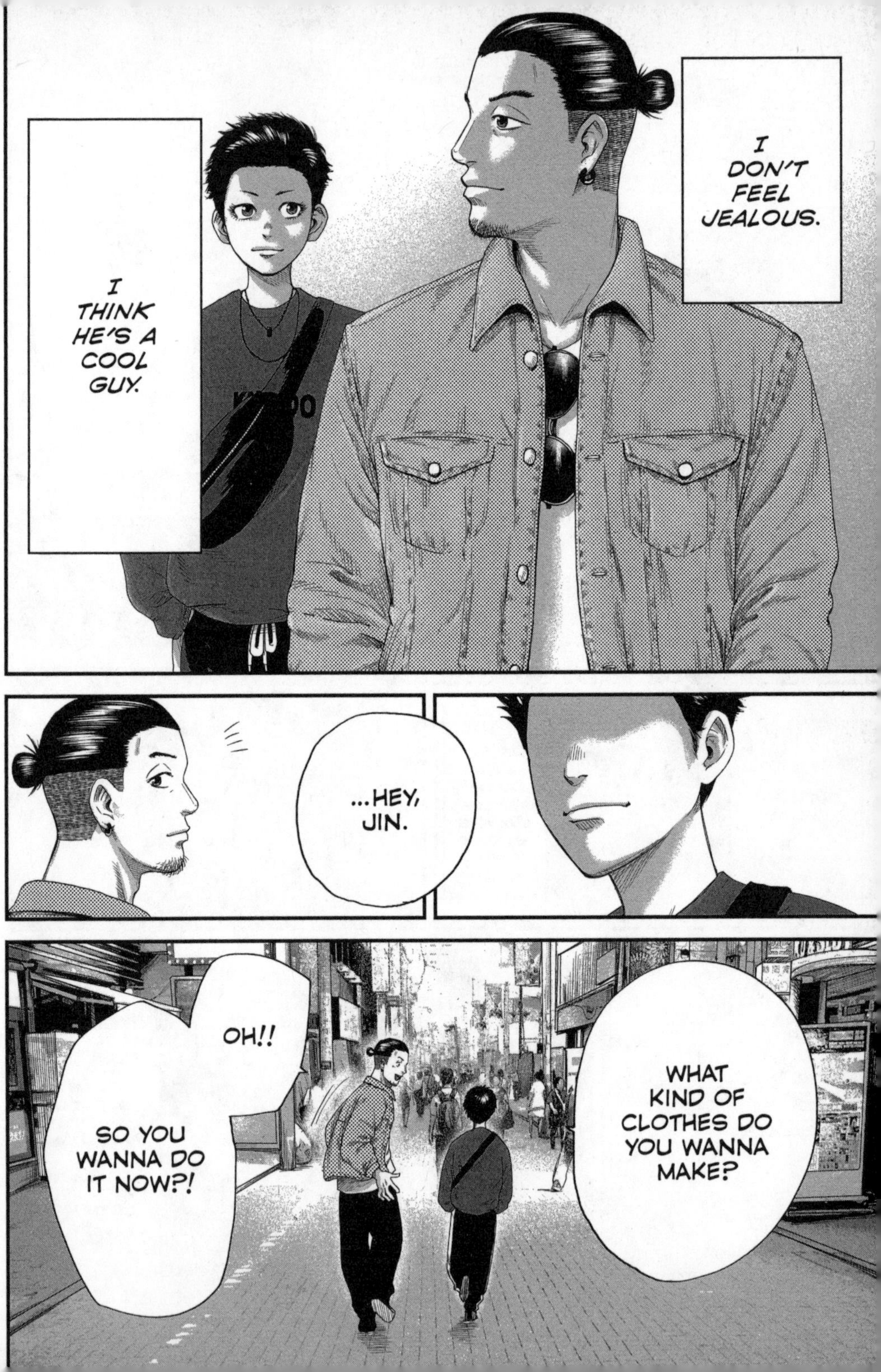
I DON'T FEEL JEALOUS.
I THINK HE'S A COOL GUY.
...HEY, JIN.
WHAT KIND OF CLOTHES DO YOU WANNA MAKE?
OH!!
SO YOU WANNA DO IT NOW?!

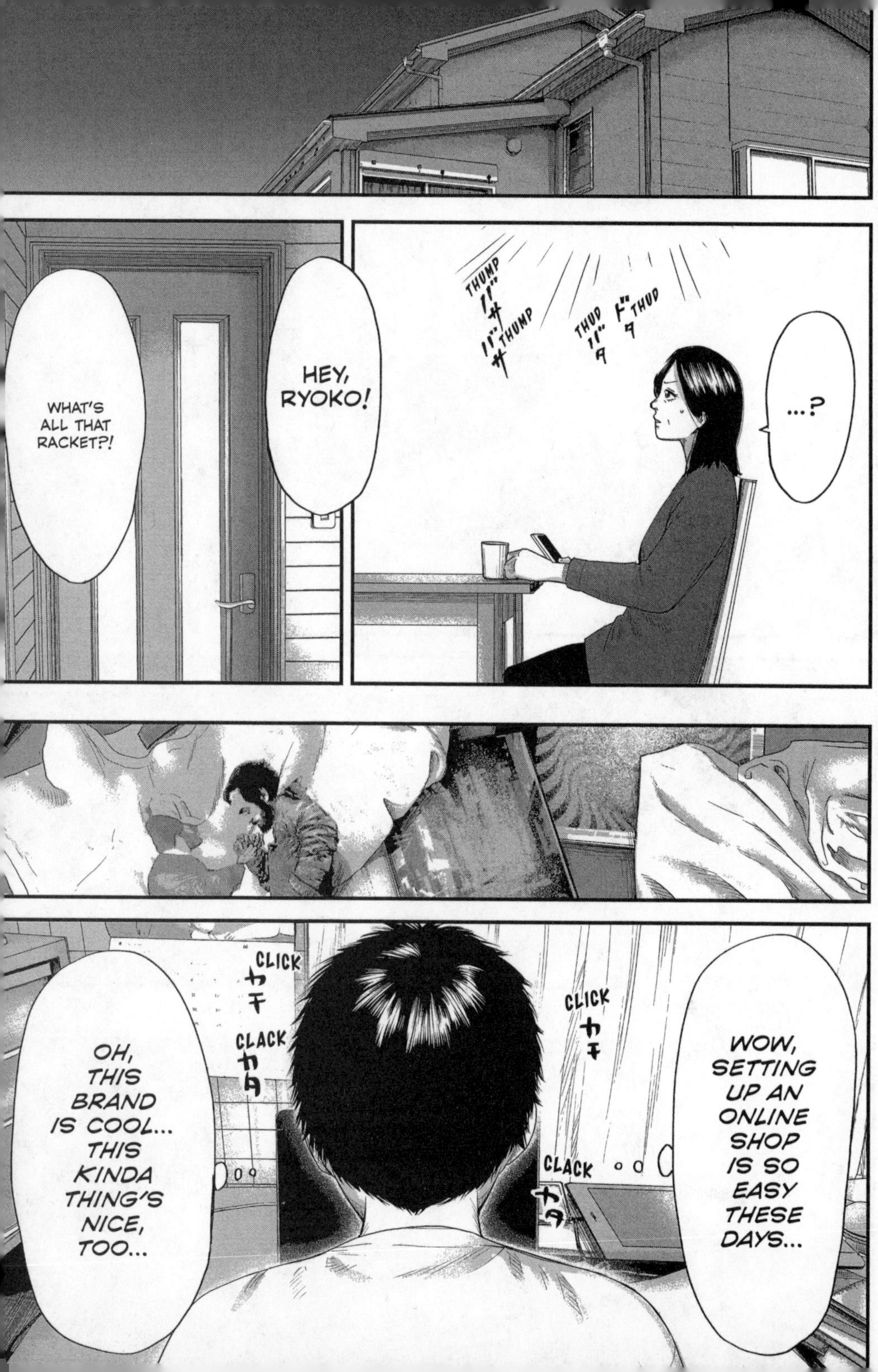
THUD ドタ
THUD バタ
THUMP バサ
THUMP バサ
...?
HEY, RYOKO!
WHAT'S ALL THAT RACKET?!
WOW, SETTING UP AN ONLINE SHOP IS SO EASY THESE DAYS...
CLICK カチ
CLACK カタ
CLICK カチ
CLACK カタ
OH, THIS BRAND IS COOL... THIS KINDA THING'S NICE, TOO...

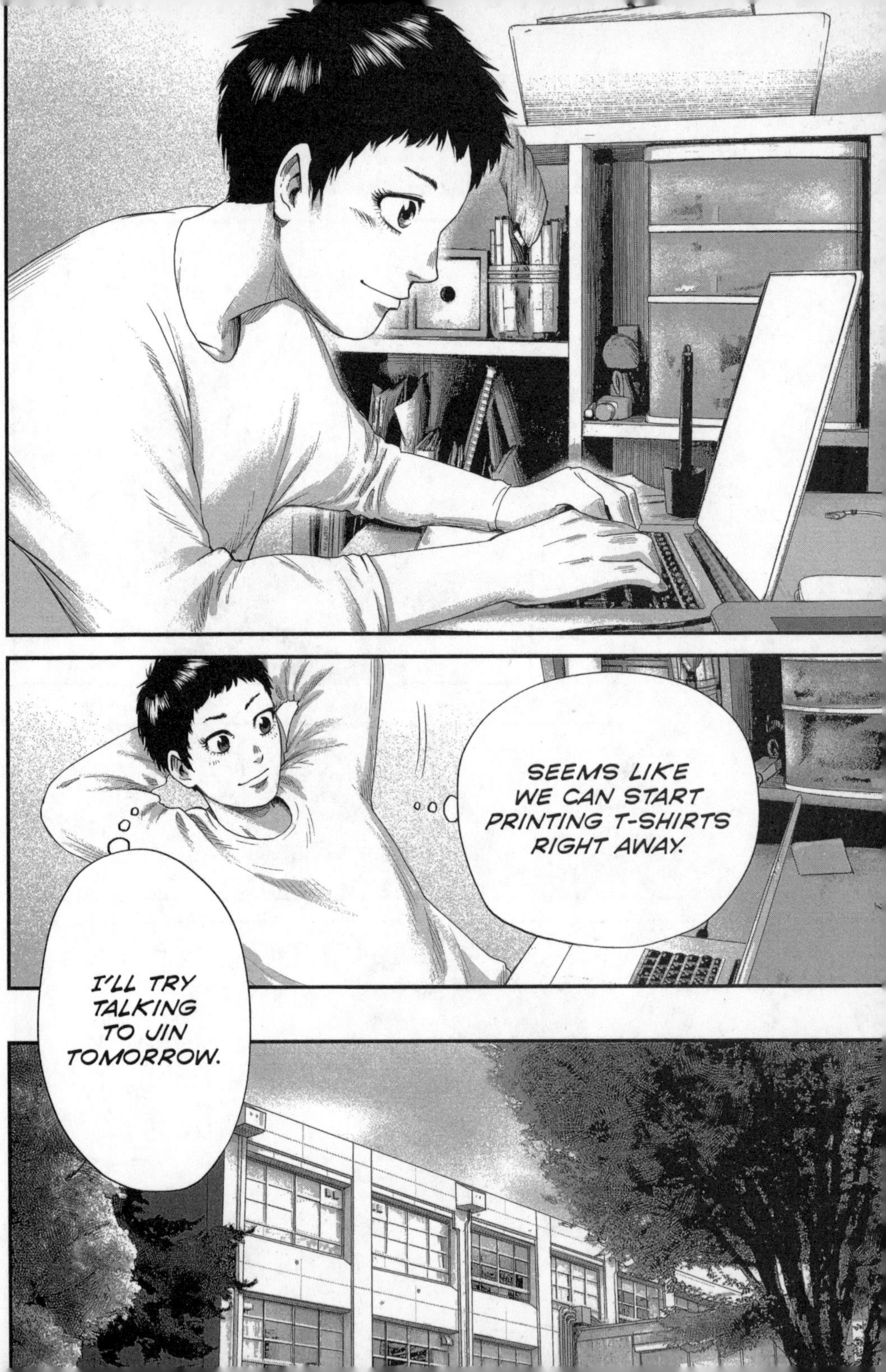
SEEMS LIKE WE CAN START PRINTING T-SHIRTS RIGHT AWAY.
I'LL TRY TALKING TO JIN TOMORROW.

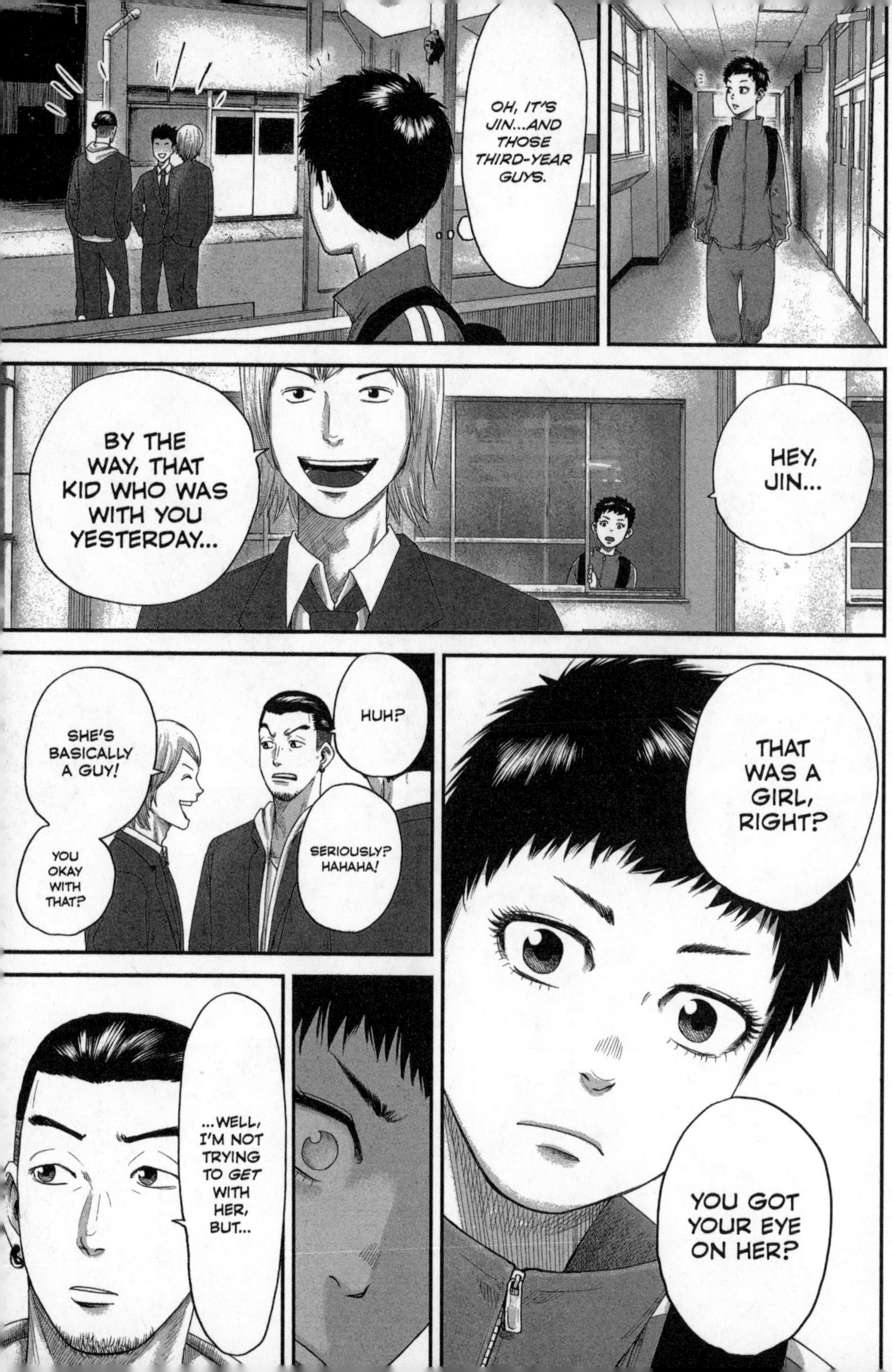
OH, IT'S JIN...AND THOSE THIRD-YEAR GUYS.
HEY, JIN...
BY THE WAY, THAT KID WHO WAS WITH YOU YESTERDAY...
THAT WAS A GIRL, RIGHT?
YOU GOT YOUR EYE ON HER?
HUH?
SERIOUSLY? HAHAHA!
SHE'S BASICALLY A GUY!
YOU OKAY WITH THAT?
...WELL, I'M NOT TRYING TO GET WITH HER, BUT...

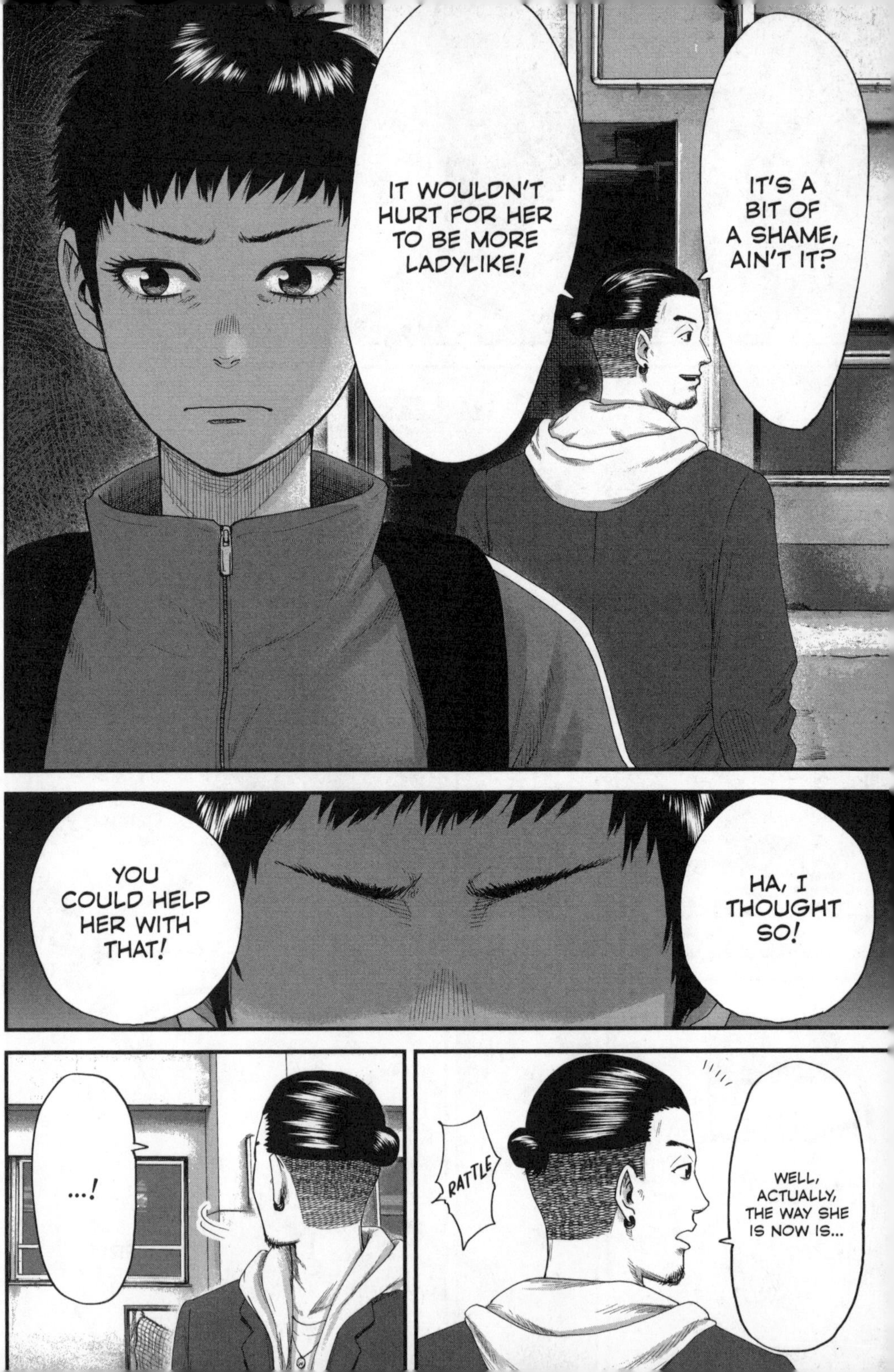
IT'S A BIT OF A SHAME, AIN'T IT?
IT WOULDN'T HURT FOR HER TO BE MORE LADYLIKE!
HA, I THOUGHT SO!
YOU COULD HELP HER WITH THAT!
WELL, ACTUALLY, THE WAY SHE IS NOW IS...
RATTLE
...!

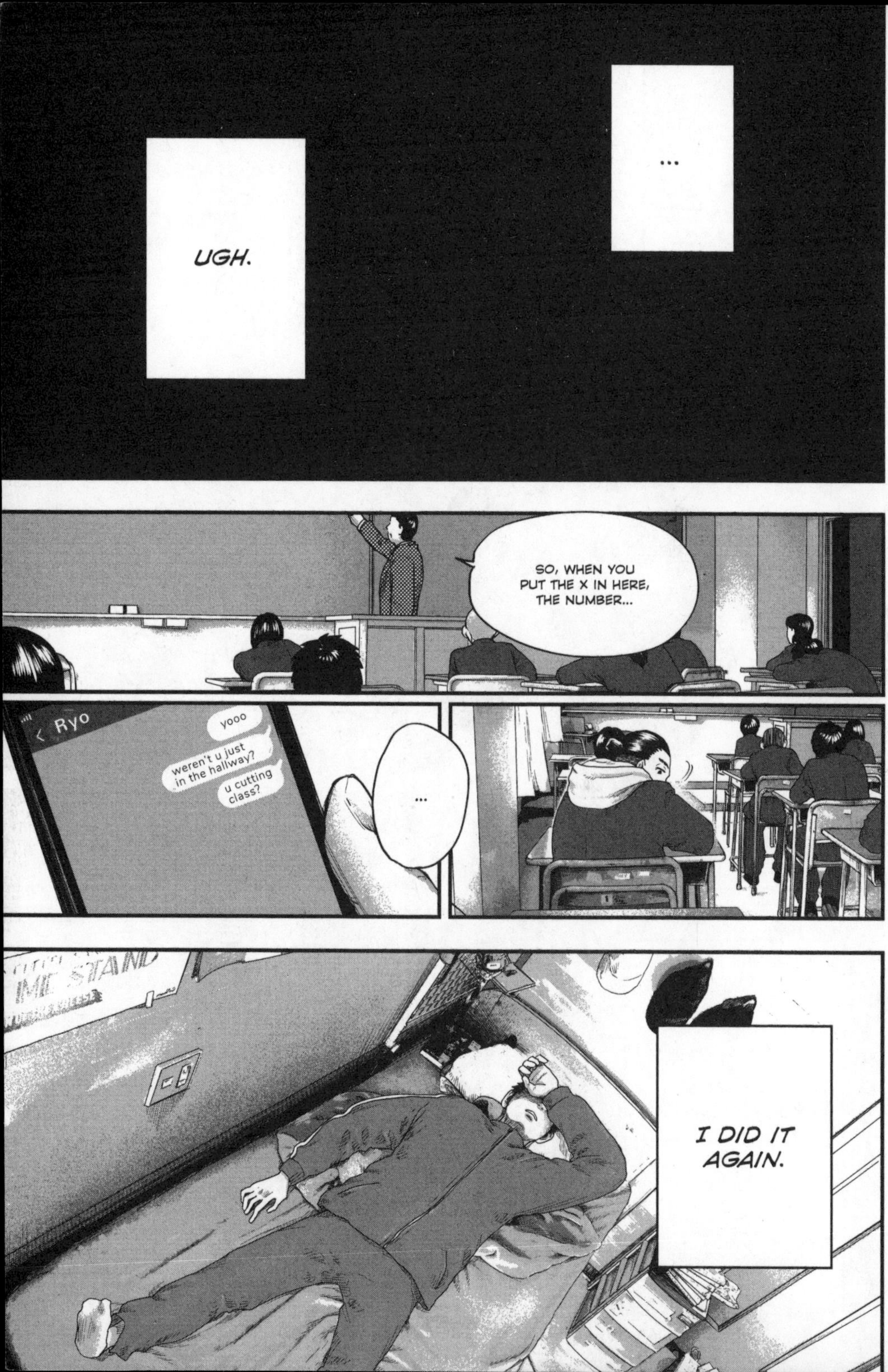
...
UGH.
SO, WHEN YOU PUT THE X IN HERE, THE NUMBER...
Ryo
yooo
weren't u just in the hallway?
u cutting class?
...
I DID IT AGAIN.

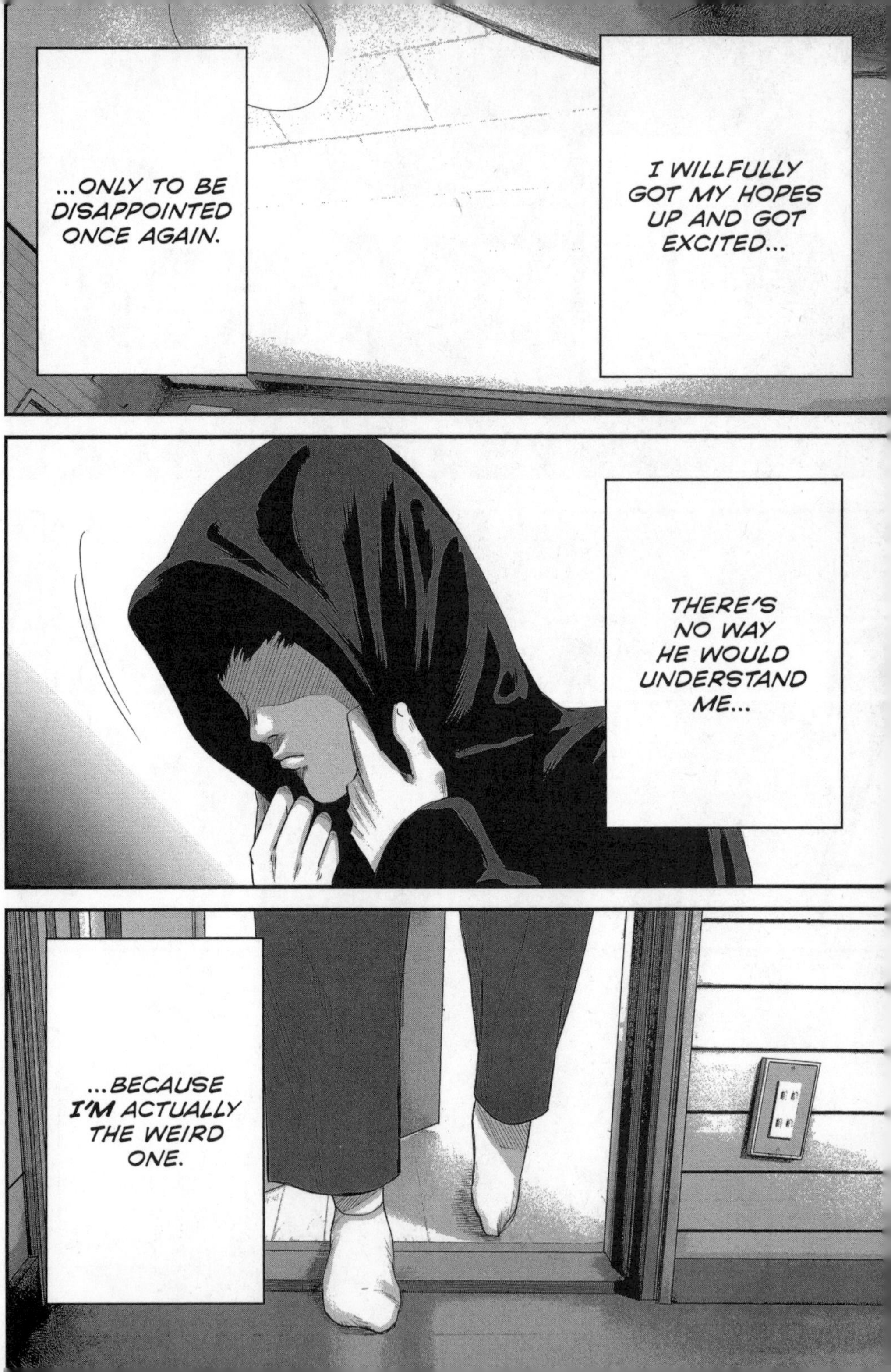
I WILLFULLY GOT MY HOPES UP AND GOT EXCITED...
...ONLY TO BE DISAPPOINTED ONCE AGAIN.
THERE'S NO WAY HE WOULD UNDERSTAND ME...
...BECAUSE I'M ACTUALLY THE WEIRD ONE.

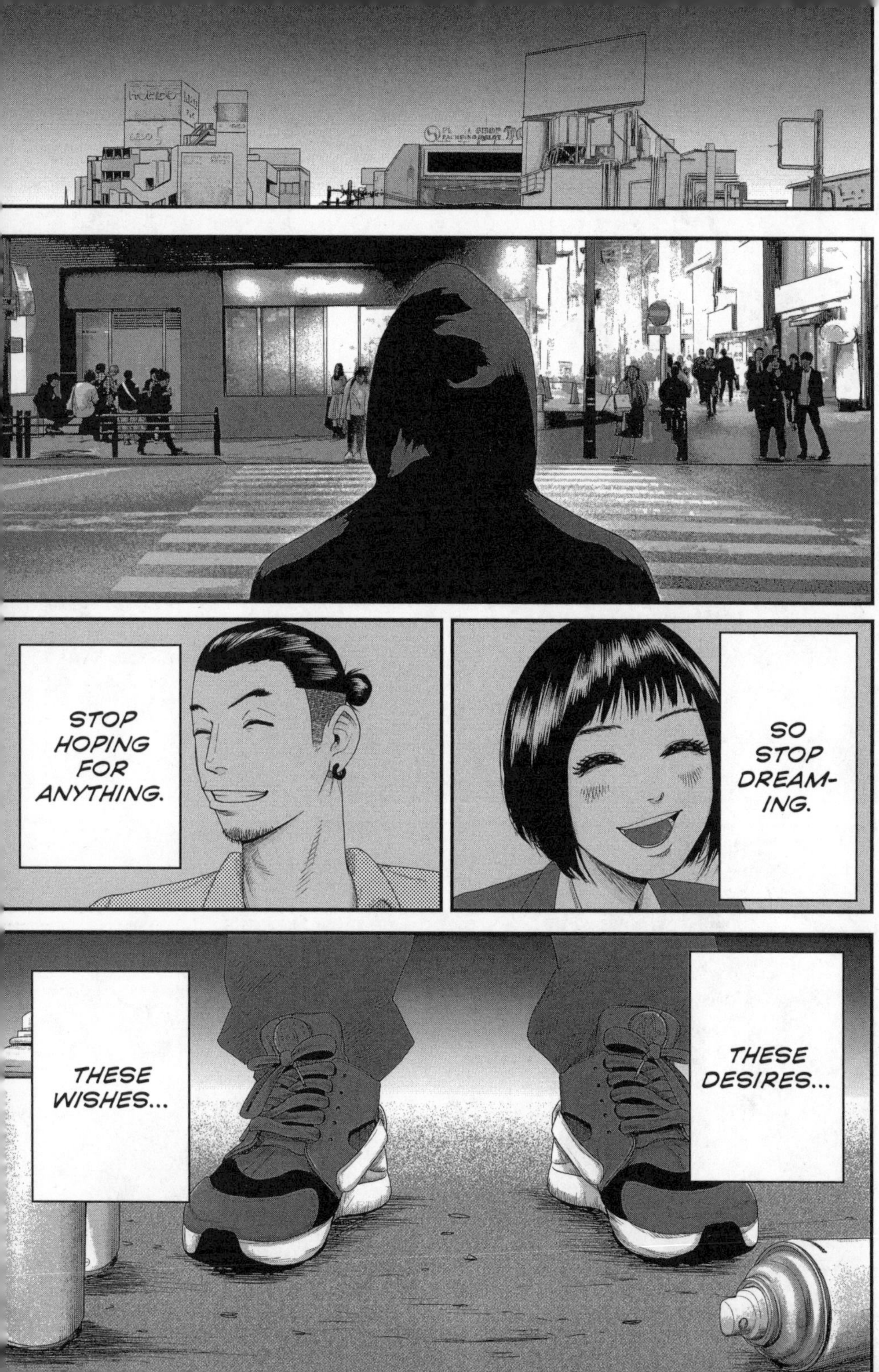
SO STOP DREAM-ING.
STOP HOPING FOR ANYTHING.
THESE DESIRES...
THESE WISHES...

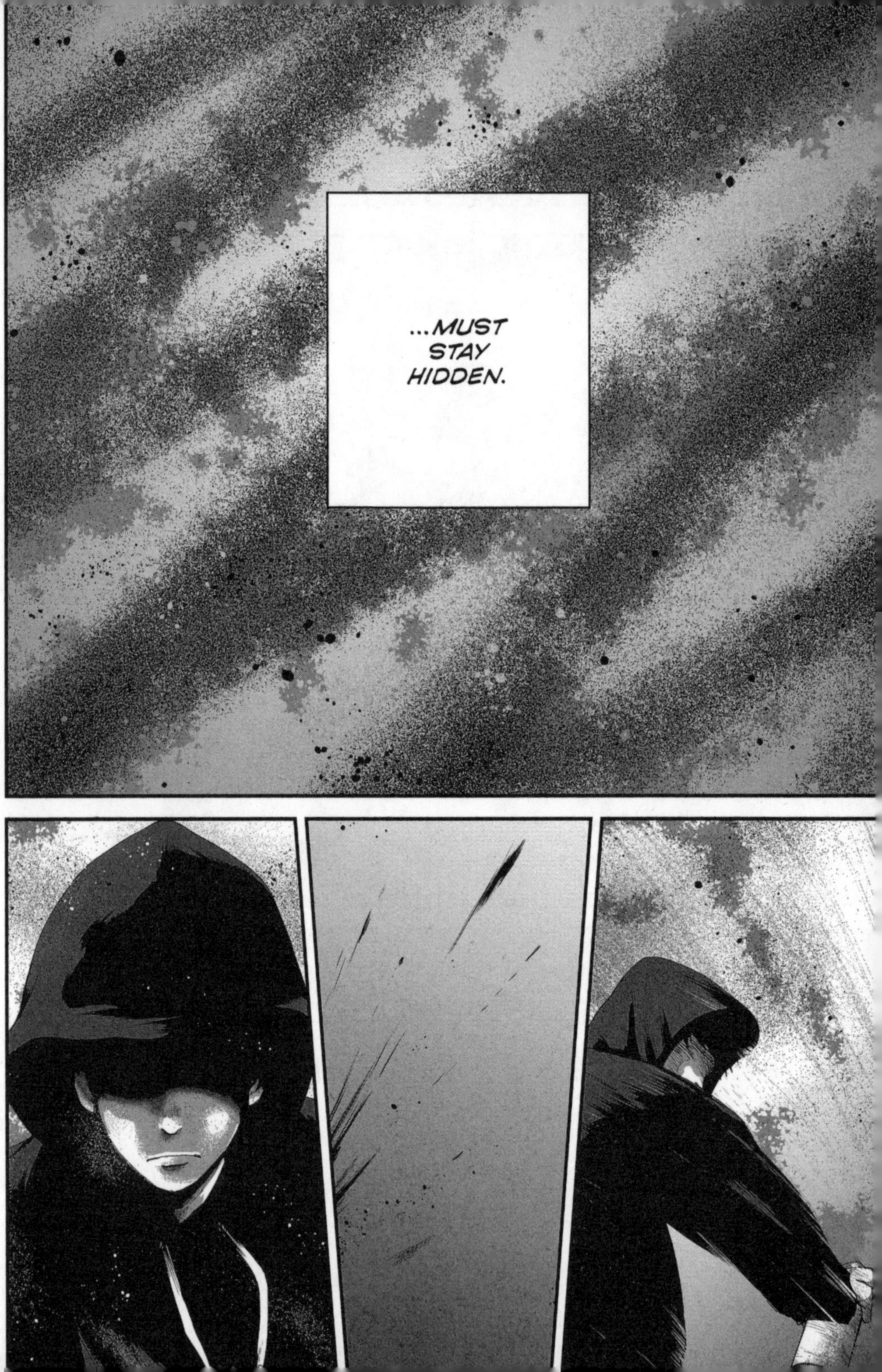
...MUST STAY HIDDEN.

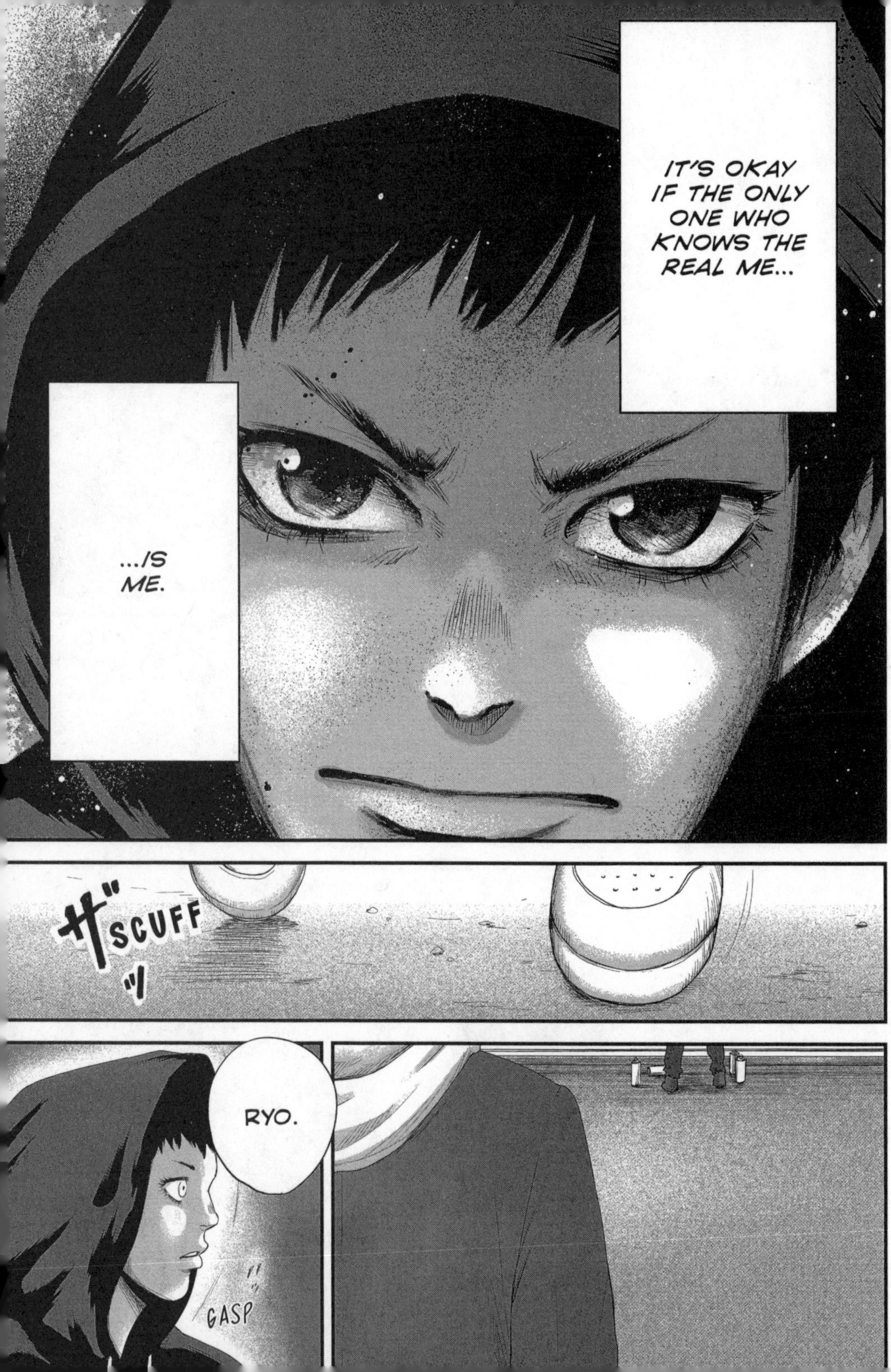
IT'S OKAY IF THE ONLY ONE WHO KNOWS THE REAL ME...
...IS ME.
ザッ SCUFF
RYO.
GASP

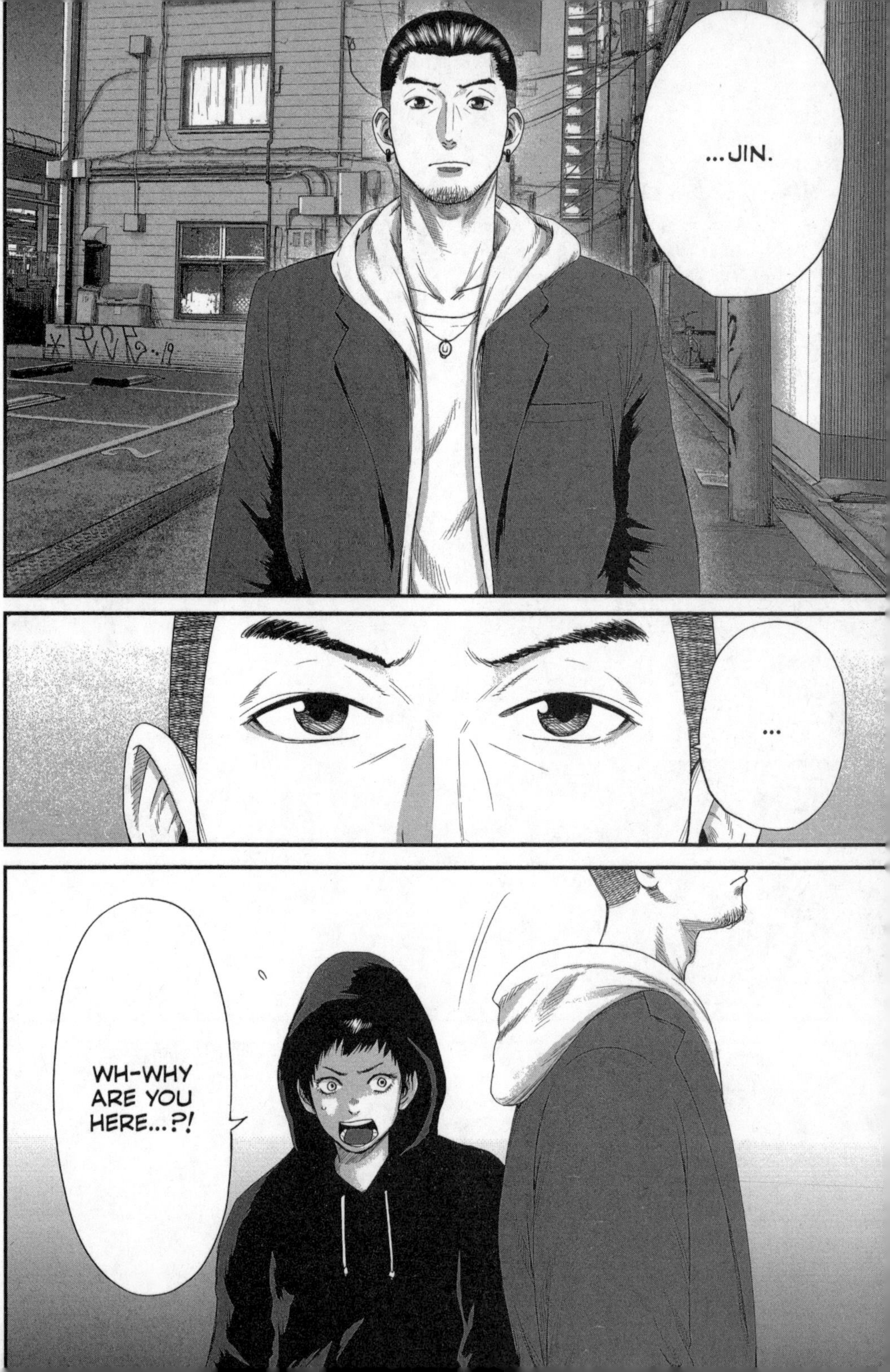
...JIN.
...
WH-WHY ARE YOU HERE...?!

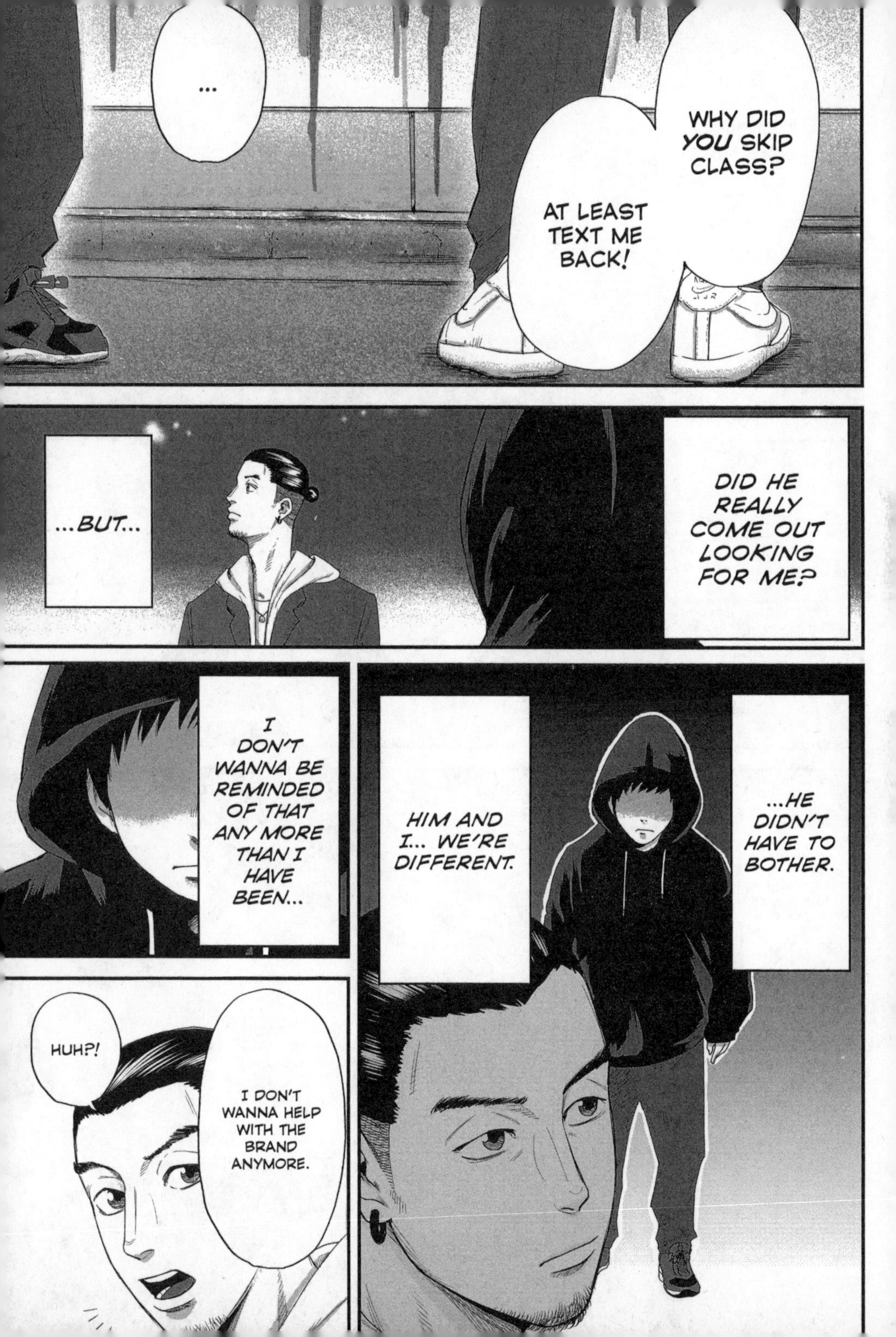
WHY DID YOU SKIP CLASS?
AT LEAST TEXT ME BACK!
...
DID HE REALLY COME OUT LOOKING FOR ME?
...BUT...
...HE DIDN'T HAVE TO BOTHER.
HIM AND I... WE'RE DIFFERENT.
I DON'T WANNA BE REMINDED OF THAT ANY MORE THAN I HAVE BEEN...
I DON'T WANNA HELP WITH THE BRAND ANYMORE.
HUH?!

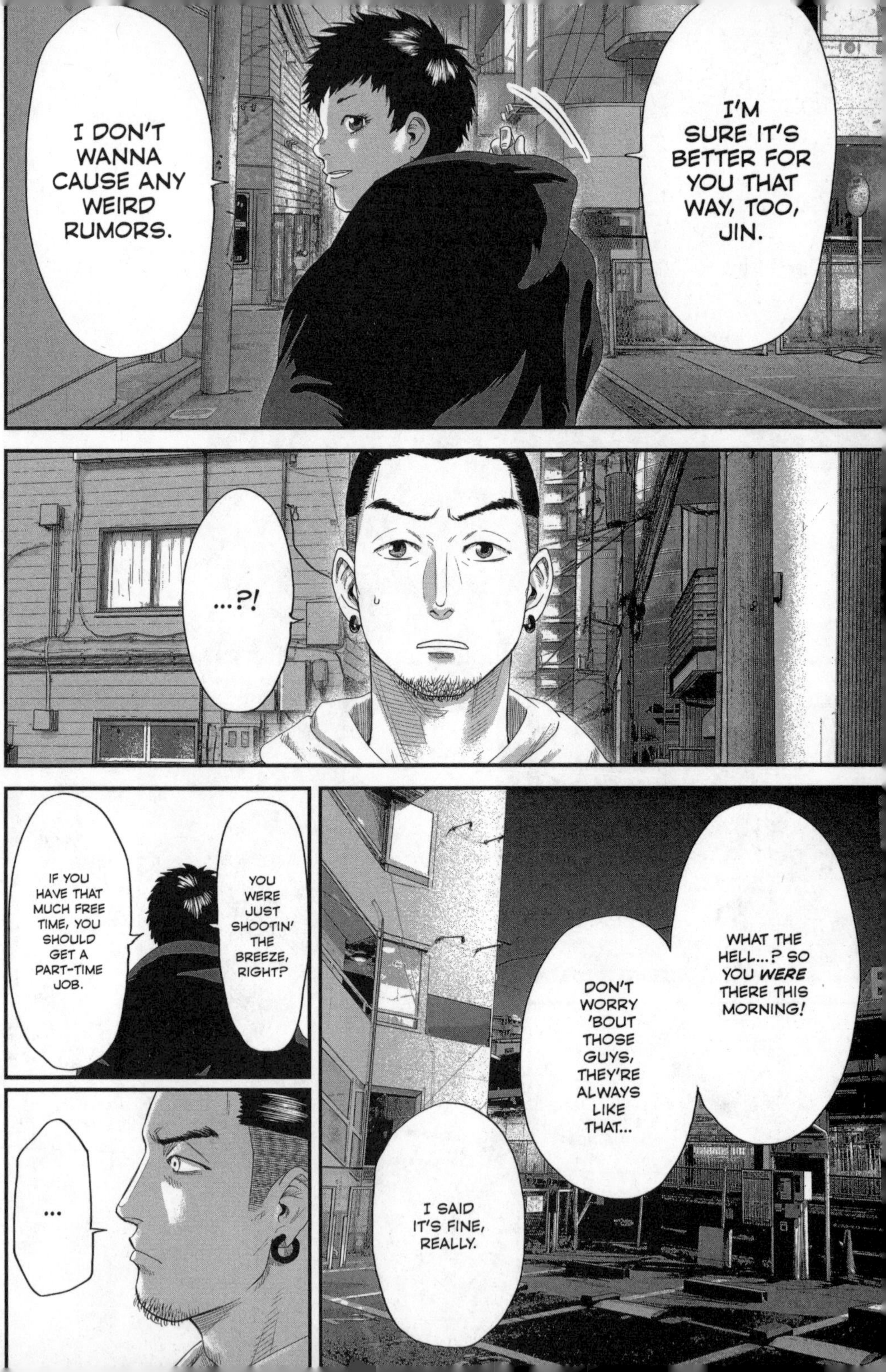
I'M SURE IT'S BETTER FOR YOU THAT WAY, TOO, JIN.
I DON'T WANNA CAUSE ANY WEIRD RUMORS.
...?!
WHAT THE HELL...? SO YOU *WERE* THERE THIS MORNING!
DON'T WORRY 'BOUT THOSE GUYS, THEY'RE ALWAYS LIKE THAT...
I SAID IT'S FINE, REALLY.
YOU WERE JUST SHOOTIN' THE BREEZE, RIGHT?
IF YOU HAVE THAT MUCH FREE TIME, YOU SHOULD GET A PART-TIME JOB.
...

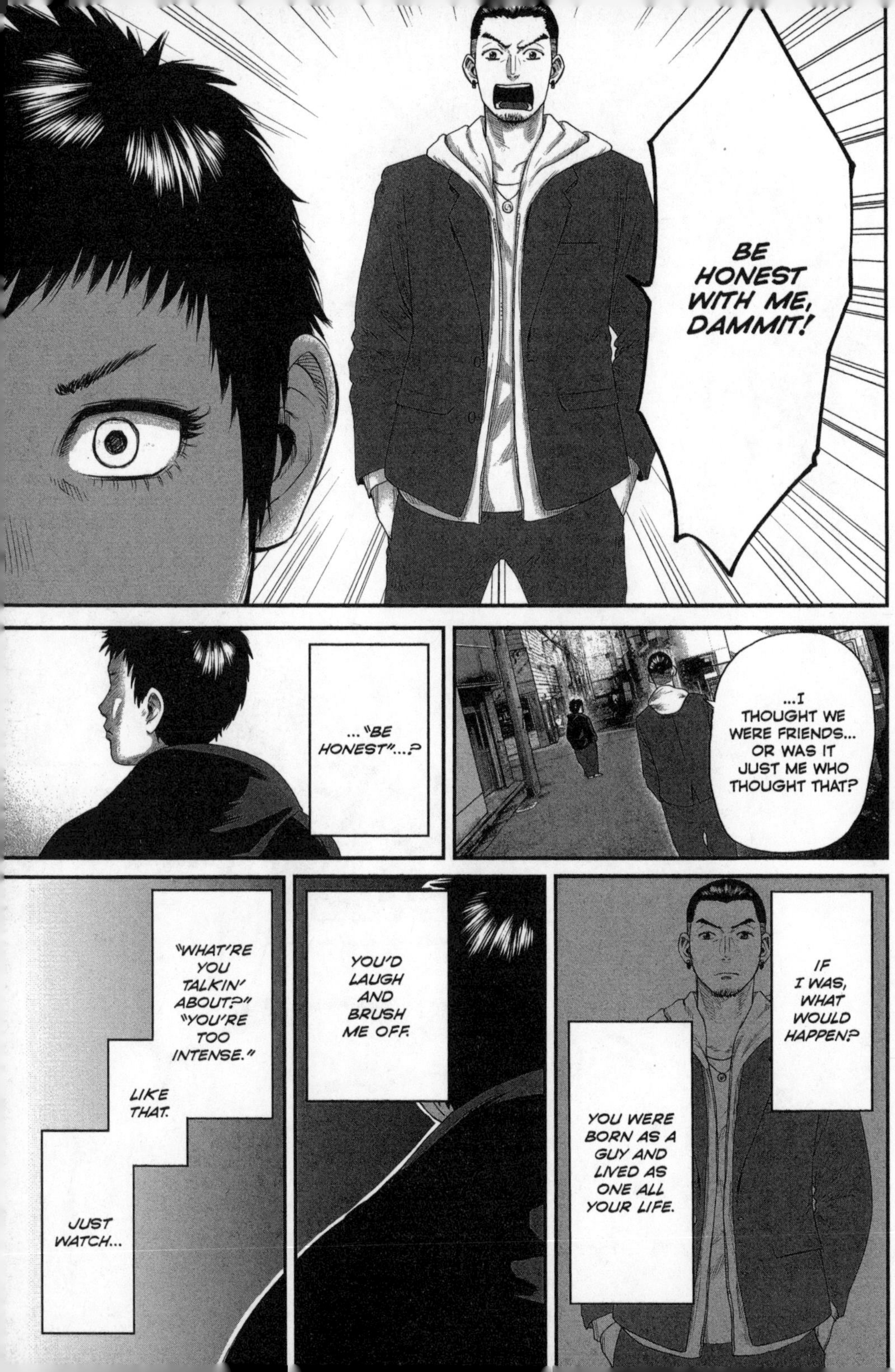
BE HONEST WITH ME, DAMMIT!
...I THOUGHT WE WERE FRIENDS... OR WAS IT JUST ME WHO THOUGHT THAT?
..."BE HONEST"...?
IF I WAS, WHAT WOULD HAPPEN?
YOU WERE BORN AS A GUY AND LIVED AS ONE ALL YOUR LIFE.
YOU'D LAUGH AND BRUSH ME OFF.
"WHAT'RE YOU TALKIN' ABOUT?" "YOU'RE TOO INTENSE."
LIKE THAT.
JUST WATCH...

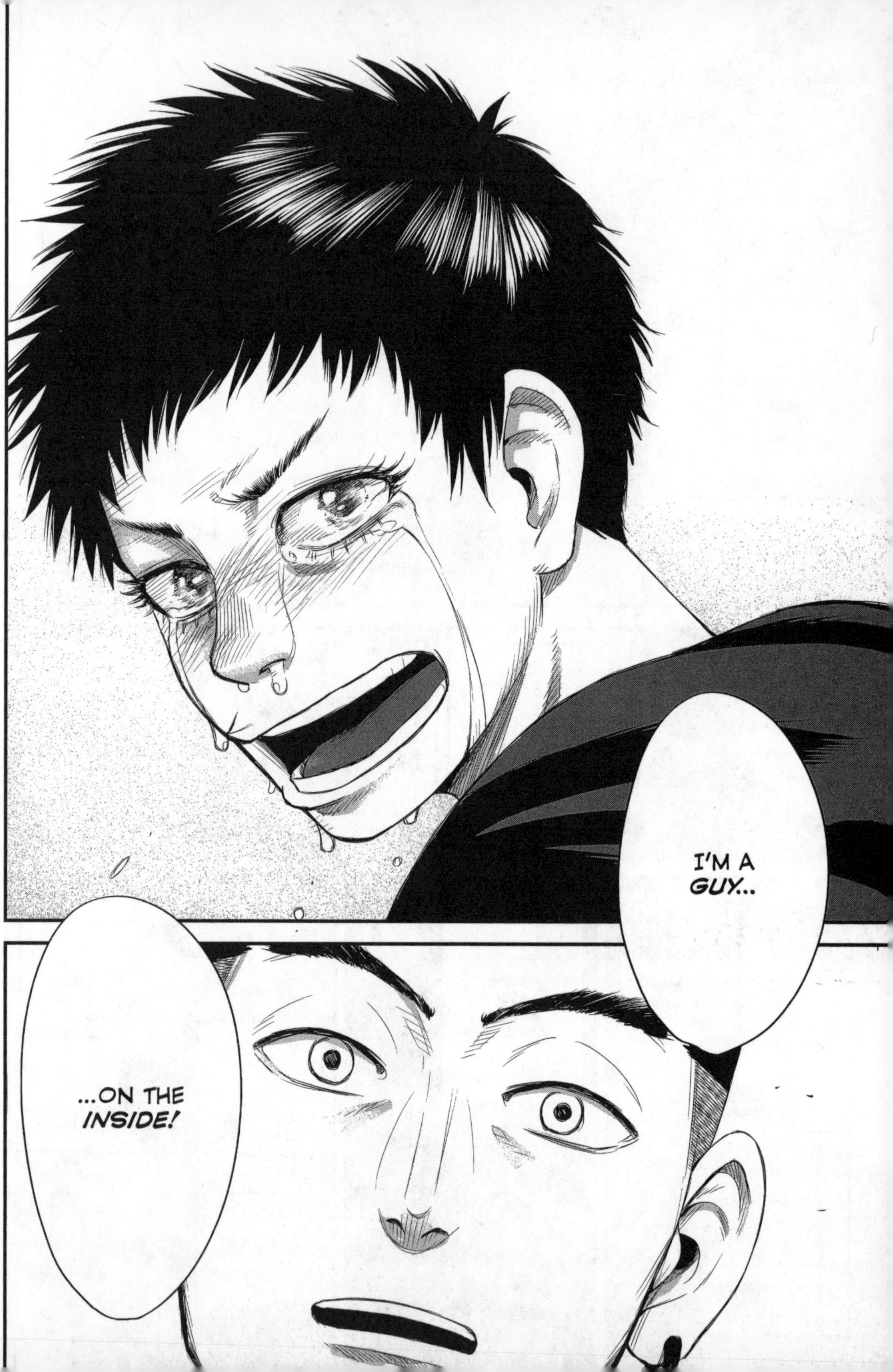
I'M A *GUY*...
...ON THE *INSIDE!*

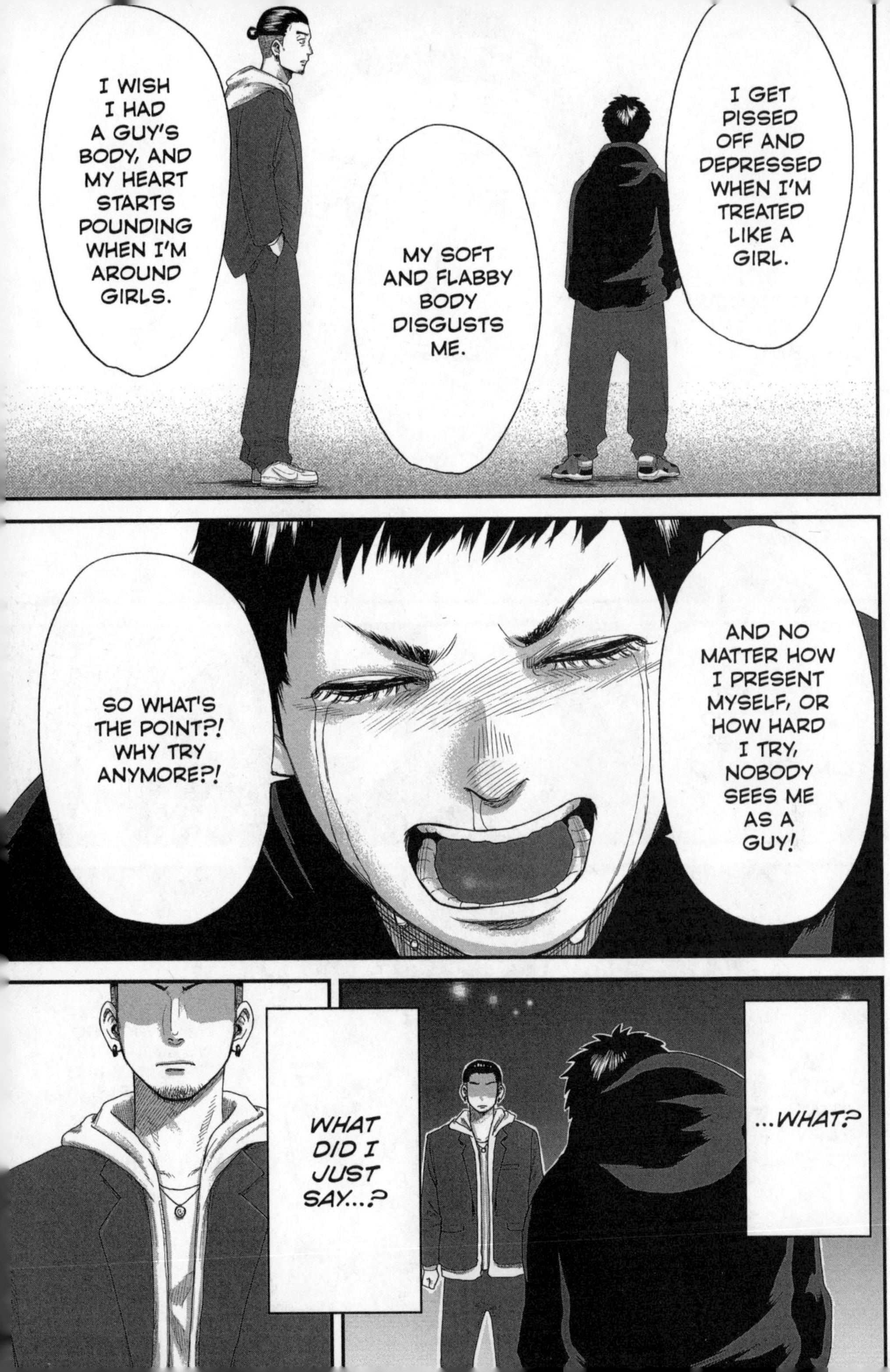
I GET PISSED OFF AND DEPRESSED WHEN I'M TREATED LIKE A GIRL.
MY SOFT AND FLABBY BODY DISGUSTS ME.
I WISH I HAD A GUY'S BODY, AND MY HEART STARTS POUNDING WHEN I'M AROUND GIRLS.
AND NO MATTER HOW I PRESENT MYSELF, OR HOW HARD I TRY, NOBODY SEES ME AS A GUY!
SO WHAT'S THE POINT?! WHY TRY ANYMORE?!
...WHAT?
WHAT DID I JUST SAY...?

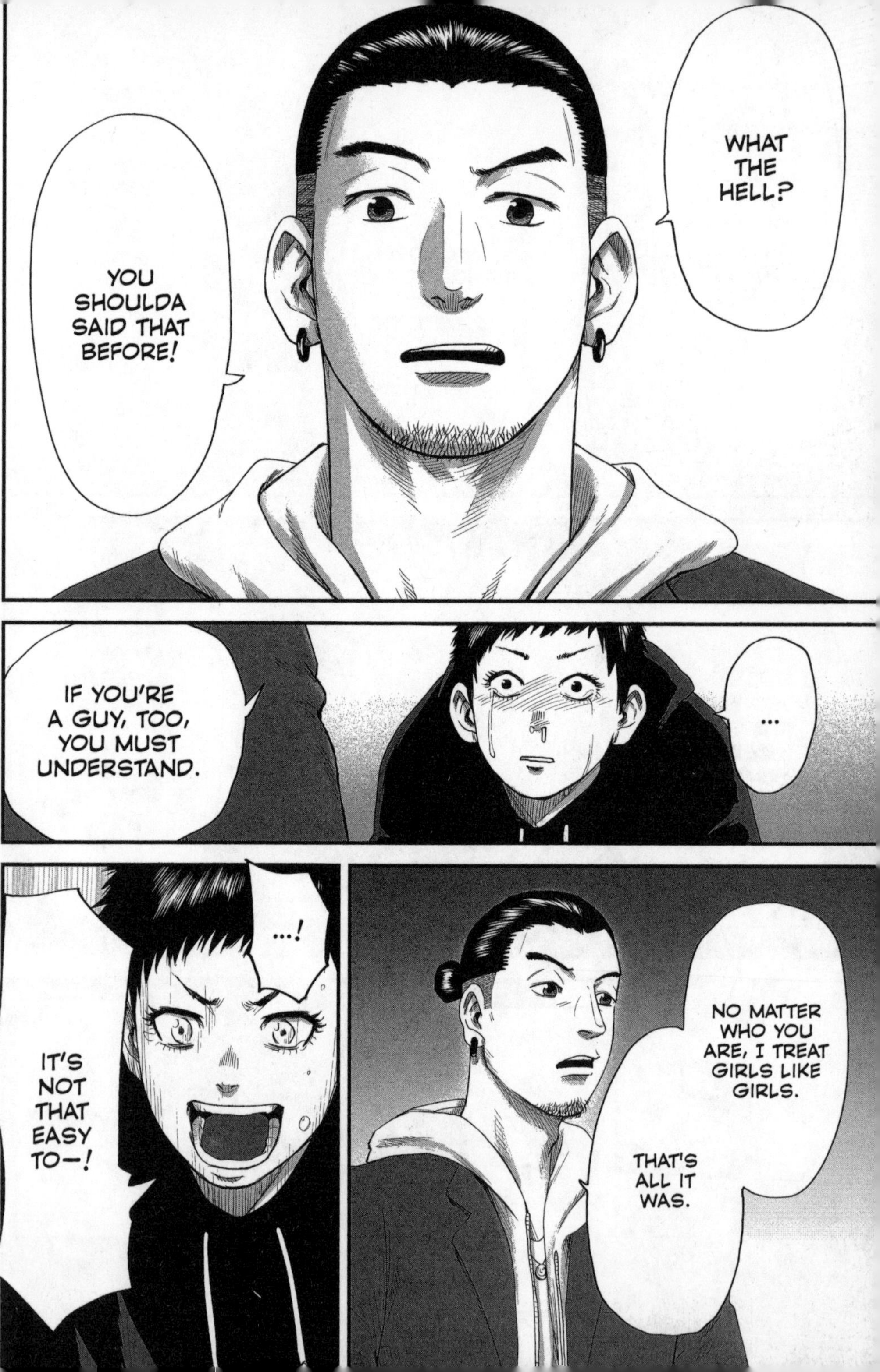
WHAT THE HELL?
YOU SHOULDA SAID THAT BEFORE!
...
IF YOU'RE A GUY, TOO, YOU MUST UNDERSTAND.
NO MATTER WHO YOU ARE, I TREAT GIRLS LIKE GIRLS.
THAT'S ALL IT WAS.
...!
IT'S NOT THAT EASY TO—!

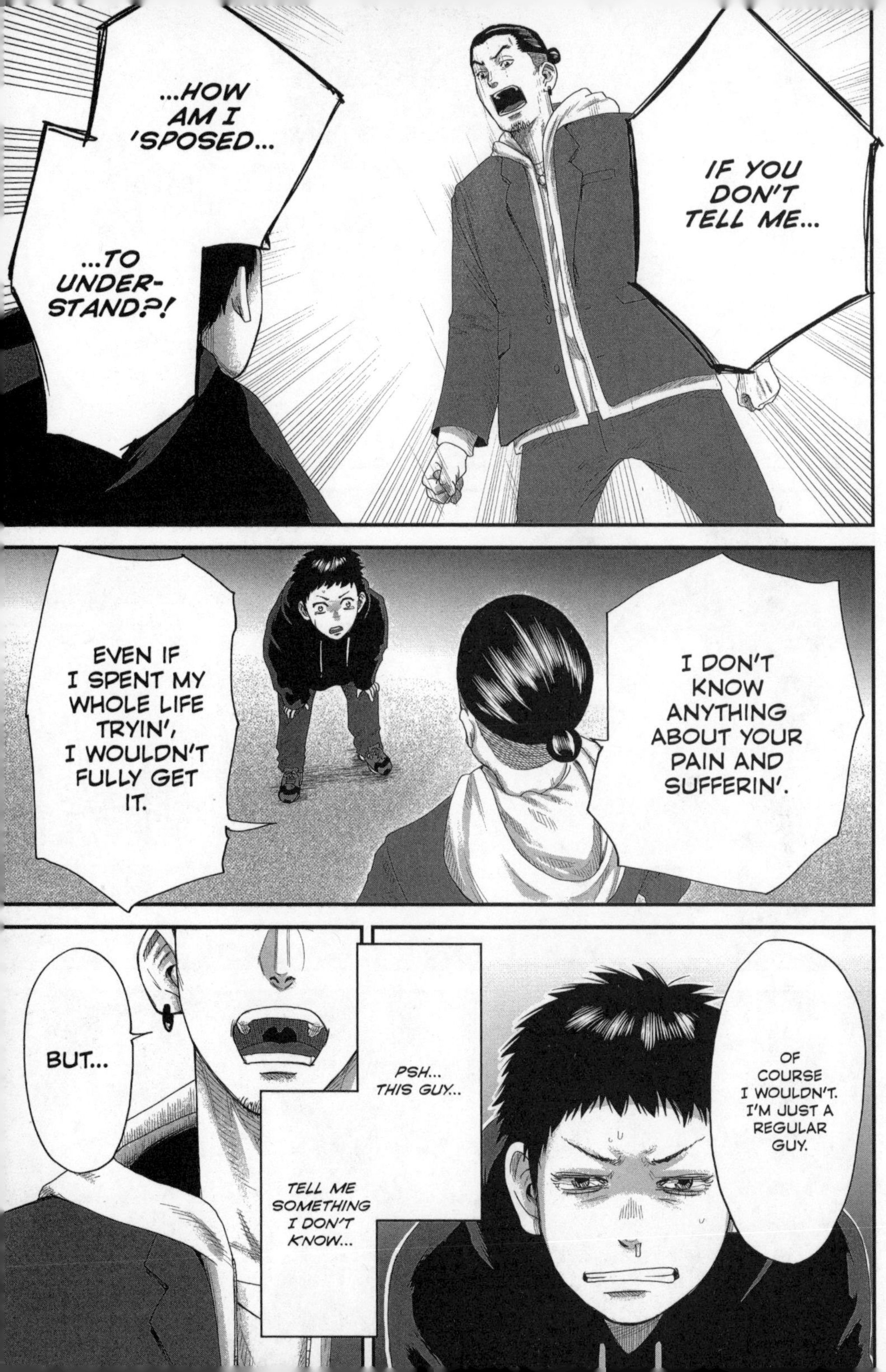
IF YOU DON'T TELL ME...
...HOW AM I 'SPOSED...
...TO UNDER-STAND?!
I DON'T KNOW ANYTHING ABOUT YOUR PAIN AND SUFFERIN'.
EVEN IF I SPENT MY WHOLE LIFE TRYIN', I WOULDN'T FULLY GET IT.
OF COURSE I WOULDN'T. I'M JUST A REGULAR GUY.
PSH... THIS GUY...
TELL ME SOMETHING I DON'T KNOW...
BUT...

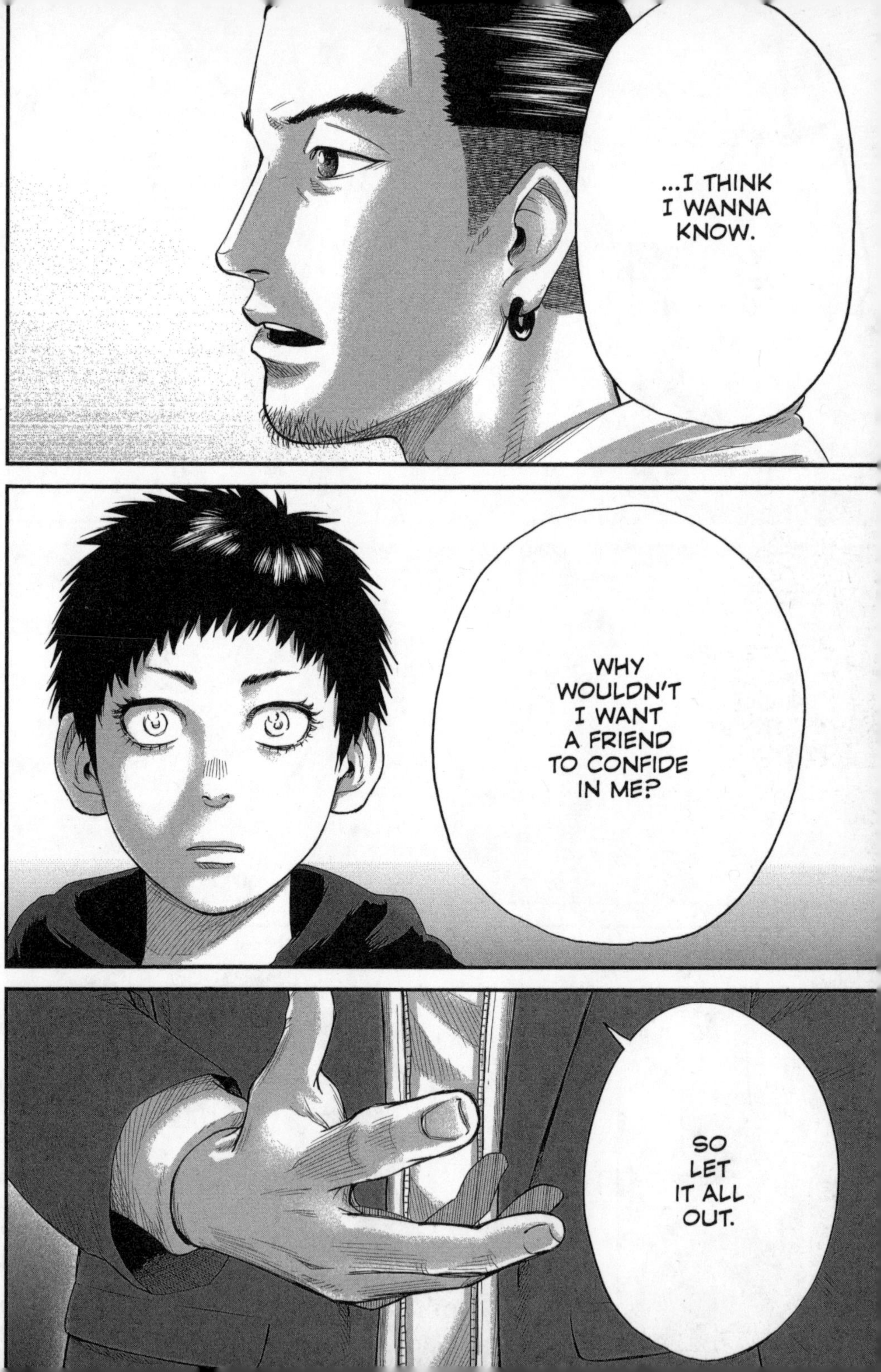
...I THINK I WANNA KNOW.
WHY WOULDN'T I WANT A FRIEND TO CONFIDE IN ME?
SO LET IT ALL OUT.

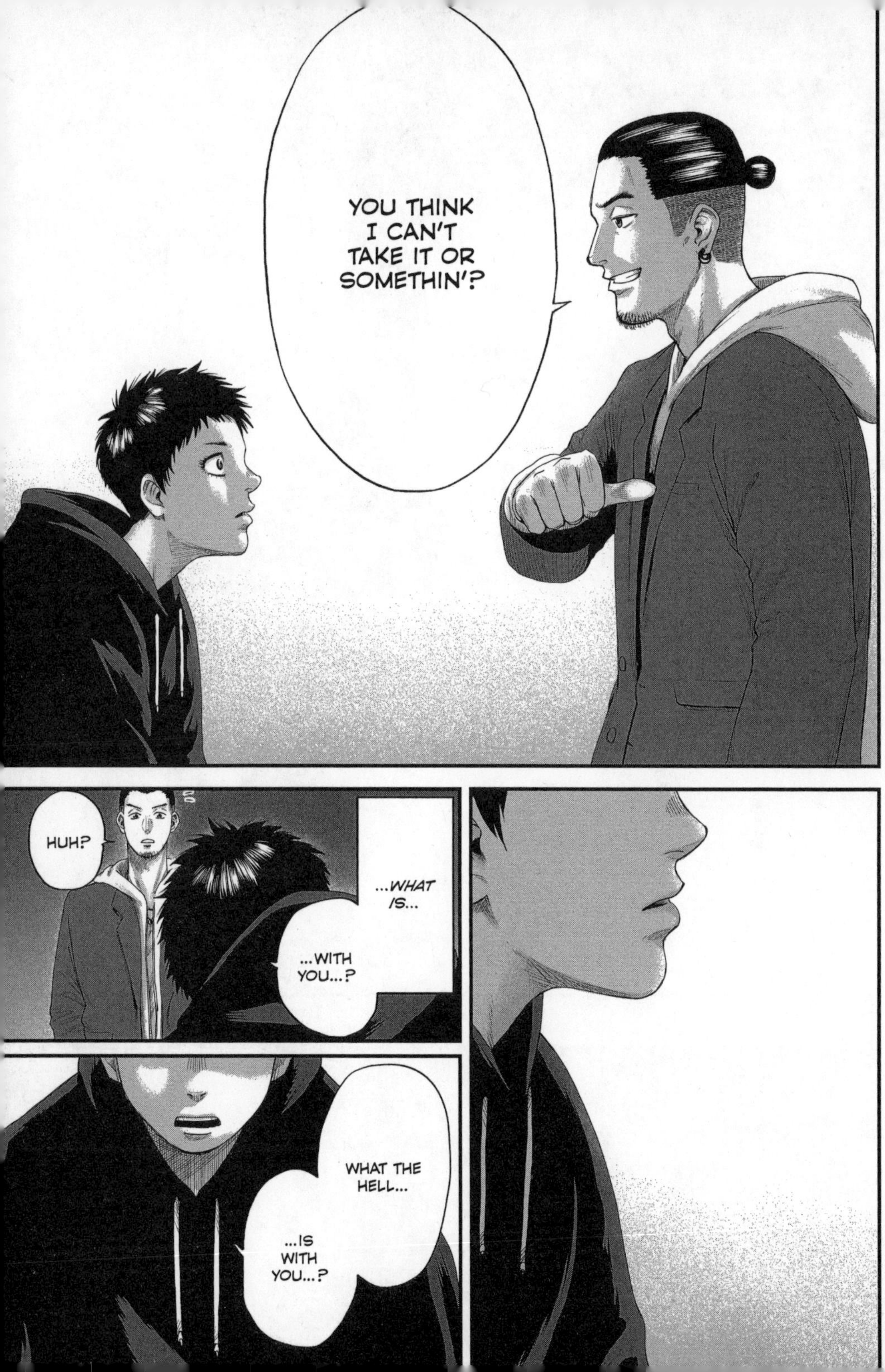

YOU THINK I CAN'T TAKE IT OR SOMETHIN'?
...WHAT IS...
...WITH YOU...?
HUH?
WHAT THE HELL...
...IS WITH YOU...?

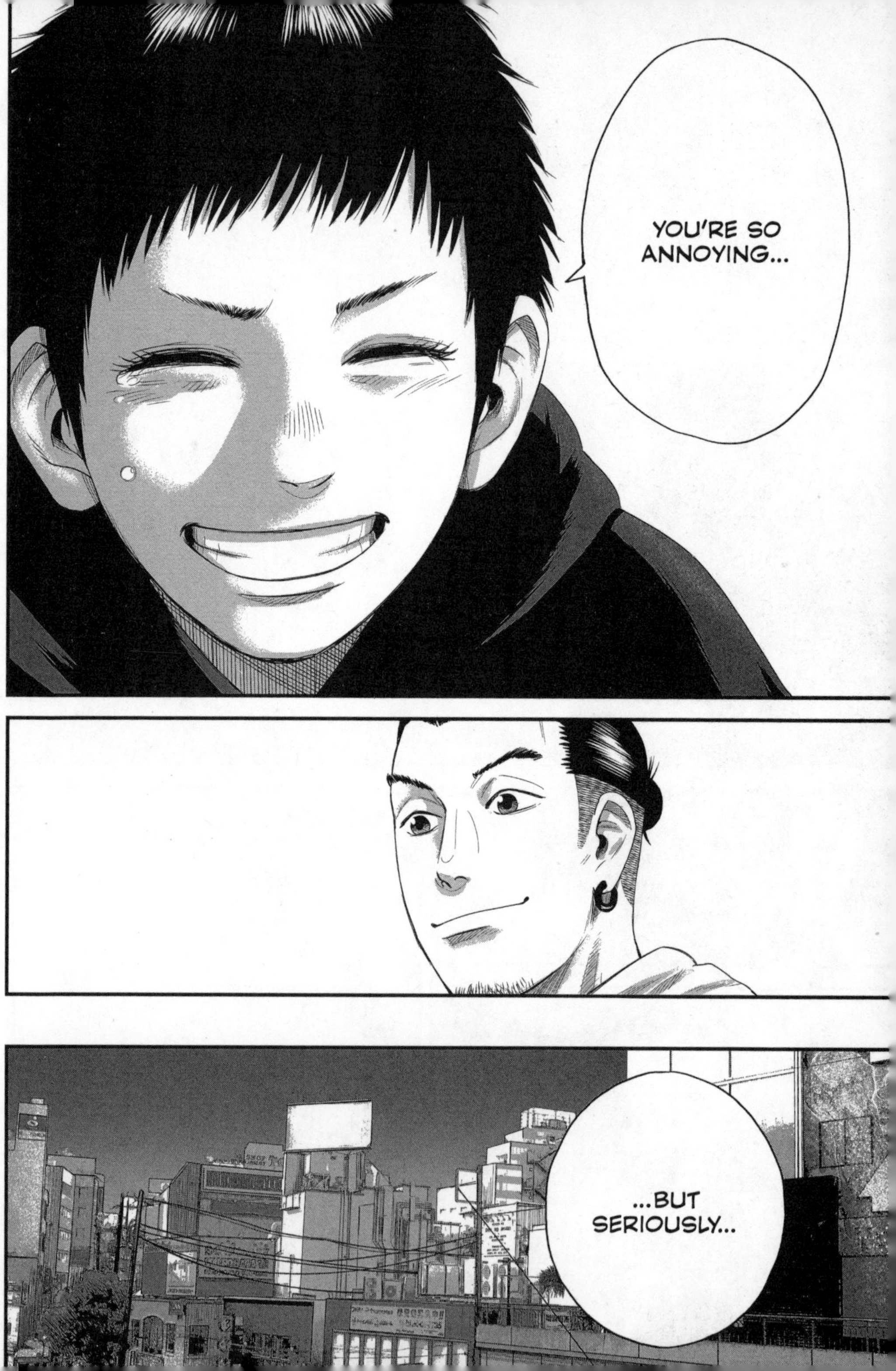
YOU'RE SO ANNOYING...
...BUT SERIOUSLY...

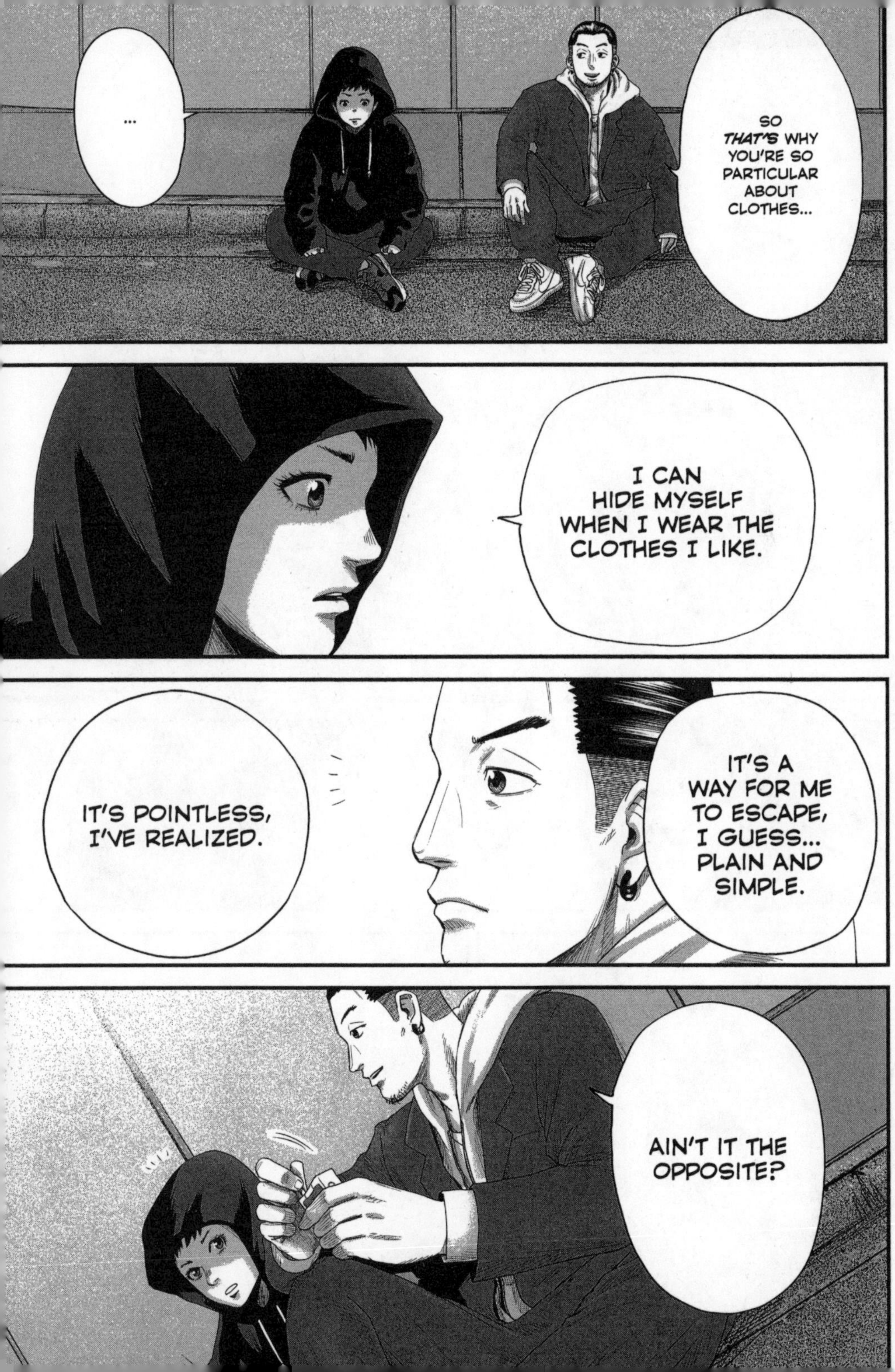
SO *THAT'S* WHY YOU'RE SO PARTICULAR ABOUT CLOTHES...
...
I CAN HIDE MYSELF WHEN I WEAR THE CLOTHES I LIKE.
IT'S A WAY FOR ME TO ESCAPE, I GUESS... PLAIN AND SIMPLE.
IT'S POINTLESS, I'VE REALIZED.
AIN'T IT THE OPPOSITE?

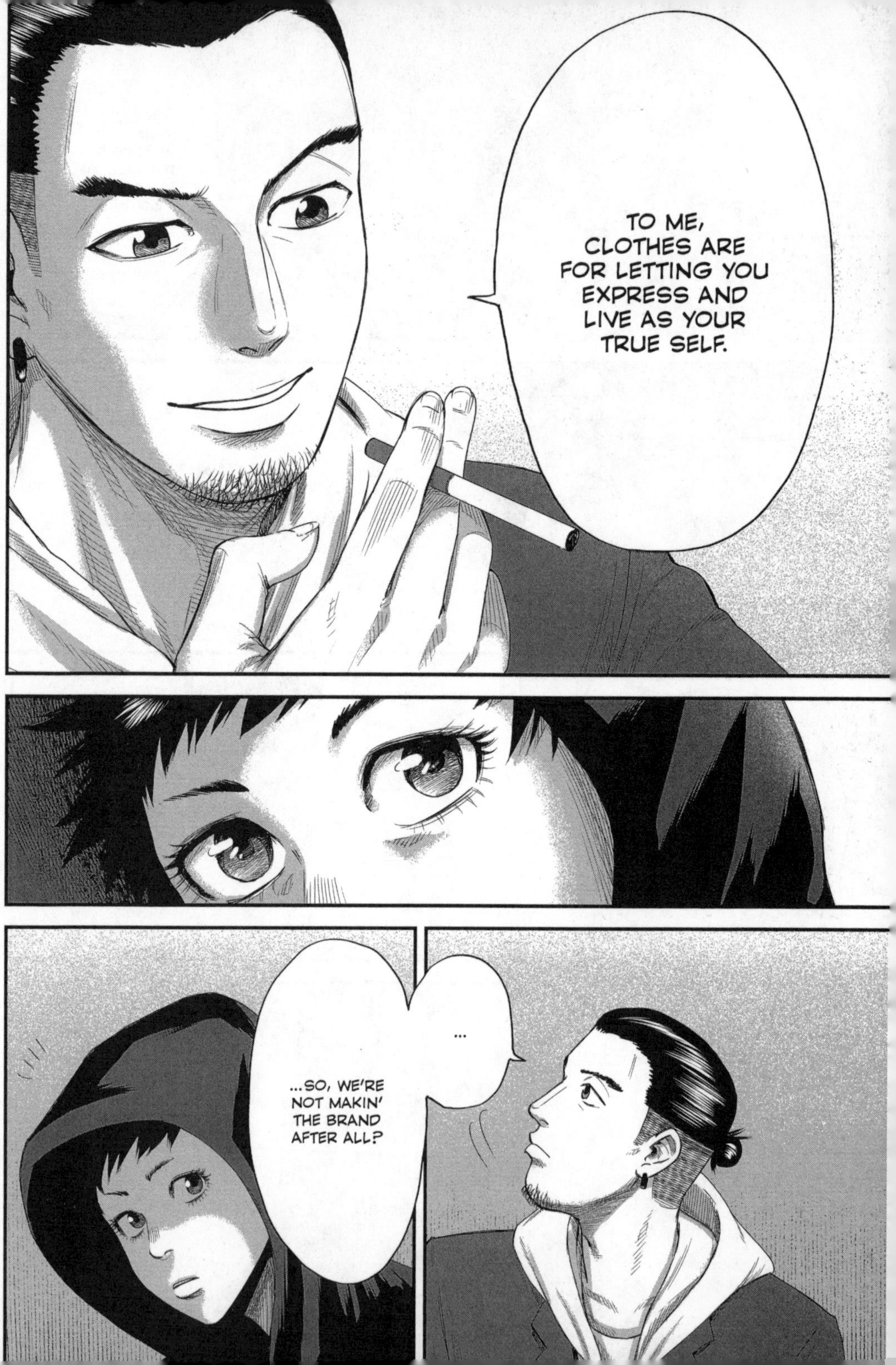
TO ME, CLOTHES ARE FOR LETTING YOU EXPRESS AND LIVE AS YOUR TRUE SELF.
...
...SO, WE'RE NOT MAKIN' THE BRAND AFTER ALL?

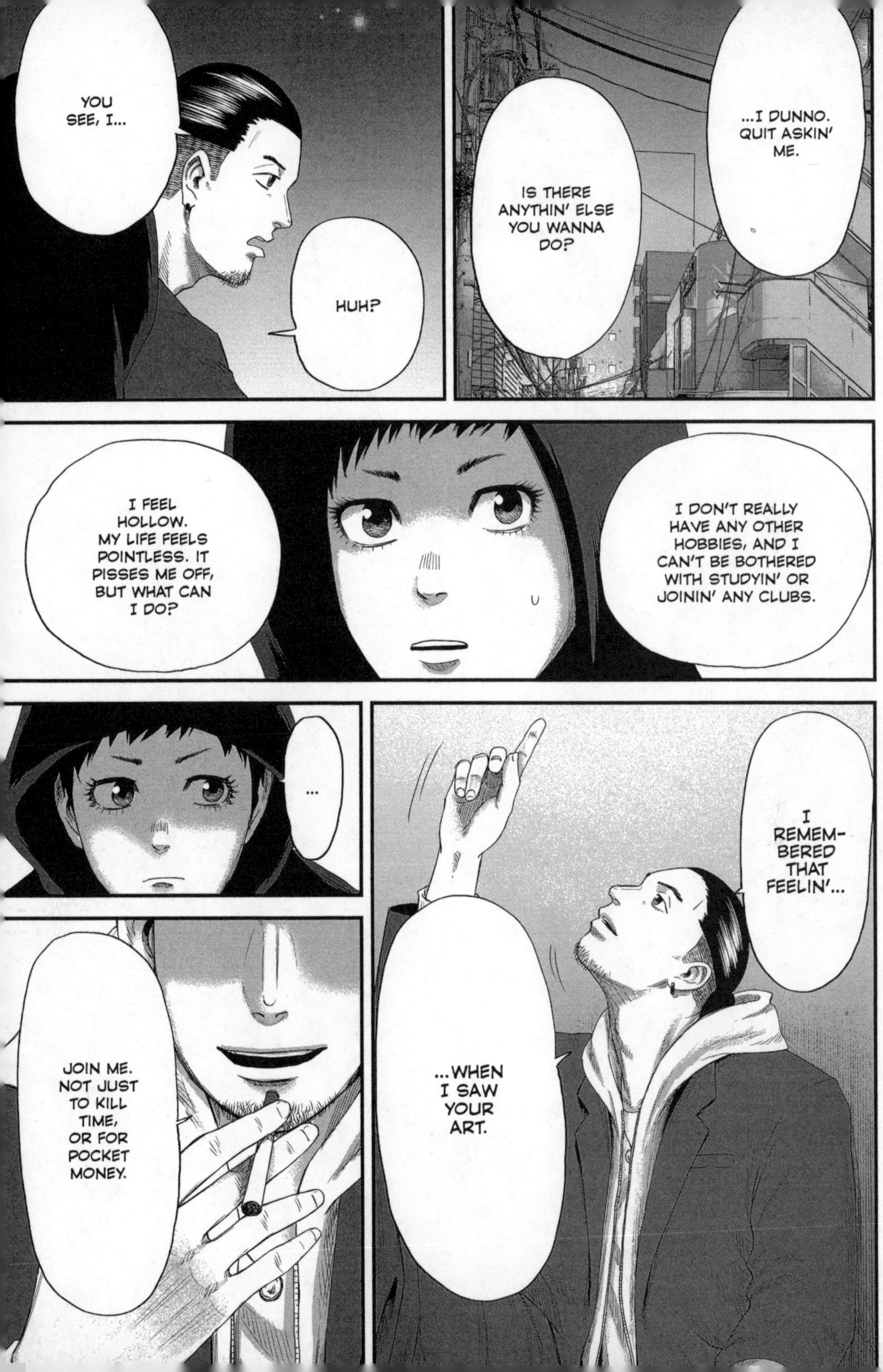
...I DUNNO. QUIT ASKIN' ME.
IS THERE ANYTHIN' ELSE YOU WANNA DO?
YOU SEE, I...
HUH?
I DON'T REALLY HAVE ANY OTHER HOBBIES, AND I CAN'T BE BOTHERED WITH STUDYIN' OR JOININ' ANY CLUBS.
I FEEL HOLLOW. MY LIFE FEELS POINTLESS. IT PISSES ME OFF, BUT WHAT CAN I DO?
I REMEMBERED THAT FEELIN'...
...WHEN I SAW YOUR ART.
...
JOIN ME. NOT JUST TO KILL TIME, OR FOR POCKET MONEY.

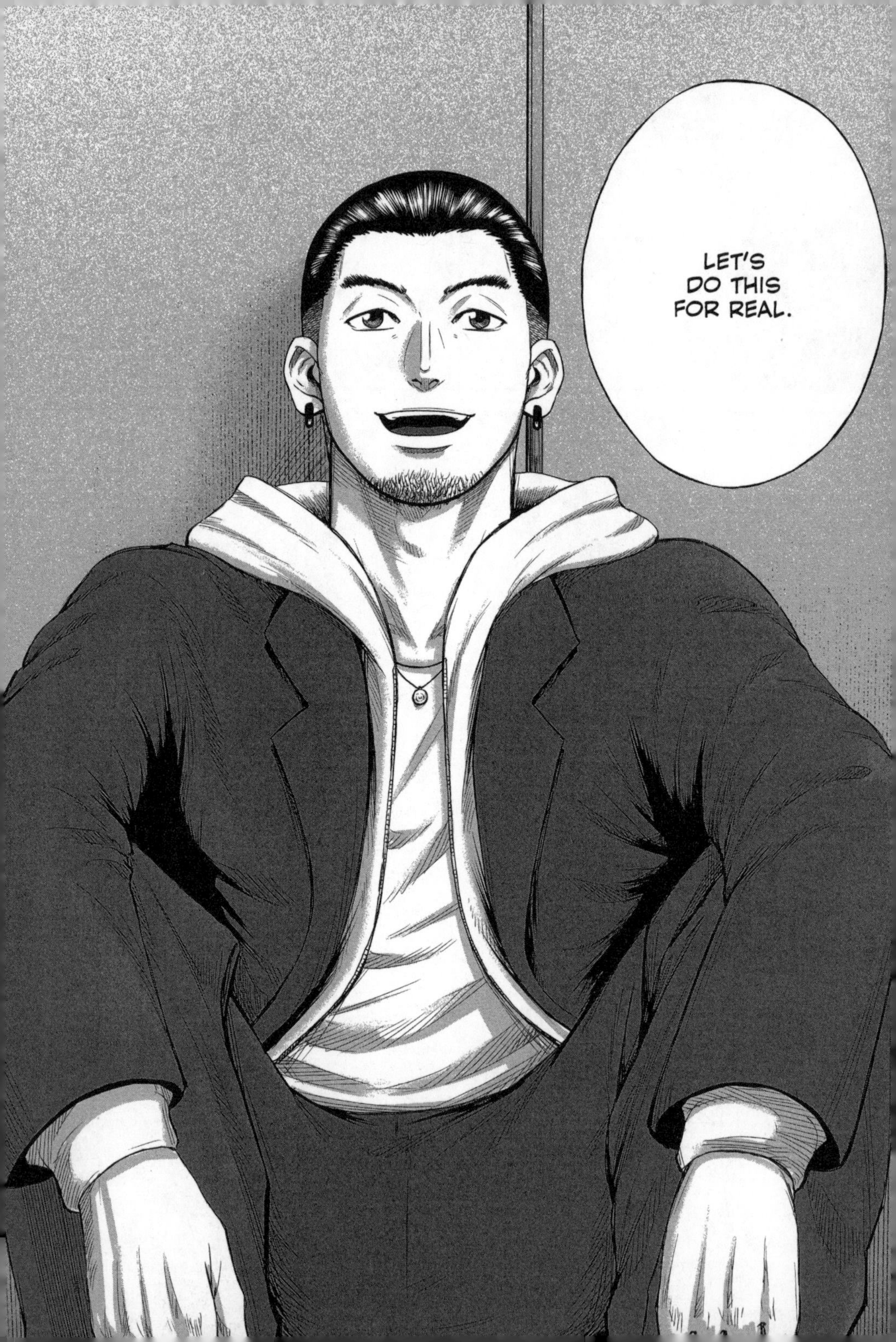
LET'S DO THIS FOR REAL.

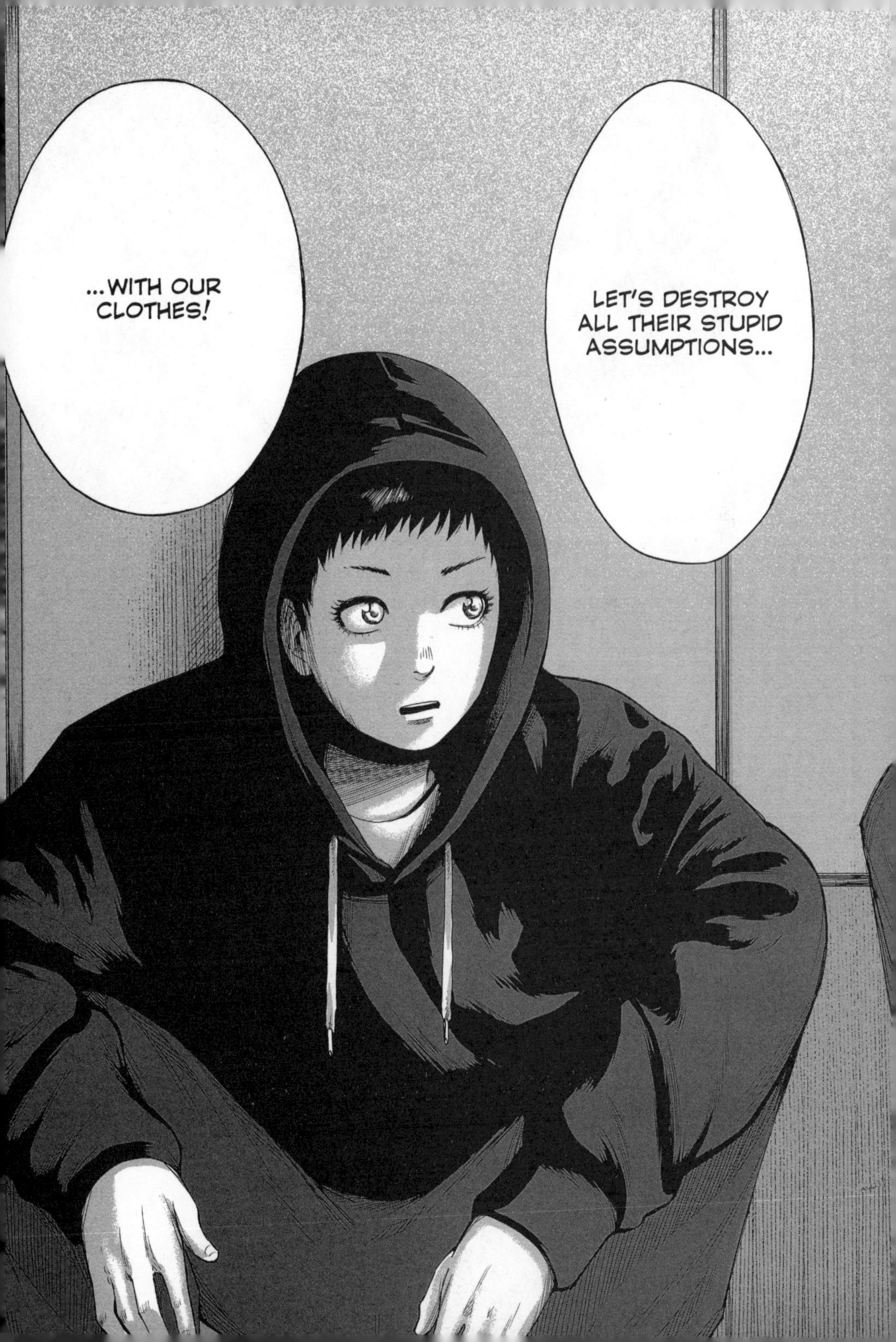
LET'S DESTROY ALL THEIR STUPID ASSUMPTIONS...
...WITH OUR CLOTHES!

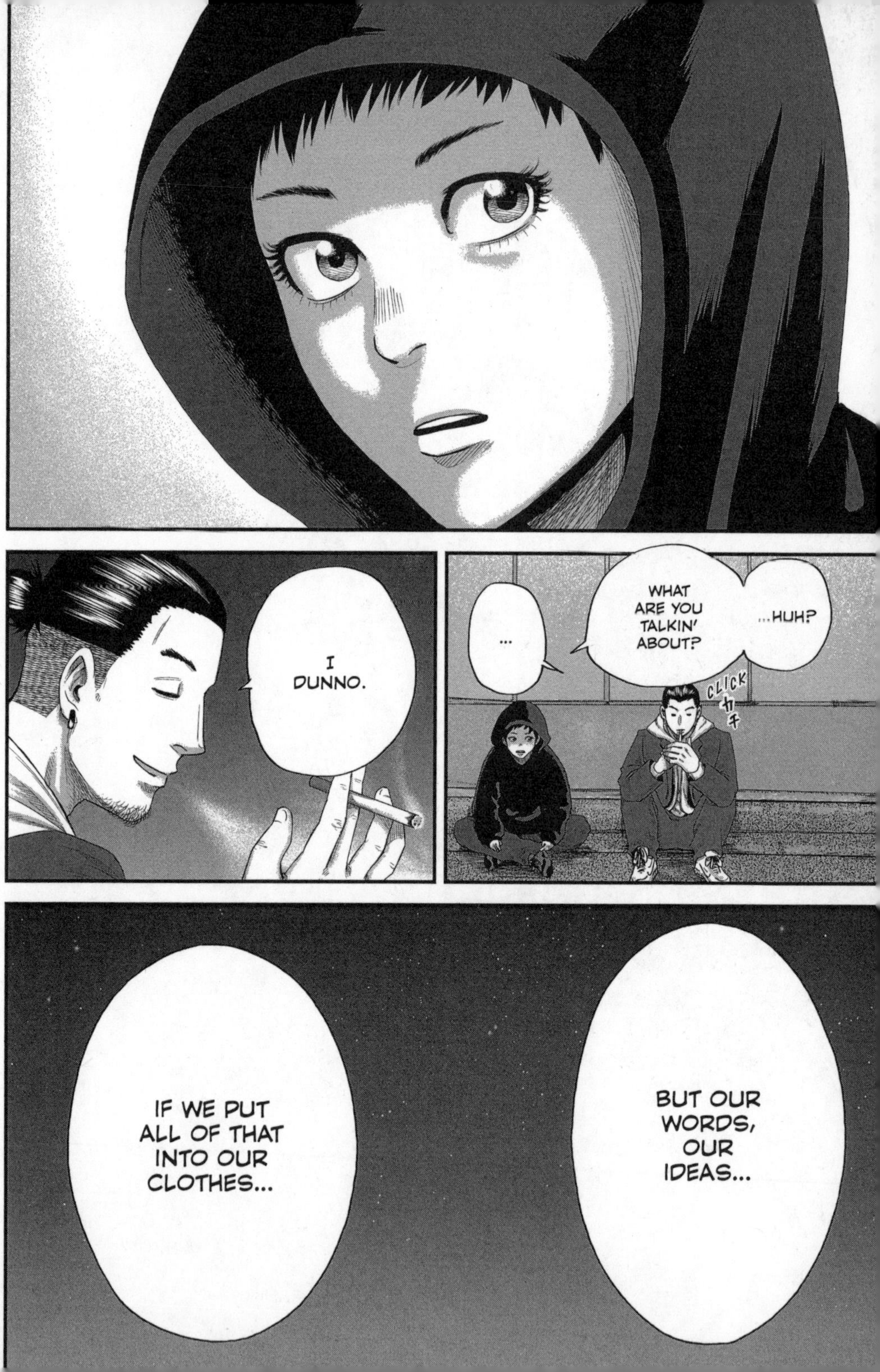
...HUH?
WHAT ARE YOU TALKIN' ABOUT?
...
CLICK カチ
I DUNNO.
BUT OUR WORDS, OUR IDEAS...
IF WE PUT ALL OF THAT INTO OUR CLOTHES...

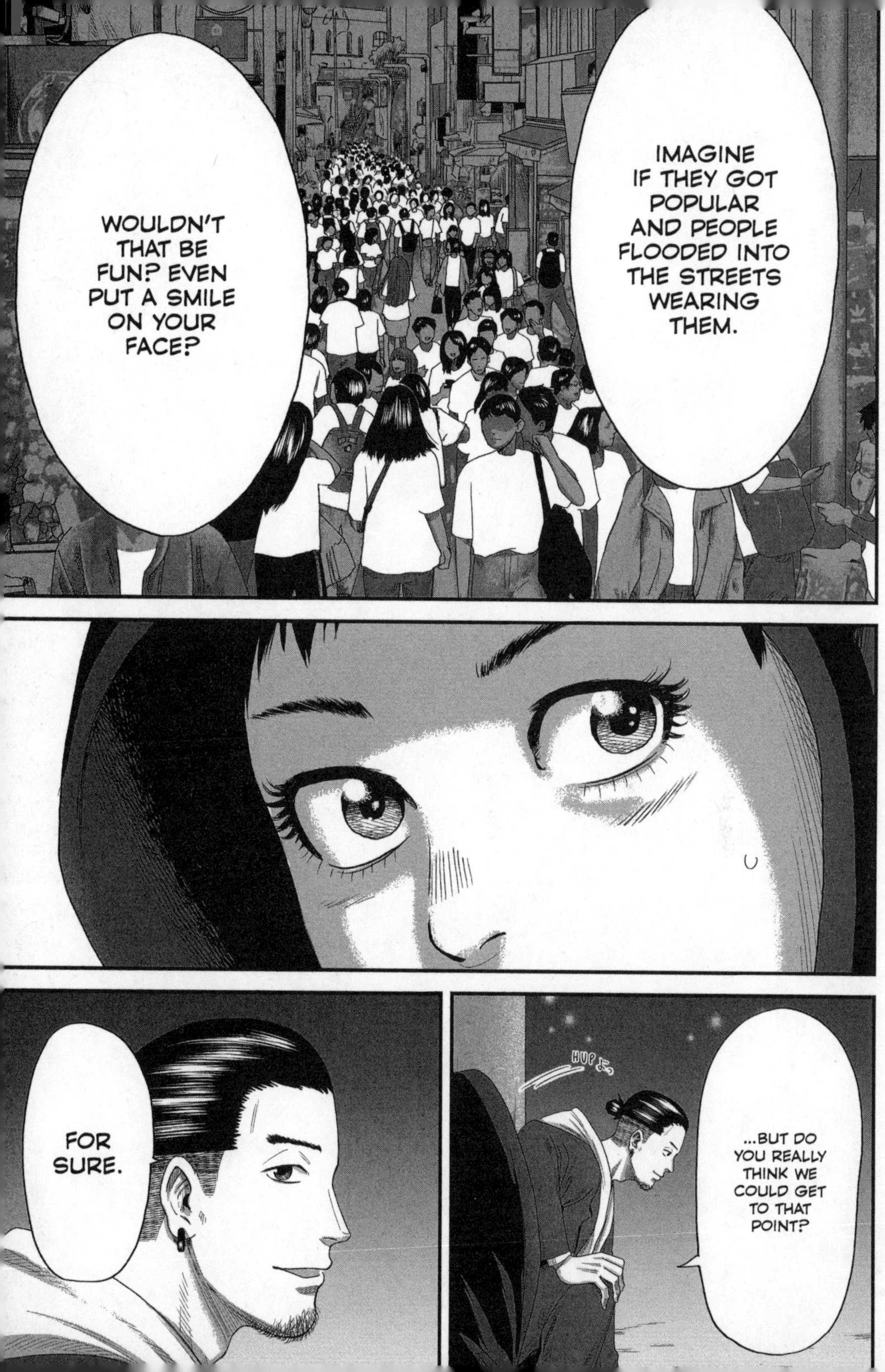
IMAGINE IF THEY GOT POPULAR AND PEOPLE FLOODED INTO THE STREETS WEARING THEM.
WOULDN'T THAT BE FUN? EVEN PUT A SMILE ON YOUR FACE?
HUP
...BUT DO YOU REALLY THINK WE COULD GET TO THAT POINT?
FOR SURE.

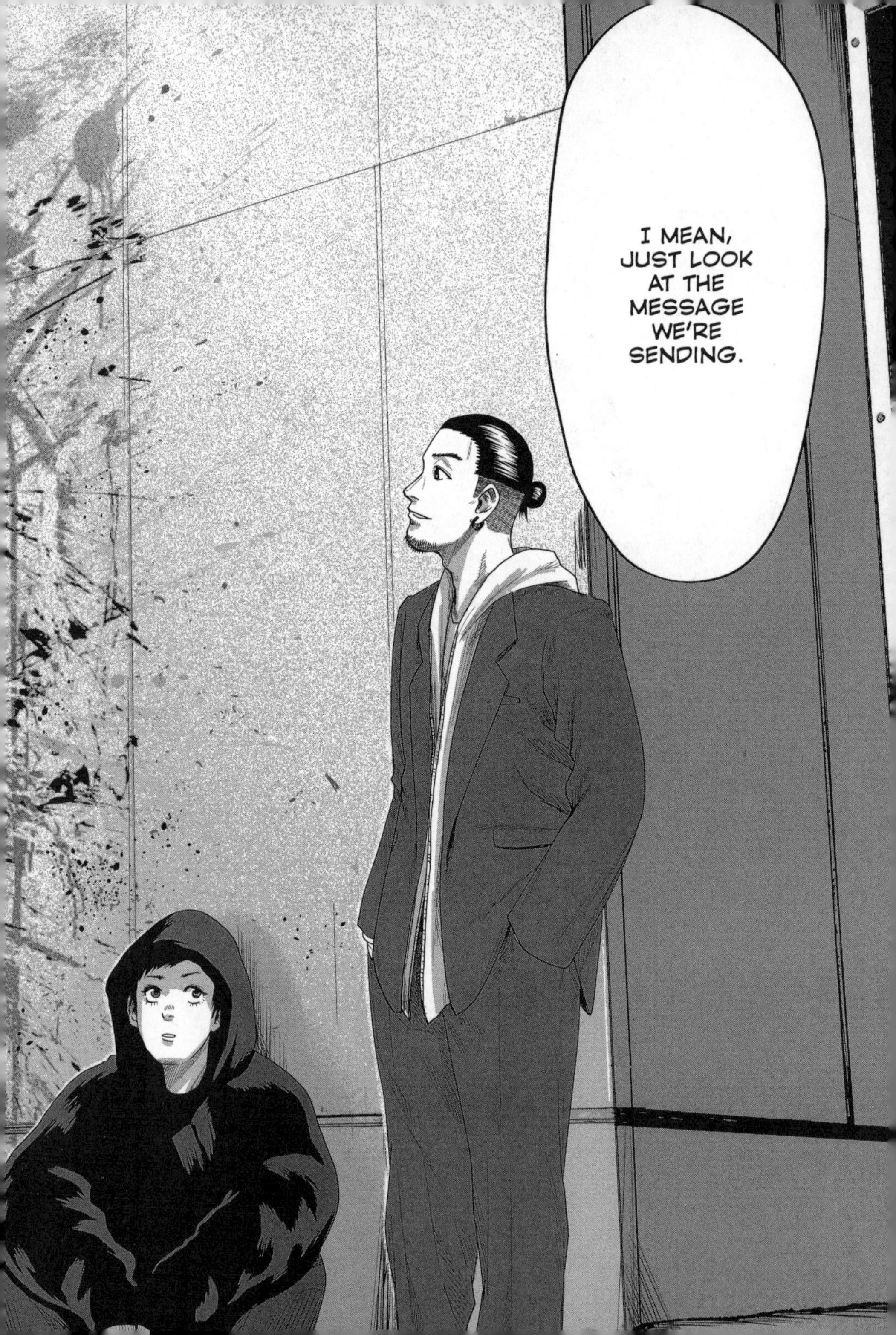
I MEAN, JUST LOOK AT THE MESSAGE WE'RE SENDING.

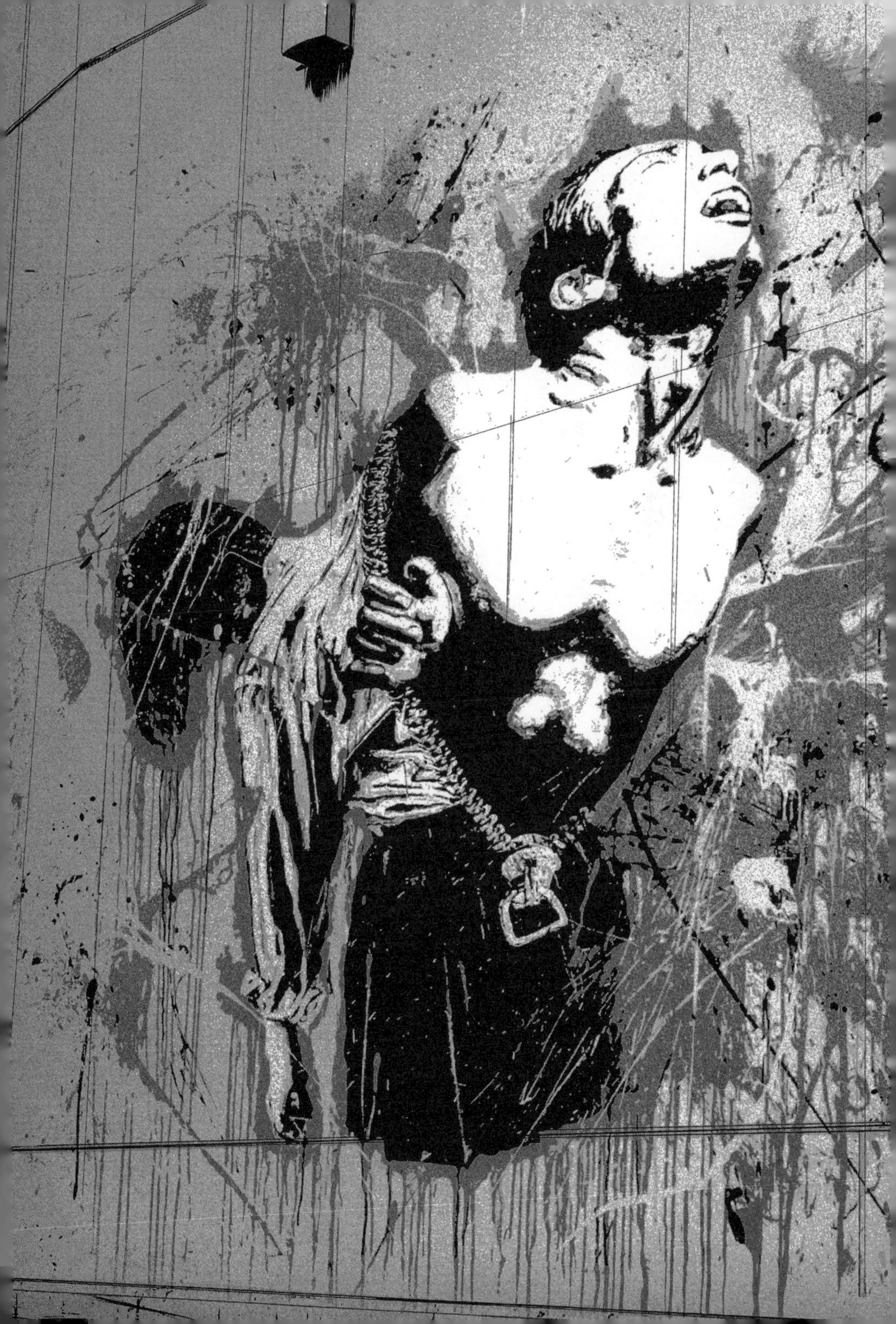

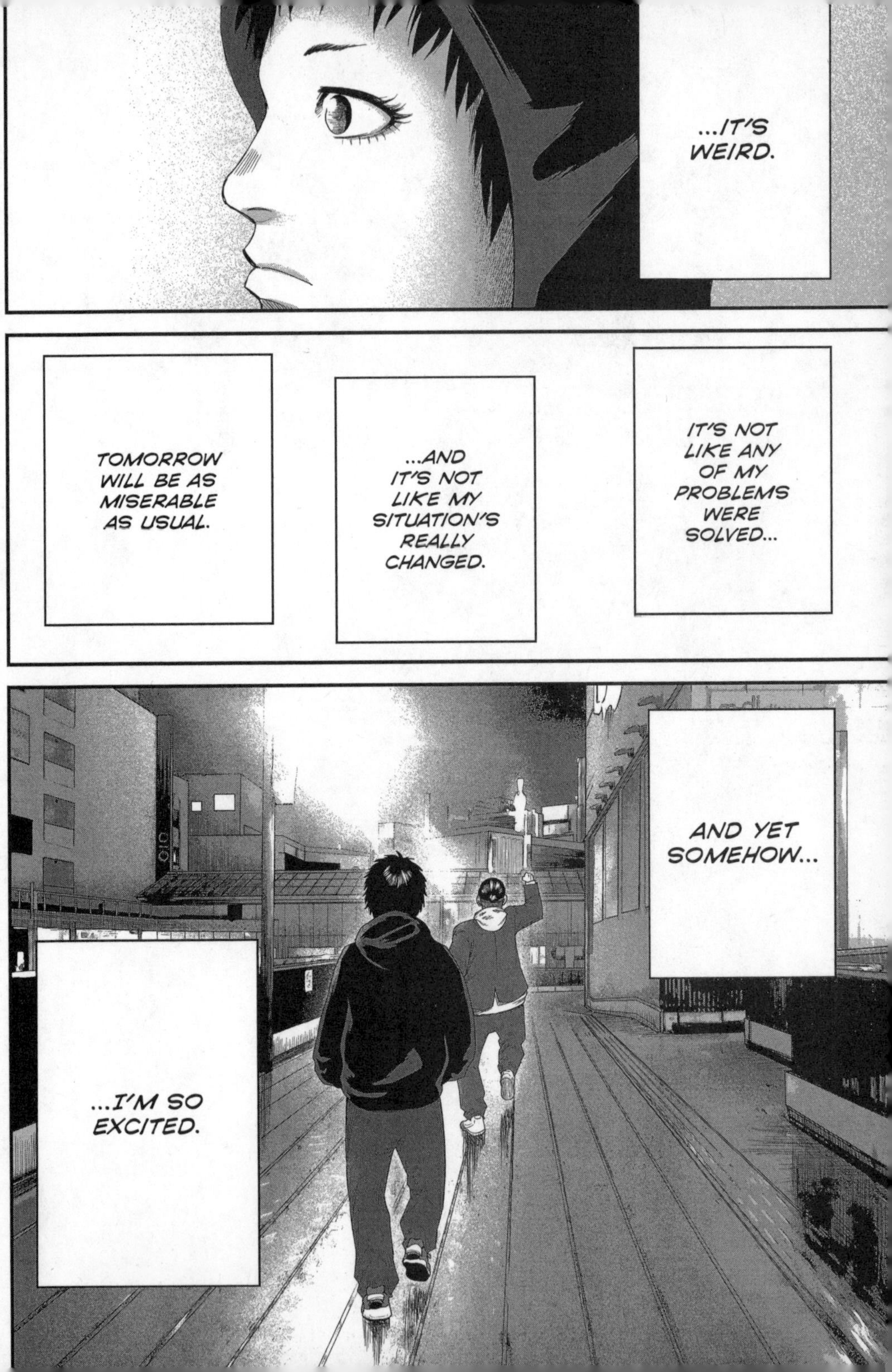
...IT'S WEIRD.
IT'S NOT LIKE ANY OF MY PROBLEMS WERE SOLVED...
...AND IT'S NOT LIKE MY SITUATION'S REALLY CHANGED.
TOMORROW WILL BE AS MISERABLE AS USUAL.
AND YET SOMEHOW...
...I'M SO EXCITED.

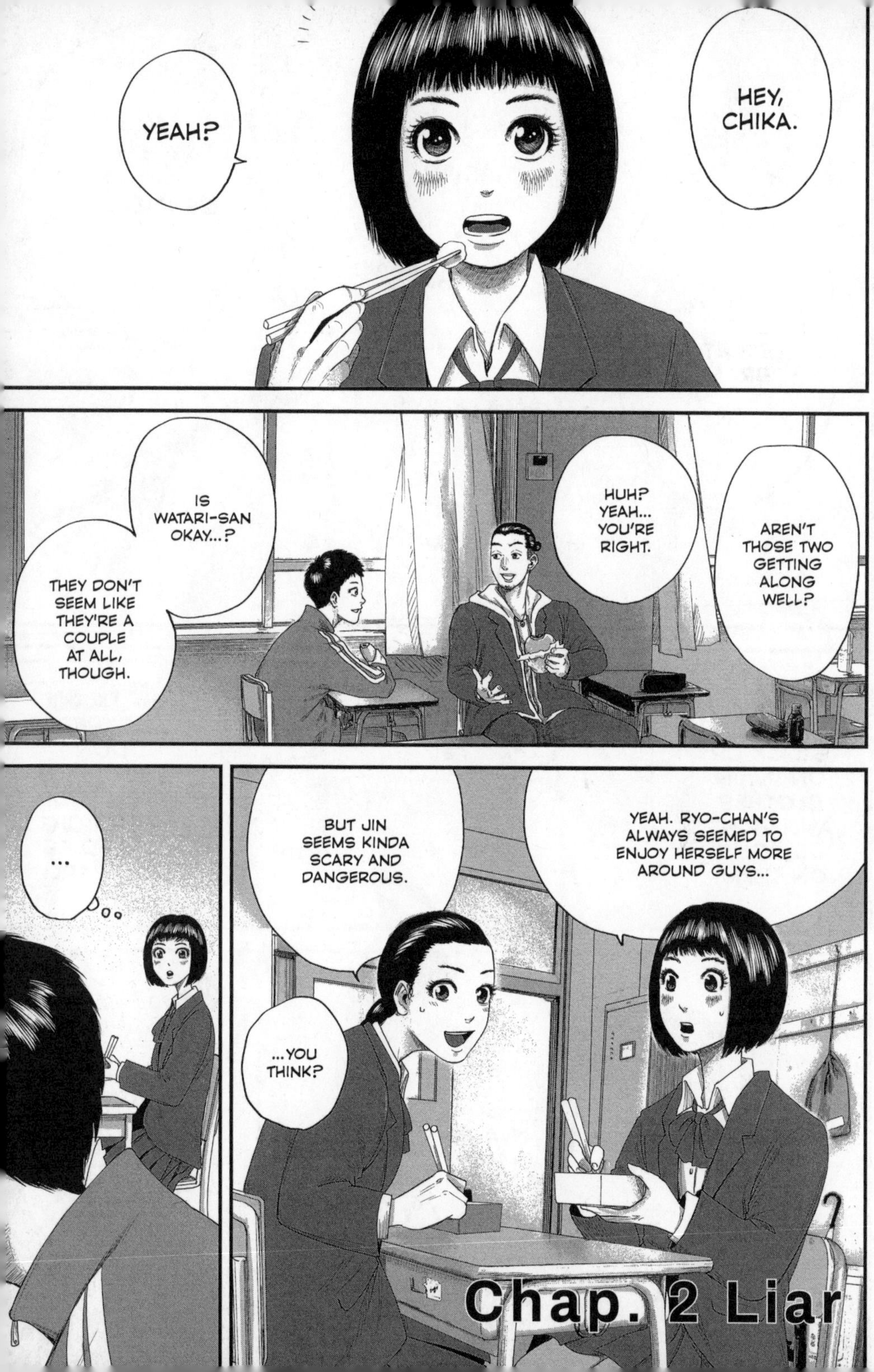
HEY, CHIKA.
YEAH?
AREN'T THOSE TWO GETTING ALONG WELL?
HUH? YEAH... YOU'RE RIGHT.
IS WATARI-SAN OKAY...?
THEY DON'T SEEM LIKE THEY'RE A COUPLE AT ALL, THOUGH.
YEAH. RYO-CHAN'S ALWAYS SEEMED TO ENJOY HERSELF MORE AROUND GUYS...
BUT JIN SEEMS KINDA SCARY AND DANGEROUS.
...YOU THINK?
Chap. 2 Liar
...

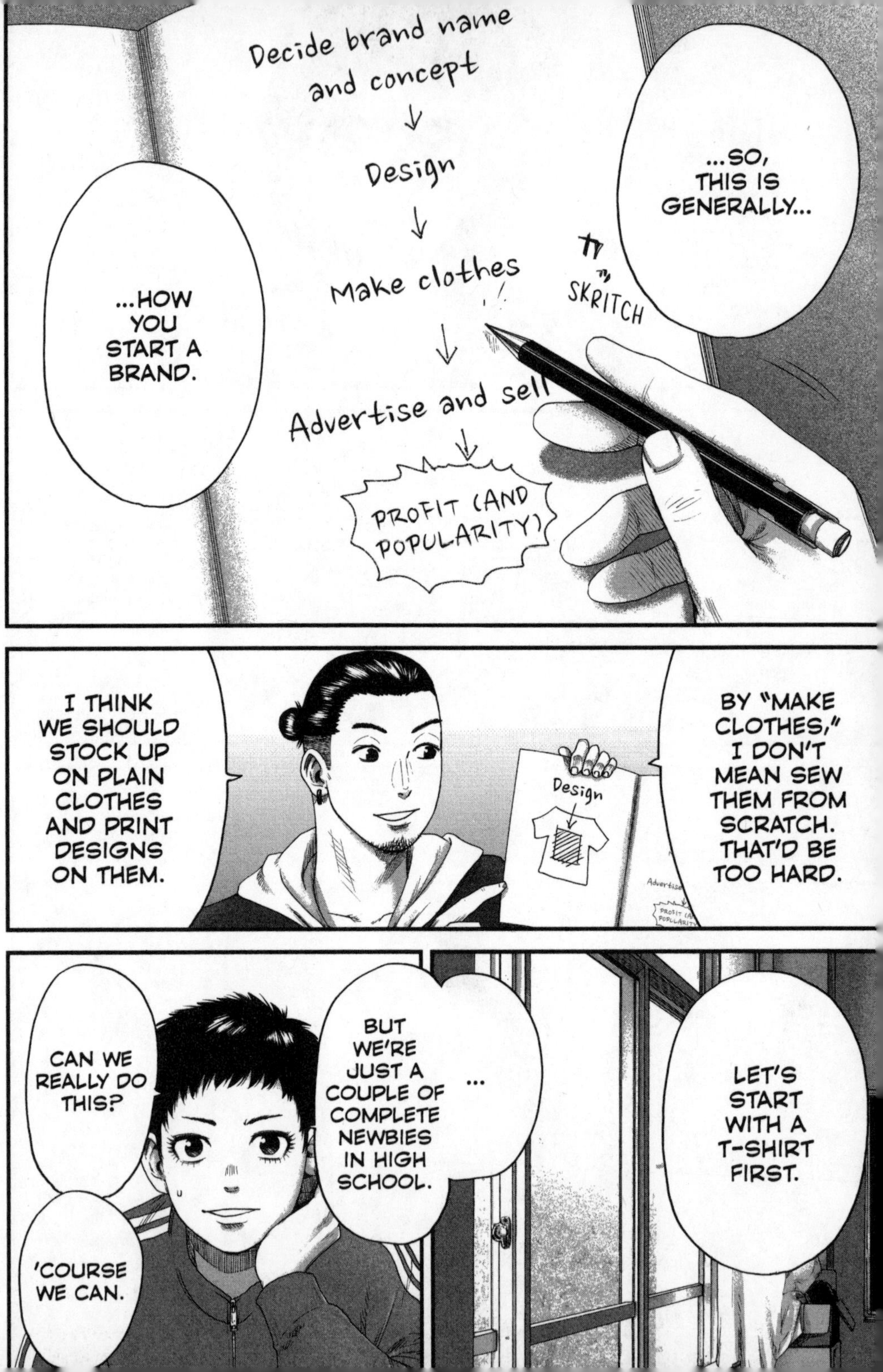
...SO, THIS IS GENERALLY...
Decide brand name and concept
Design
Make clothes
Advertise and sell
PROFIT (AND POPULARITY)
SKRITCH
...HOW YOU START A BRAND.
BY "MAKE CLOTHES," I DON'T MEAN SEW THEM FROM SCRATCH. THAT'D BE TOO HARD.
Design
I THINK WE SHOULD STOCK UP ON PLAIN CLOTHES AND PRINT DESIGNS ON THEM.
LET'S START WITH A T-SHIRT FIRST.
BUT WE'RE JUST A COUPLE OF COMPLETE NEWBIES IN HIGH SCHOOL.
...
CAN WE REALLY DO THIS?
'COURSE WE CAN.

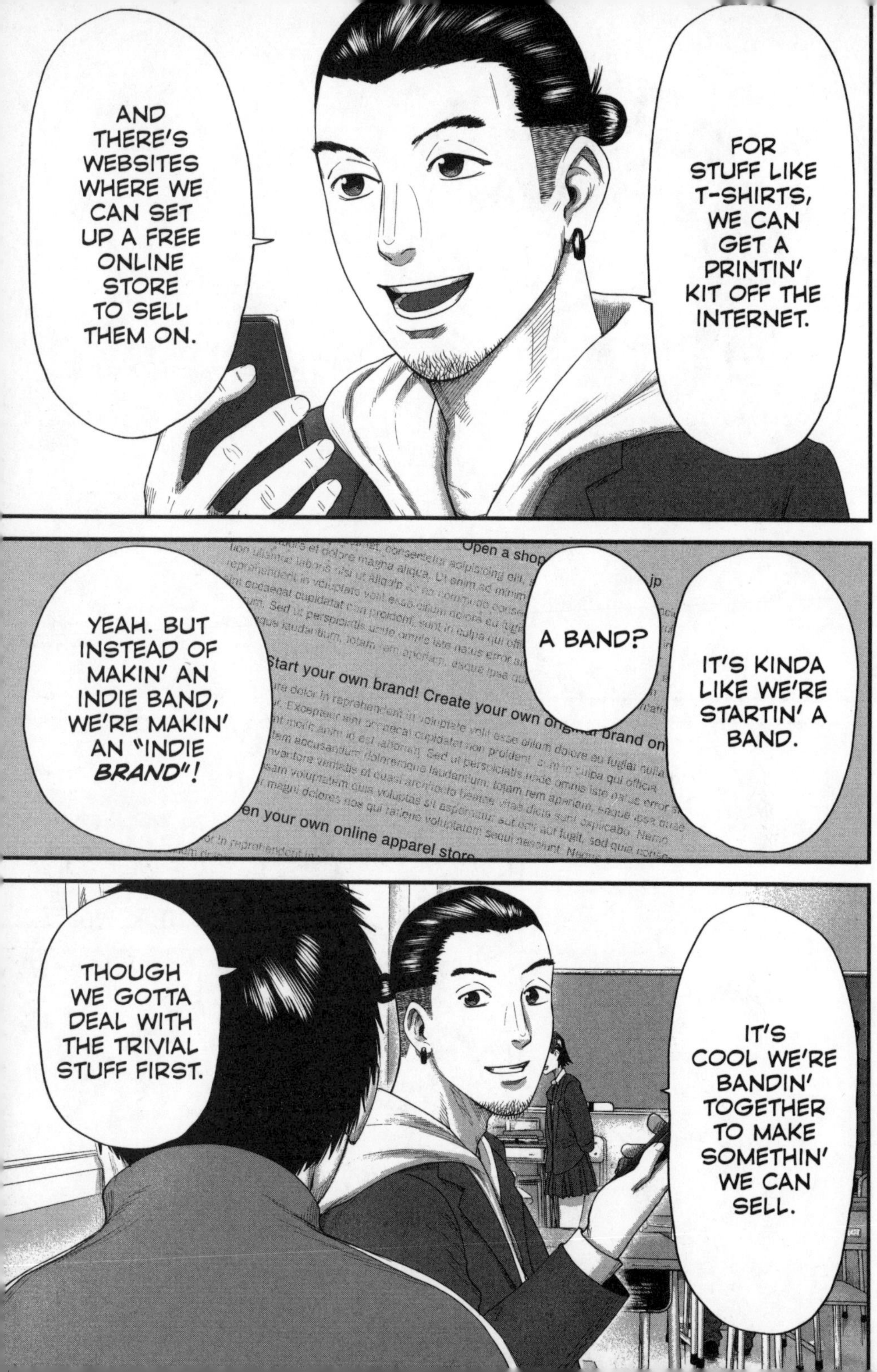
FOR STUFF LIKE T-SHIRTS, WE CAN GET A PRINTIN' KIT OFF THE INTERNET.
AND THERE'S WEBSITES WHERE WE CAN SET UP A FREE ONLINE STORE TO SELL THEM ON.
IT'S KINDA LIKE WE'RE STARTIN' A BAND.
A BAND?
YEAH. BUT INSTEAD OF MAKIN' AN INDIE BAND, WE'RE MAKIN' AN "INDIE *BRAND*"!
Open a shop
Start your own brand!
your own online apparel store
IT'S COOL WE'RE BANDIN' TOGETHER TO MAKE SOMETHIN' WE CAN SELL.
THOUGH WE GOTTA DEAL WITH THE TRIVIAL STUFF FIRST.

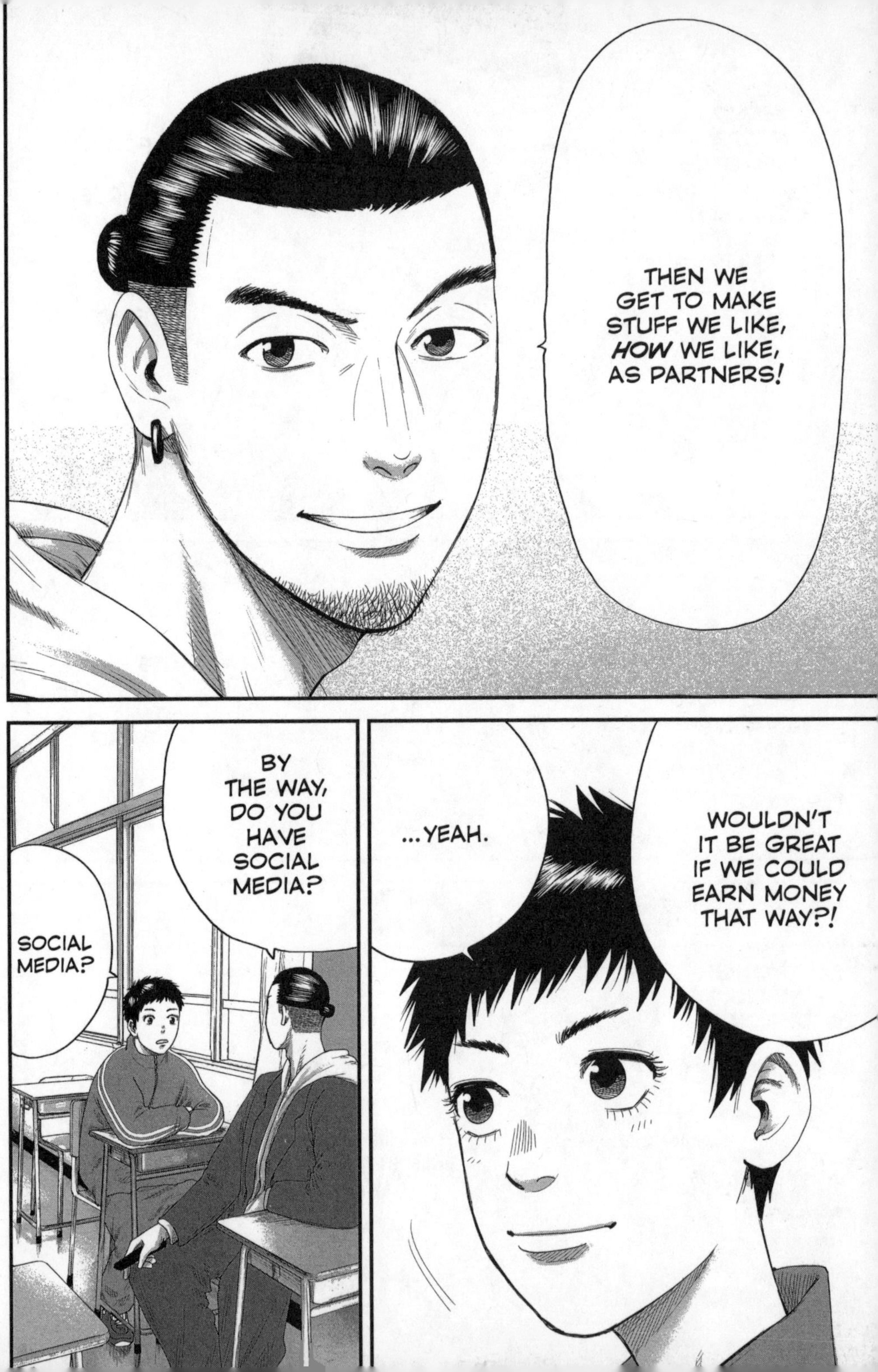
THEN WE GET TO MAKE STUFF WE LIKE, *HOW* WE LIKE, AS PARTNERS!
WOULDN'T IT BE GREAT IF WE COULD EARN MONEY THAT WAY?!
...YEAH.
BY THE WAY, DO YOU HAVE SOCIAL MEDIA?
SOCIAL MEDIA?

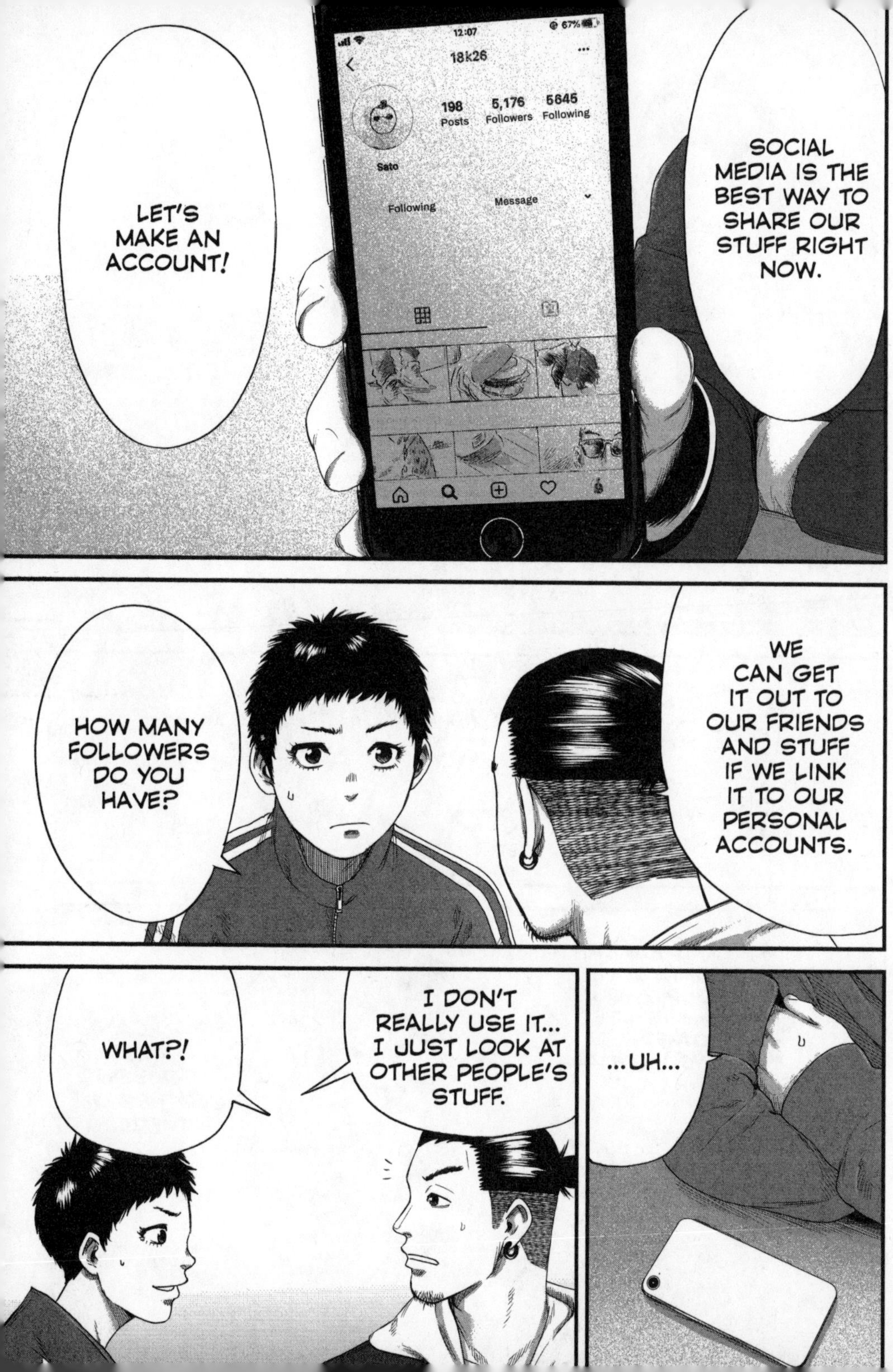
SOCIAL MEDIA IS THE BEST WAY TO SHARE OUR STUFF RIGHT NOW.
12:07
67%
18k26
198 Posts
5,176 Followers
5645 Following
Sato
Following
Message
LET'S MAKE AN ACCOUNT!
WE CAN GET IT OUT TO OUR FRIENDS AND STUFF IF WE LINK IT TO OUR PERSONAL ACCOUNTS.
HOW MANY FOLLOWERS DO YOU HAVE?
...UH...
I DON'T REALLY USE IT... I JUST LOOK AT OTHER PEOPLE'S STUFF.
WHAT?!

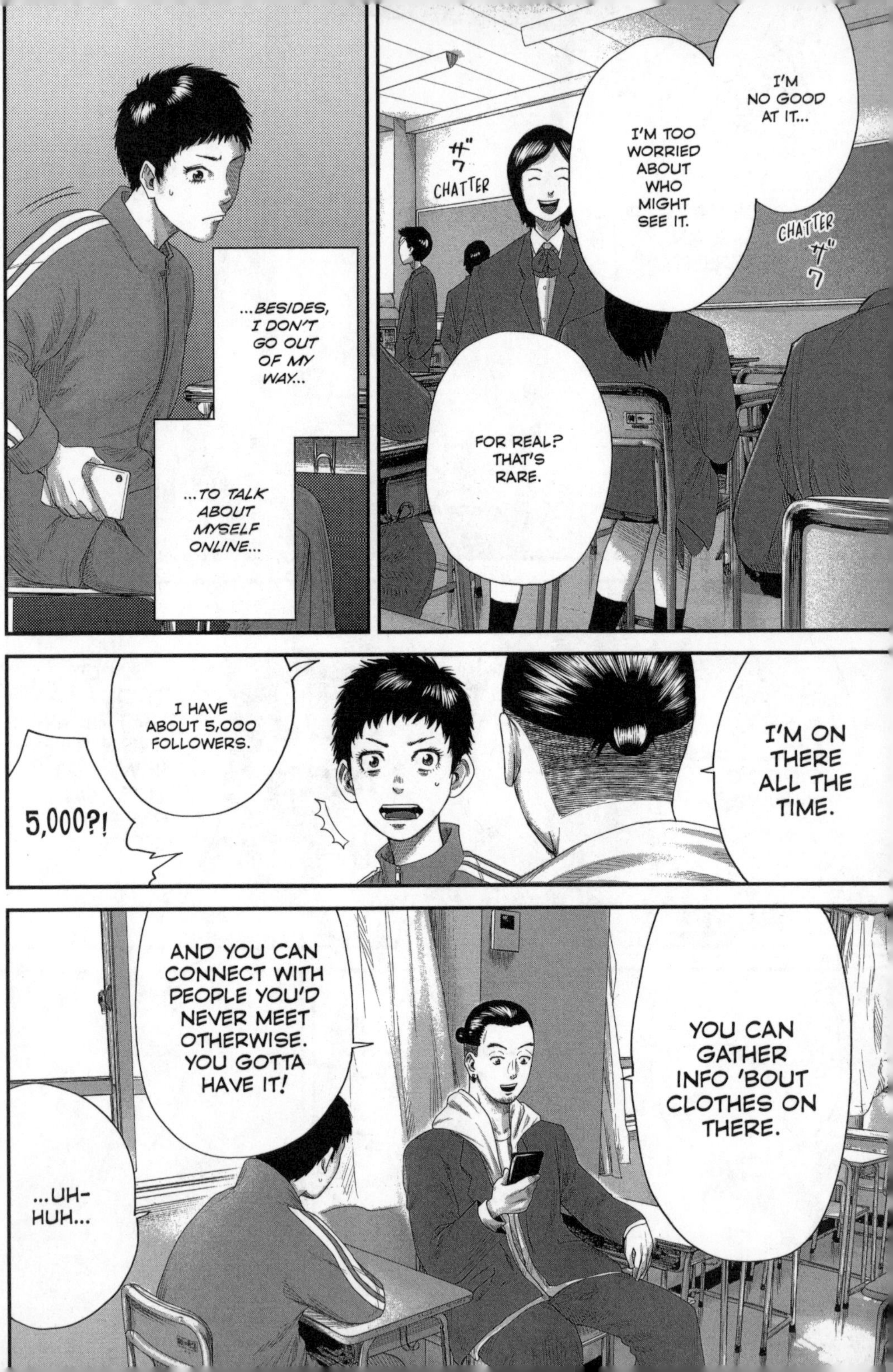

I'M NO GOOD AT IT...
I'M TOO WORRIED ABOUT WHO MIGHT SEE IT.
ザワ CHATTER
ザワ CHATTER
FOR REAL? THAT'S RARE.
...BESIDES, I DON'T GO OUT OF MY WAY...
...TO TALK ABOUT MYSELF ONLINE...
I'M ON THERE ALL THE TIME.
I HAVE ABOUT 5,000 FOLLOWERS.
5,000?!
YOU CAN GATHER INFO 'BOUT CLOTHES ON THERE.
AND YOU CAN CONNECT WITH PEOPLE YOU'D NEVER MEET OTHERWISE. YOU GOTTA HAVE IT!
...UH-HUH...

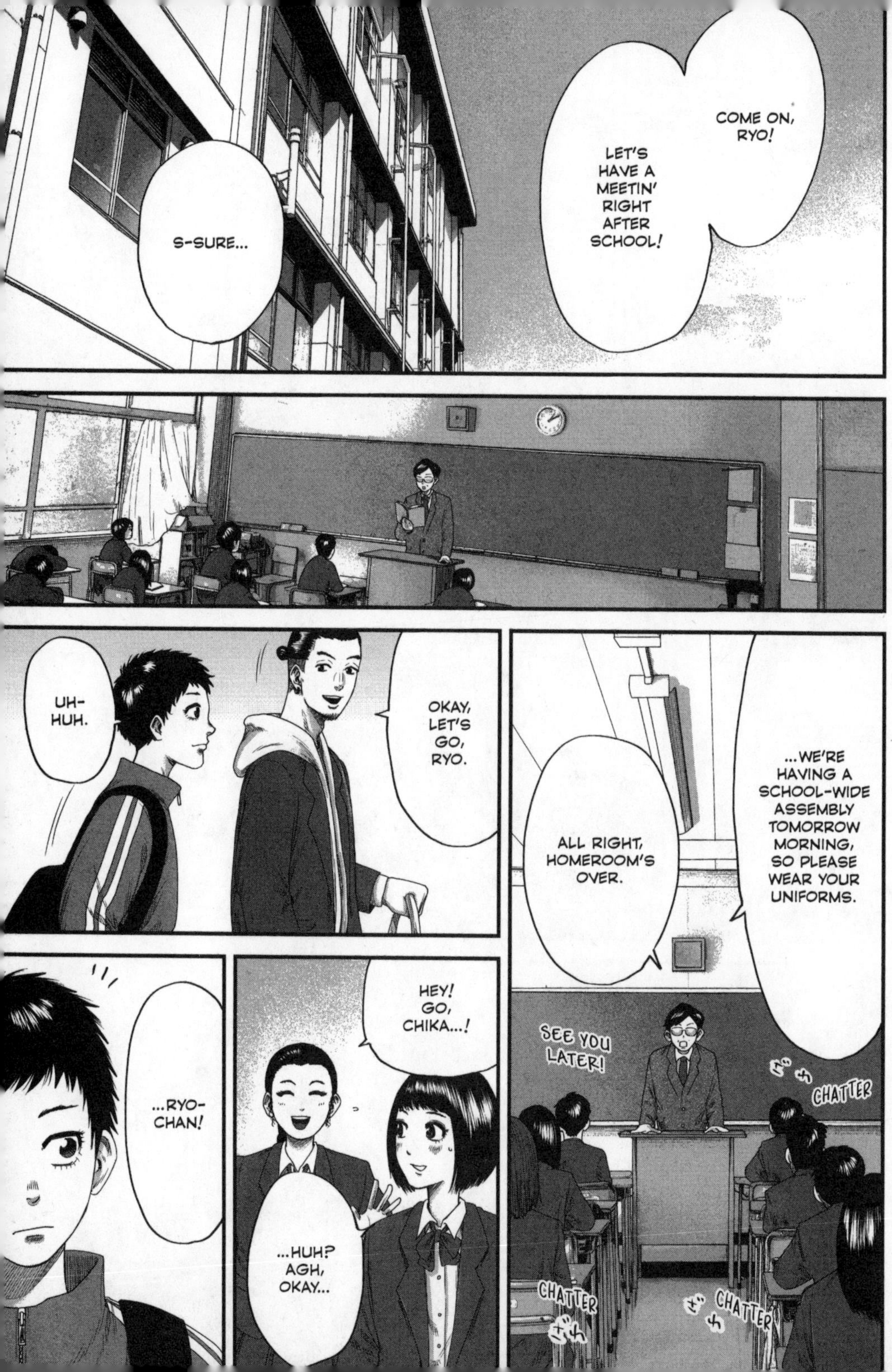
COME ON, RYO!
LET'S HAVE A MEETIN' RIGHT AFTER SCHOOL!
S-SURE...
...WE'RE HAVING A SCHOOL-WIDE ASSEMBLY TOMORROW MORNING, SO PLEASE WEAR YOUR UNIFORMS.
ALL RIGHT, HOMEROOM'S OVER.
CHATTER
SEE YOU LATER!
CHATTER
CHATTER
OKAY, LET'S GO, RYO.
UH-HUH.
HEY! GO, CHIKA...!
...HUH? AGH, OKAY...
...RYO-CHAN!

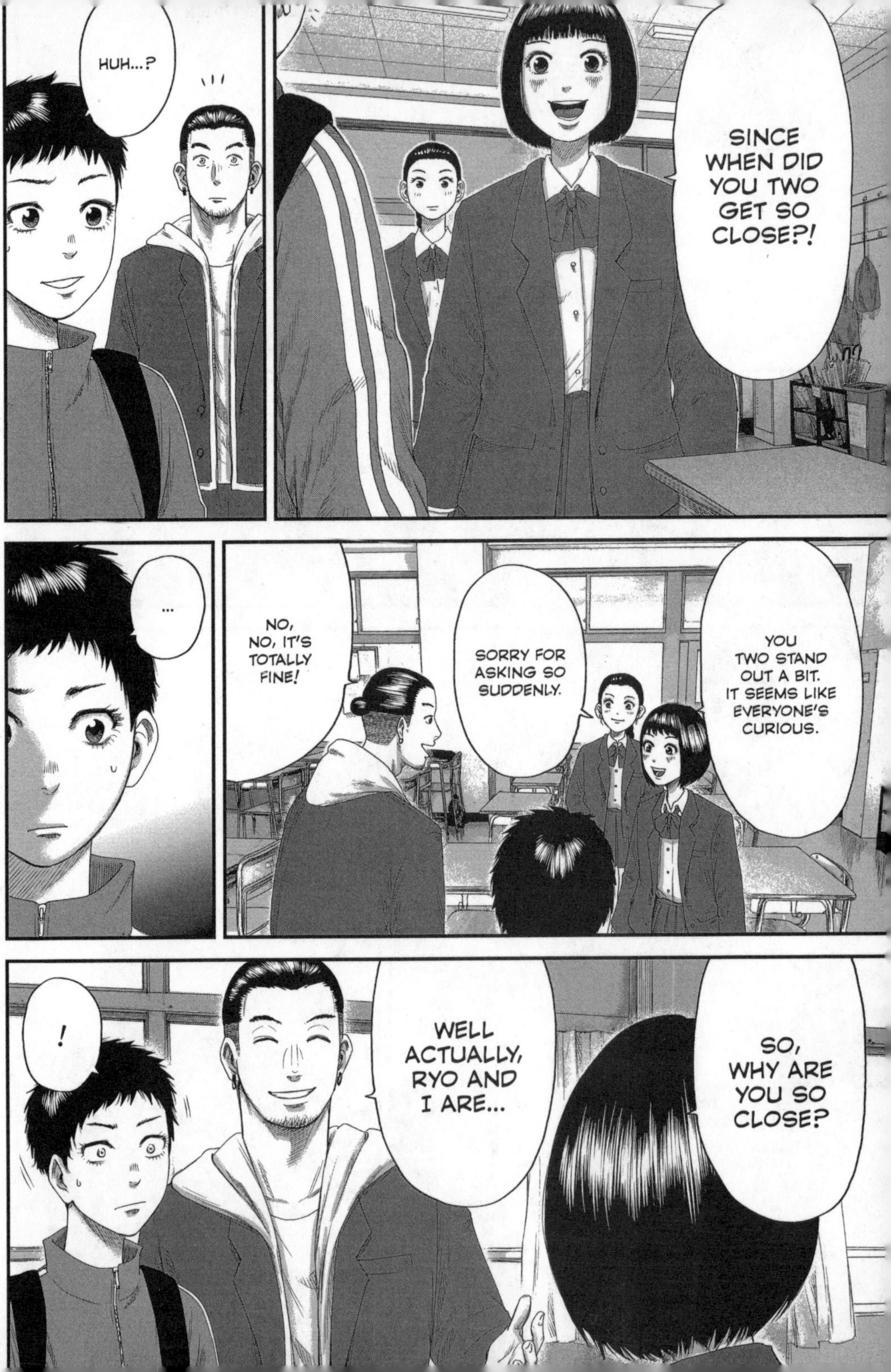
SINCE WHEN DID YOU TWO GET SO CLOSE?!
HUH...?
YOU TWO STAND OUT A BIT. IT SEEMS LIKE EVERYONE'S CURIOUS.
SORRY FOR ASKING SO SUDDENLY.
NO, NO, IT'S TOTALLY FINE!
...
SO, WHY ARE YOU SO CLOSE?
WELL ACTUALLY, RYO AND I ARE...
!

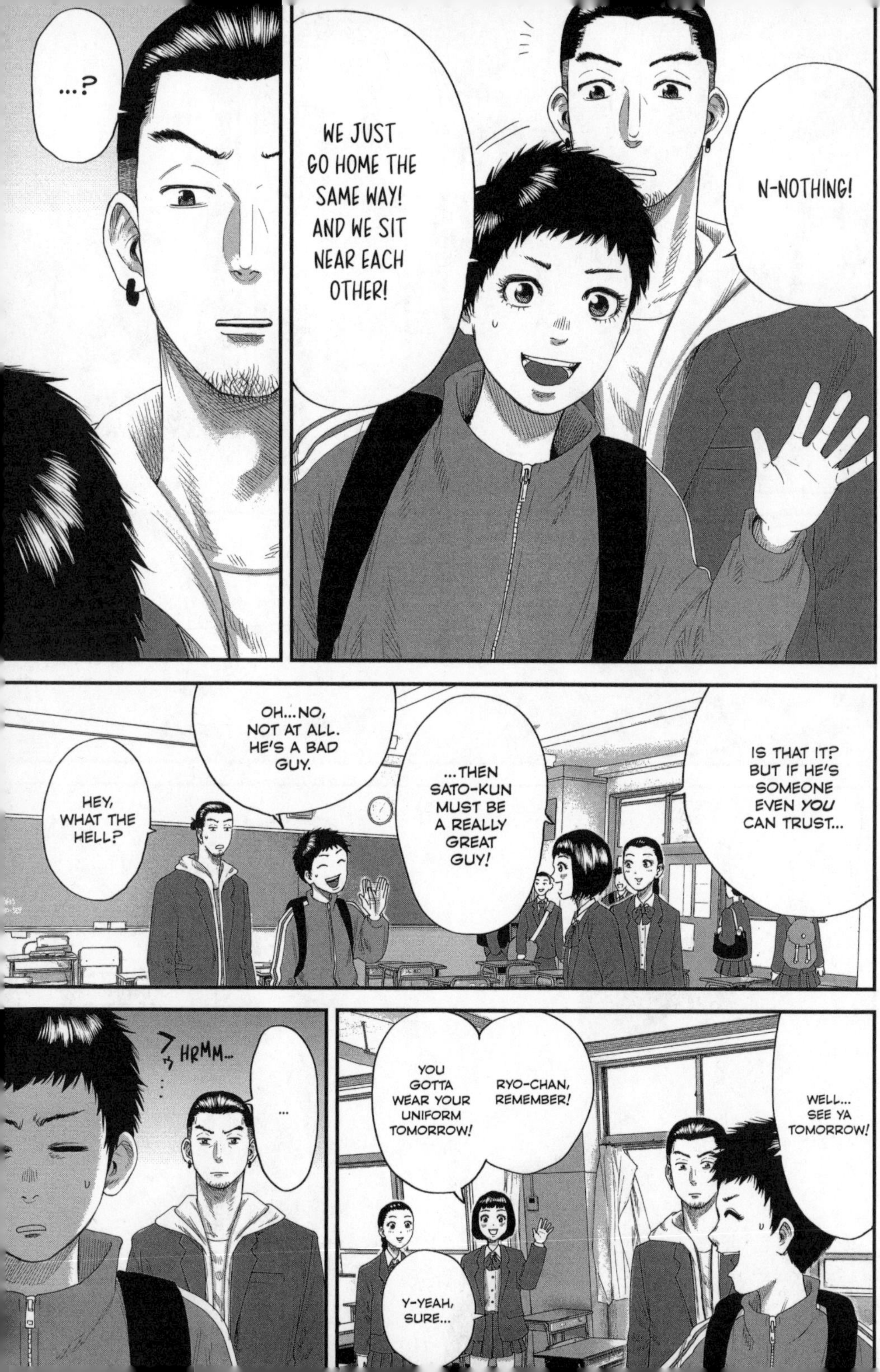
N-NOTHING!
WE JUST GO HOME THE SAME WAY! AND WE SIT NEAR EACH OTHER!
...?
IS THAT IT? BUT IF HE'S SOMEONE EVEN *YOU* CAN TRUST...
...THEN SATO-KUN MUST BE A REALLY GREAT GUY!
OH...NO, NOT AT ALL. HE'S A BAD GUY.
HEY, WHAT THE HELL?
WELL... SEE YA TOMORROW!
RYO-CHAN, REMEMBER!
YOU GOTTA WEAR YOUR UNIFORM TOMORROW!
Y-YEAH, SURE...
HRMM...
...
...

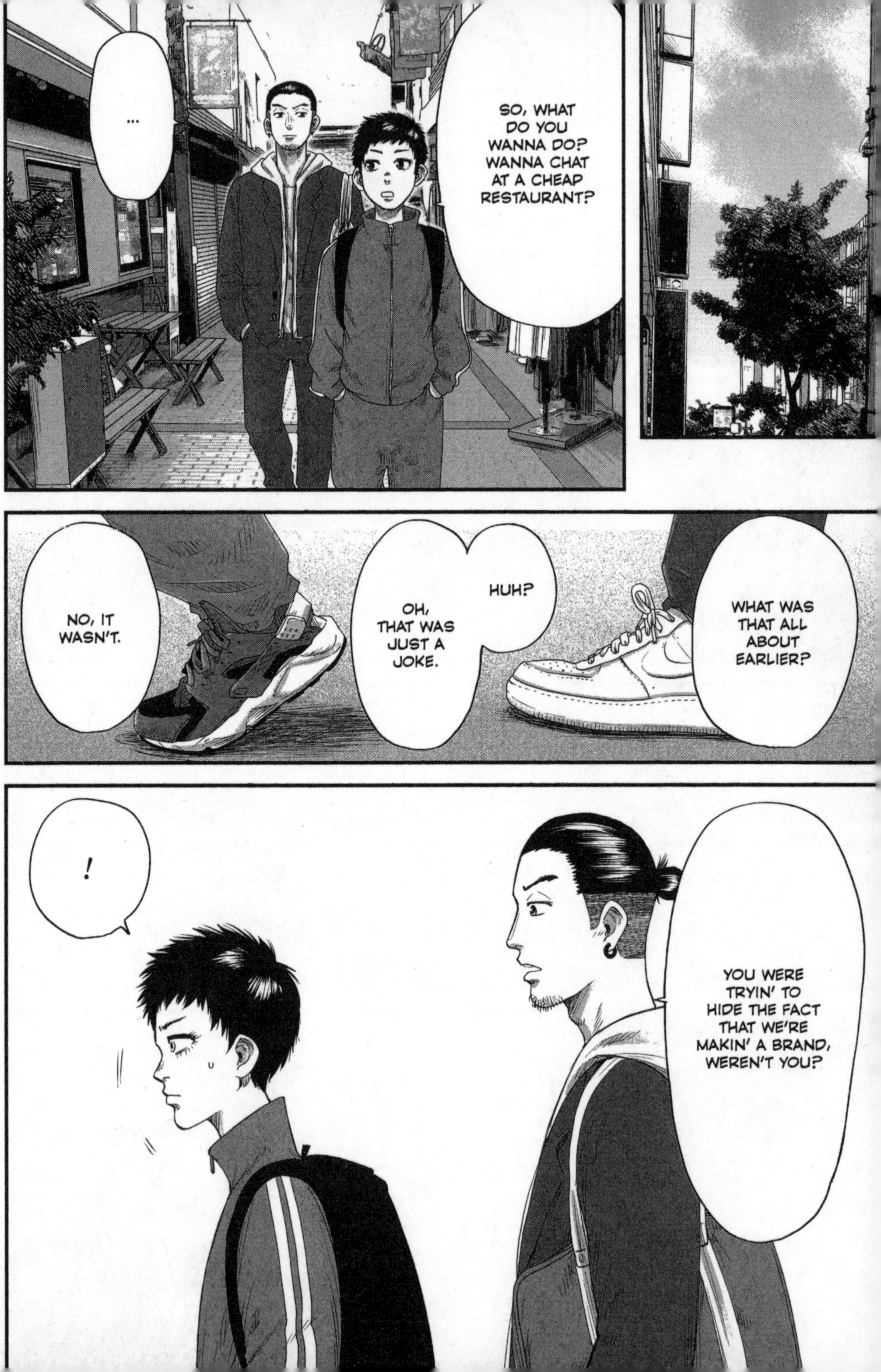
SO, WHAT DO YOU WANNA DO? WANNA CHAT AT A CHEAP RESTAURANT?
...
WHAT WAS THAT ALL ABOUT EARLIER?
HUH?
OH, THAT WAS JUST A JOKE.
NO, IT WASN'T.
YOU WERE TRYIN' TO HIDE THE FACT THAT WE'RE MAKIN' A BRAND, WEREN'T YOU?
!

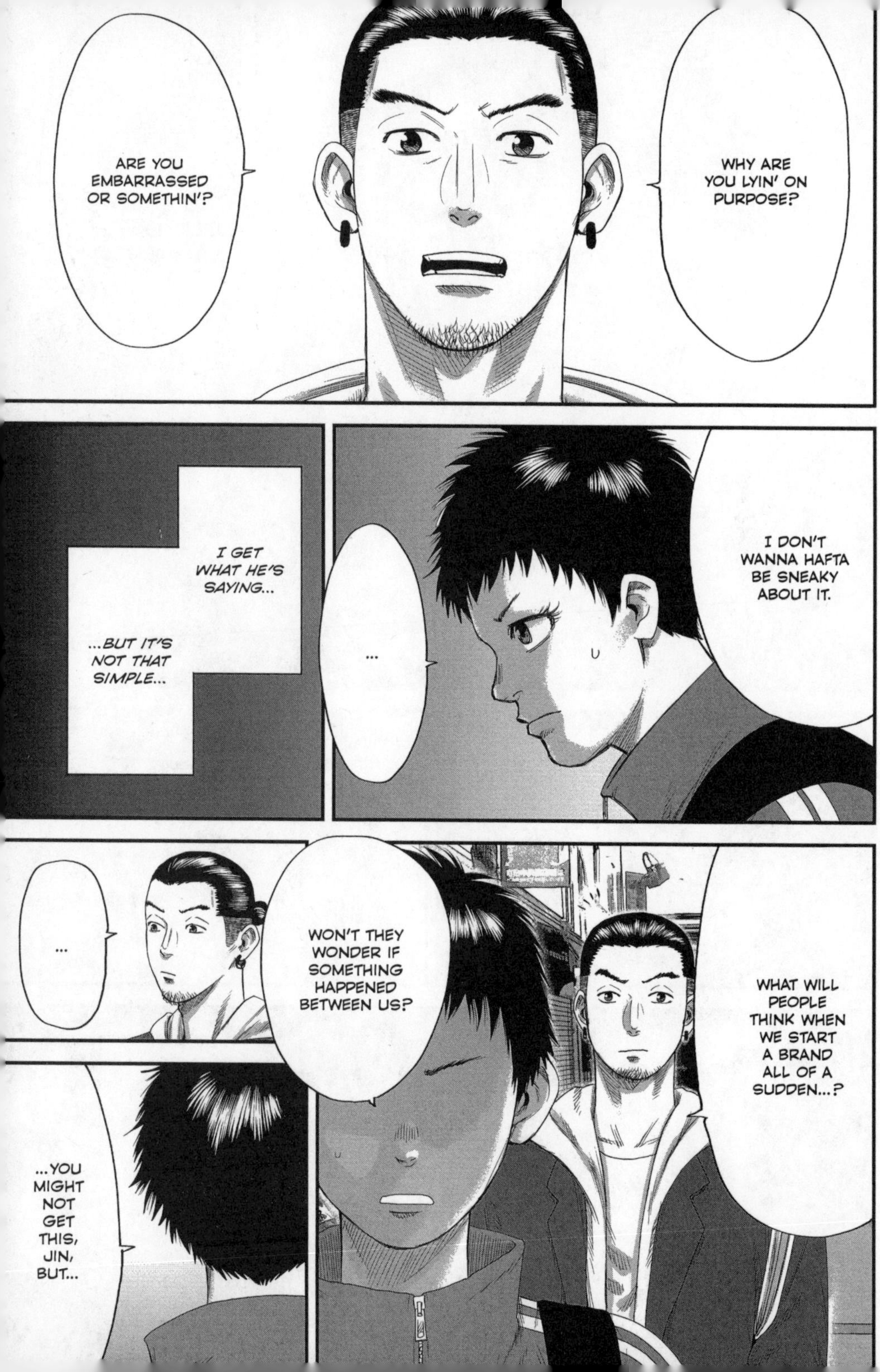
WHY ARE YOU LYIN' ON PURPOSE?
ARE YOU EMBARRASSED OR SOMETHIN'?
I DON'T WANNA HAFTA BE SNEAKY ABOUT IT.
...
I GET WHAT HE'S SAYING...
...BUT IT'S NOT THAT SIMPLE...
WHAT WILL PEOPLE THINK WHEN WE START A BRAND ALL OF A SUDDEN...?
WON'T THEY WONDER IF SOMETHING HAPPENED BETWEEN US?
...
...YOU MIGHT NOT GET THIS, JIN, BUT...

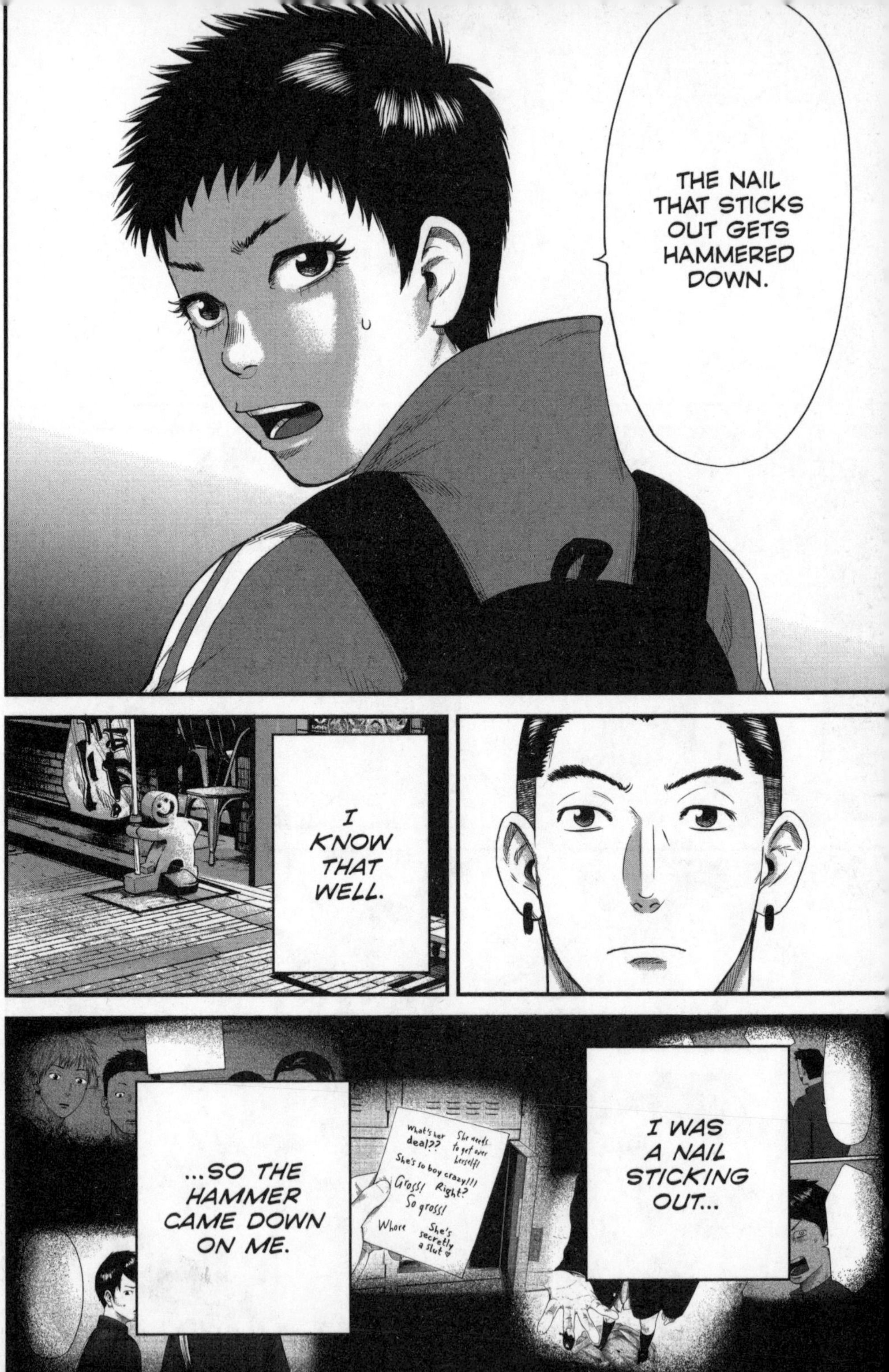
THE NAIL THAT STICKS OUT GETS HAMMERED DOWN.
I KNOW THAT WELL.
I WAS A NAIL STICKING OUT...
What's her deal??
She needs to get over herself!
She's so boy crazy!!!
Gross!
Right?
So gross!
Whore
She's secretly a slut♥
...SO THE HAMMER CAME DOWN ON ME.

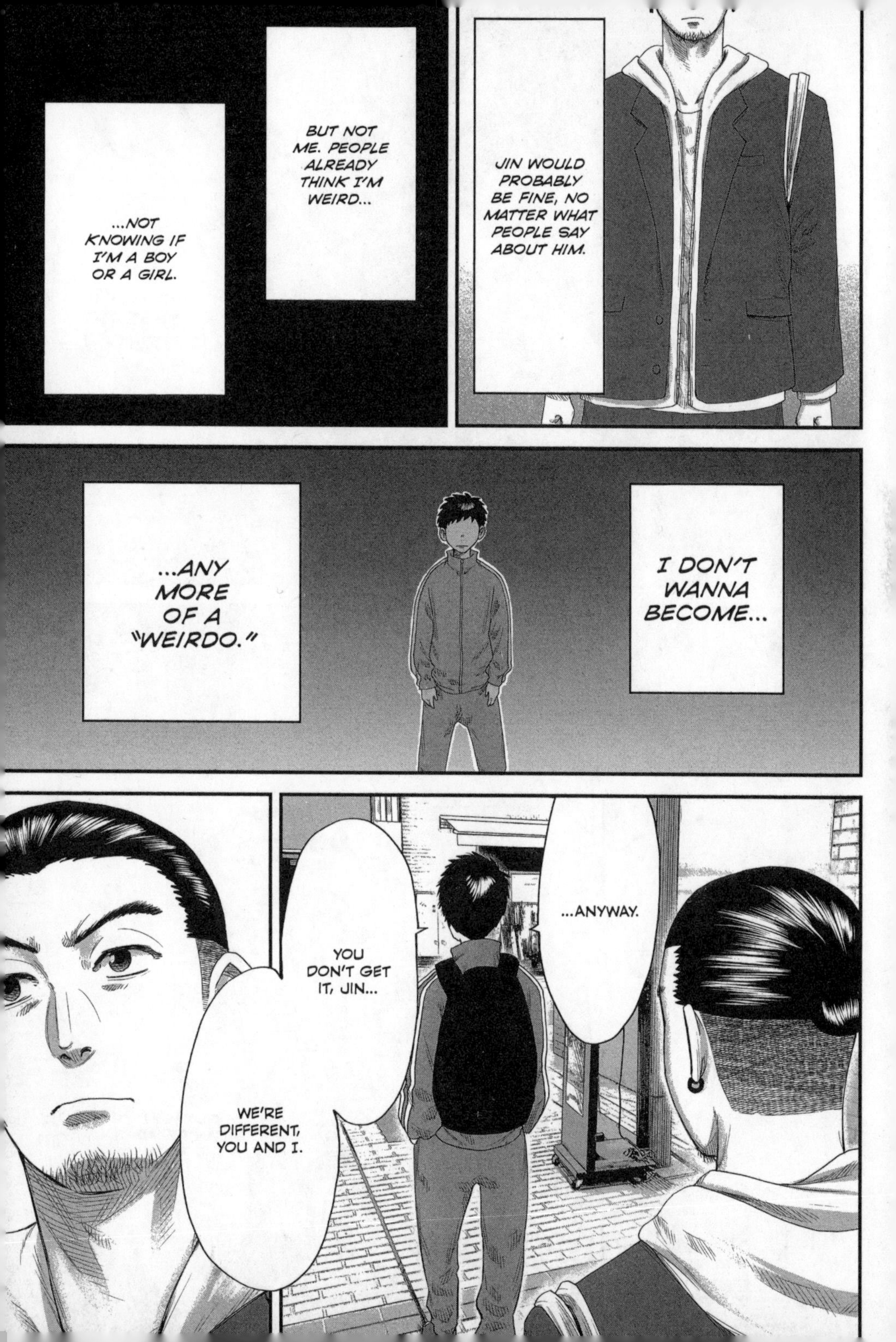
JIN WOULD PROBABLY BE FINE, NO MATTER WHAT PEOPLE SAY ABOUT HIM.
BUT NOT ME. PEOPLE ALREADY THINK I'M WEIRD...
...NOT KNOWING IF I'M A BOY OR A GIRL.
I DON'T WANNA BECOME...
...ANY MORE OF A "WEIRDO."
...ANYWAY.
YOU DON'T GET IT, JIN...
WE'RE DIFFERENT, YOU AND I.

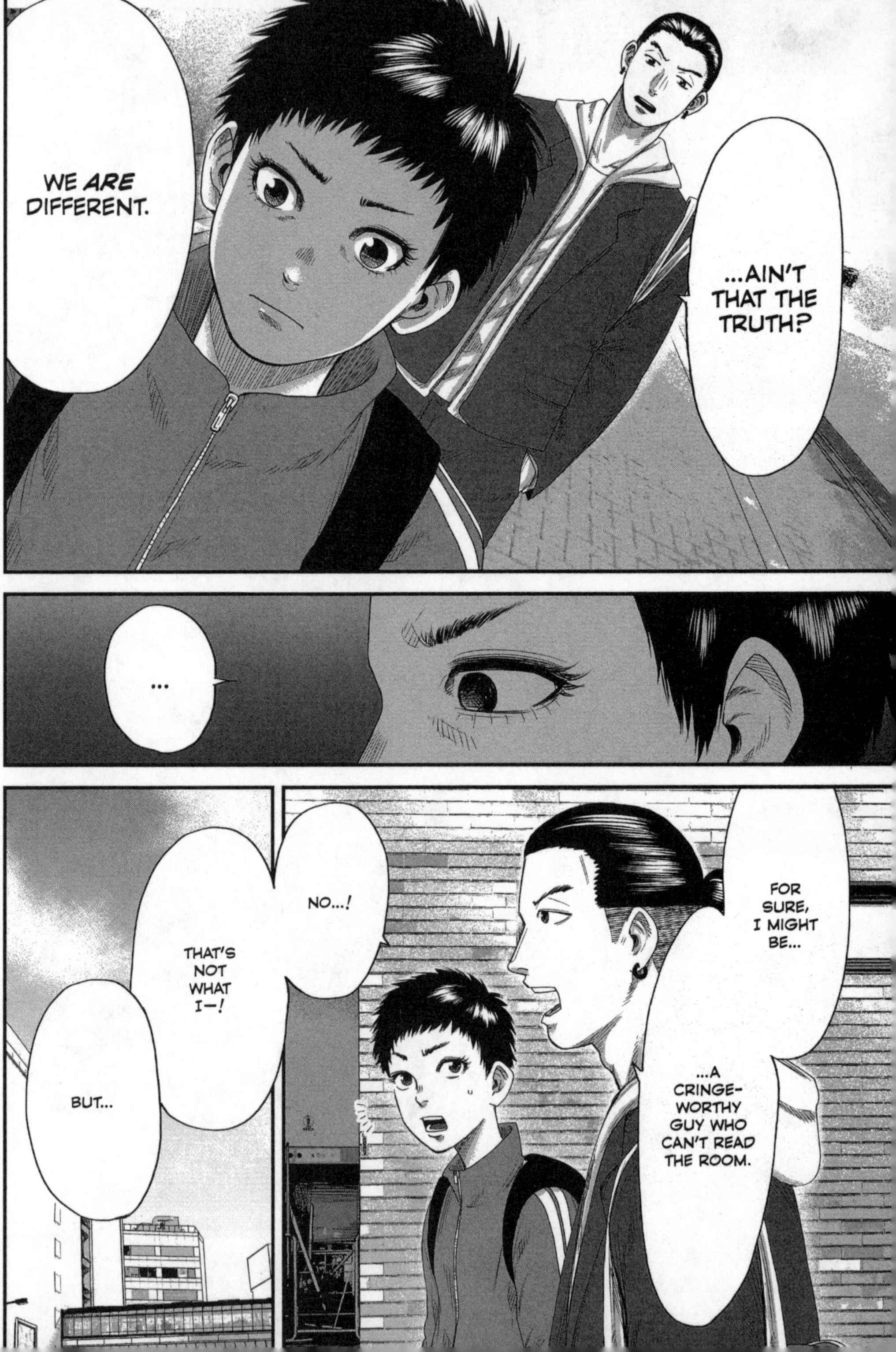
...AIN'T THAT THE TRUTH?
WE ARE DIFFERENT.
...
FOR SURE, I MIGHT BE...
...A CRINGE-WORTHY GUY WHO CAN'T READ THE ROOM.
NO...!
THAT'S NOT WHAT I—!
BUT...

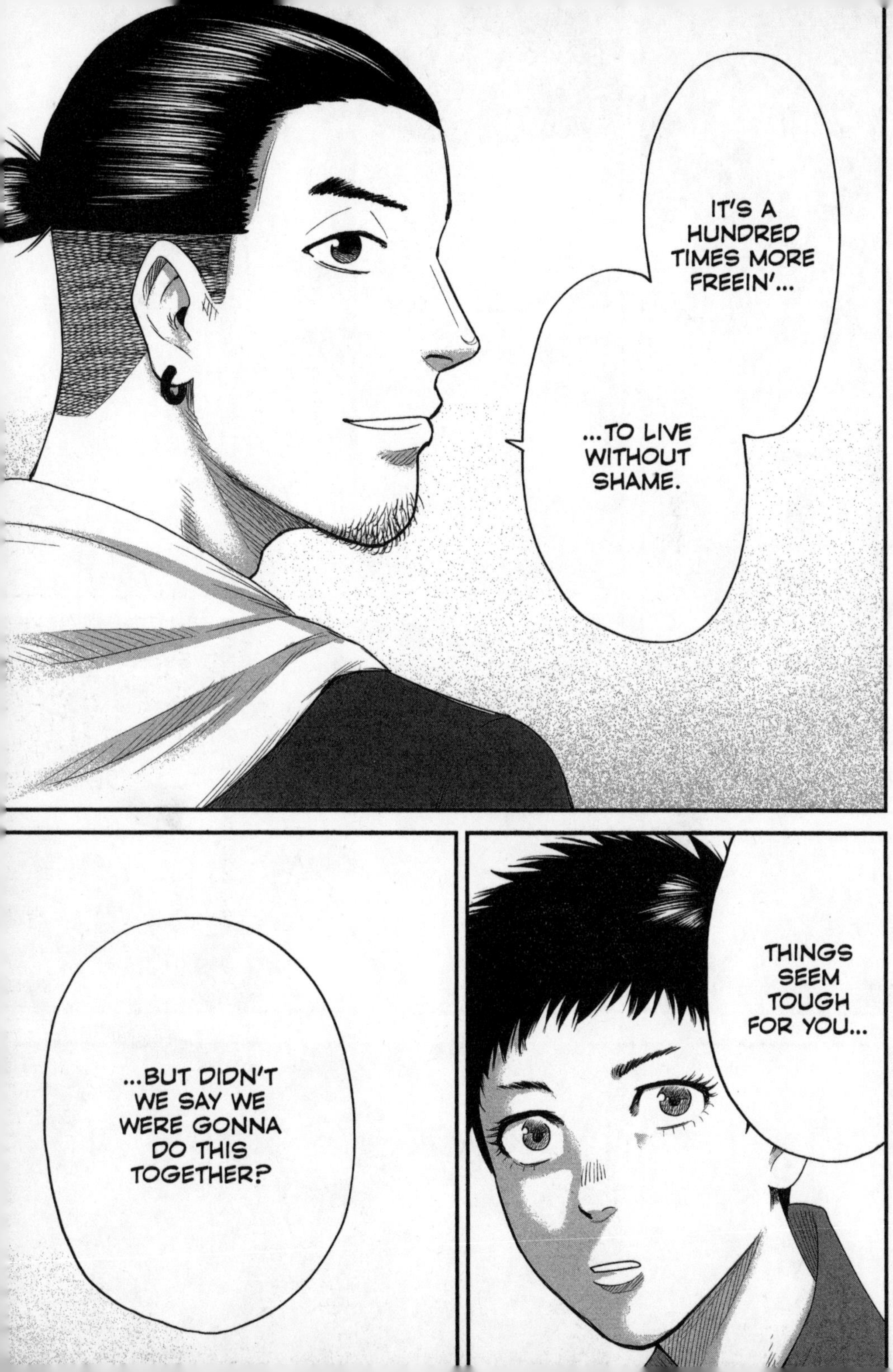
IT'S A HUNDRED TIMES MORE FREEIN'...
...TO LIVE WITHOUT SHAME.
THINGS SEEM TOUGH FOR YOU...
...BUT DIDN'T WE SAY WE WERE GONNA DO THIS TOGETHER?

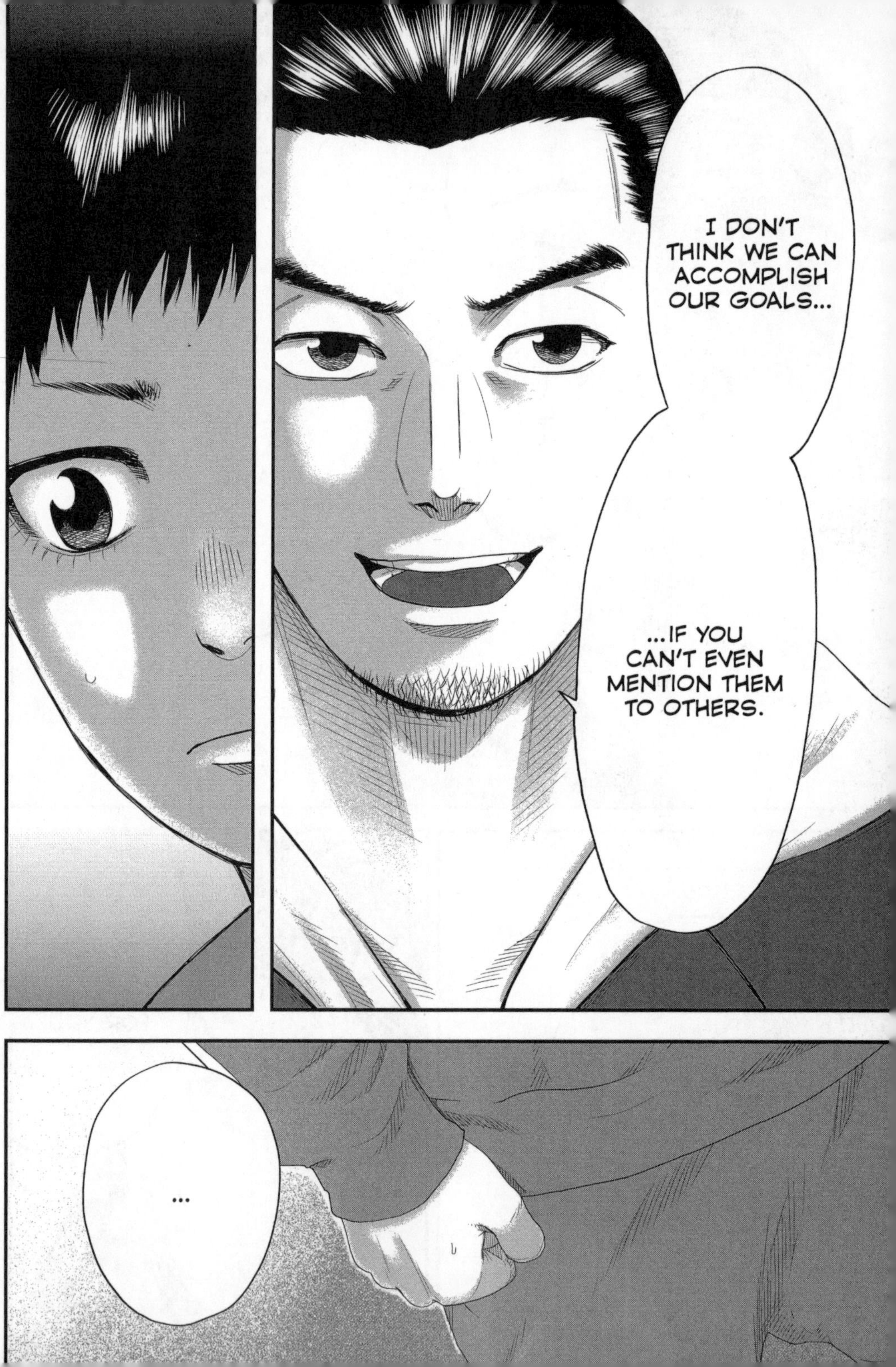
I DON'T THINK WE CAN ACCOMPLISH OUR GOALS...
...IF YOU CAN'T EVEN MENTION THEM TO OTHERS.
...

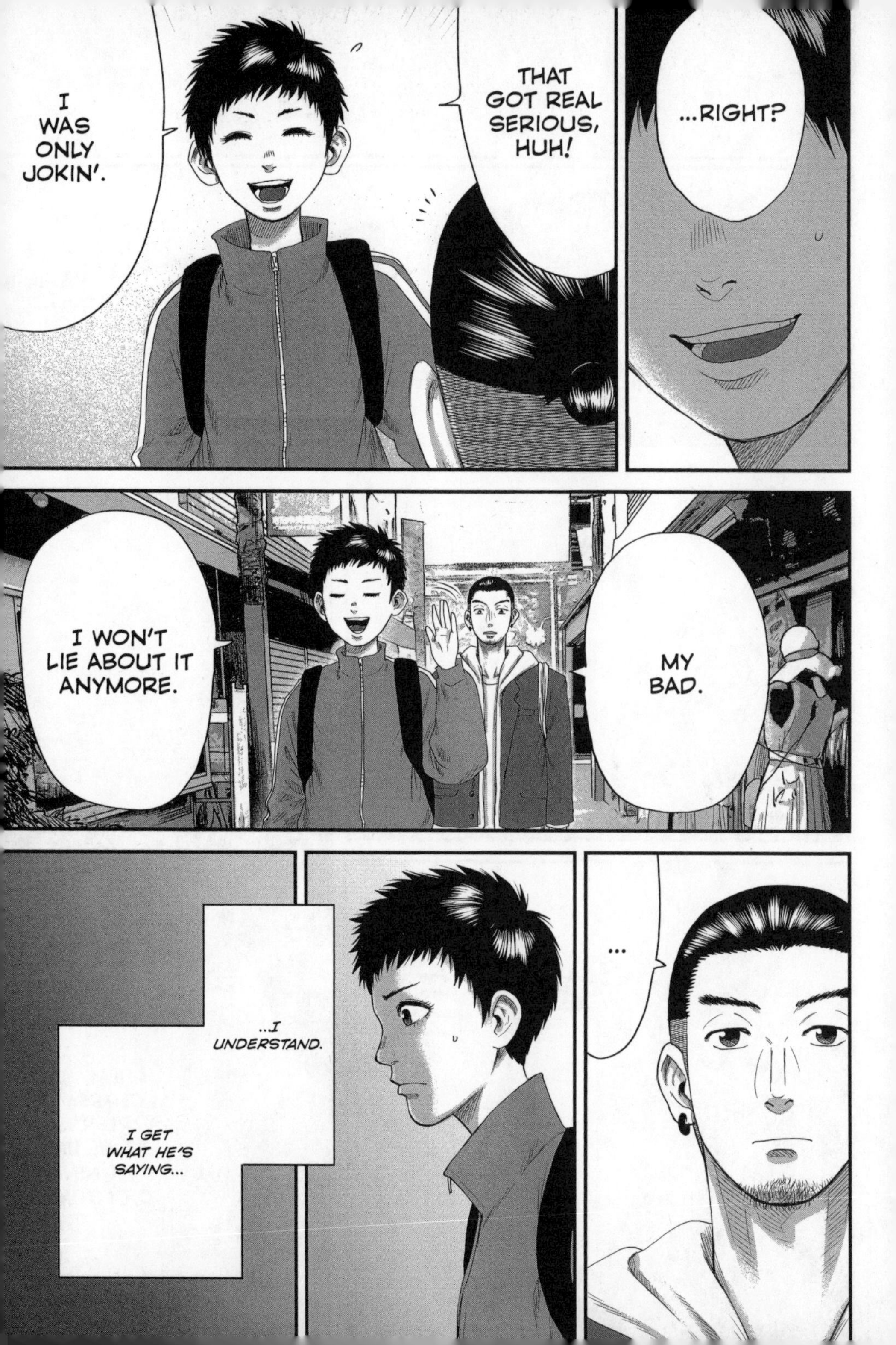
...RIGHT?
THAT GOT REAL SERIOUS, HUH!
I WAS ONLY JOKIN'.
MY BAD.
I WON'T LIE ABOUT IT ANYMORE.
...
...I UNDERSTAND.
I GET WHAT HE'S SAYING...

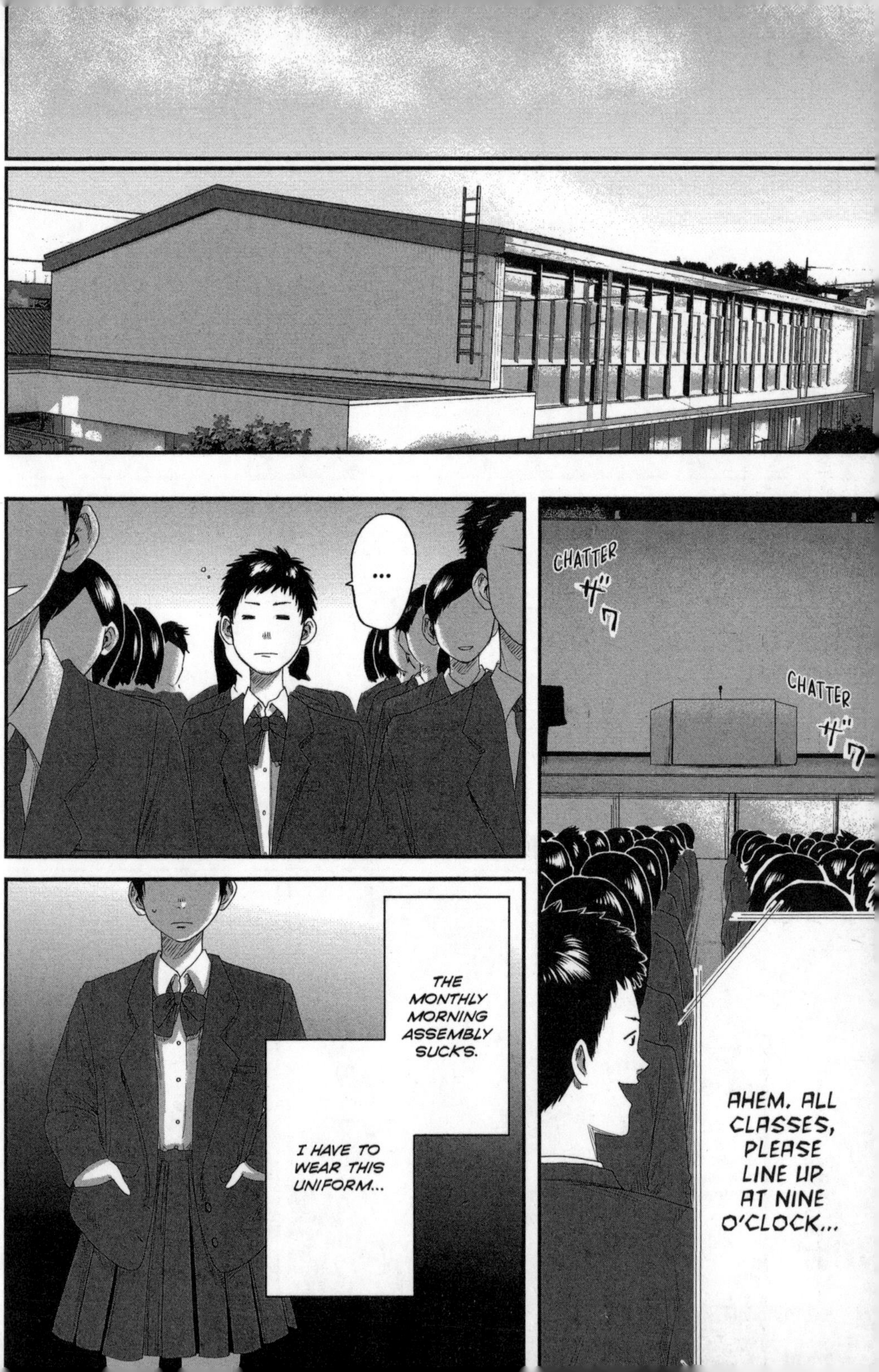
CHATTER
ザワ
CHATTER
ザワ
AHEM. ALL CLASSES, PLEASE LINE UP AT NINE O'CLOCK...
...
THE MONTHLY MORNING ASSEMBLY SUCKS.
I HAVE TO WEAR THIS UNIFORM...

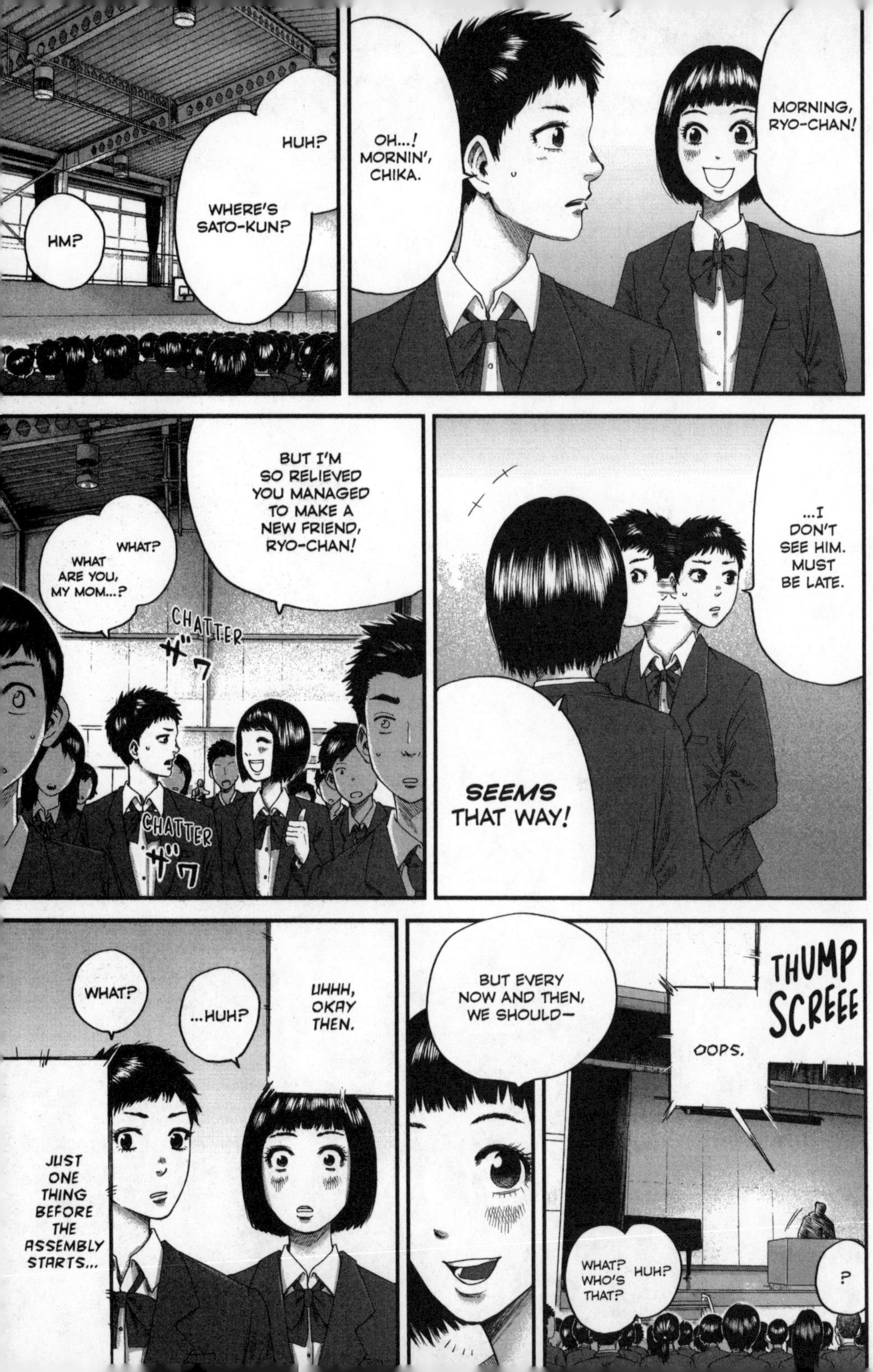
MORNING, RYO-CHAN!
OH...! MORNIN', CHIKA.
HUH?
WHERE'S SATO-KUN?
HM?
...I DON'T SEE HIM. MUST BE LATE.
SEEMS THAT WAY!
BUT I'M SO RELIEVED YOU MANAGED TO MAKE A NEW FRIEND, RYO-CHAN!
WHAT? WHAT ARE YOU, MY MOM...?
CHATTER ザワ
CHATTER ザワ
THUMP SCREEE
BUT EVERY NOW AND THEN, WE SHOULD—
OOPS.
?
HUH?
WHAT? WHO'S THAT?
UHHH, OKAY THEN.
...HUH?
WHAT?
JUST ONE THING BEFORE THE ASSEMBLY STARTS...

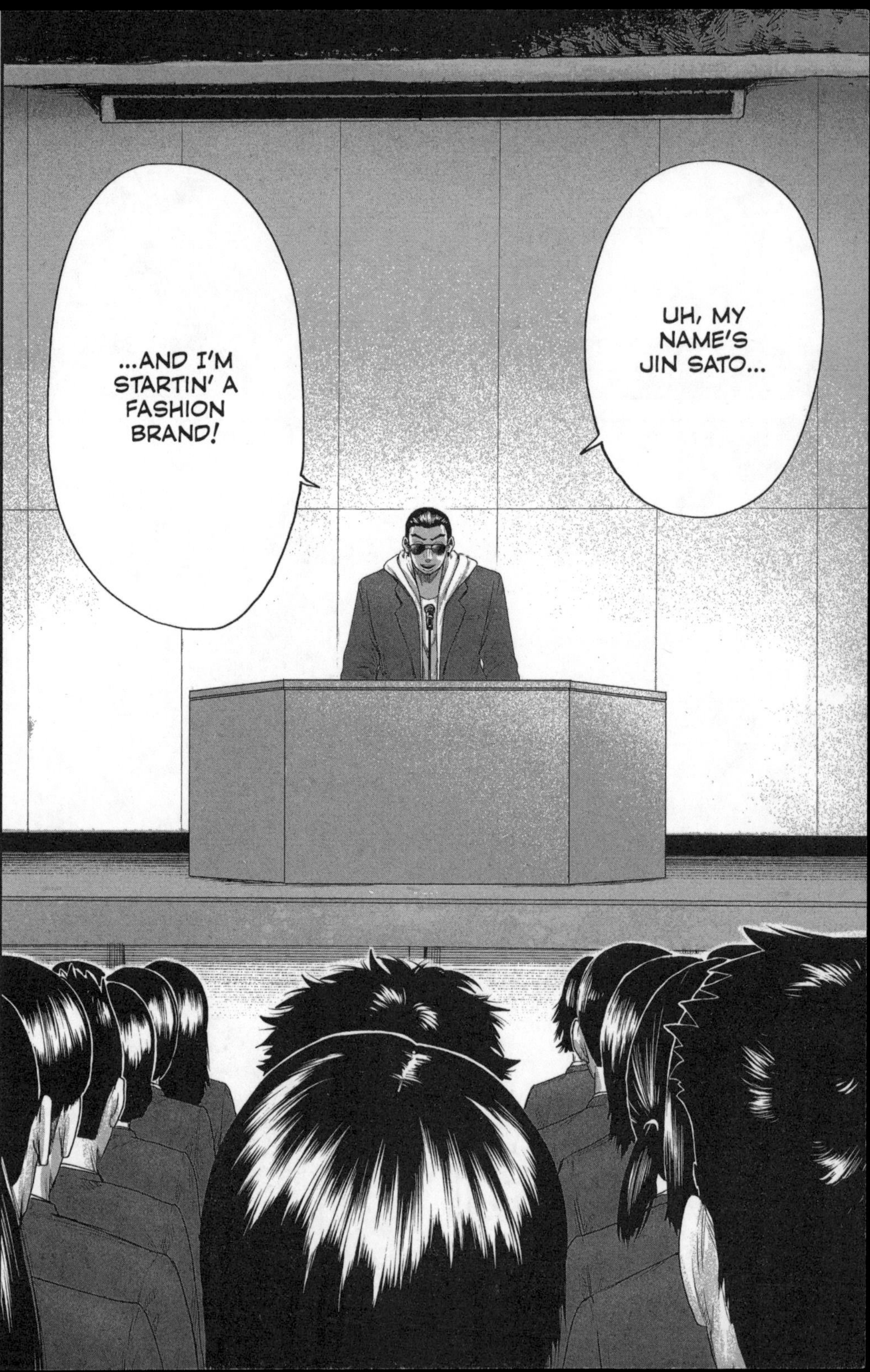
UH, MY NAME'S JIN SATO...
...AND I'M STARTIN' A FASHION BRAND!

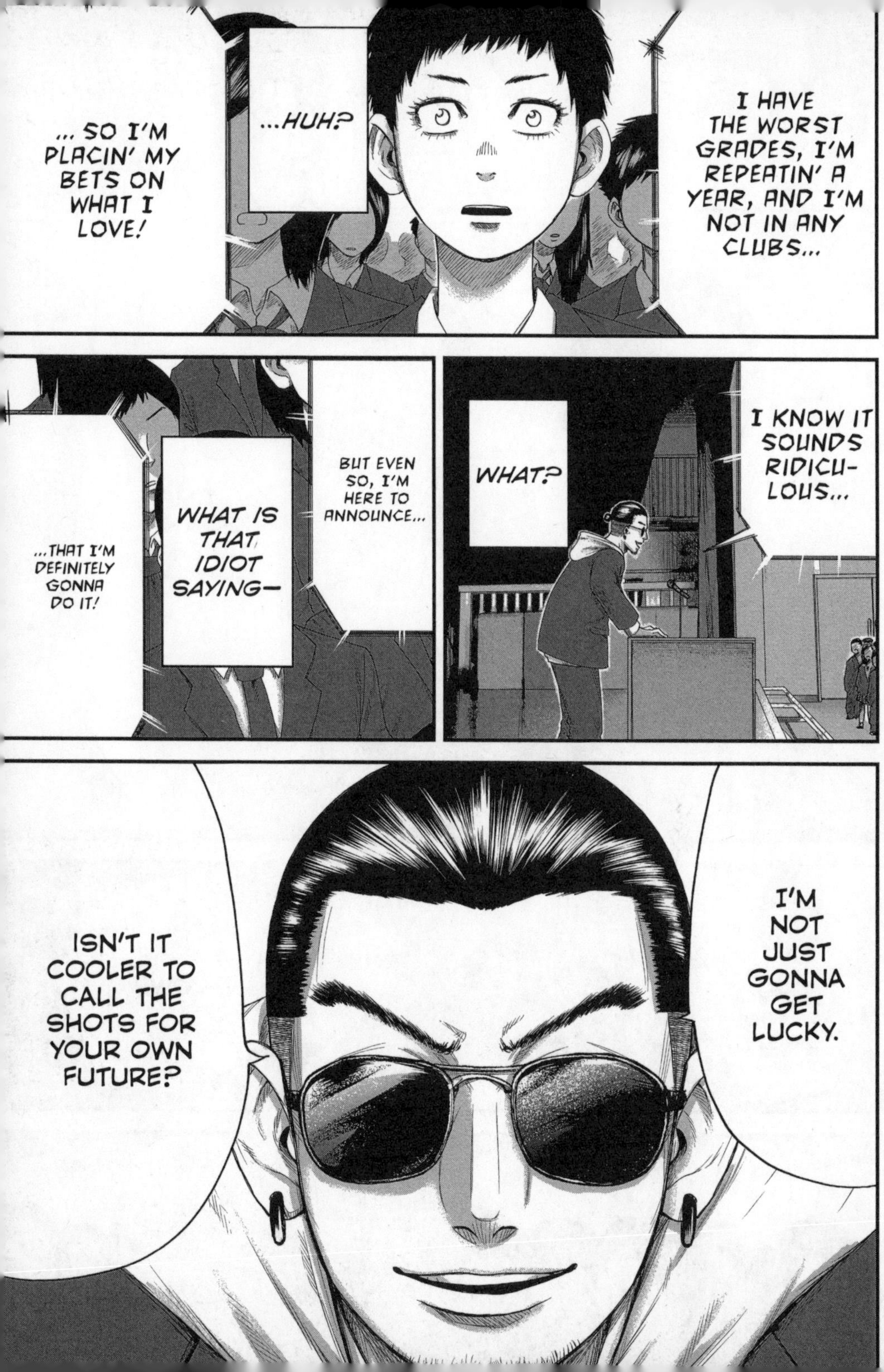
I HAVE THE WORST GRADES, I'M REPEATIN' A YEAR, AND I'M NOT IN ANY CLUBS...
...HUH?
...SO I'M PLACIN' MY BETS ON WHAT I LOVE!
I KNOW IT SOUNDS RIDICU-LOUS...
WHAT?
BUT EVEN SO, I'M HERE TO ANNOUNCE...
WHAT IS THAT IDIOT SAYING—
...THAT I'M DEFINITELY GONNA DO IT!
I'M NOT JUST GONNA GET LUCKY.
ISN'T IT COOLER TO CALL THE SHOTS FOR YOUR OWN FUTURE?

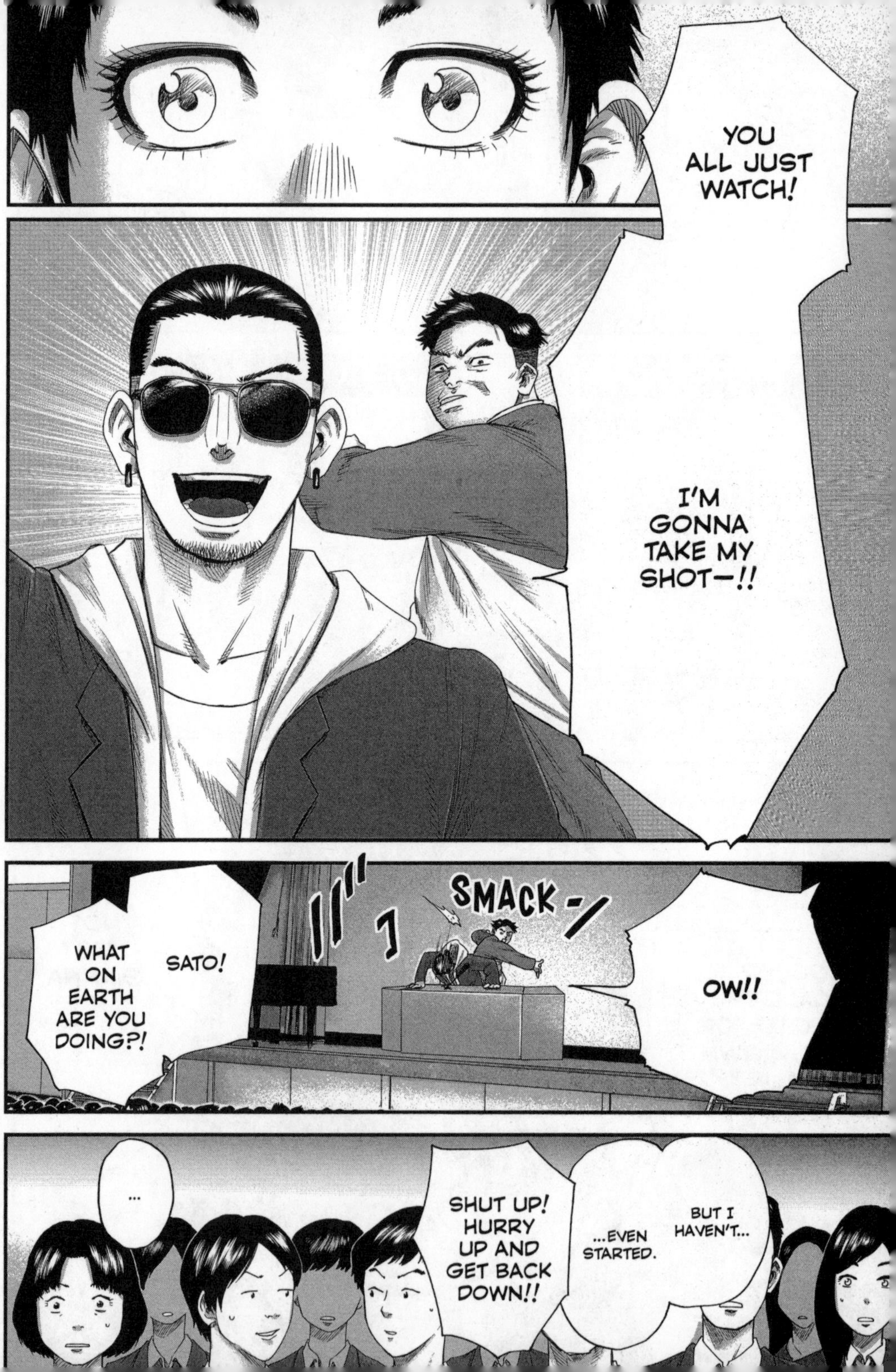
YOU ALL JUST WATCH!
I'M GONNA TAKE MY SHOT—!!
OW!!
SMACK-
SATO!
WHAT ON EARTH ARE YOU DOING?!
BUT I HAVEN'T...
...EVEN STARTED.
SHUT UP! HURRY UP AND GET BACK DOWN!!
...

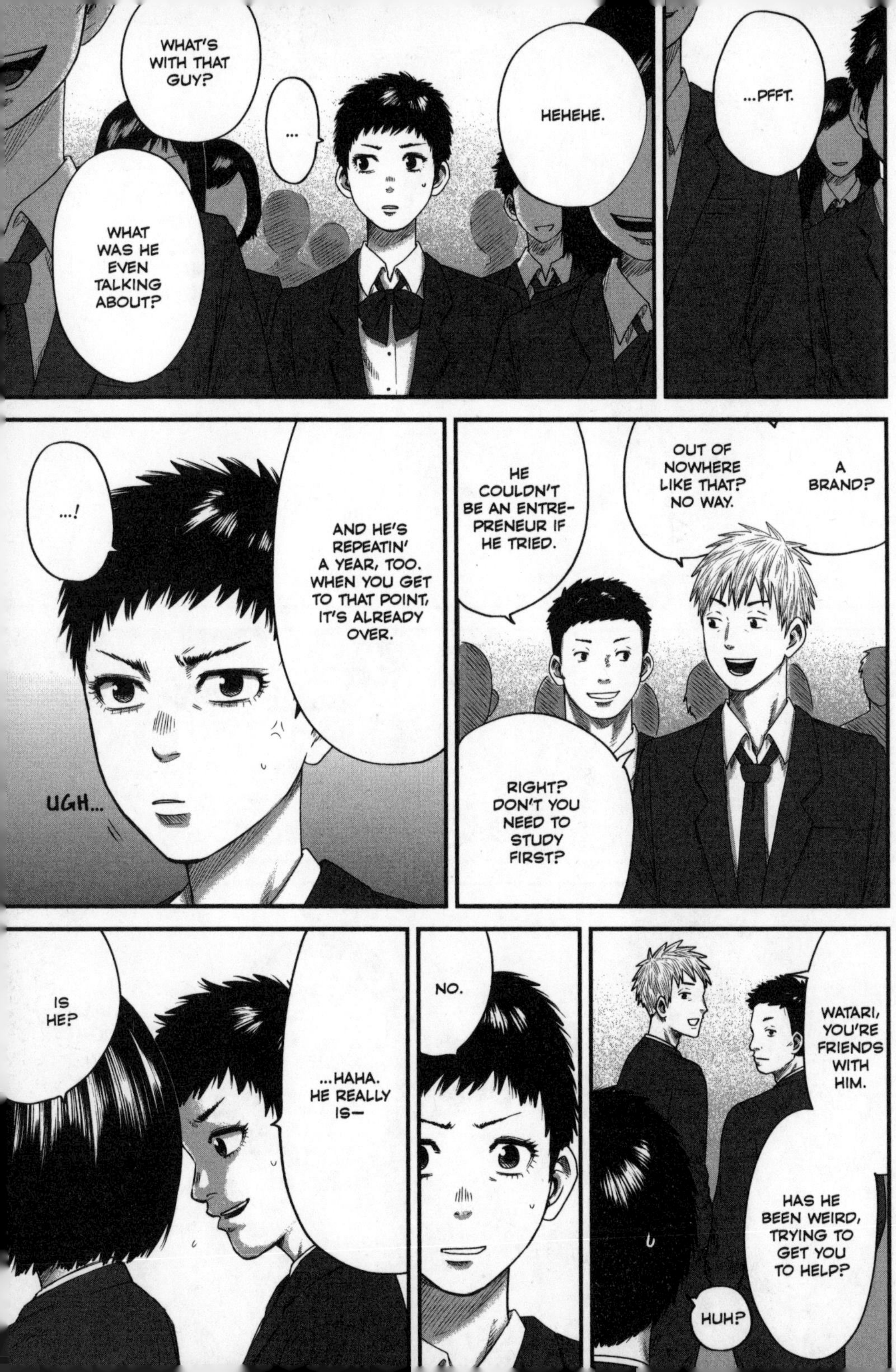
...PFFT.
HEHEHE.
...
WHAT'S WITH THAT GUY?
WHAT WAS HE EVEN TALKING ABOUT?
A BRAND?
OUT OF NOWHERE LIKE THAT? NO WAY.
HE COULDN'T BE AN ENTREPRENEUR IF HE TRIED.
RIGHT? DON'T YOU NEED TO STUDY FIRST?
AND HE'S REPEATIN' A YEAR, TOO. WHEN YOU GET TO THAT POINT, IT'S ALREADY OVER.
...!
UGH...
WATARI, YOU'RE FRIENDS WITH HIM.
HAS HE BEEN WEIRD, TRYING TO GET YOU TO HELP?
HUH?
NO.
IS HE?
...HAHA. HE REALLY IS—

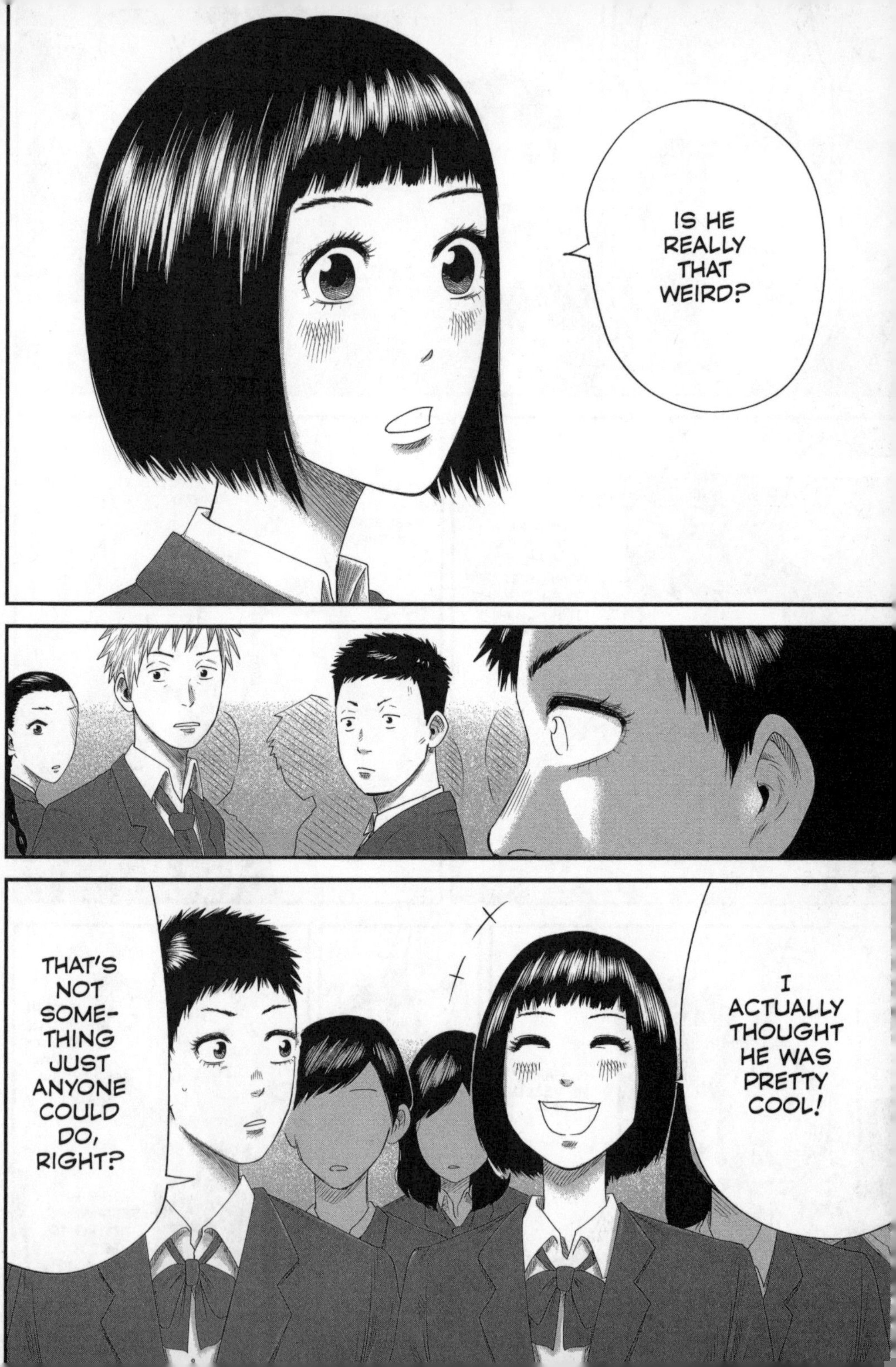
IS HE REALLY THAT WEIRD?
I ACTUALLY THOUGHT HE WAS PRETTY COOL!
THAT'S NOT SOME-THING JUST ANYONE COULD DO, RIGHT?

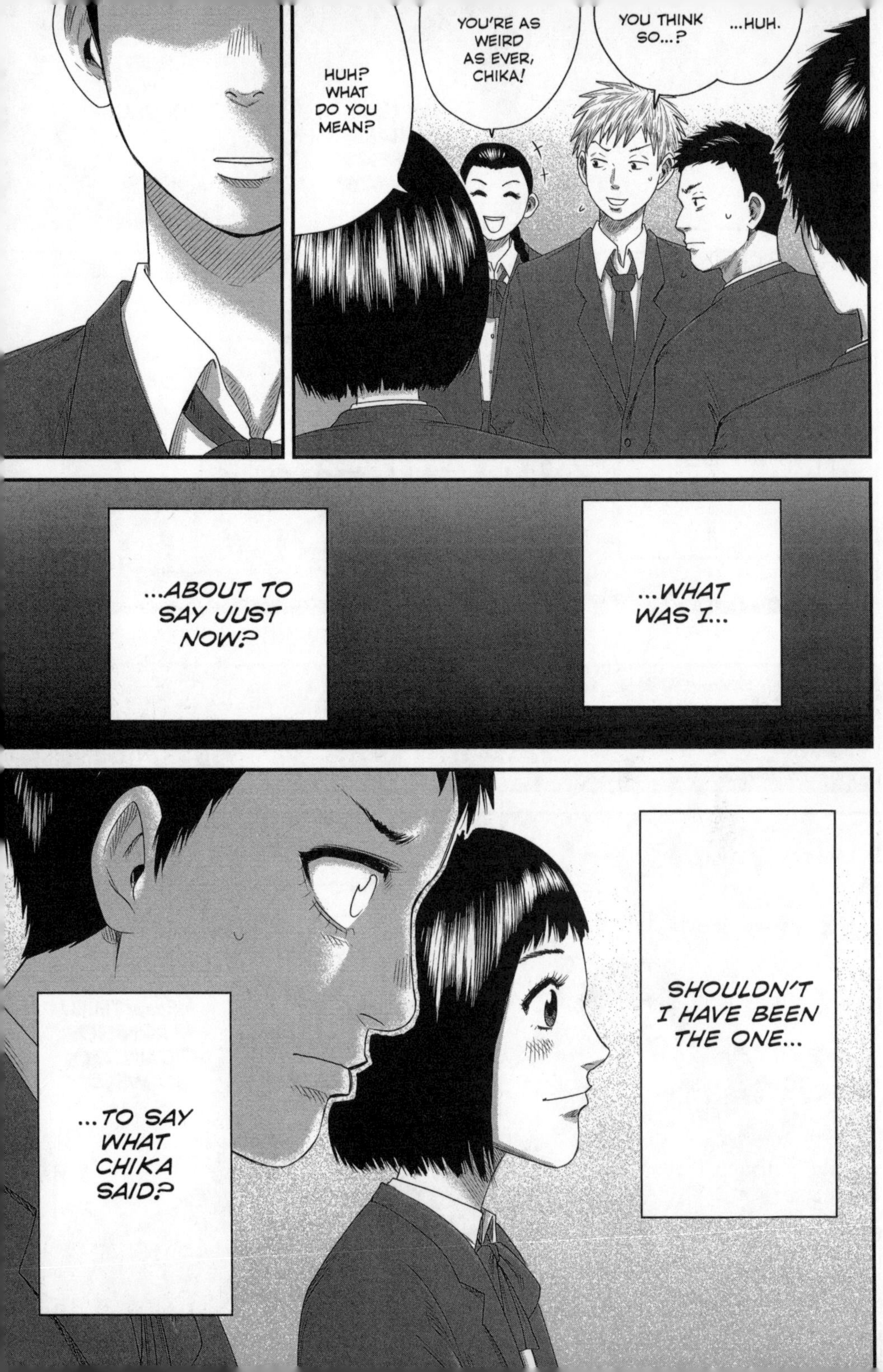
...HUH.
YOU THINK SO...?
YOU'RE AS WEIRD AS EVER, CHIKA!
HUH? WHAT DO YOU MEAN?
...WHAT WAS I...
...ABOUT TO SAY JUST NOW?
SHOULDN'T I HAVE BEEN THE ONE...
...TO SAY WHAT CHIKA SAID?

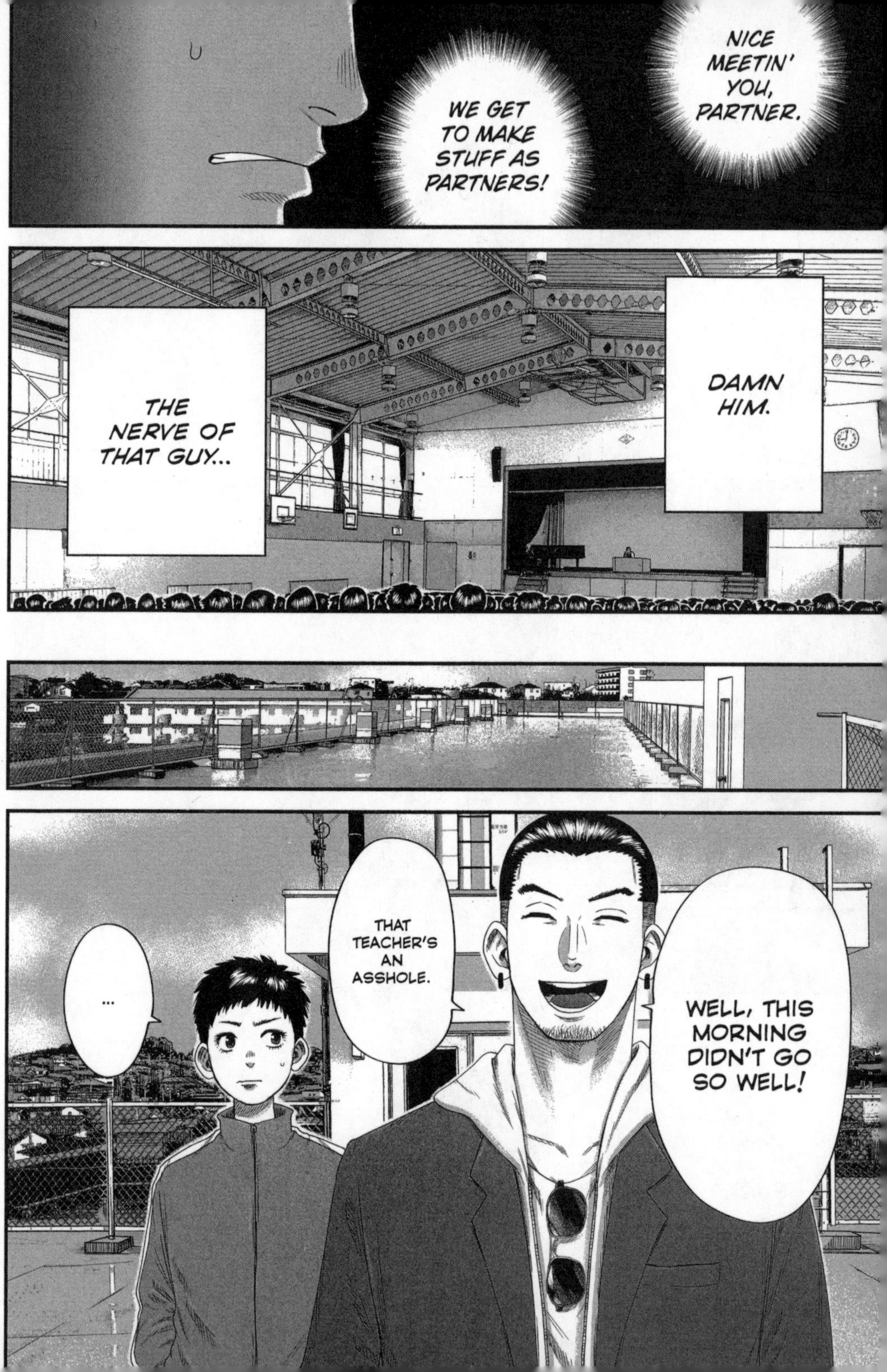
NICE MEETIN' YOU, PARTNER.
WE GET TO MAKE STUFF AS PARTNERS!
DAMN HIM.
THE NERVE OF THAT GUY...
WELL, THIS MORNING DIDN'T GO SO WELL!
THAT TEACHER'S AN ASSHOLE.
...

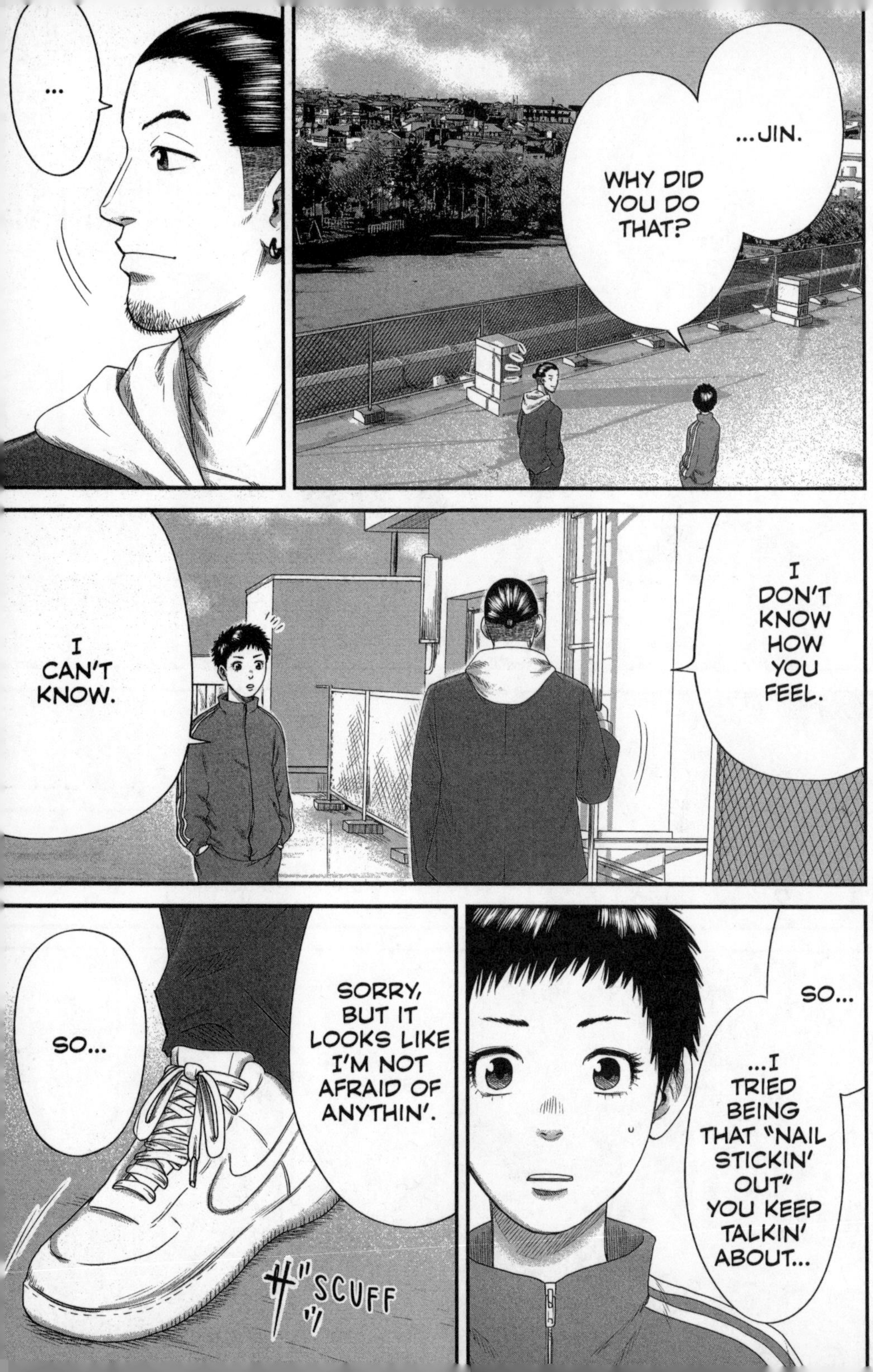
...JIN.
WHY DID YOU DO THAT?
...
I DON'T KNOW HOW YOU FEEL.
I CAN'T KNOW.
SO...
...I TRIED BEING THAT "NAIL STICKIN' OUT" YOU KEEP TALKIN' ABOUT...
SORRY, BUT IT LOOKS LIKE I'M NOT AFRAID OF ANYTHIN'.
SO...
SCUFF

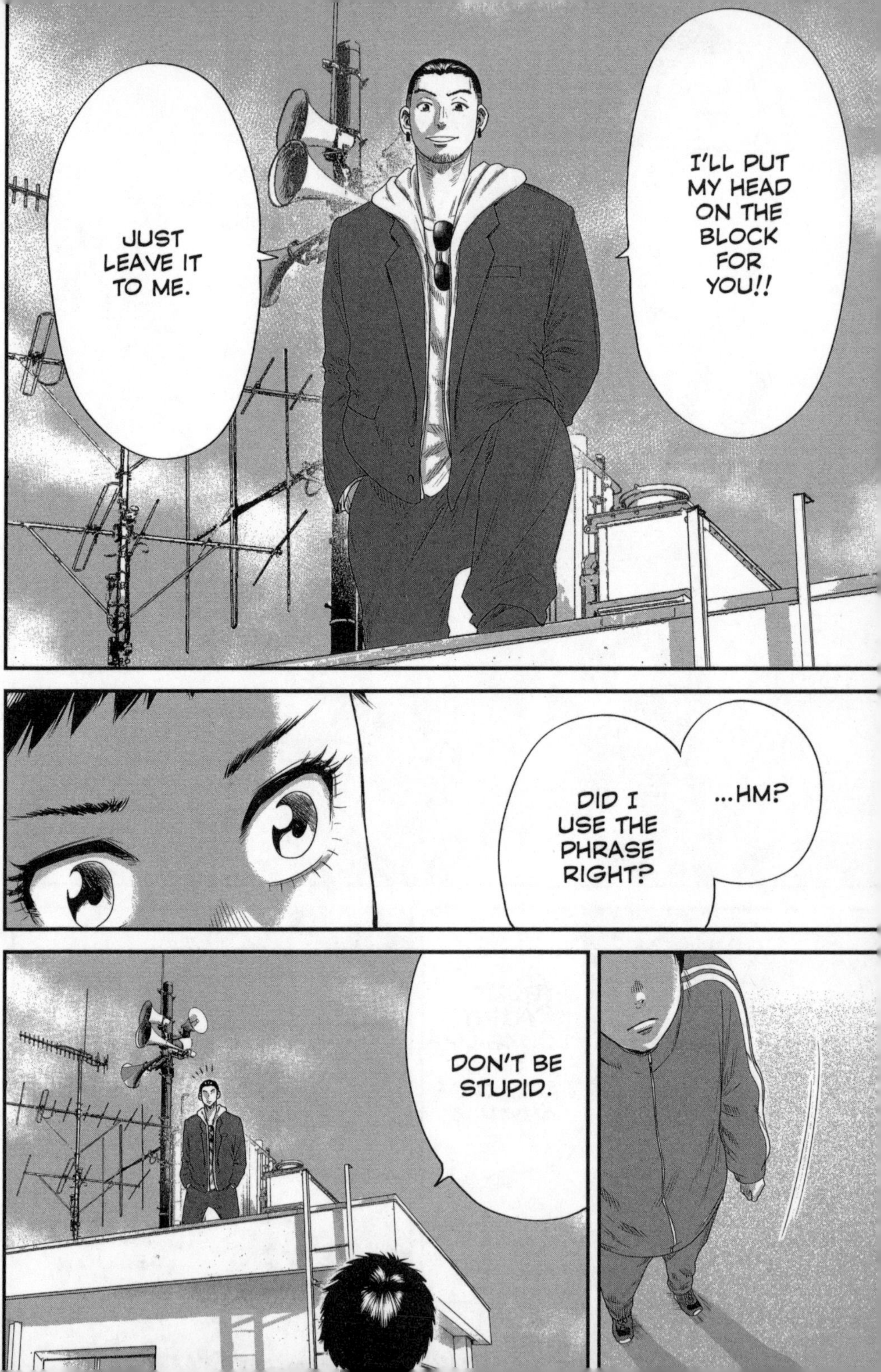
I'LL PUT MY HEAD ON THE BLOCK FOR YOU!!
JUST LEAVE IT TO ME.
...HM?
DID I USE THE PHRASE RIGHT?
DON'T BE STUPID.

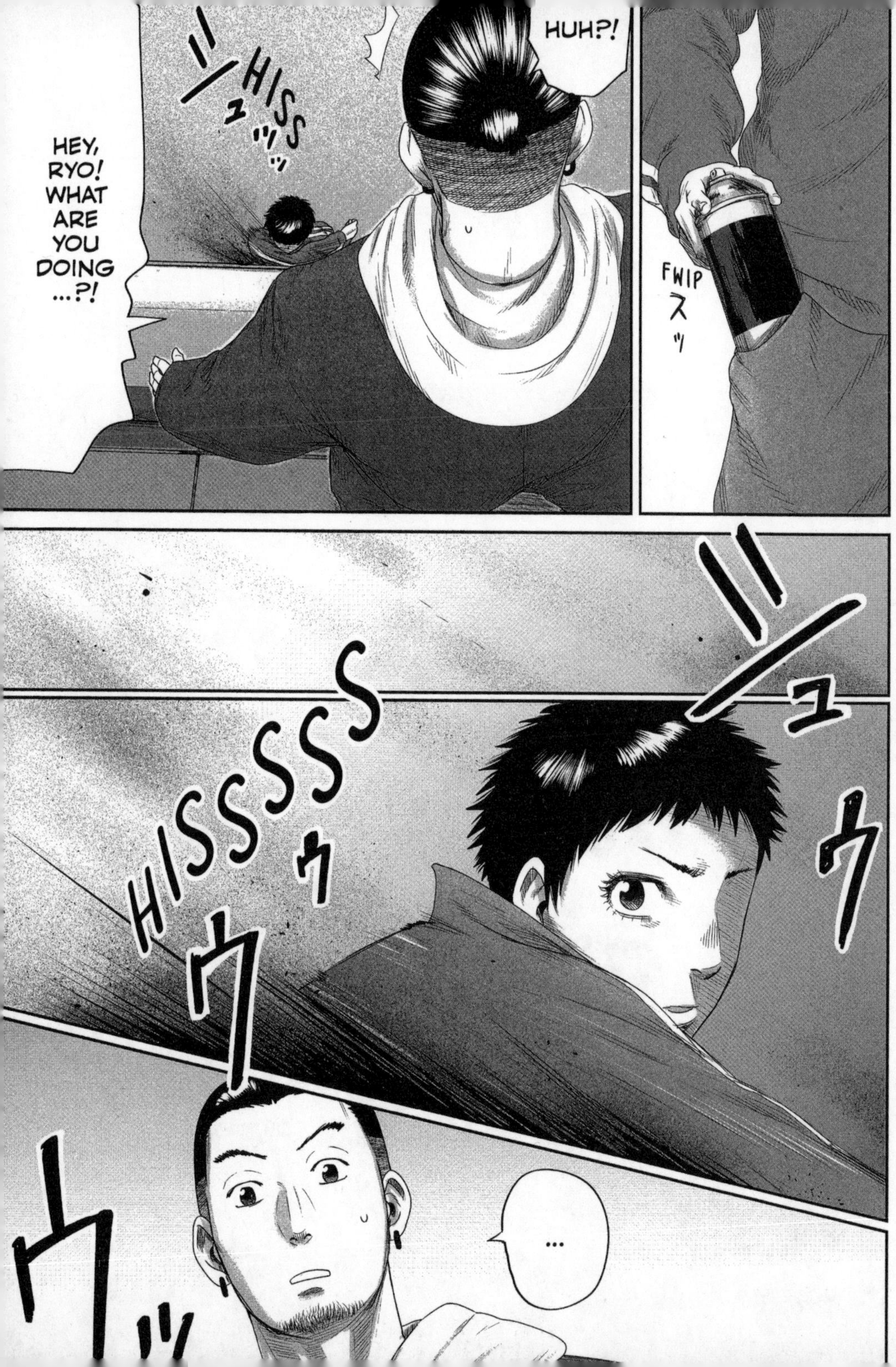
FWIP
スッ
HUH?!
HISS
シュッッ
HEY, RYO! WHAT ARE YOU DOING ...?!
HISSSSS
ジュウウウ
...

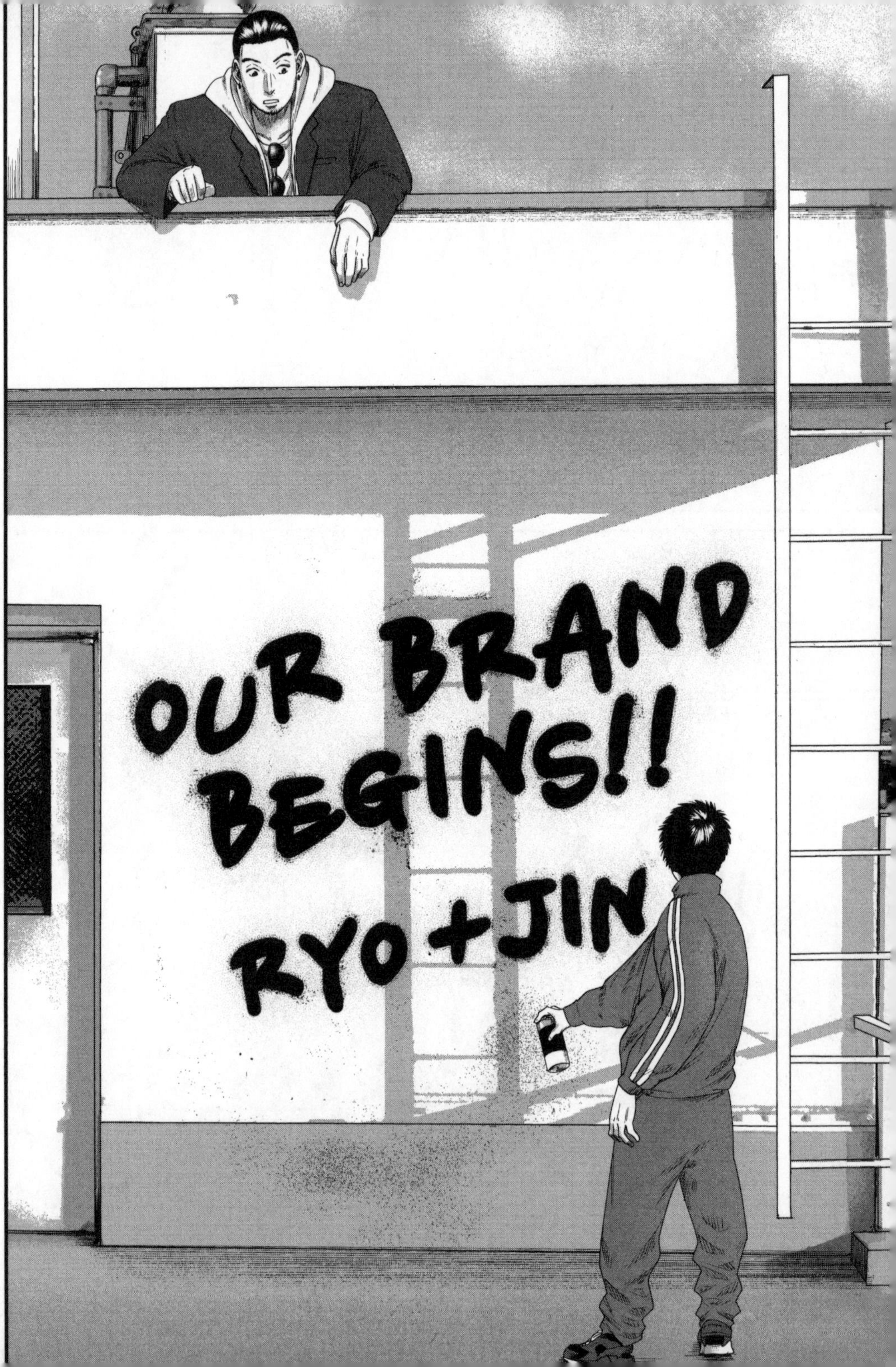
OUR BRAND BEGINS!!
RYO+JIN

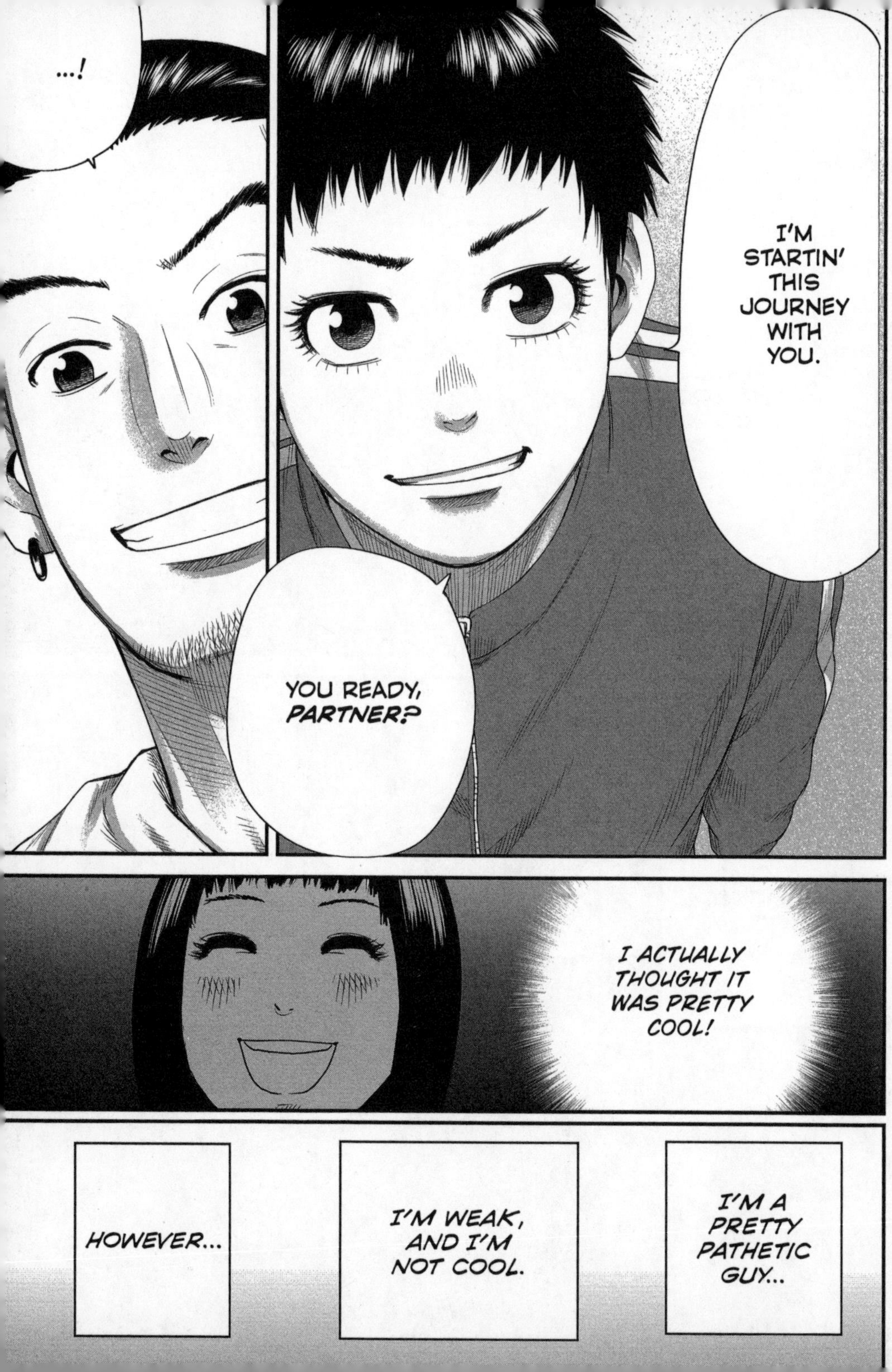
I'M STARTIN' THIS JOURNEY WITH YOU.
YOU READY, *PARTNER?*
...!
I ACTUALLY THOUGHT IT WAS PRETTY COOL!
I'M A PRETTY PATHETIC GUY...
I'M WEAK, AND I'M NOT COOL.
HOWEVER...

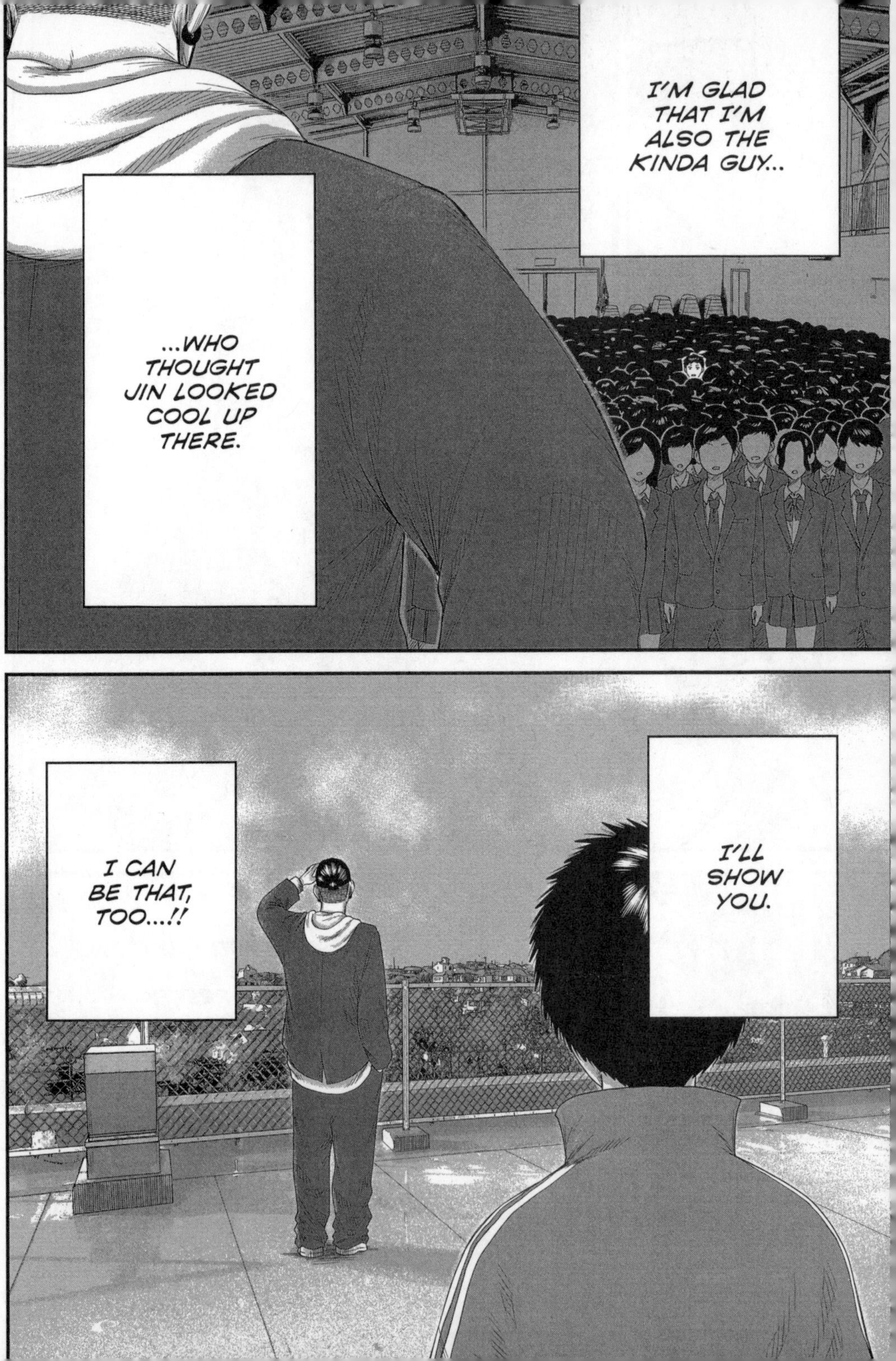
I'M GLAD THAT I'M ALSO THE KINDA GUY...
...WHO THOUGHT JIN LOOKED COOL UP THERE.
I'LL SHOW YOU.
I CAN BE THAT, TOO...!!

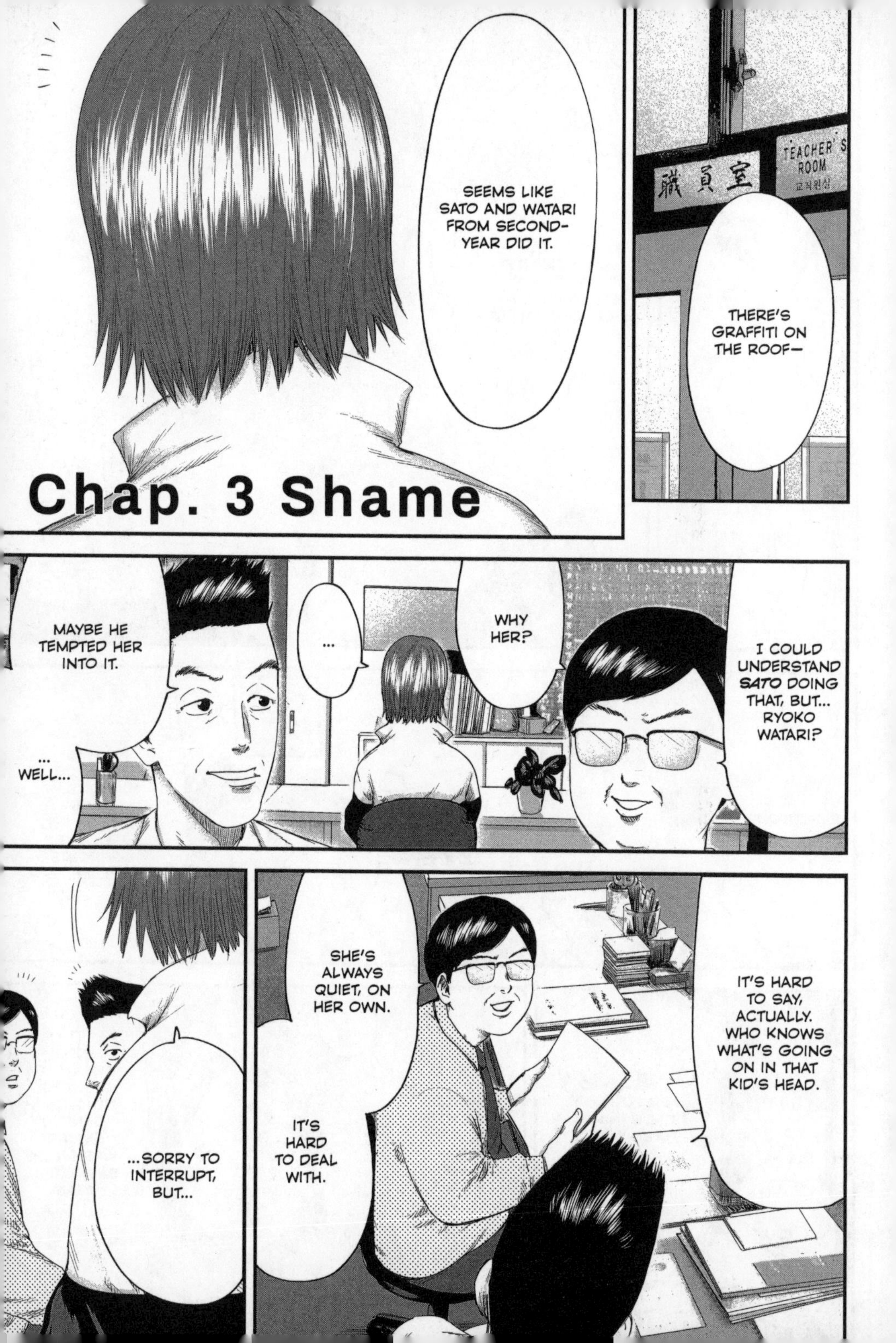

TEACHER'S ROOM
職員室
교직원실
THERE'S GRAFFITI ON THE ROOF—
SEEMS LIKE SATO AND WATARI FROM SECOND-YEAR DID IT.
Chap. 3 Shame
I COULD UNDERSTAND SATO DOING THAT, BUT... RYOKO WATARI?
WHY HER?
...
MAYBE HE TEMPTED HER INTO IT.
... WELL...
IT'S HARD TO SAY, ACTUALLY. WHO KNOWS WHAT'S GOING ON IN THAT KID'S HEAD.
SHE'S ALWAYS QUIET, ON HER OWN.
IT'S HARD TO DEAL WITH.
...SORRY TO INTERRUPT, BUT...

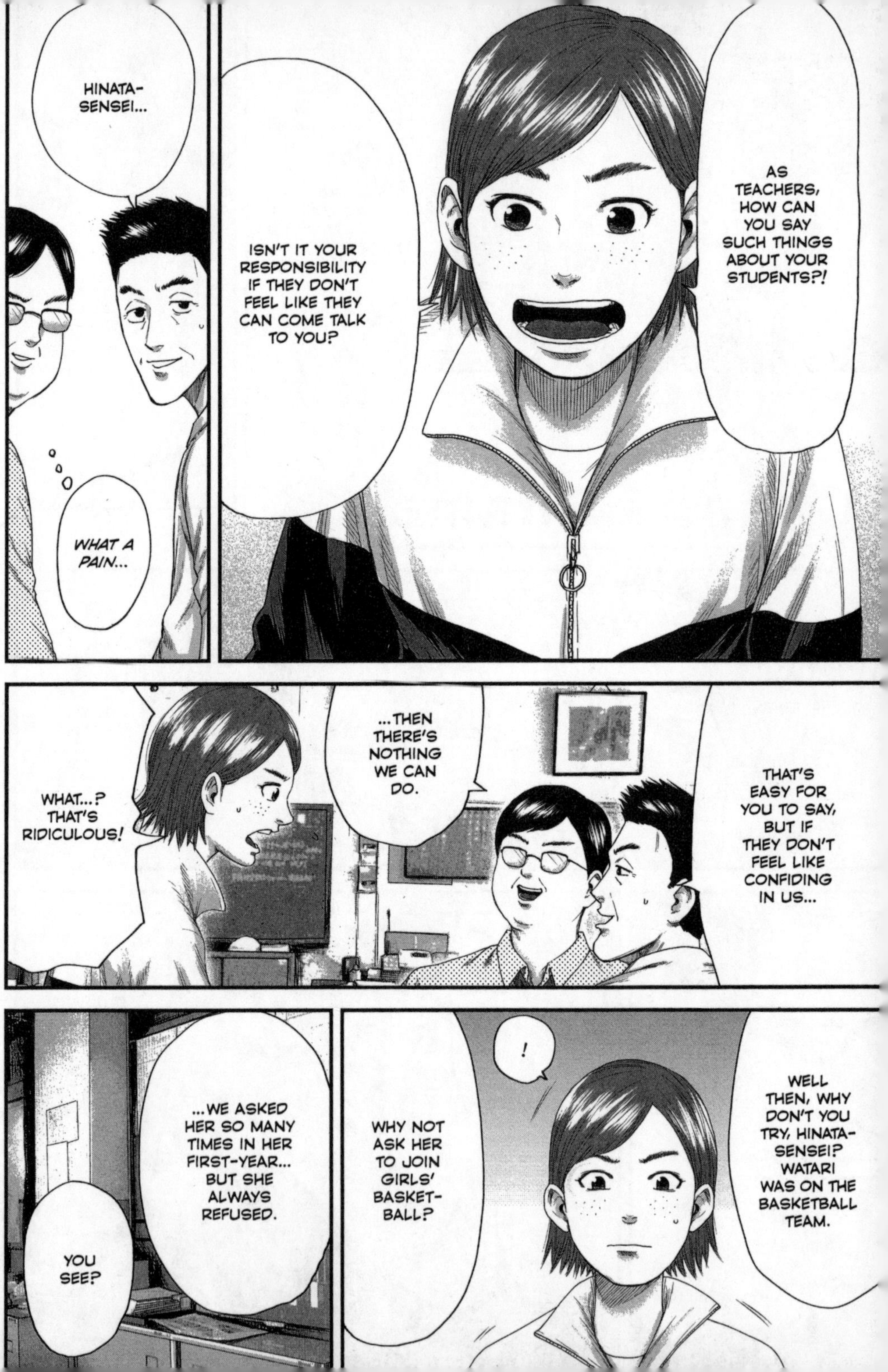
AS TEACHERS, HOW CAN YOU SAY SUCH THINGS ABOUT YOUR STUDENTS?!
ISN'T IT YOUR RESPONSIBILITY IF THEY DON'T FEEL LIKE THEY CAN COME TALK TO YOU?
HINATA-SENSEI...
WHAT A PAIN...
THAT'S EASY FOR YOU TO SAY, BUT IF THEY DON'T FEEL LIKE CONFIDING IN US...
...THEN THERE'S NOTHING WE CAN DO.
WHAT...? THAT'S RIDICULOUS!
WELL THEN, WHY DON'T YOU TRY, HINATA-SENSEI? WATARI WAS ON THE BASKETBALL TEAM.
!
WHY NOT ASK HER TO JOIN GIRLS' BASKETBALL?
...WE ASKED HER SO MANY TIMES IN HER FIRST-YEAR... BUT SHE ALWAYS REFUSED.
YOU SEE?

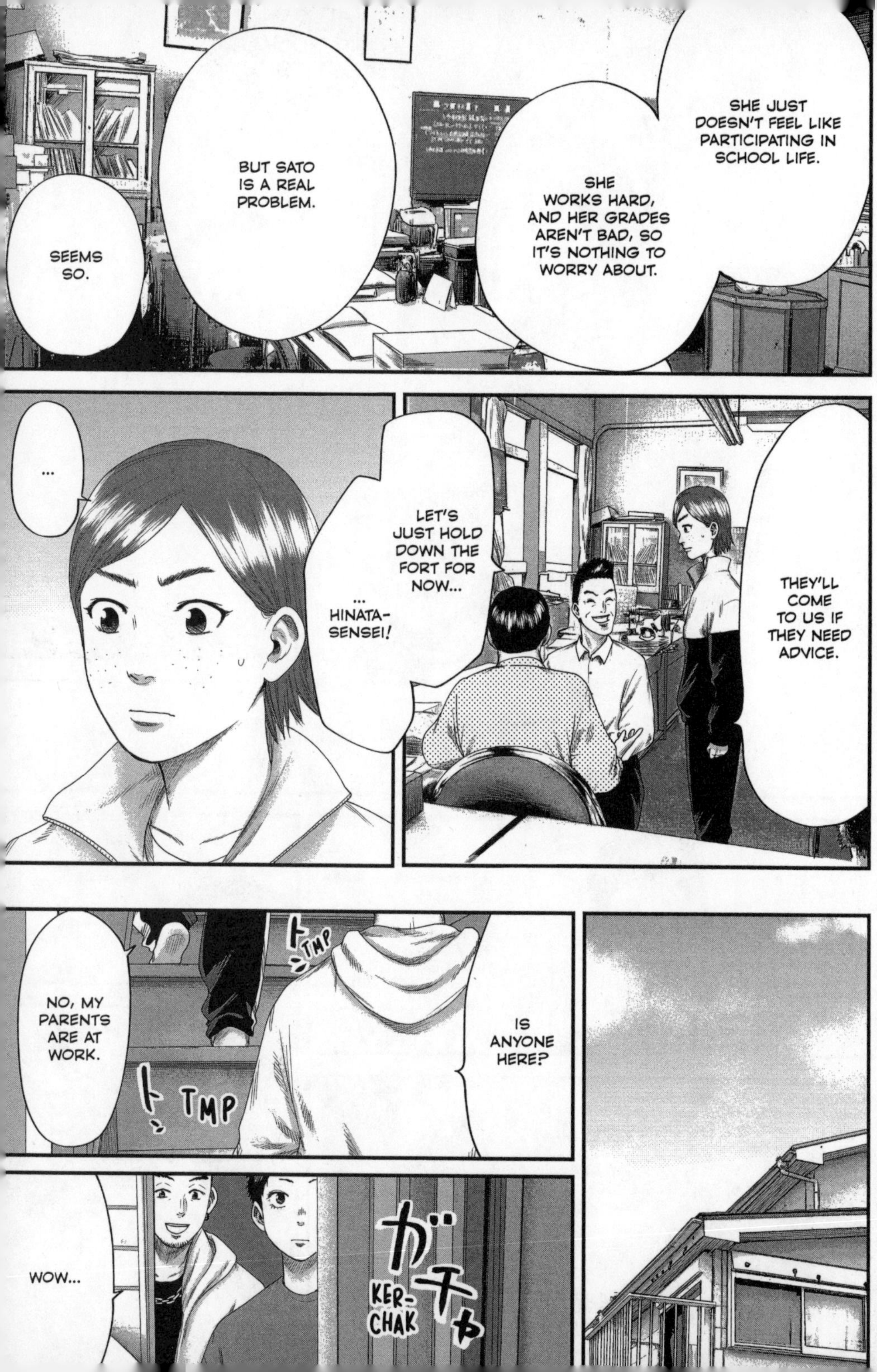
SHE JUST DOESN'T FEEL LIKE PARTICIPATING IN SCHOOL LIFE.
SHE WORKS HARD, AND HER GRADES AREN'T BAD, SO IT'S NOTHING TO WORRY ABOUT.
BUT SATO IS A REAL PROBLEM.
SEEMS SO.
THEY'LL COME TO US IF THEY NEED ADVICE.
LET'S JUST HOLD DOWN THE FORT FOR NOW...
... HINATA-SENSEI!
...
TMP
IS ANYONE HERE?
TMP
NO, MY PARENTS ARE AT WORK.
ガチャ
KER-CHAK
WOW...

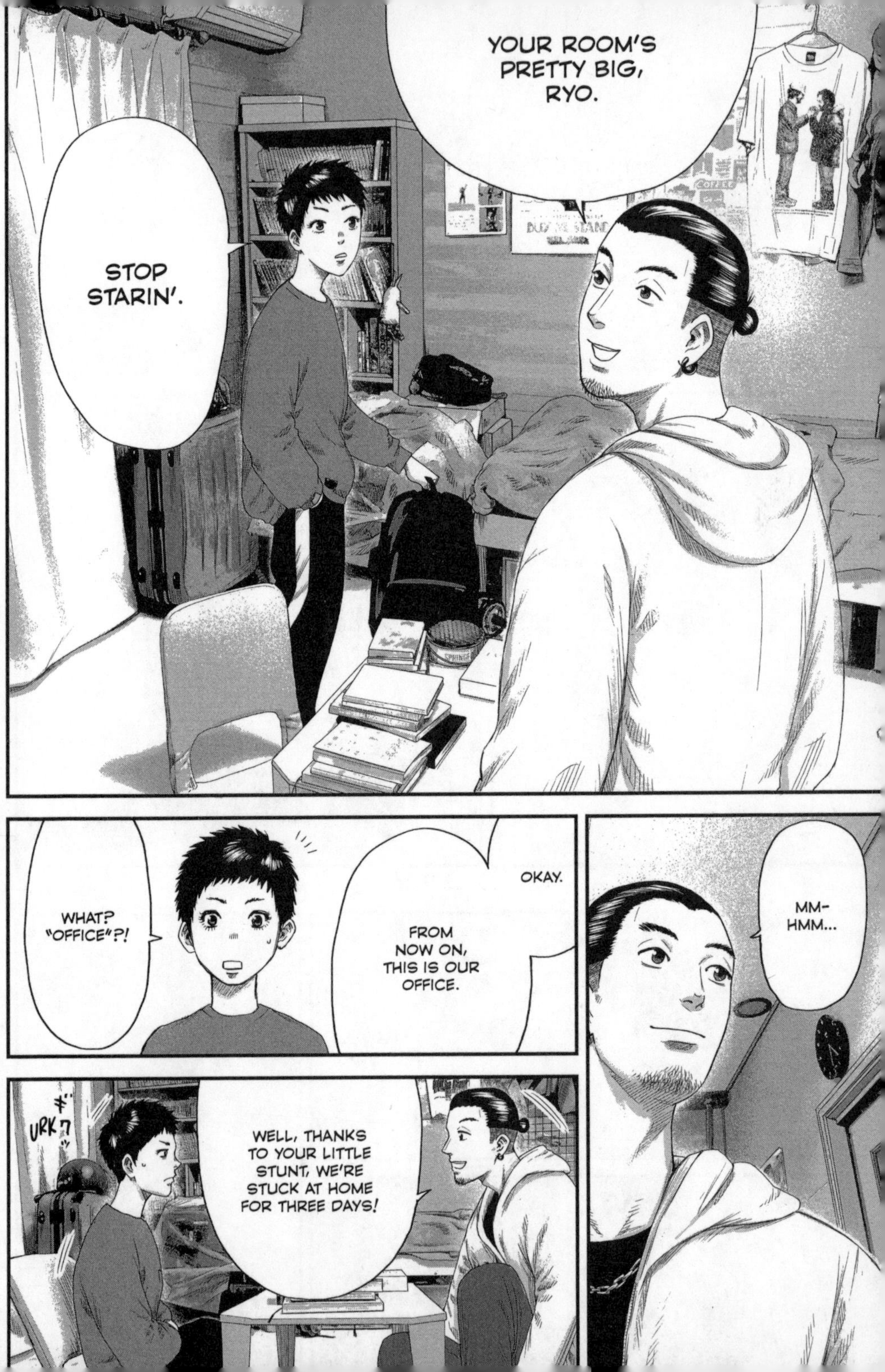
YOUR ROOM'S PRETTY BIG, RYO.
STOP STARIN'.
MM-HMM...
OKAY.
FROM NOW ON, THIS IS OUR OFFICE.
WHAT? "OFFICE"?!
WELL, THANKS TO YOUR LITTLE STUNT, WE'RE STUCK AT HOME FOR THREE DAYS!
URK ギクッ

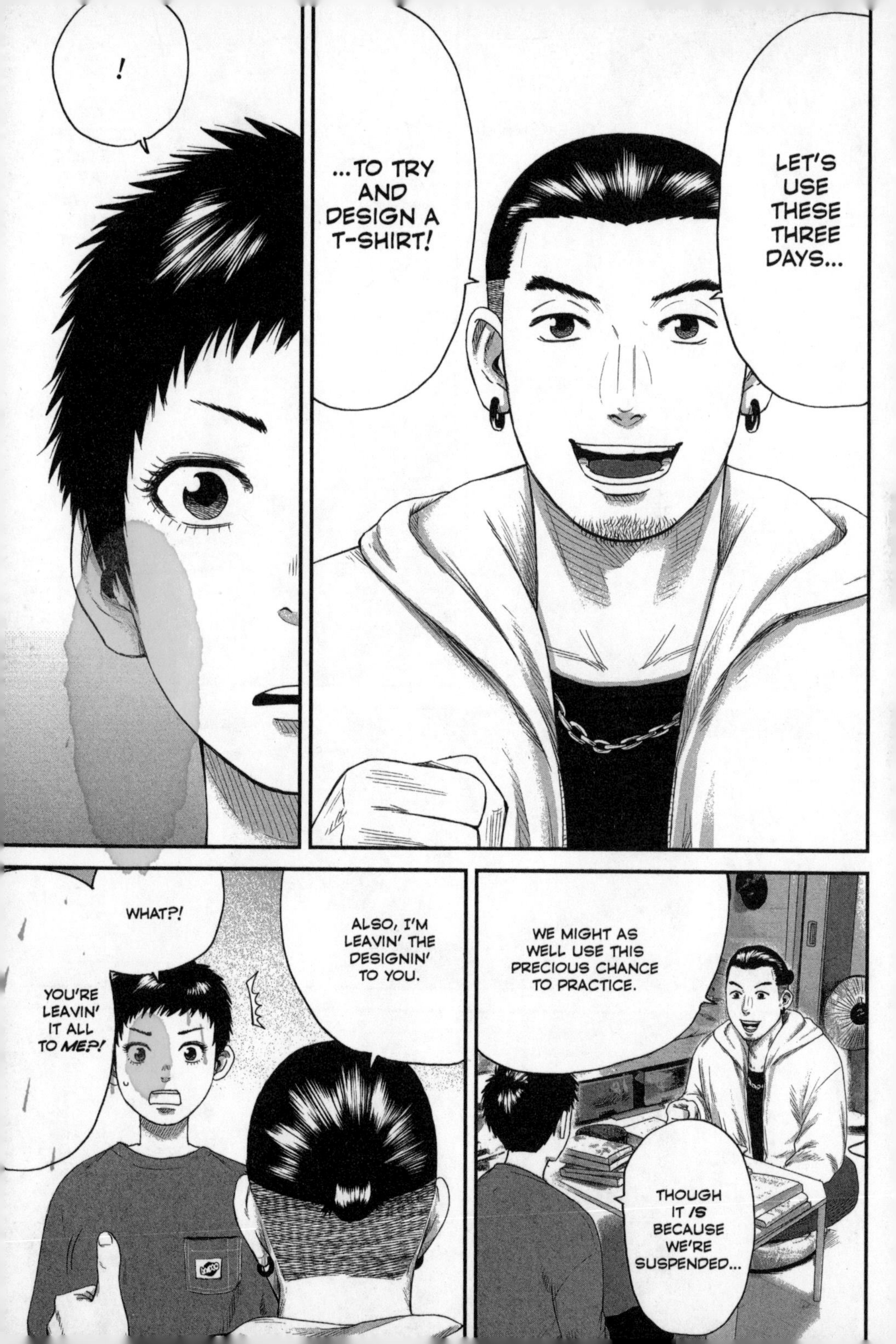
LET'S USE THESE THREE DAYS...
...TO TRY AND DESIGN A T-SHIRT!
!
WE MIGHT AS WELL USE THIS PRECIOUS CHANCE TO PRACTICE.
THOUGH IT *IS* BECAUSE WE'RE SUSPENDED...
ALSO, I'M LEAVIN' THE DESIGNIN' TO YOU.
WHAT?!
YOU'RE LEAVIN' IT ALL TO *ME*?!

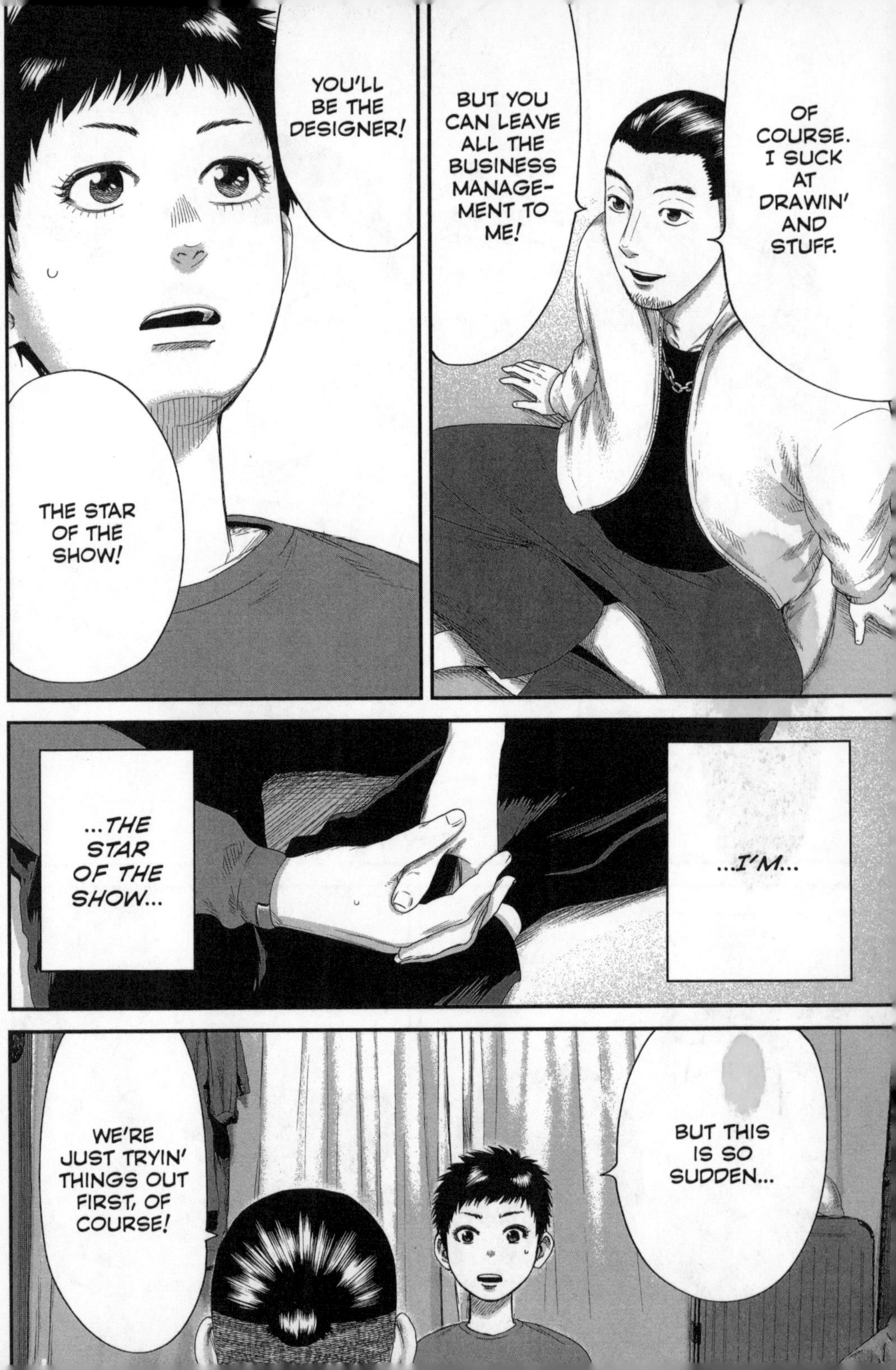
OF COURSE. I SUCK AT DRAWIN' AND STUFF.
BUT YOU CAN LEAVE ALL THE BUSINESS MANAGE-MENT TO ME!
YOU'LL BE THE DESIGNER!
THE STAR OF THE SHOW!
...I'M...
...THE STAR OF THE SHOW...
BUT THIS IS SO SUDDEN...
WE'RE JUST TRYIN' THINGS OUT FIRST, OF COURSE!

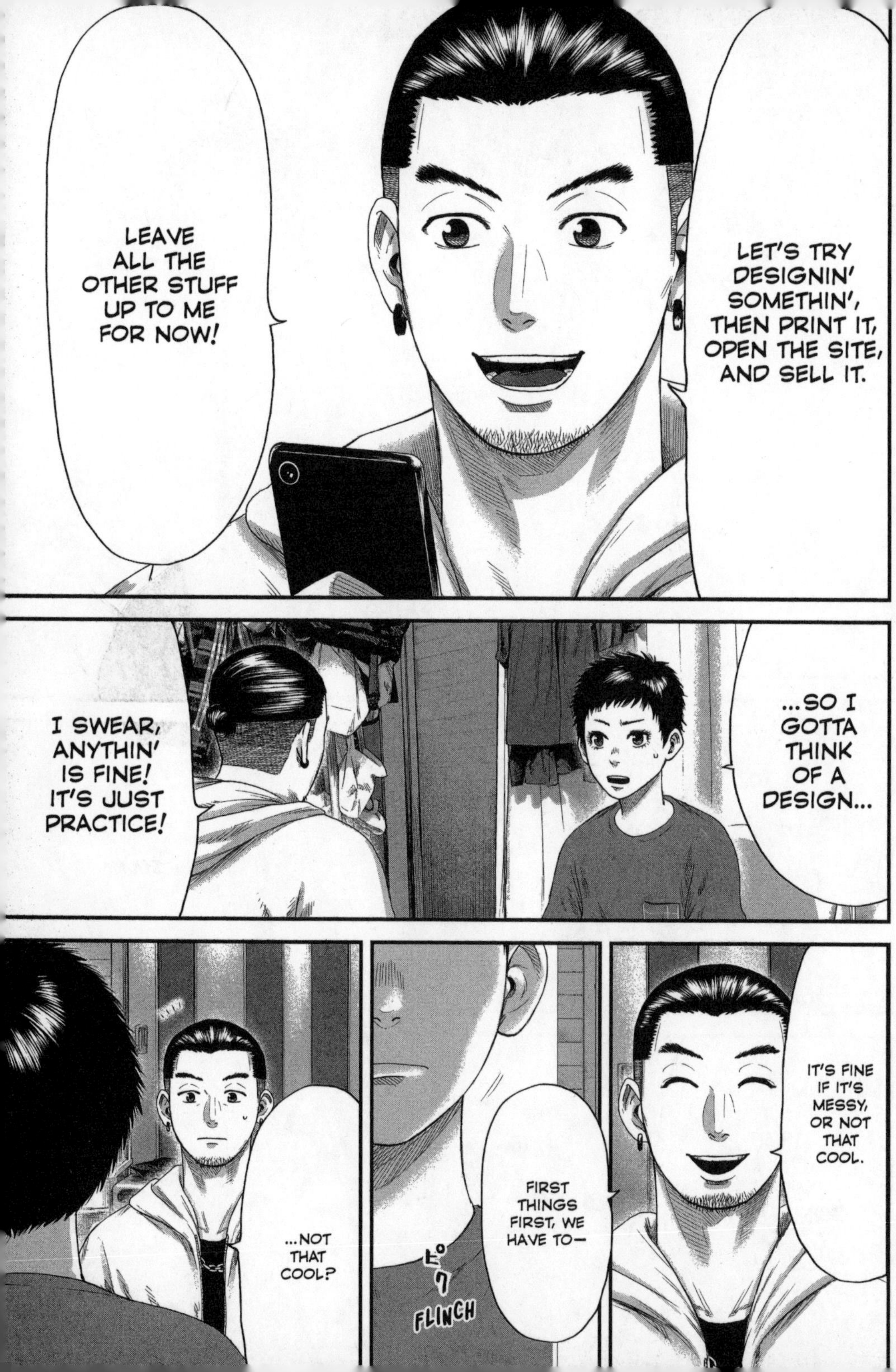
LET'S TRY DESIGNIN' SOMETHIN', THEN PRINT IT, OPEN THE SITE, AND SELL IT.
LEAVE ALL THE OTHER STUFF UP TO ME FOR NOW!
...SO I GOTTA THINK OF A DESIGN...
I SWEAR, ANYTHIN' IS FINE! IT'S JUST PRACTICE!
IT'S FINE IF IT'S MESSY, OR NOT THAT COOL.
FIRST THINGS FIRST, WE HAVE TO—
ピク
FLINCH
...NOT THAT COOL?

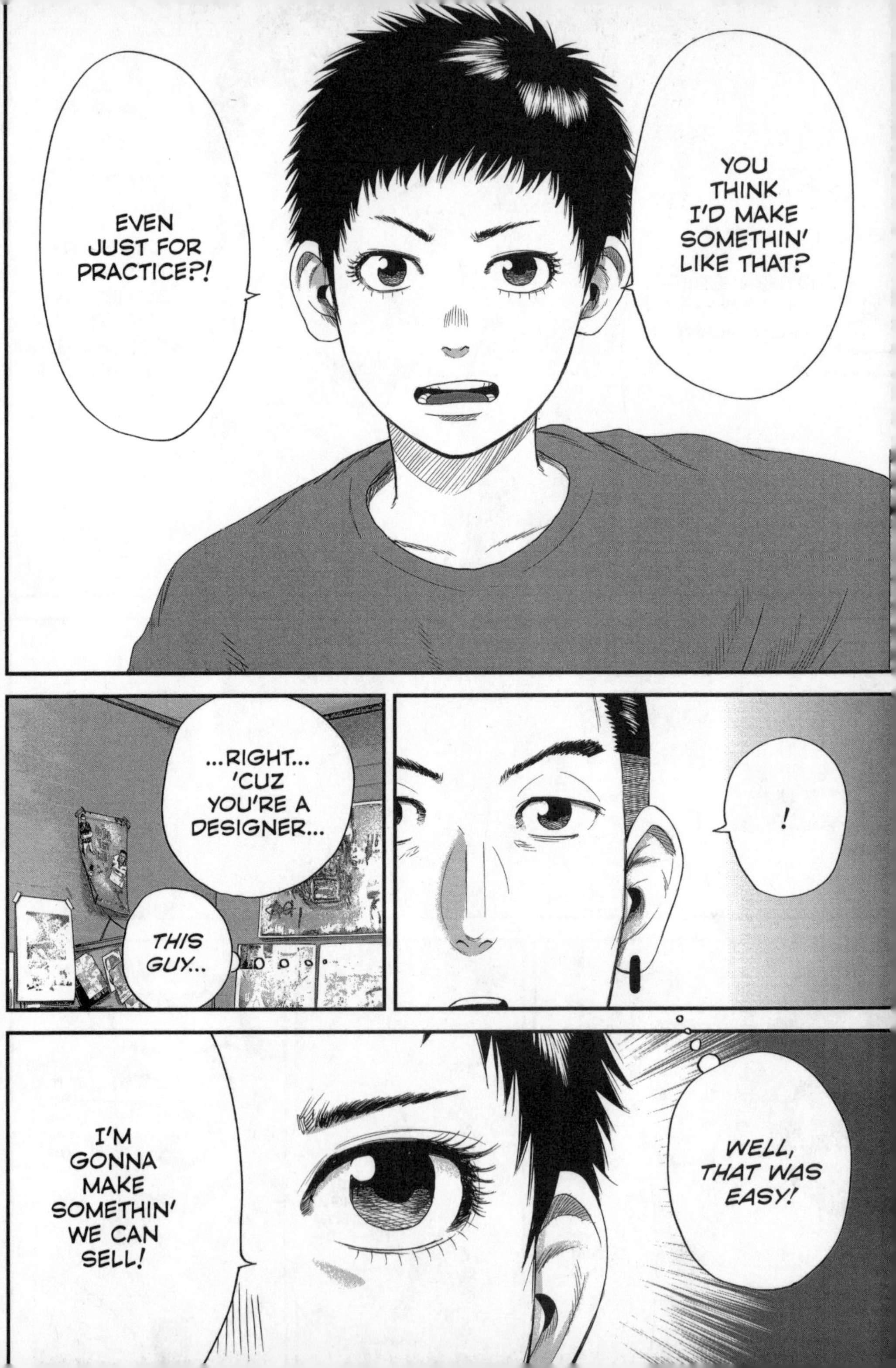
YOU THINK I'D MAKE SOMETHIN' LIKE THAT?
EVEN JUST FOR PRACTICE?!
!
...RIGHT... 'CUZ YOU'RE A DESIGNER...
THIS GUY...
WELL, THAT WAS EASY!
I'M GONNA MAKE SOMETHIN' WE CAN SELL!

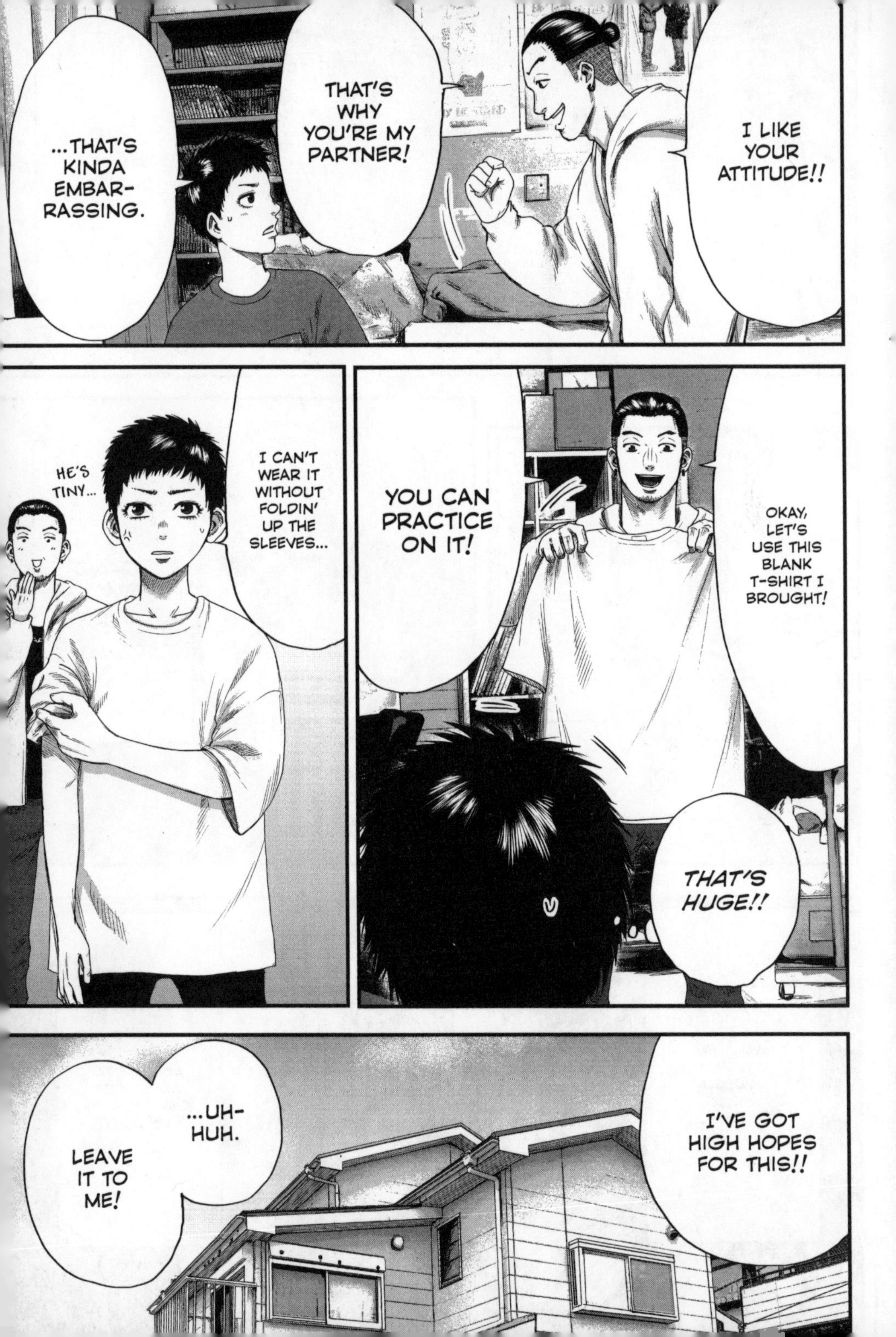
I LIKE YOUR ATTITUDE!!
THAT'S WHY YOU'RE MY PARTNER!
...THAT'S KINDA EMBARRASSING.
OKAY, LET'S USE THIS BLANK T-SHIRT I BROUGHT!
YOU CAN PRACTICE ON IT!
THAT'S HUGE!!
I CAN'T WEAR IT WITHOUT FOLDIN' UP THE SLEEVES...
HE'S TINY...
I'VE GOT HIGH HOPES FOR THIS!!
...UH-HUH.
LEAVE IT TO ME!

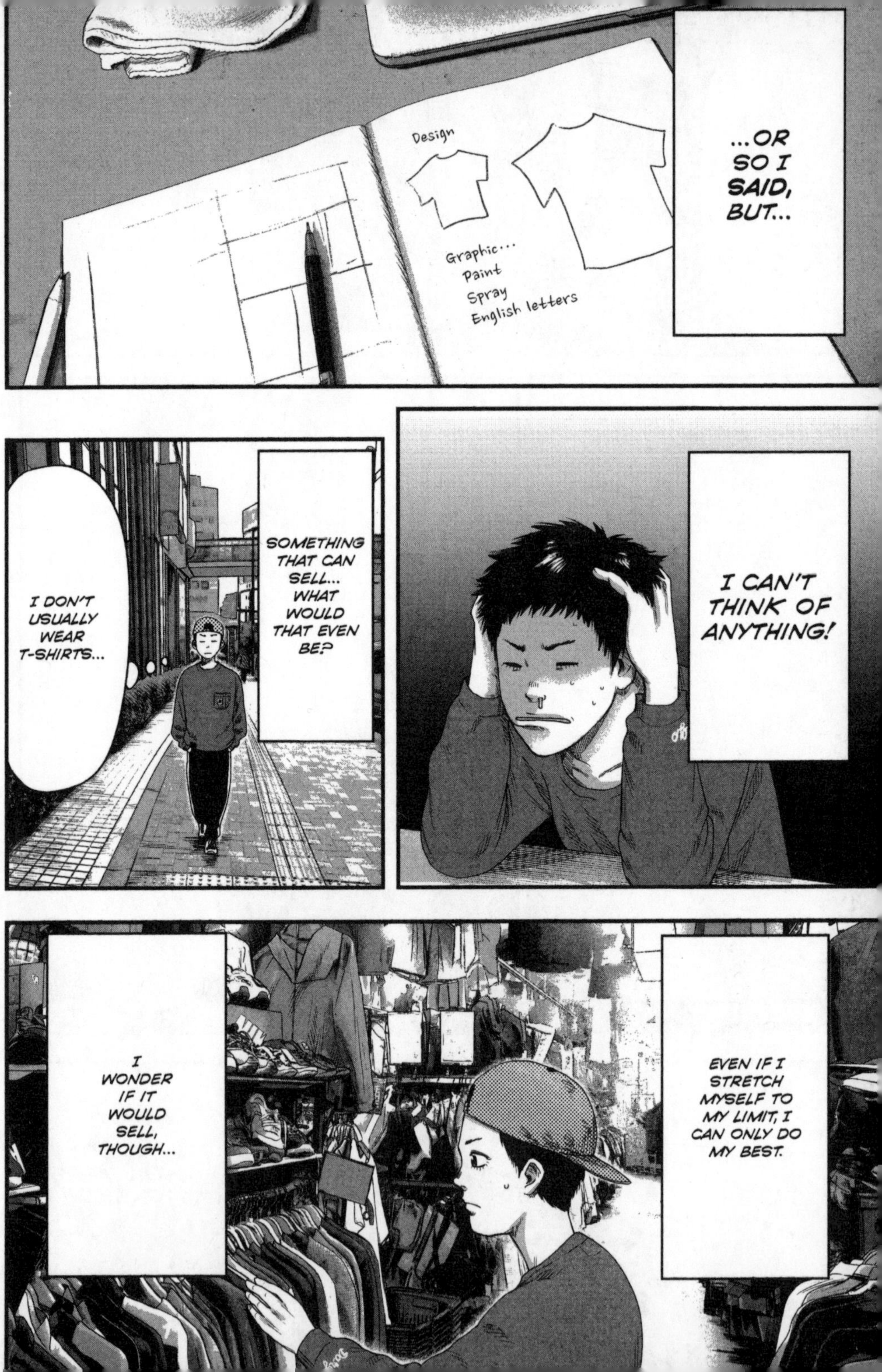
...OR SO I SAID, BUT...
Design
Graphic...
Paint
Spray
English letters
I CAN'T THINK OF ANYTHING!
SOMETHING THAT CAN SELL... WHAT WOULD THAT EVEN BE?
I DON'T USUALLY WEAR T-SHIRTS...
EVEN IF I STRETCH MYSELF TO MY LIMIT, I CAN ONLY DO MY BEST.
I WONDER IF IT WOULD SELL, THOUGH...

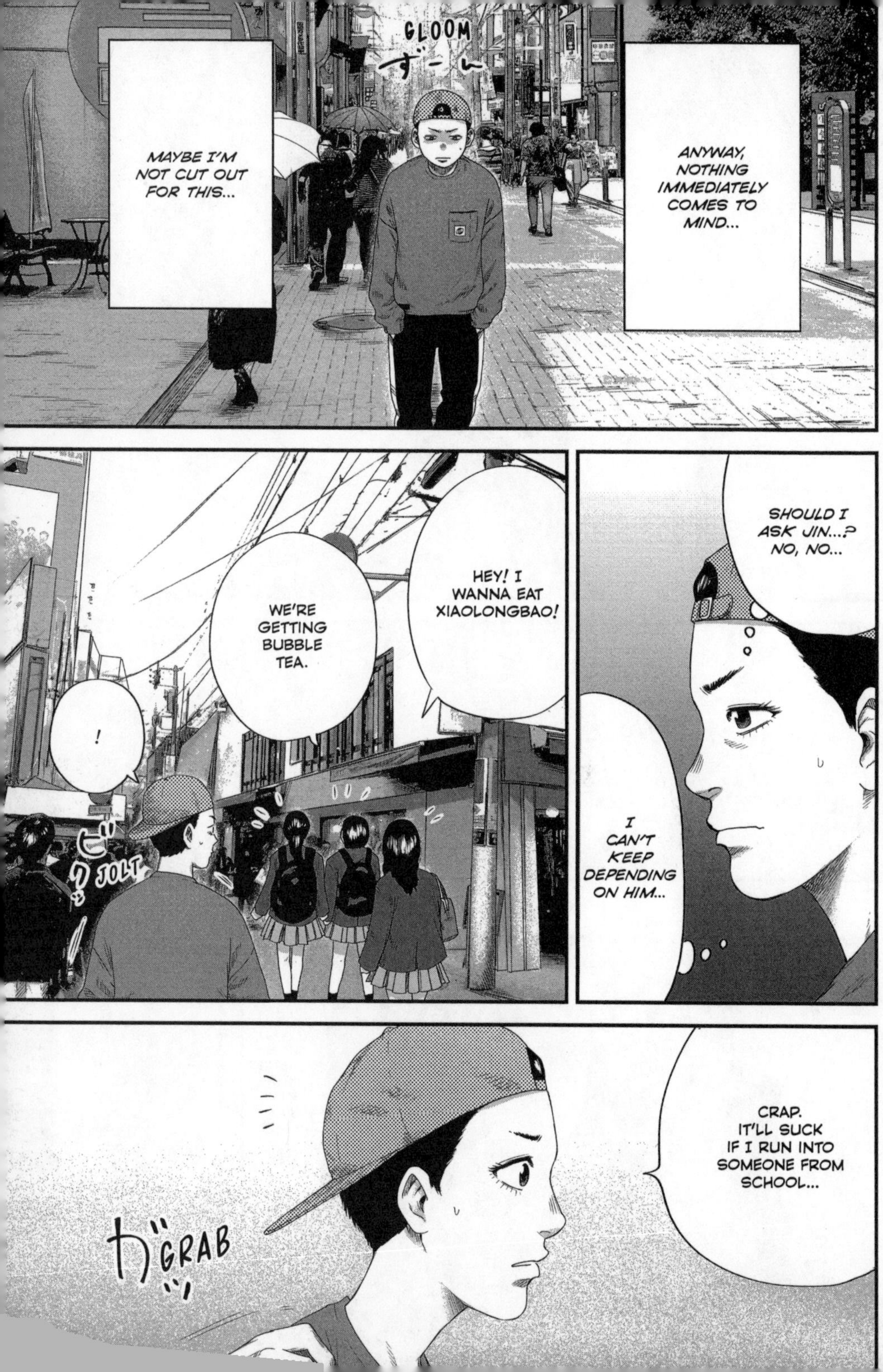
ANYWAY, NOTHING IMMEDIATELY COMES TO MIND...
GLOOM
ずーん
MAYBE I'M NOT CUT OUT FOR THIS...
SHOULD I ASK JIN...? NO, NO...
I CAN'T KEEP DEPENDING ON HIM...
HEY! I WANNA EAT XIAOLONGBAO!
WE'RE GETTING BUBBLE TEA.
!
JOLT
CRAP. IT'LL SUCK IF I RUN INTO SOMEONE FROM SCHOOL...
GRAB

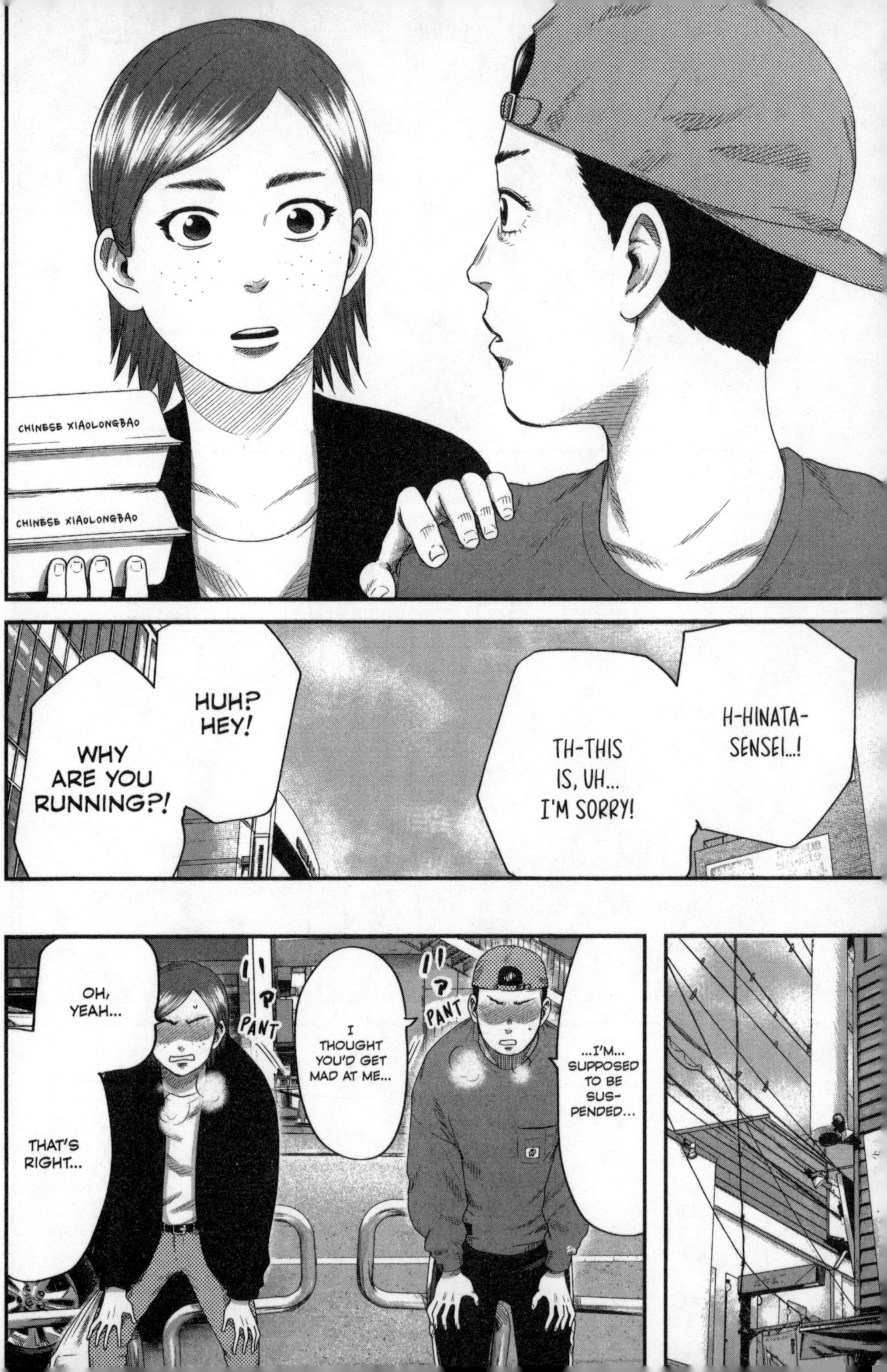
CHINESE XIAOLONGBAO
CHINESE XIAOLONGBAO
H-HINATA-SENSEI...!
TH-THIS IS, UH... I'M SORRY!
HUH? HEY!
WHY ARE YOU RUNNING?!
...I'M... SUPPOSED TO BE SUS-PENDED...
PANT
I THOUGHT YOU'D GET MAD AT ME...
PANT
OH, YEAH...
THAT'S RIGHT...

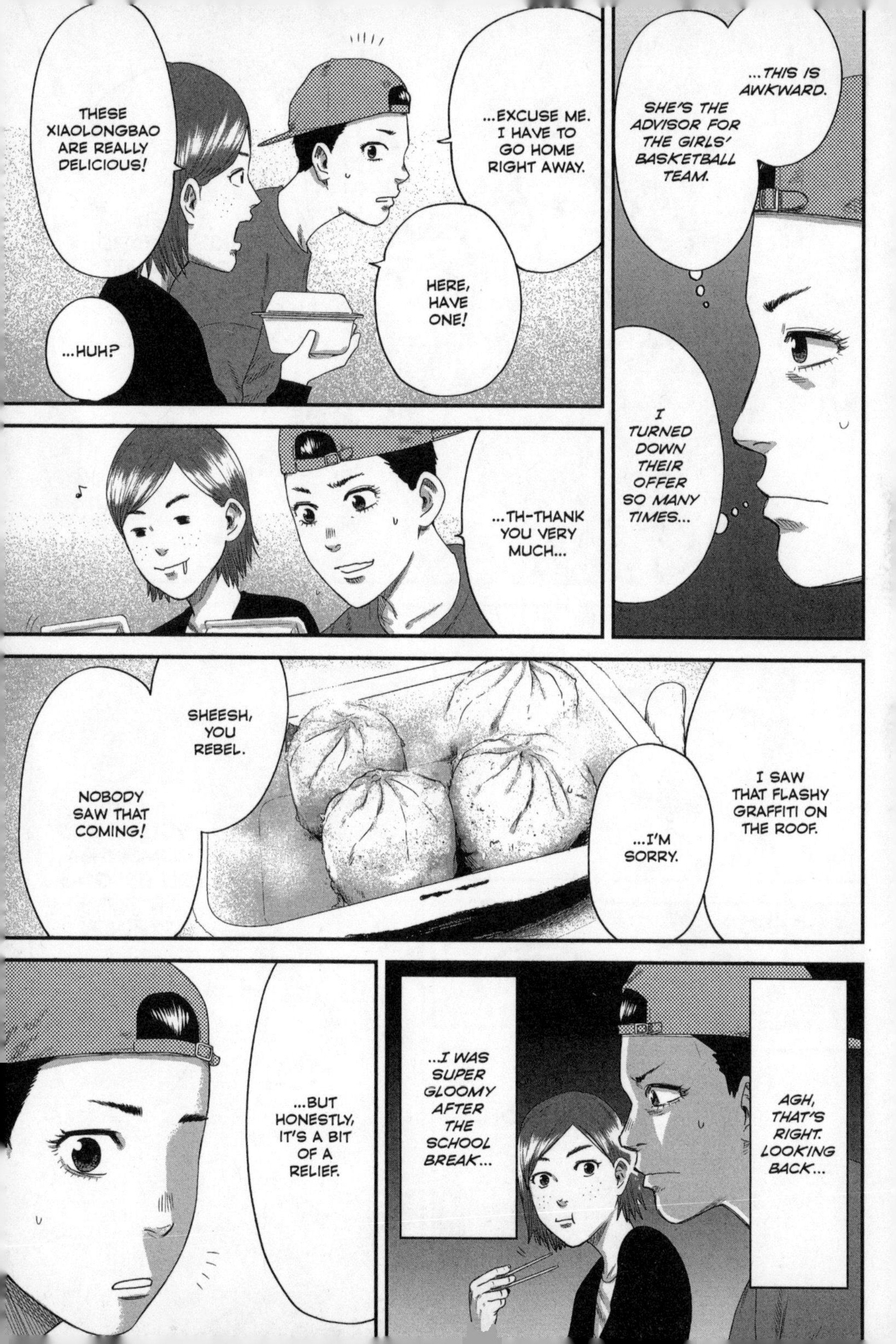
...THIS IS AWKWARD.
SHE'S THE ADVISOR FOR THE GIRLS' BASKETBALL TEAM.
I TURNED DOWN THEIR OFFER SO MANY TIMES...
...EXCUSE ME. I HAVE TO GO HOME RIGHT AWAY.
THESE XIAOLONGBAO ARE REALLY DELICIOUS!
HERE, HAVE ONE!
...HUH?
...TH-THANK YOU VERY MUCH...
I SAW THAT FLASHY GRAFFITI ON THE ROOF.
...I'M SORRY.
SHEESH, YOU REBEL.
NOBODY SAW THAT COMING!
AGH, THAT'S RIGHT. LOOKING BACK...
...I WAS SUPER GLOOMY AFTER THE SCHOOL BREAK...
...BUT HONESTLY, IT'S A BIT OF A RELIEF.

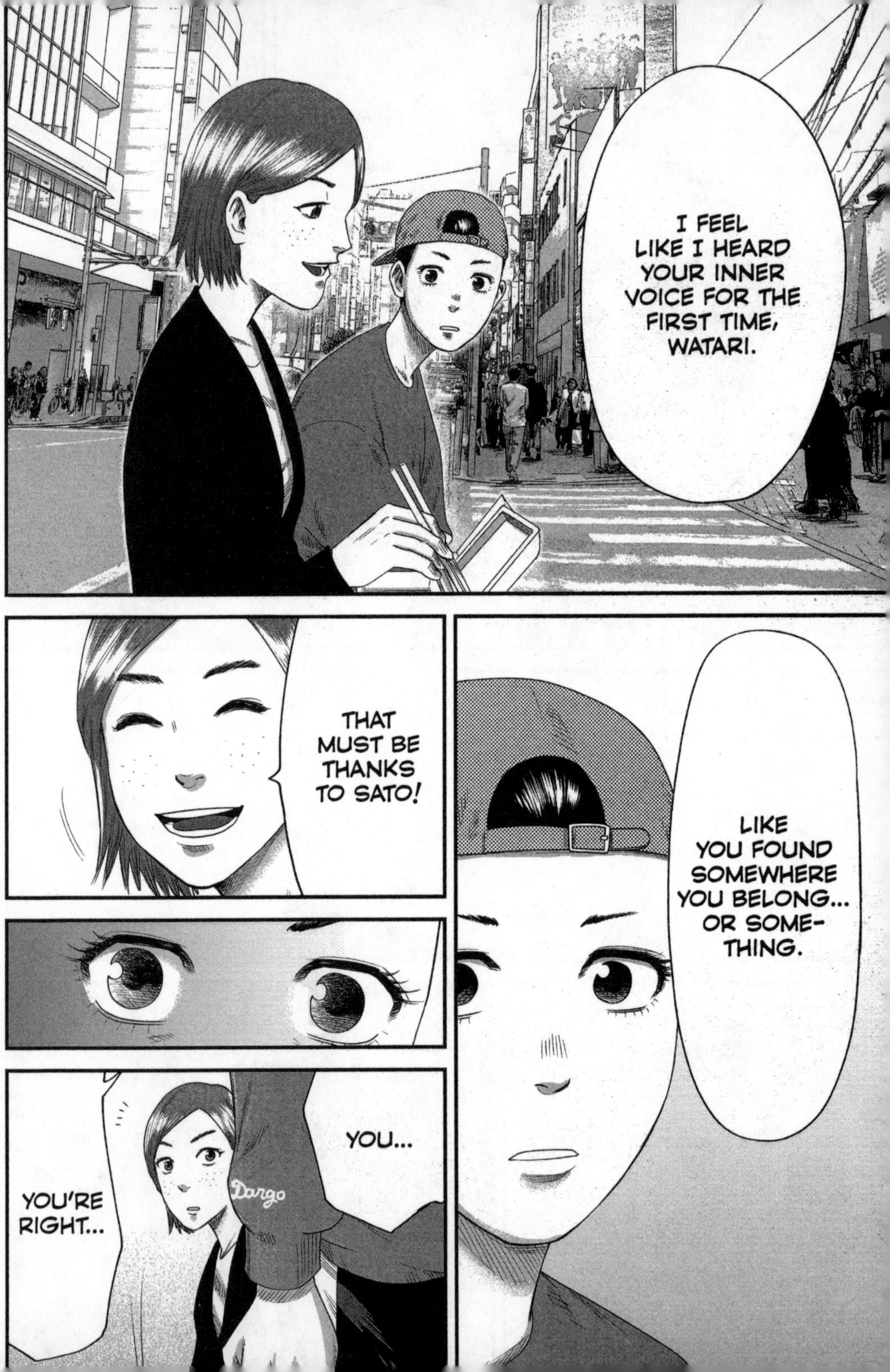
I FEEL LIKE I HEARD YOUR INNER VOICE FOR THE FIRST TIME, WATARI.
LIKE YOU FOUND SOMEWHERE YOU BELONG... OR SOME-THING.
THAT MUST BE THANKS TO SATO!
YOU...
YOU'RE RIGHT...
Dargo

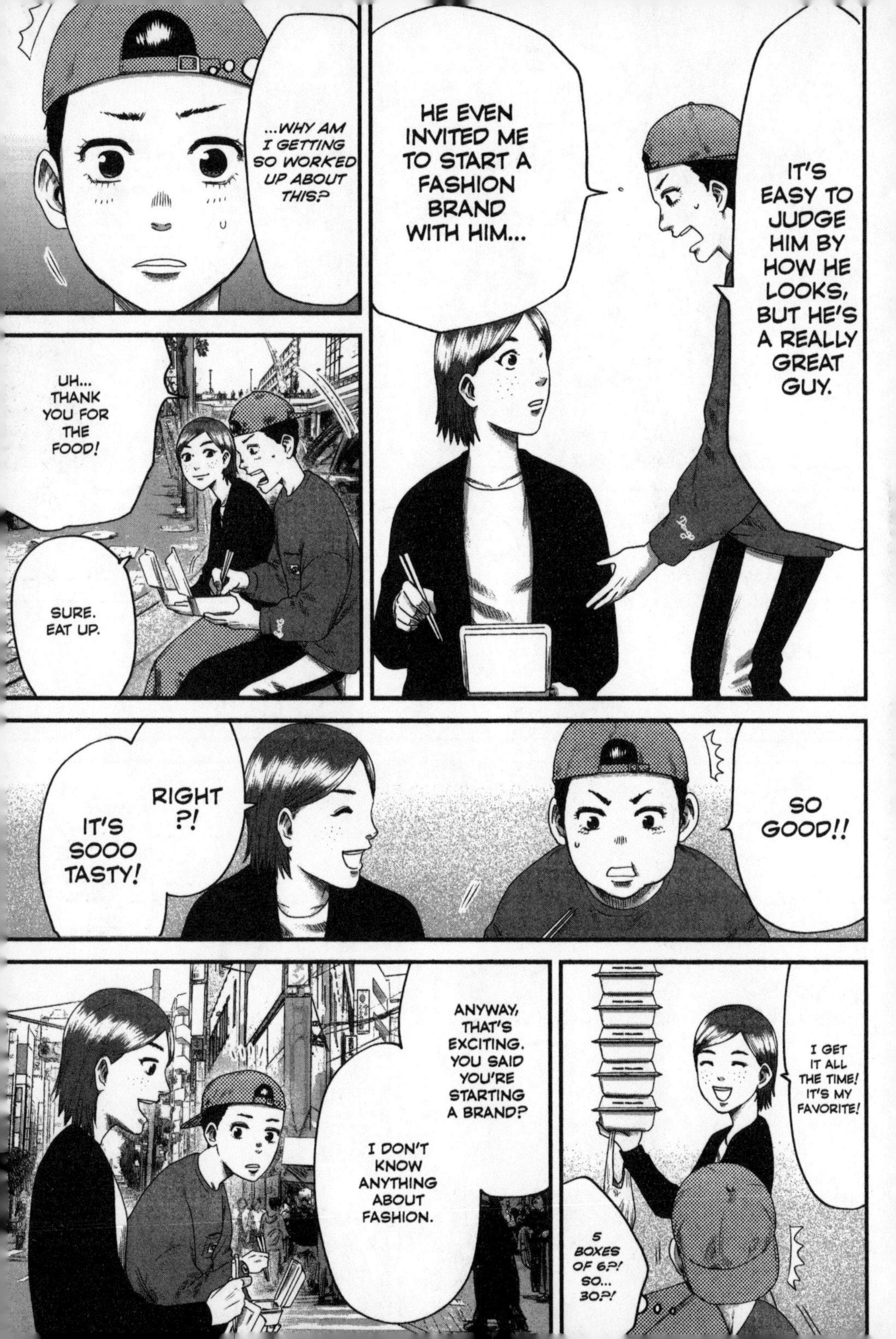
IT'S EASY TO JUDGE HIM BY HOW HE LOOKS, BUT HE'S A REALLY GREAT GUY.
HE EVEN INVITED ME TO START A FASHION BRAND WITH HIM...
...WHY AM I GETTING SO WORKED UP ABOUT THIS?
UH... THANK YOU FOR THE FOOD!
SURE. EAT UP.
SO GOOD!!
RIGHT?!
IT'S SOOO TASTY!
I GET IT ALL THE TIME! IT'S MY FAVORITE!
5 BOXES OF 6?! SO... 30?!
ANYWAY, THAT'S EXCITING. YOU SAID YOU'RE STARTING A BRAND?
I DON'T KNOW ANYTHING ABOUT FASHION.

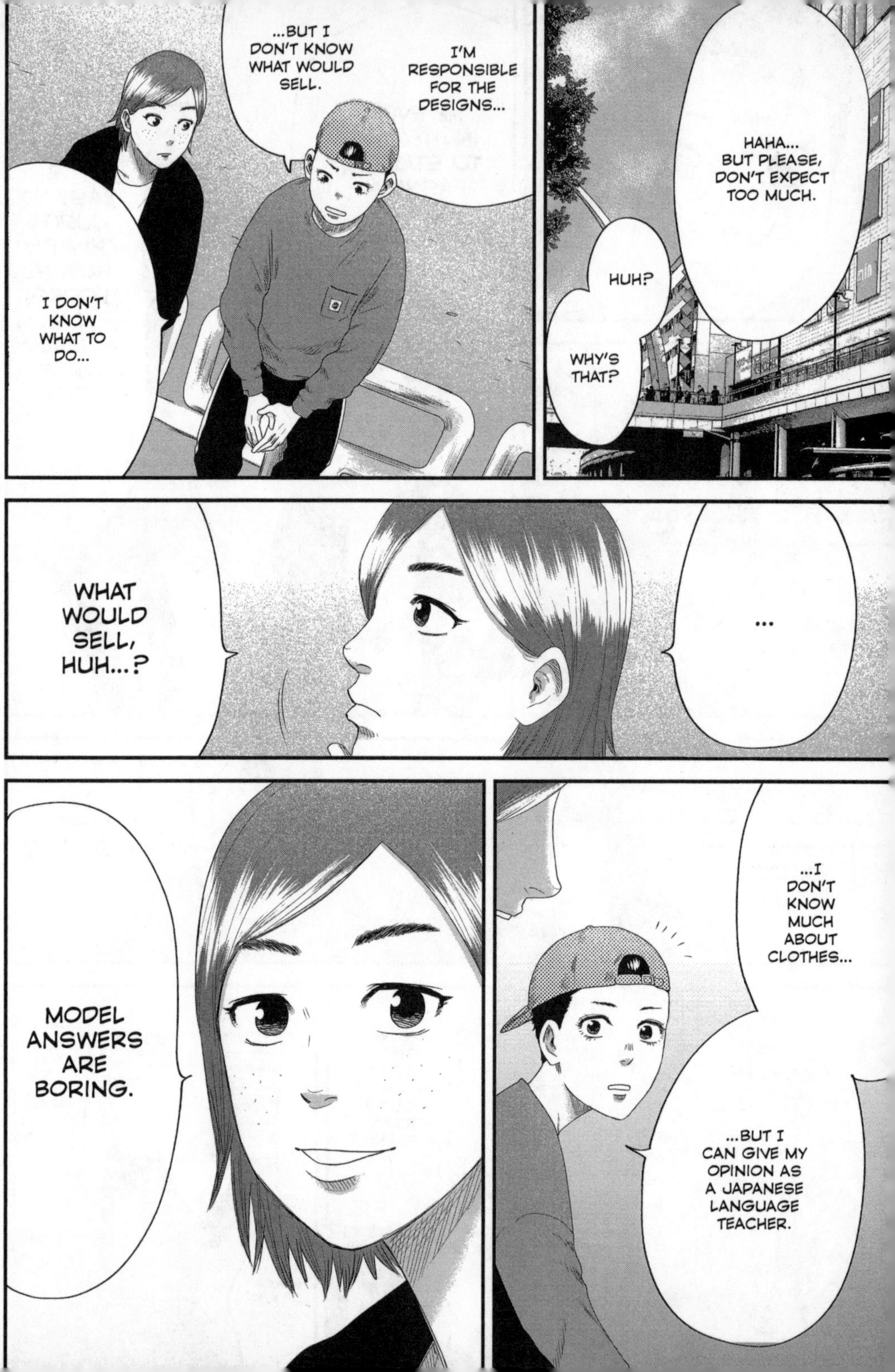
HAHA... BUT PLEASE, DON'T EXPECT TOO MUCH.
HUH?
WHY'S THAT?
I'M RESPONSIBLE FOR THE DESIGNS...
...BUT I DON'T KNOW WHAT WOULD SELL.
I DON'T KNOW WHAT TO DO...
...
WHAT WOULD SELL, HUH...?
...I DON'T KNOW MUCH ABOUT CLOTHES...
...BUT I CAN GIVE MY OPINION AS A JAPANESE LANGUAGE TEACHER.
MODEL ANSWERS ARE BORING.

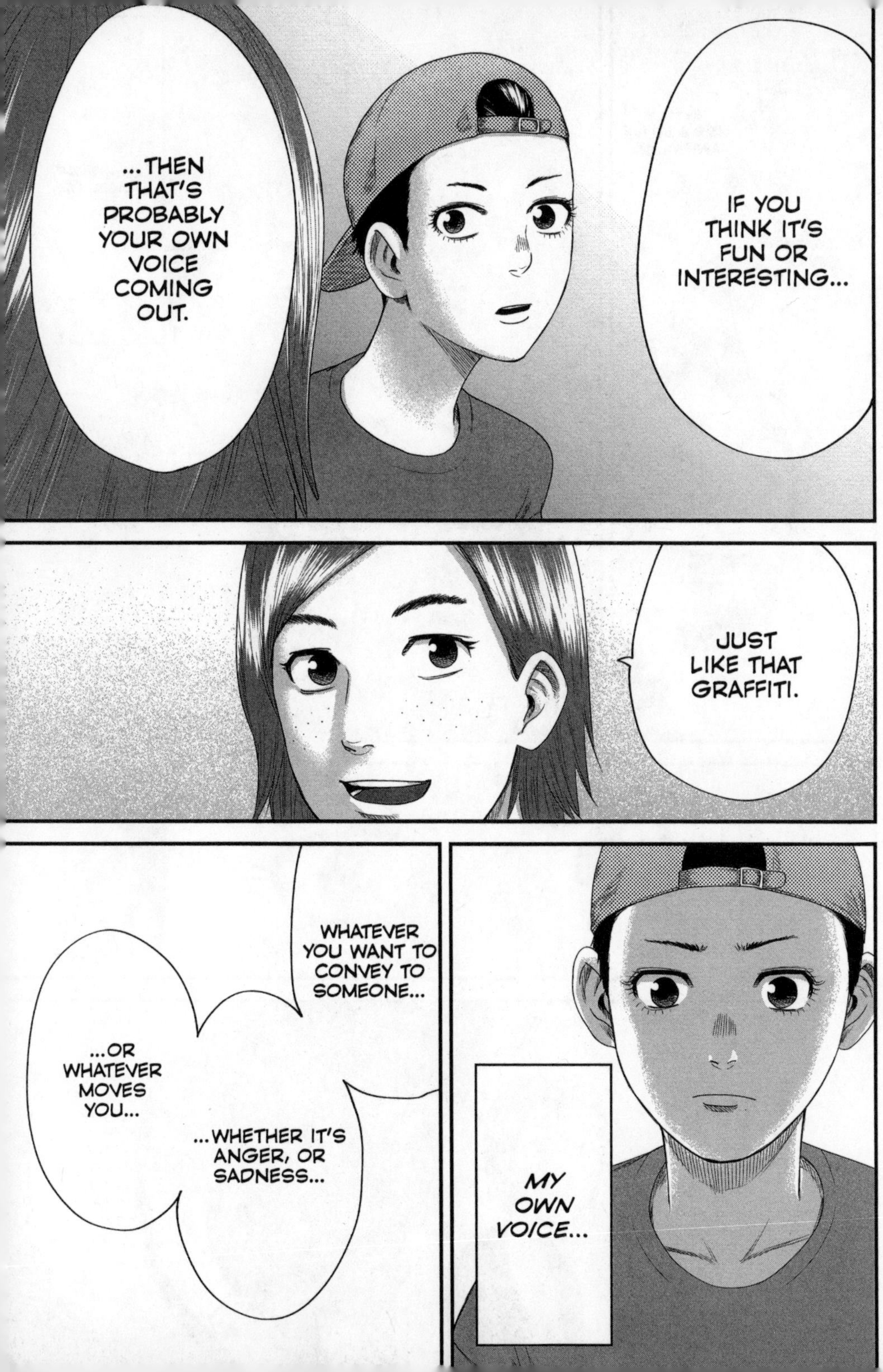
IF YOU THINK IT'S FUN OR INTERESTING...
...THEN THAT'S PROBABLY YOUR OWN VOICE COMING OUT.
JUST LIKE THAT GRAFFITI.
MY OWN VOICE...
WHATEVER YOU WANT TO CONVEY TO SOMEONE...
...OR WHATEVER MOVES YOU...
...WHETHER IT'S ANGER, OR SADNESS...

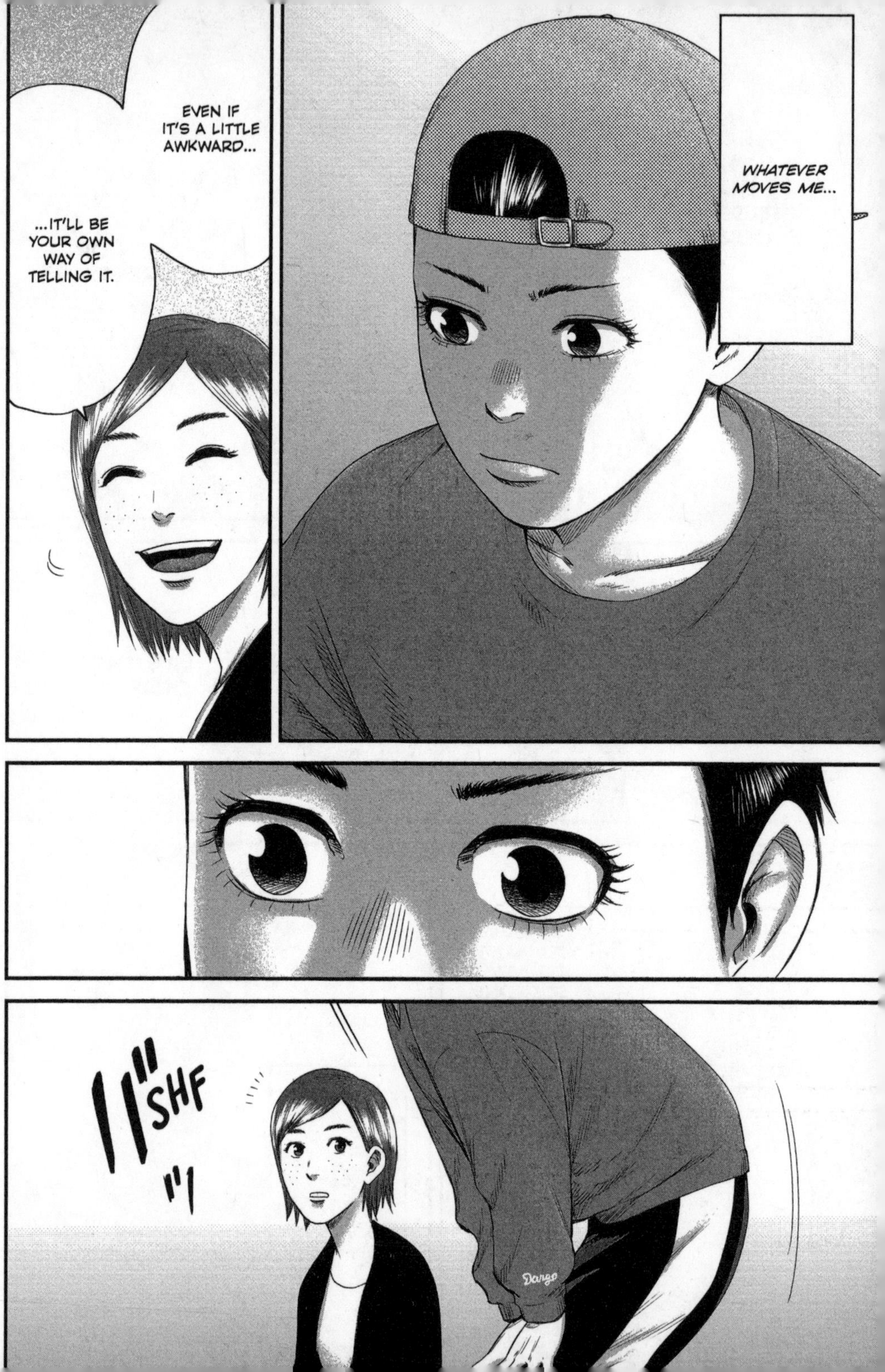
WHATEVER MOVES ME...
EVEN IF IT'S A LITTLE AWKWARD...
...IT'LL BE YOUR OWN WAY OF TELLING IT.
SHF
Dargo

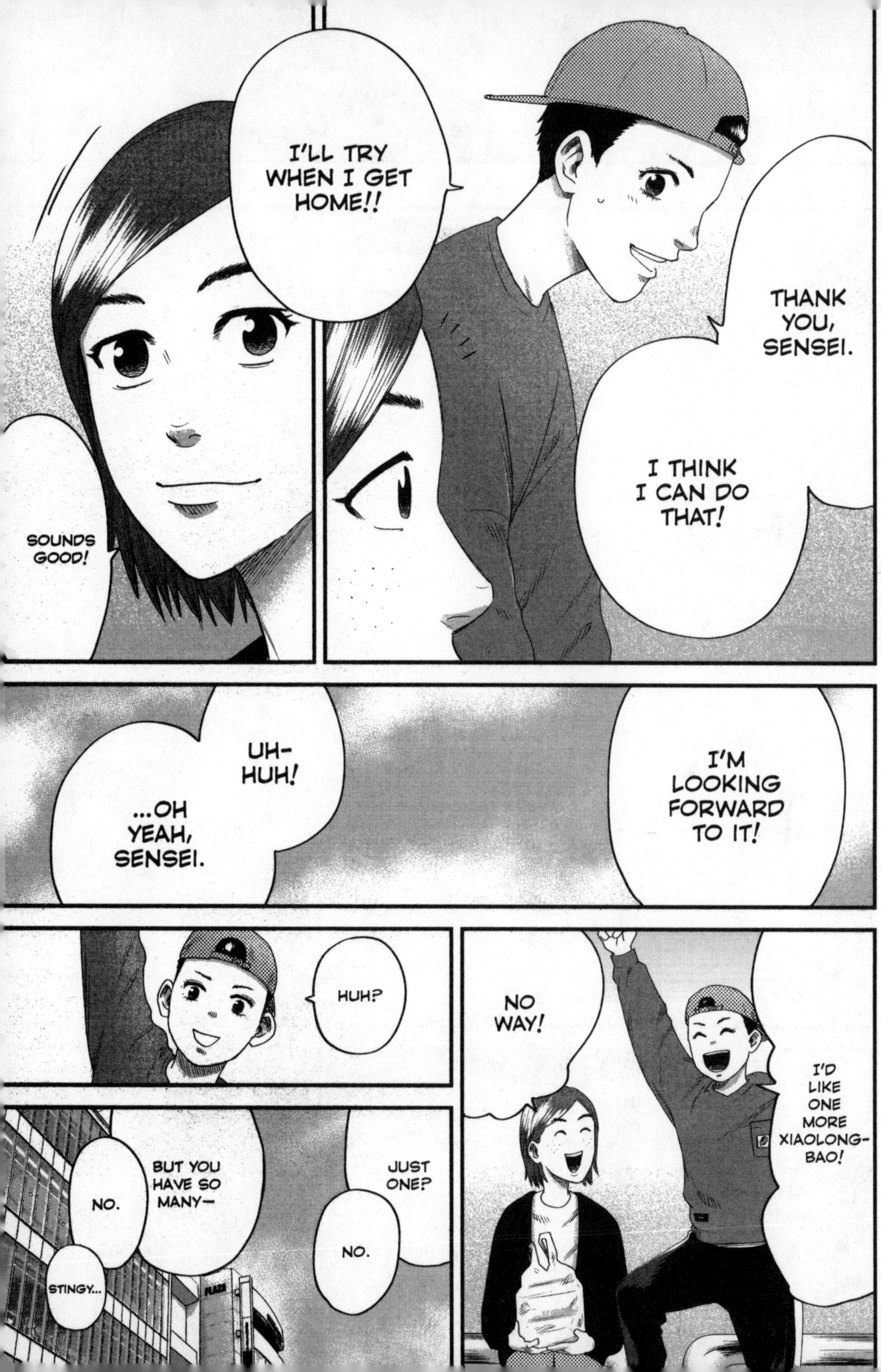
THANK YOU, SENSEI.
I THINK I CAN DO THAT!
I'LL TRY WHEN I GET HOME!!
SOUNDS GOOD!
I'M LOOKING FORWARD TO IT!
UH-HUH!
...OH YEAH, SENSEI.
I'D LIKE ONE MORE XIAOLONG-BAO!
NO WAY!
HUH?
JUST ONE?
NO.
BUT YOU HAVE SO MANY—
NO.
STINGY...

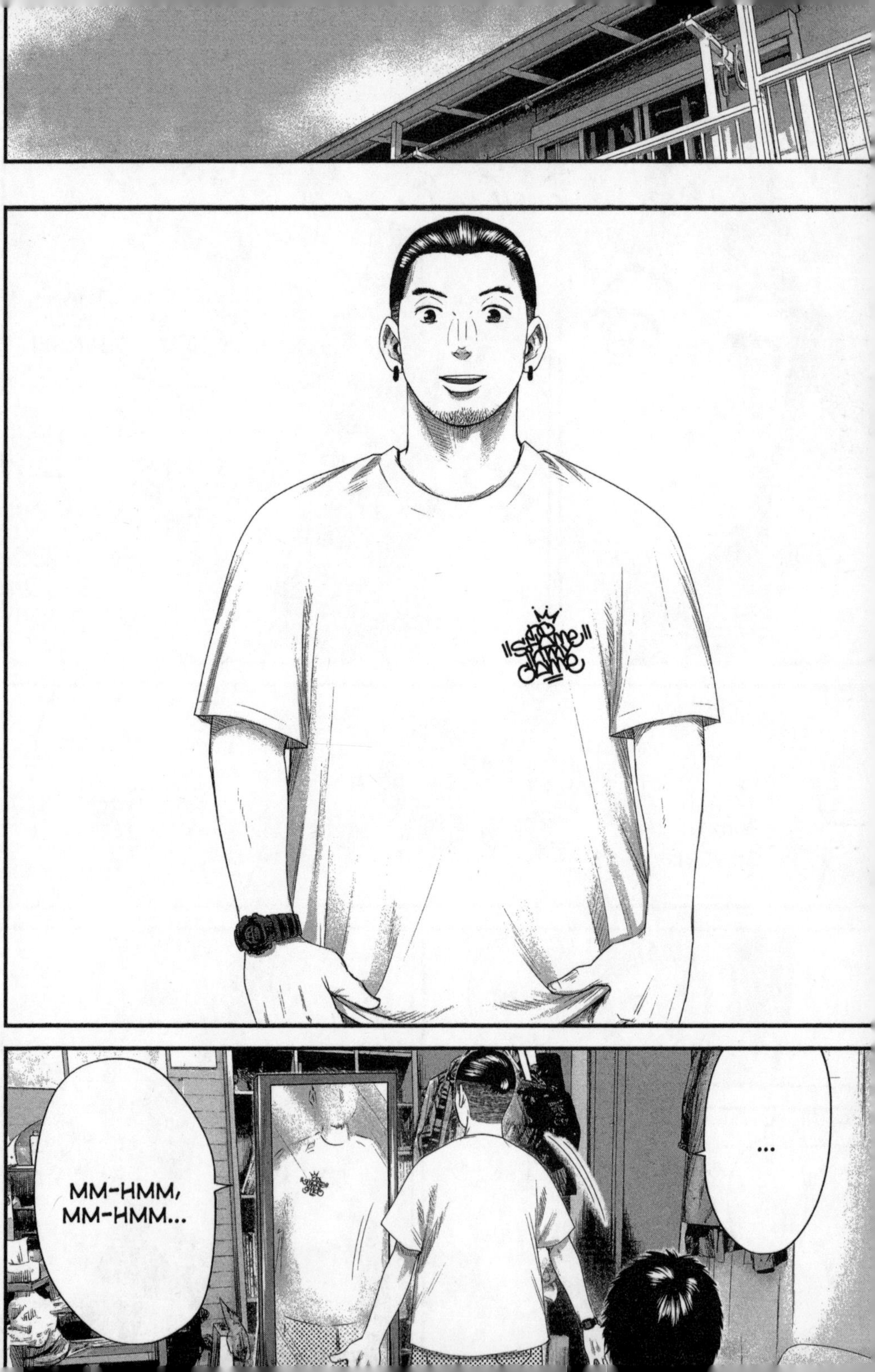
...
MM-HMM,
MM-HMM...

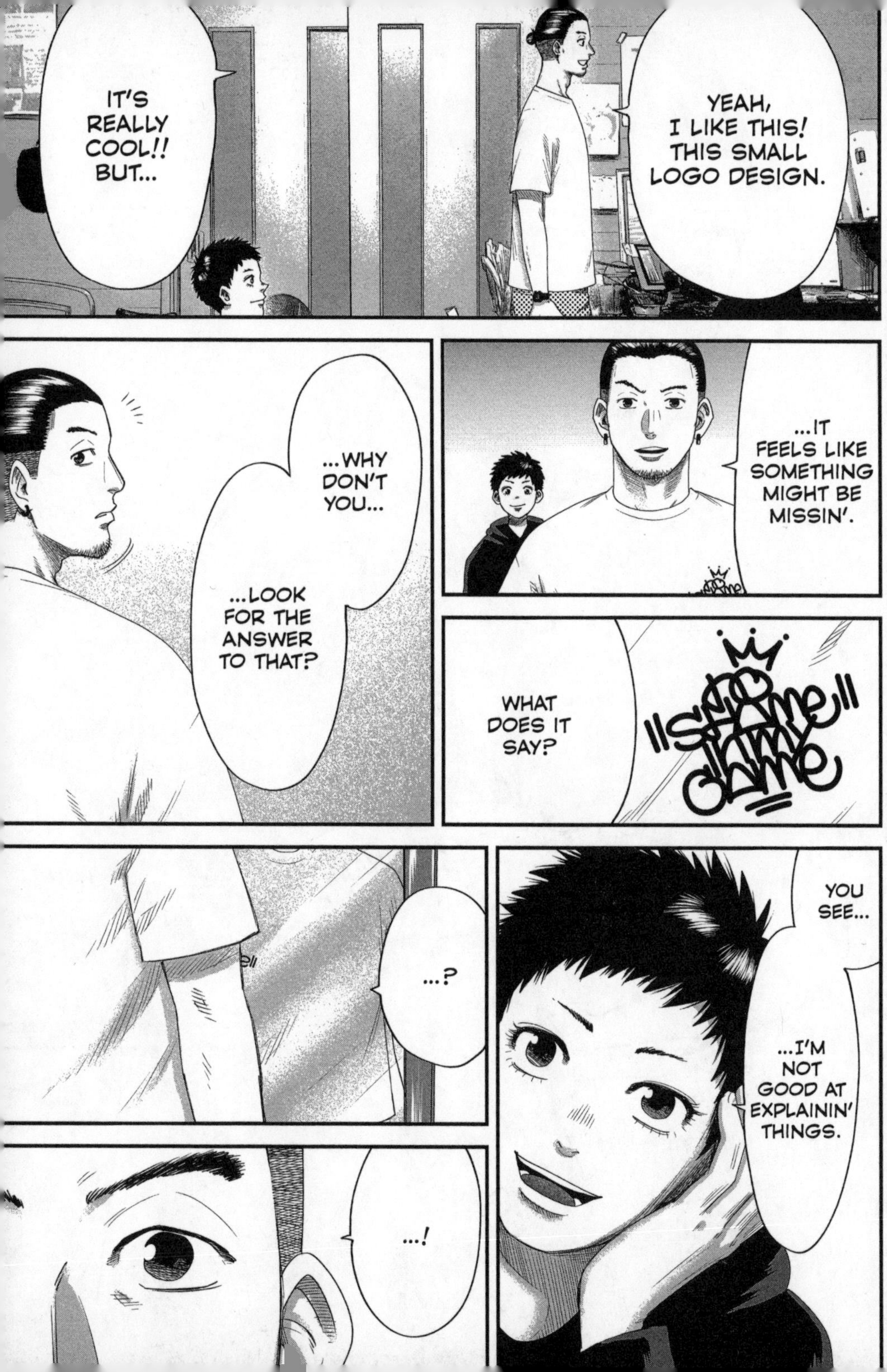
YEAH, I LIKE THIS! THIS SMALL LOGO DESIGN.
IT'S REALLY COOL!! BUT...
...IT FEELS LIKE SOMETHING MIGHT BE MISSIN'.
WHAT DOES IT SAY?
...WHY DON'T YOU...
...LOOK FOR THE ANSWER TO THAT?
YOU SEE...
...I'M NOT GOOD AT EXPLAININ' THINGS.
...?
...!

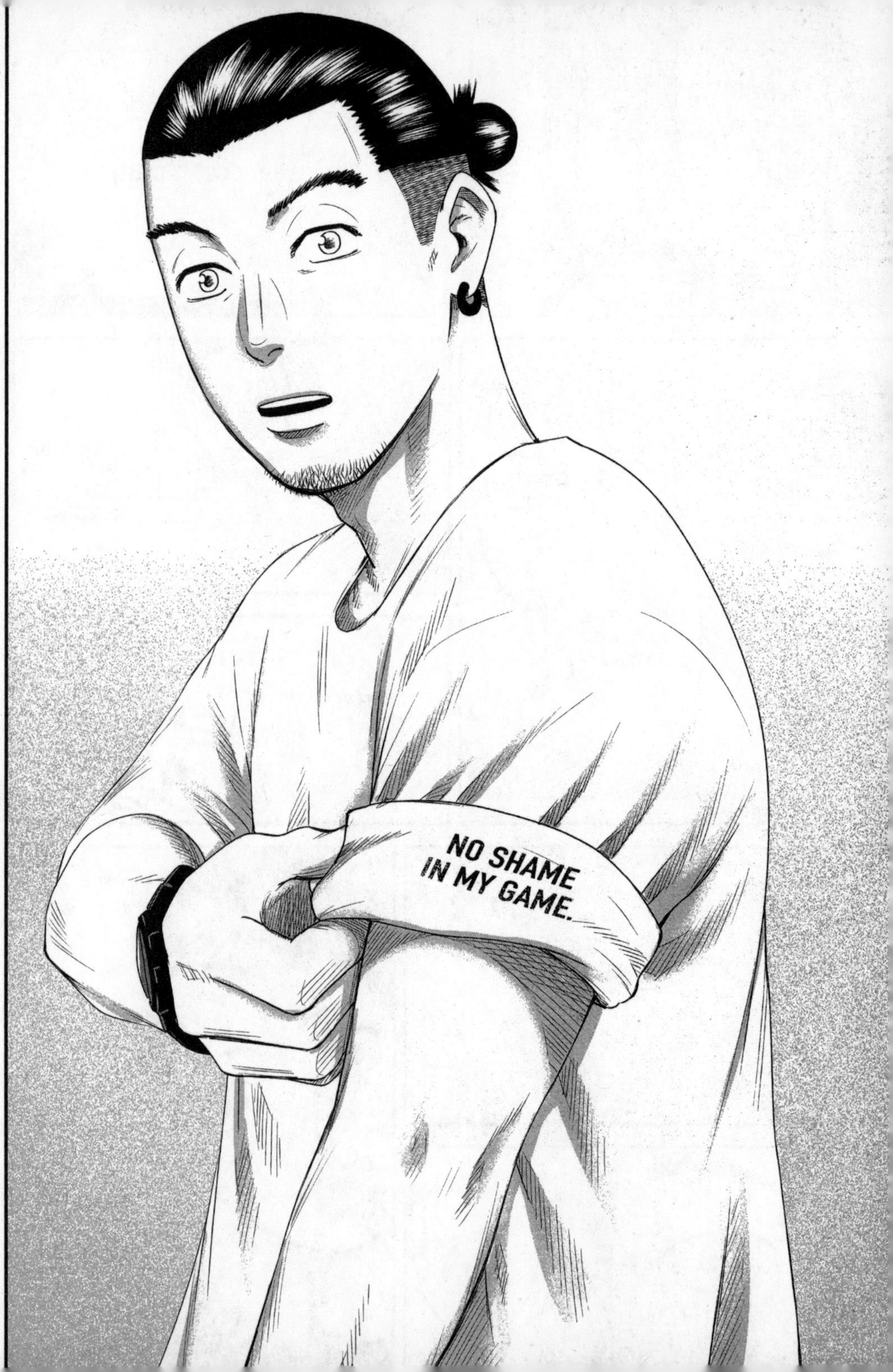
NO SHAME
IN MY GAME.

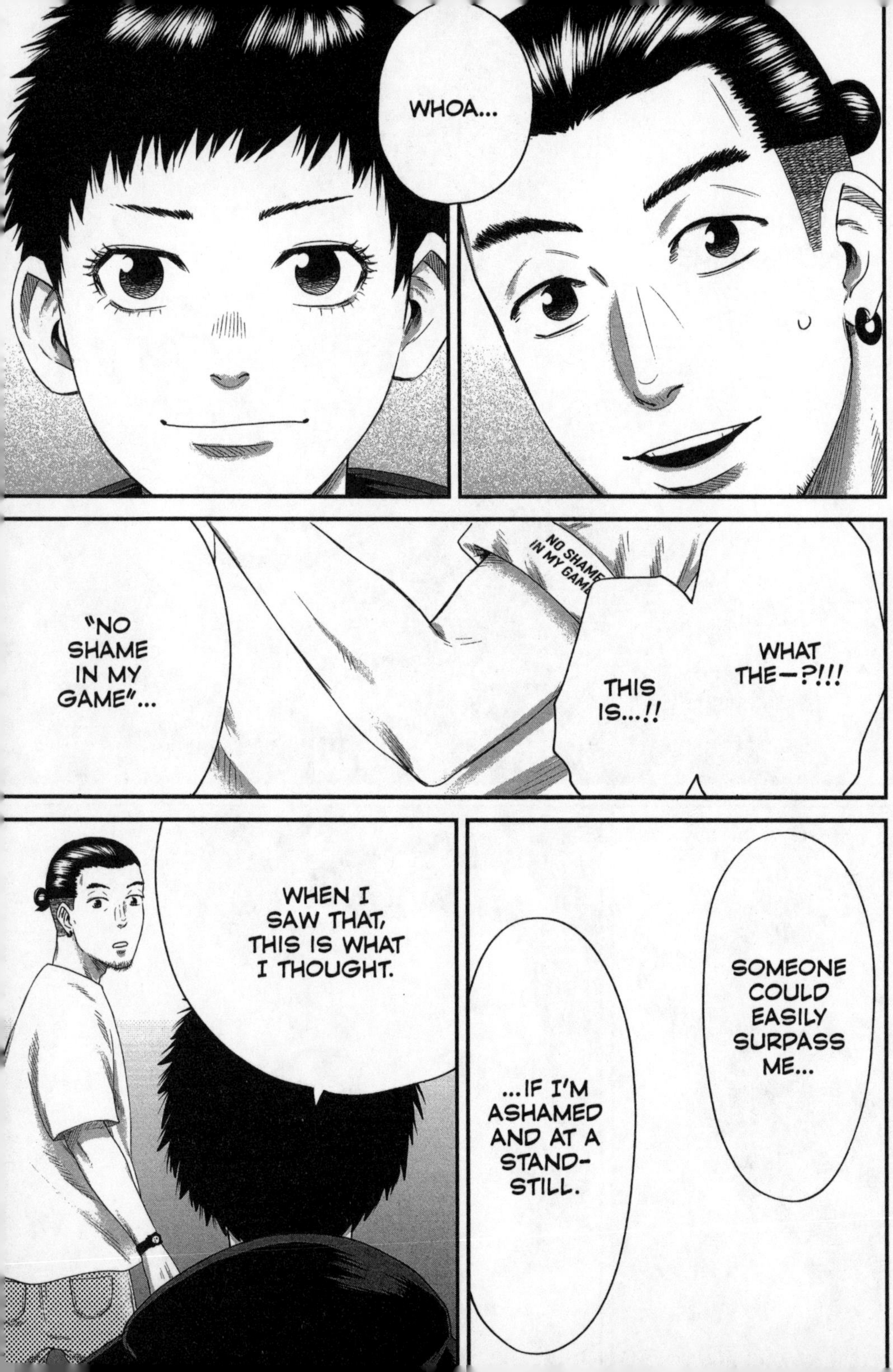
WHOA...
WHAT THE—?!!!
THIS IS...!!
NO SHAME IN MY GAM
"NO SHAME IN MY GAME"...
SOMEONE COULD EASILY SURPASS ME...
...IF I'M ASHAMED AND AT A STAND-STILL.
WHEN I SAW THAT, THIS IS WHAT I THOUGHT.

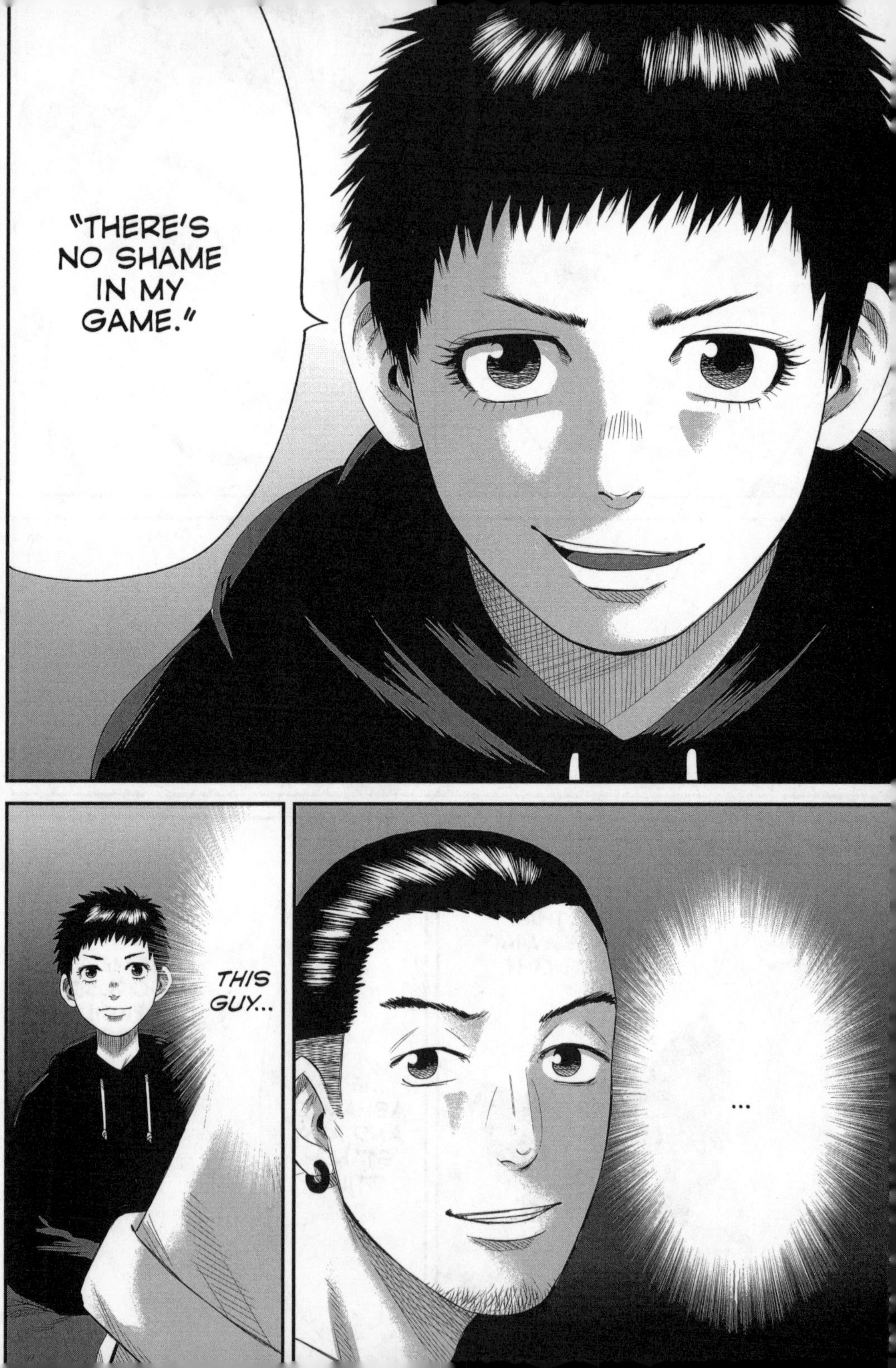
"THERE'S NO SHAME IN MY GAME."
...
THIS GUY...

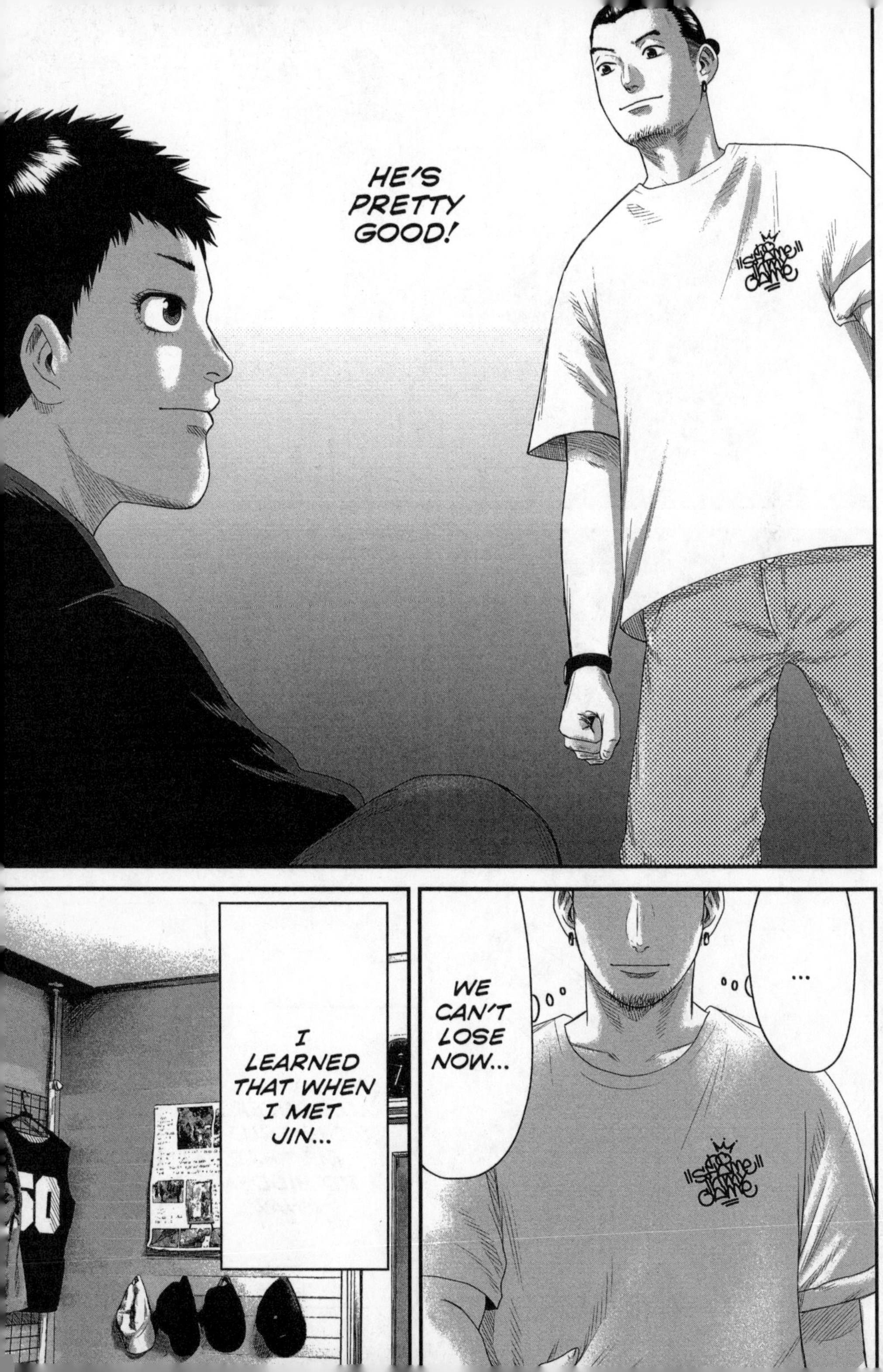
HE'S PRETTY GOOD!
...
WE CAN'T LOSE NOW...
I LEARNED THAT WHEN I MET JIN...

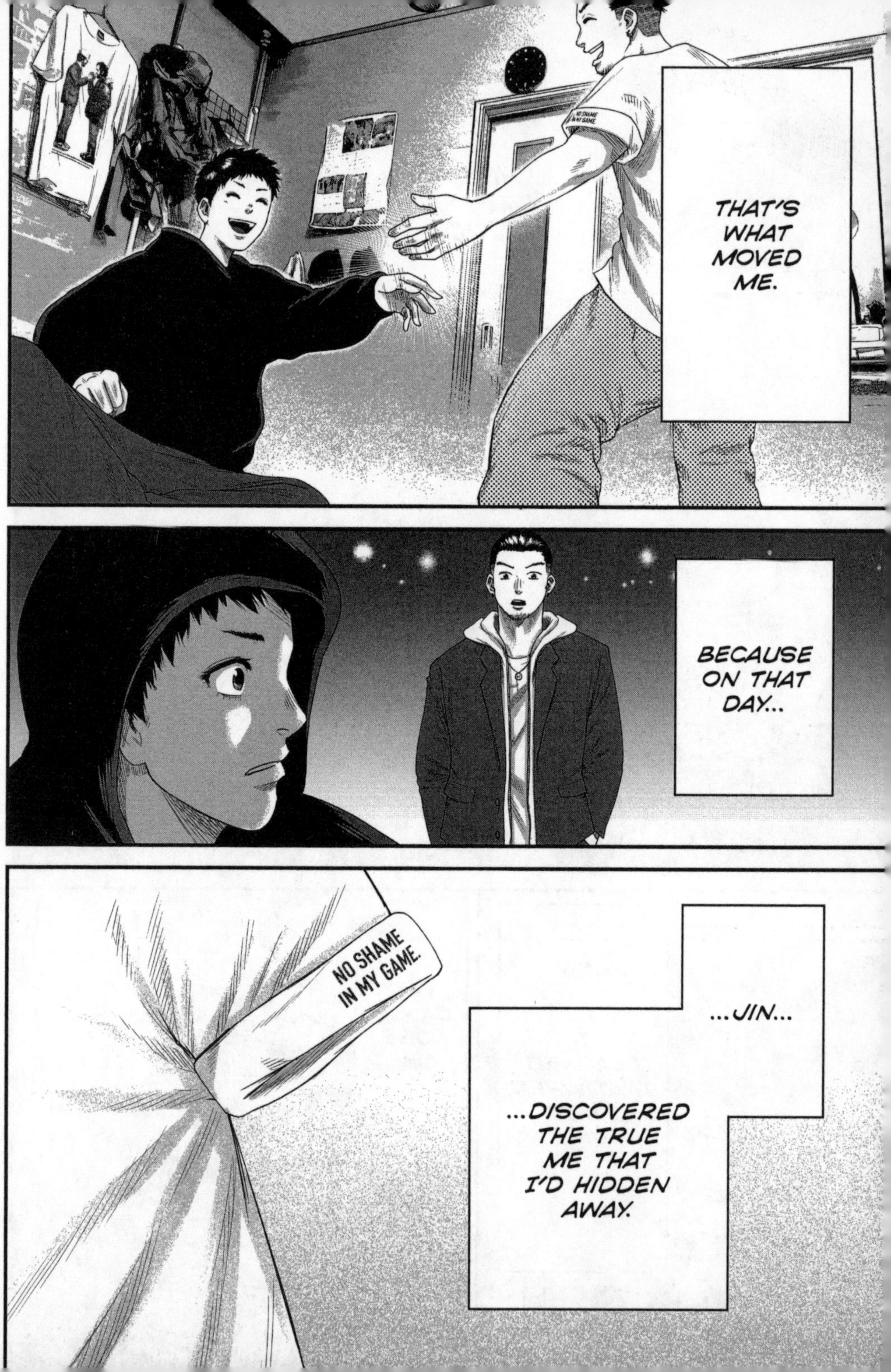
NO SHAME IN MY GAME
THAT'S WHAT MOVED ME.
BECAUSE ON THAT DAY...
NO SHAME IN MY GAME.
...JIN...
...DISCOVERED THE TRUE ME THAT I'D HIDDEN AWAY.

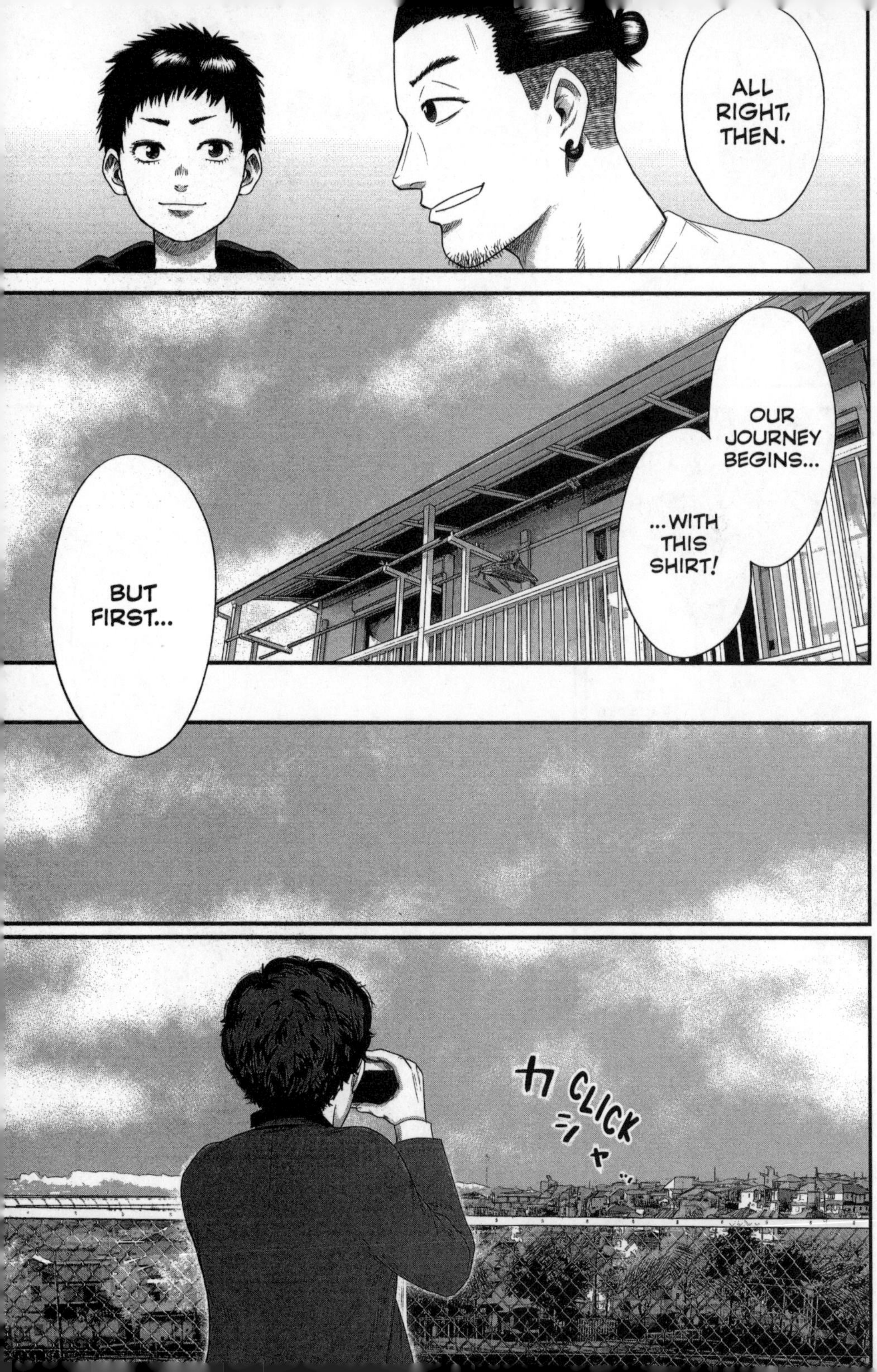
ALL RIGHT, THEN.
OUR JOURNEY BEGINS...
...WITH THIS SHIRT!
BUT FIRST...
カシャ
CLICK

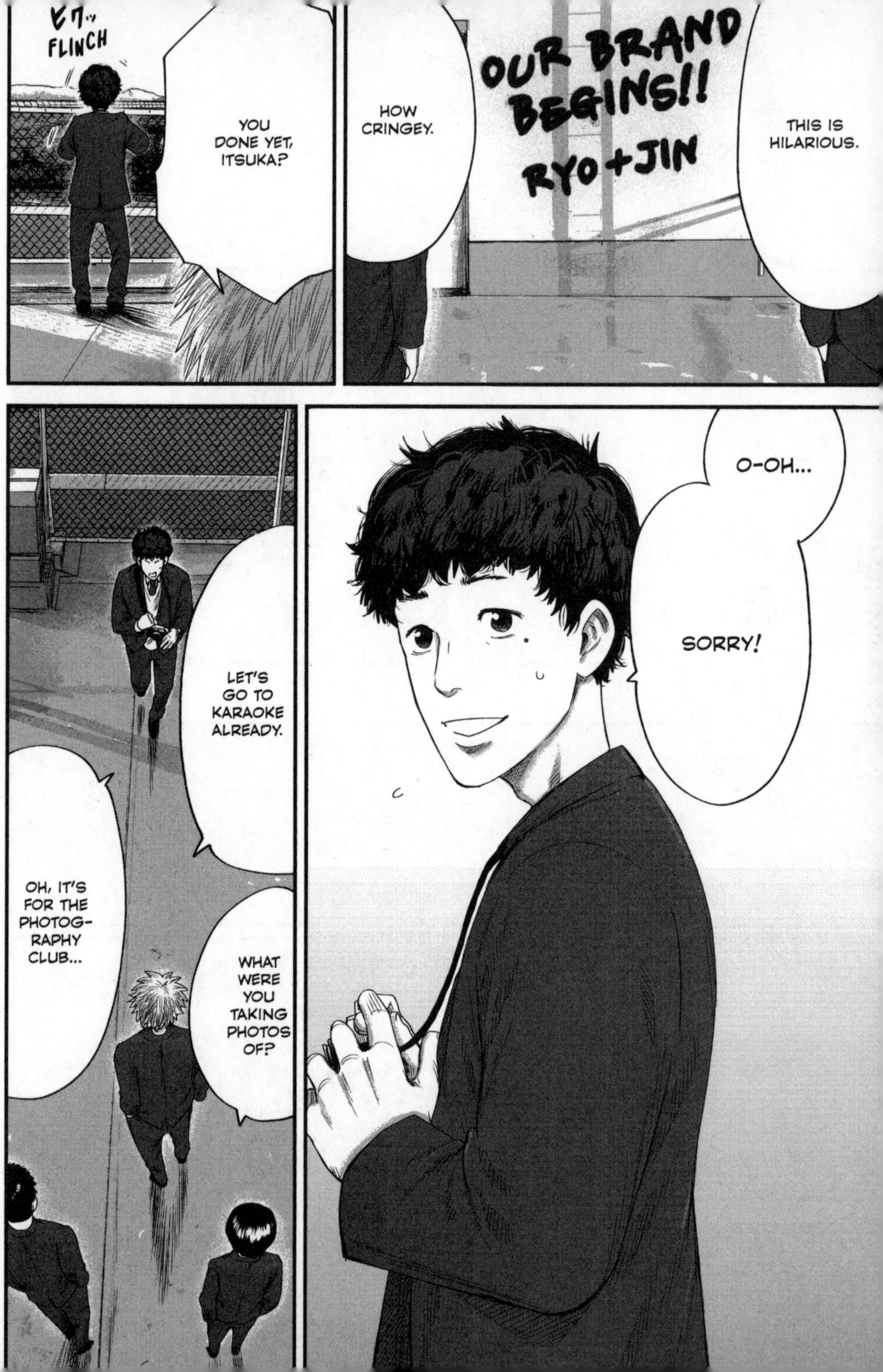
THIS IS HILARIOUS.
OUR BRAND BEGINS!! RYO+JIN
HOW CRINGEY.
YOU DONE YET, ITSUKA?
ヒクッ
FLINCH
O-OH...
SORRY!
LET'S GO TO KARAOKE ALREADY.
WHAT WERE YOU TAKING PHOTOS OF?
OH, IT'S FOR THE PHOTOG-RAPHY CLUB...

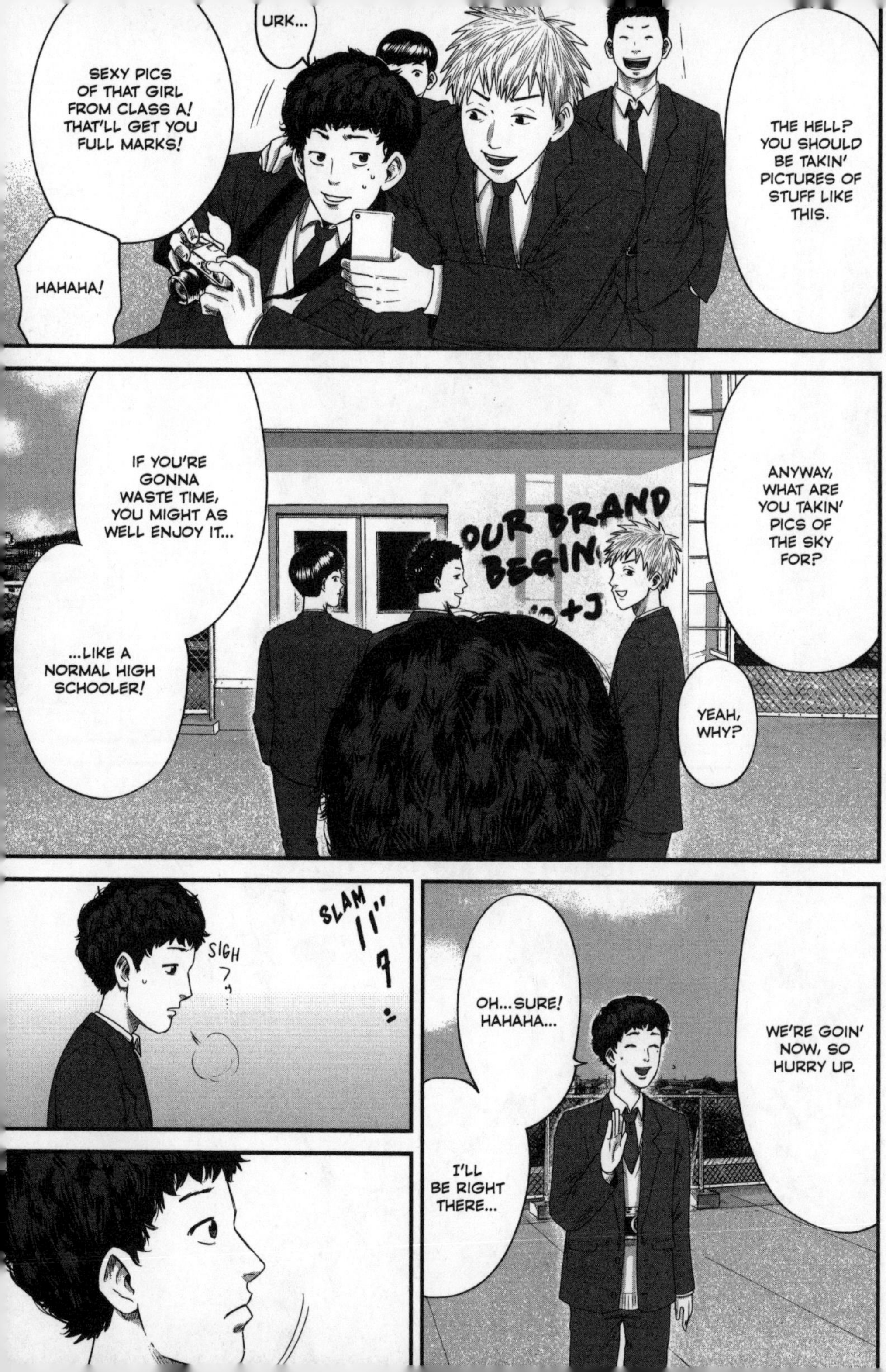
THE HELL? YOU SHOULD BE TAKIN' PICTURES OF STUFF LIKE THIS.
URK...
SEXY PICS OF THAT GIRL FROM CLASS A! THAT'LL GET YOU FULL MARKS!
HAHAHA!
ANYWAY, WHAT ARE YOU TAKIN' PICS OF THE SKY FOR?
YEAH, WHY?
IF YOU'RE GONNA WASTE TIME, YOU MIGHT AS WELL ENJOY IT...
...LIKE A NORMAL HIGH SCHOOLER!
WE'RE GOIN' NOW, SO HURRY UP.
OH...SURE! HAHAHA...
I'LL BE RIGHT THERE...
SLAM
SIGH

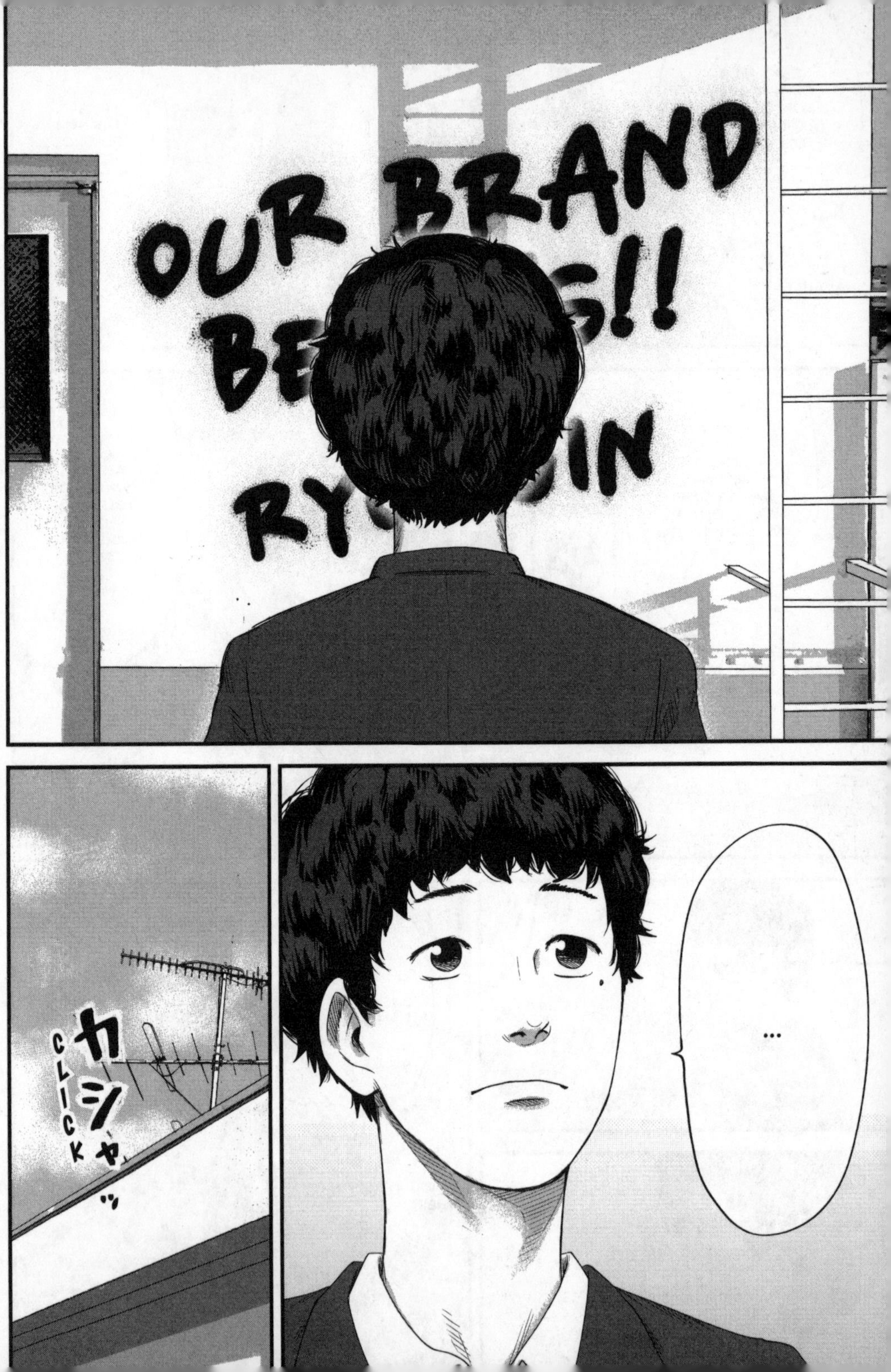
OUR BRAND
...
カシャッ
CLICK

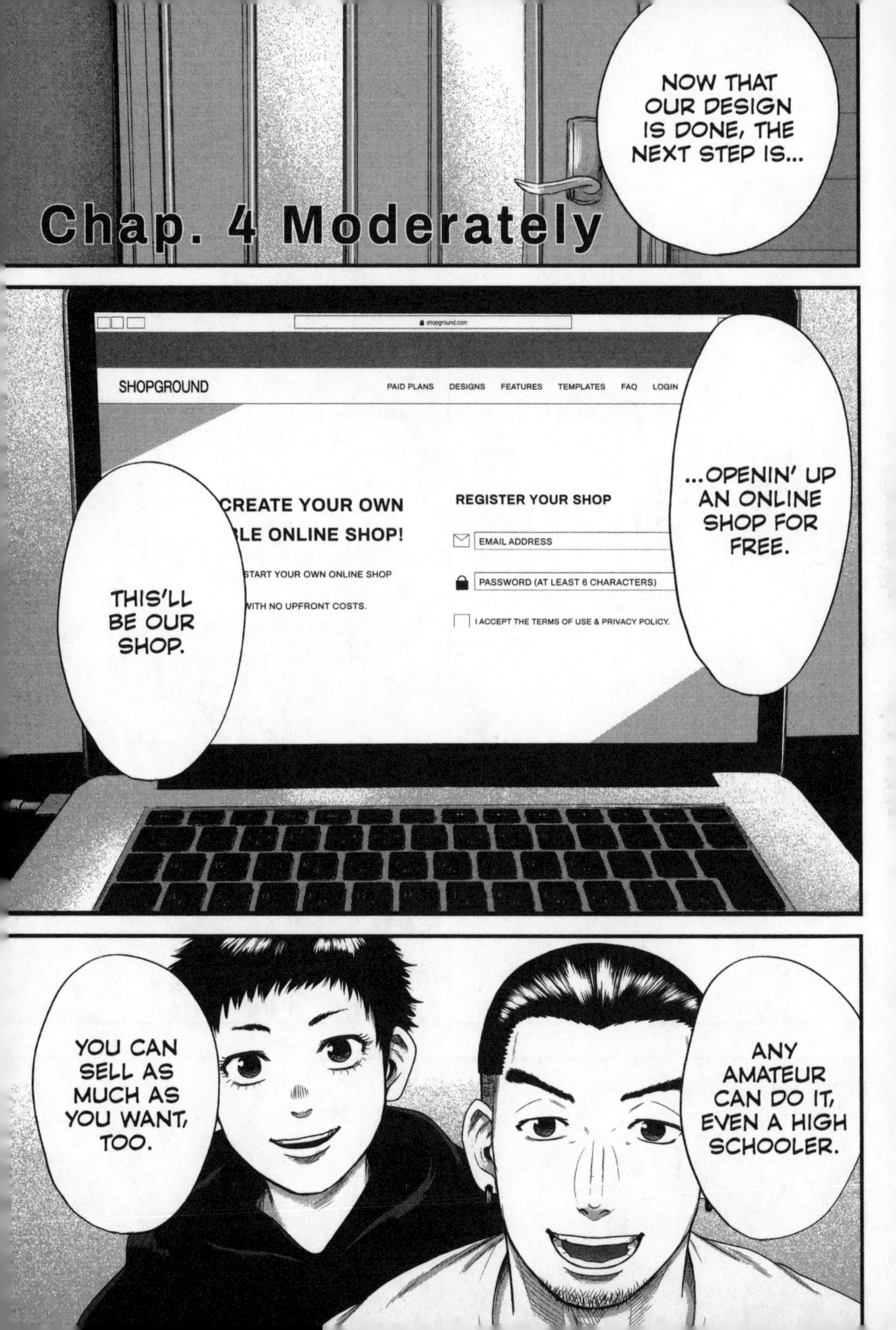
Chap. 4 Moderately
NOW THAT OUR DESIGN IS DONE, THE NEXT STEP IS...
shopground.com
SHOPGROUND
PAID PLANS DESIGNS FEATURES TEMPLATES FAQ LOGIN
CREATE YOUR OWN
ONLINE SHOP!
START YOUR OWN ONLINE SHOP
WITH NO UPFRONT COSTS.
REGISTER YOUR SHOP
EMAIL ADDRESS
PASSWORD (AT LEAST 6 CHARACTERS)
I ACCEPT THE TERMS OF USE & PRIVACY POLICY.
...OPENIN' UP AN ONLINE SHOP FOR FREE.
THIS'LL BE OUR SHOP.
ANY AMATEUR CAN DO IT, EVEN A HIGH SCHOOLER.
YOU CAN SELL AS MUCH AS YOU WANT, TOO.

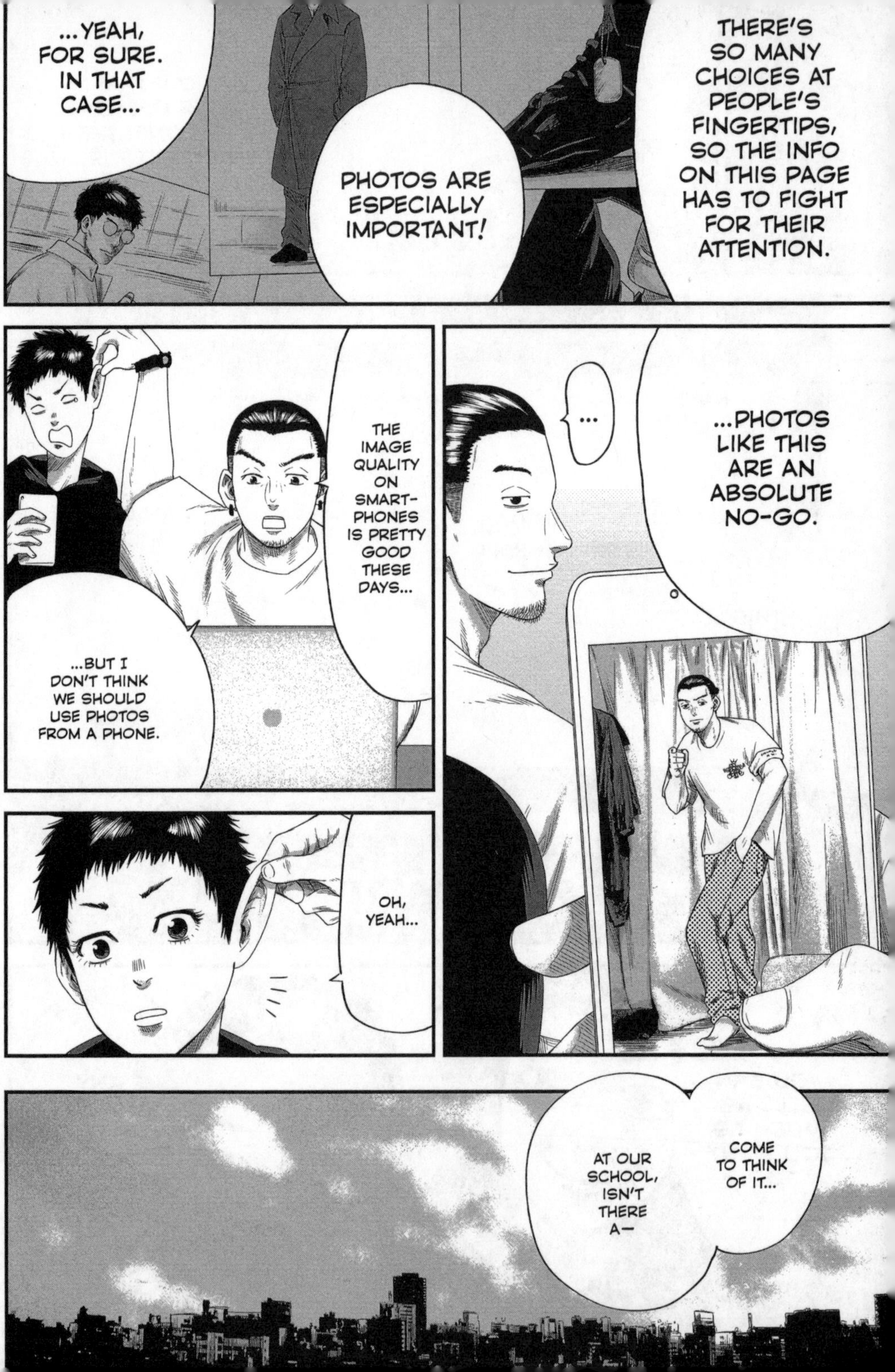
THERE'S SO MANY CHOICES AT PEOPLE'S FINGERTIPS, SO THE INFO ON THIS PAGE HAS TO FIGHT FOR THEIR ATTENTION.
PHOTOS ARE ESPECIALLY IMPORTANT!
...YEAH, FOR SURE. IN THAT CASE...
...
...PHOTOS LIKE THIS ARE AN ABSOLUTE NO-GO.
THE IMAGE QUALITY ON SMART-PHONES IS PRETTY GOOD THESE DAYS...
...BUT I DON'T THINK WE SHOULD USE PHOTOS FROM A PHONE.
OH, YEAH...
COME TO THINK OF IT...
AT OUR SCHOOL, ISN'T THERE A—

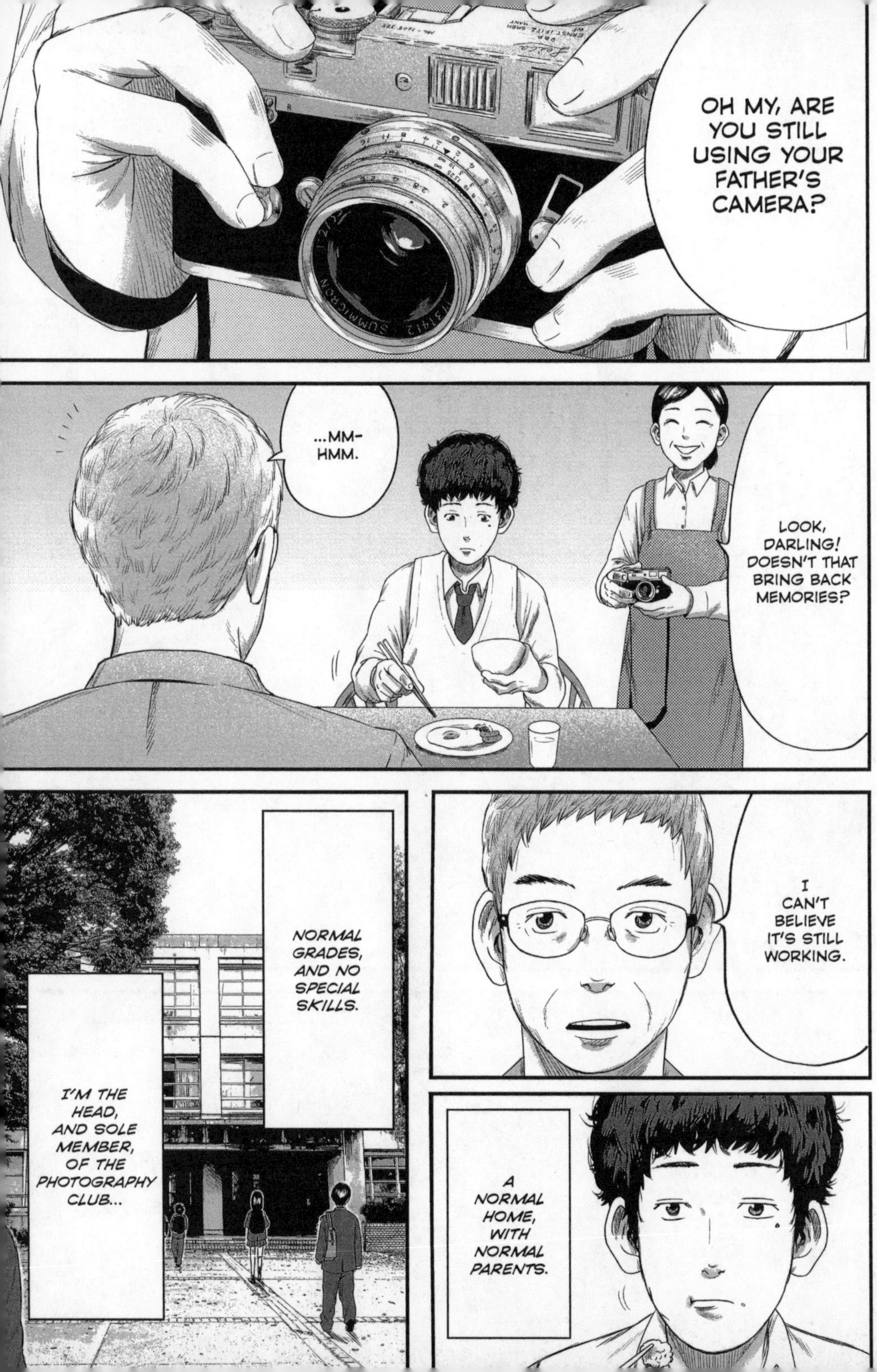
OH MY, ARE YOU STILL USING YOUR FATHER'S CAMERA?
LOOK, DARLING! DOESN'T THAT BRING BACK MEMORIES?
...MM-HMM.
I CAN'T BELIEVE IT'S STILL WORKING.
A NORMAL HOME, WITH NORMAL PARENTS.
NORMAL GRADES, AND NO SPECIAL SKILLS.
I'M THE HEAD, AND SOLE MEMBER, OF THE PHOTOGRAPHY CLUB...

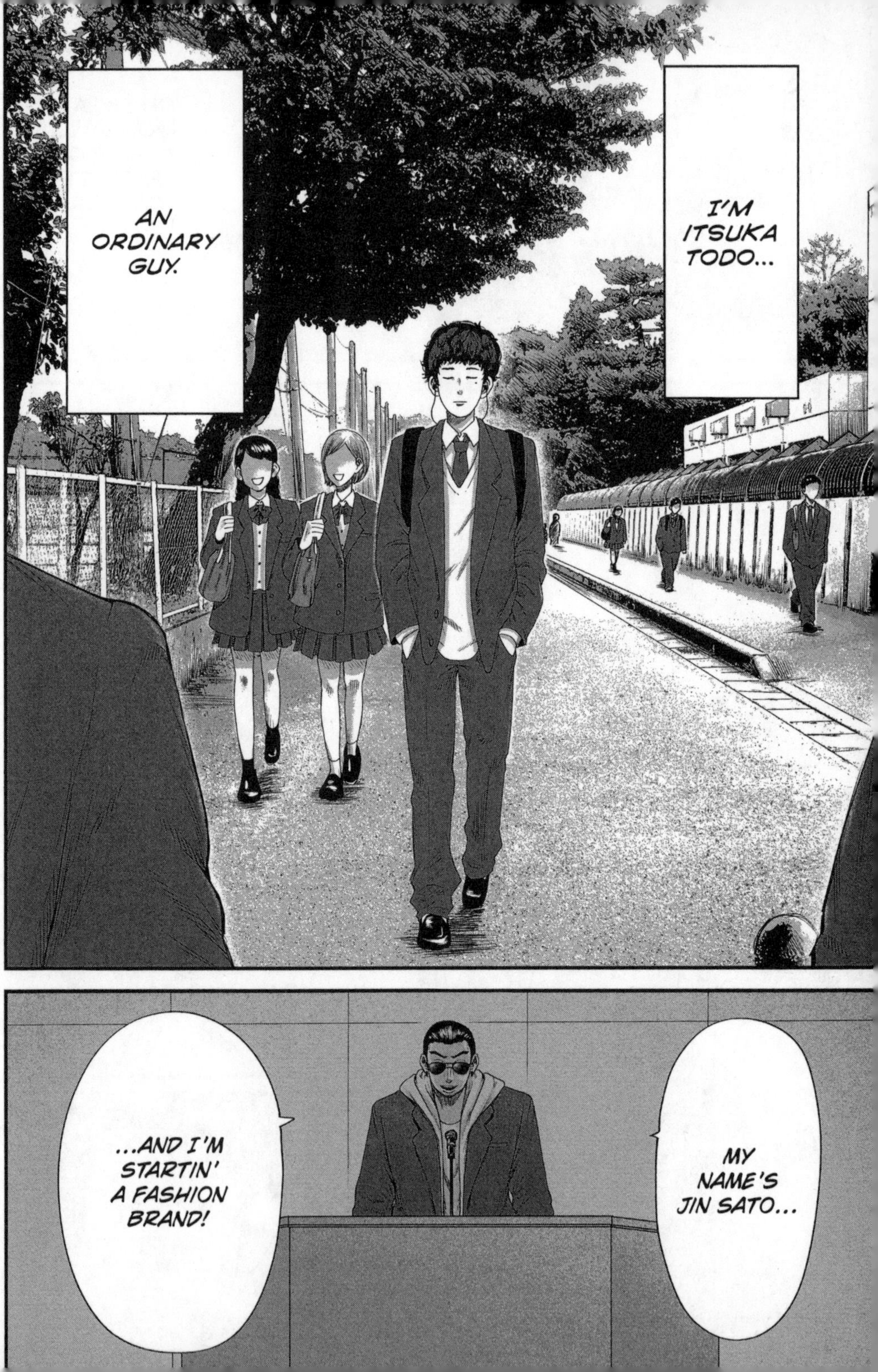
I'M ITSUKA TODO...
AN ORDINARY GUY.
MY NAME'S JIN SATO...
...AND I'M STARTIN' A FASHION BRAND!

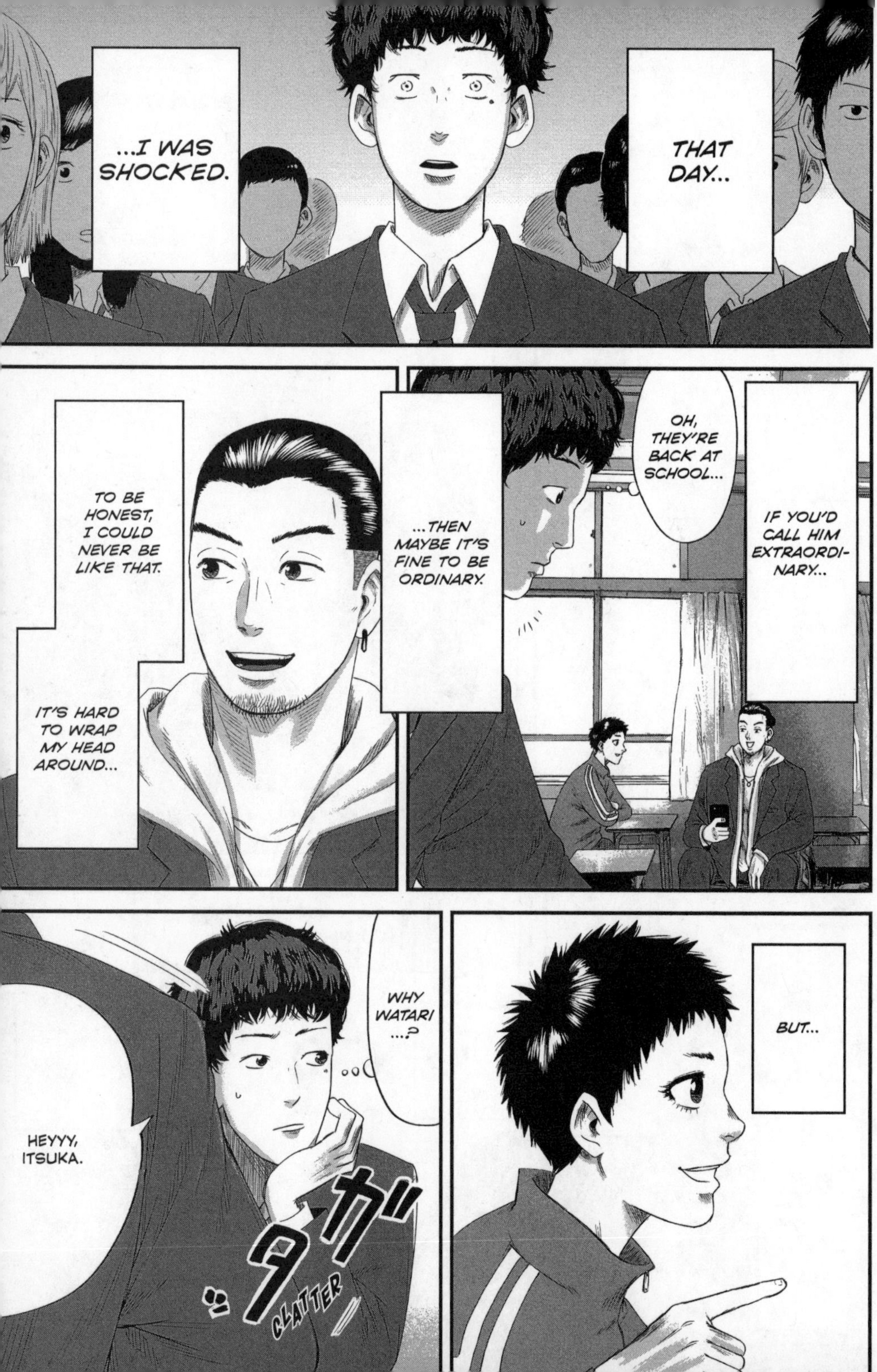
THAT DAY...
...I WAS SHOCKED.
IF YOU'D CALL HIM EXTRAORDINARY...
OH, THEY'RE BACK AT SCHOOL...
...THEN MAYBE IT'S FINE TO BE ORDINARY.
TO BE HONEST, I COULD NEVER BE LIKE THAT.
IT'S HARD TO WRAP MY HEAD AROUND...
BUT...
WHY WATARI ...?
HEYYY, ITSUKA.
ガタ
CLATTER

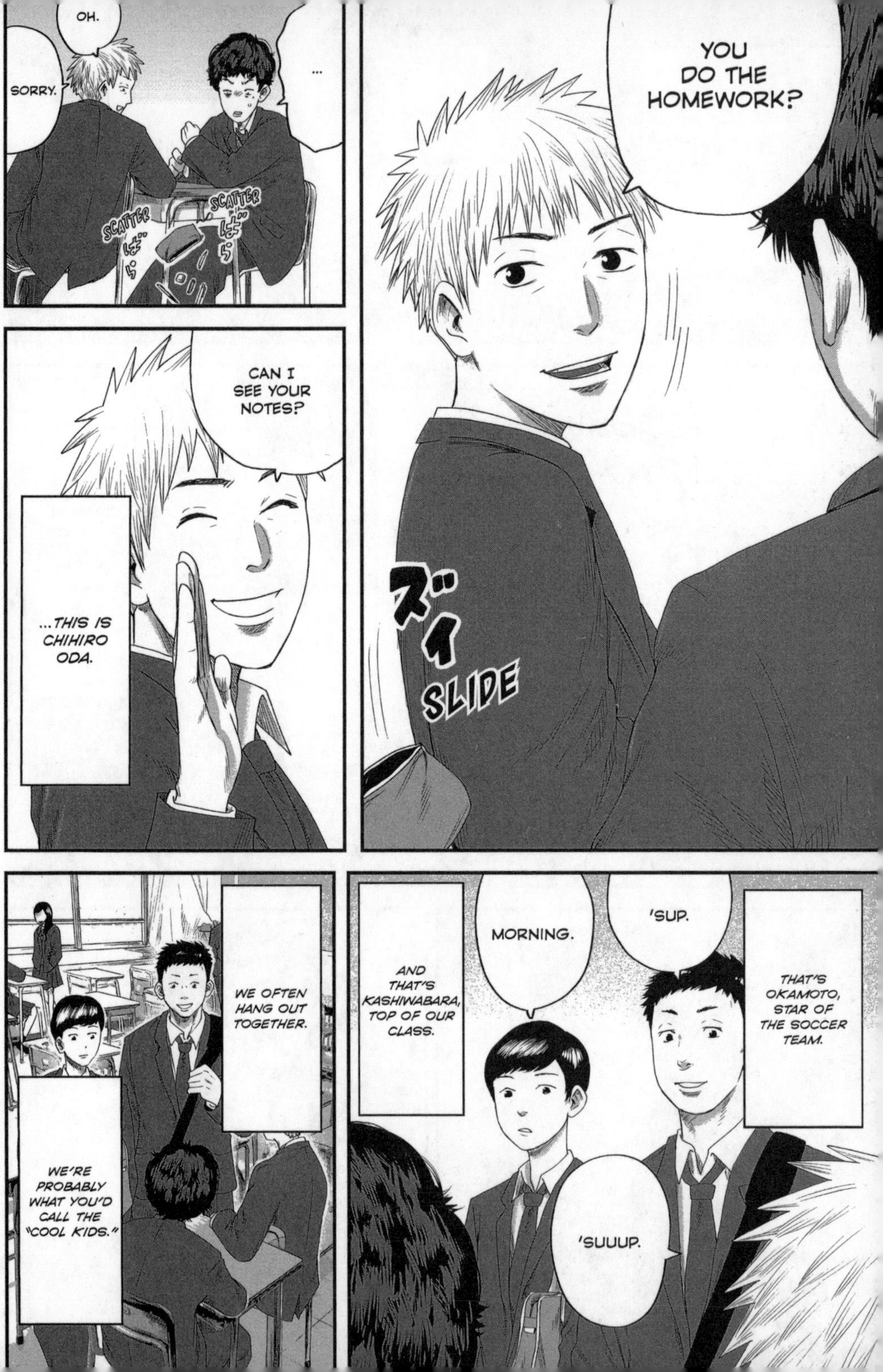
YOU DO THE HOMEWORK?
ズイ
SLIDE
...
OH.
SORRY.
SCATTER
ばら
SCATTER
ばら
CAN I SEE YOUR NOTES?
...THIS IS CHIHIRO ODA.
'SUP.
MORNING.
THAT'S OKAMOTO, STAR OF THE SOCCER TEAM.
AND THAT'S KASHIWABARA, TOP OF OUR CLASS.
'SUUUP.
WE OFTEN HANG OUT TOGETHER.
WE'RE PROBABLY WHAT YOU'D CALL THE "COOL KIDS."

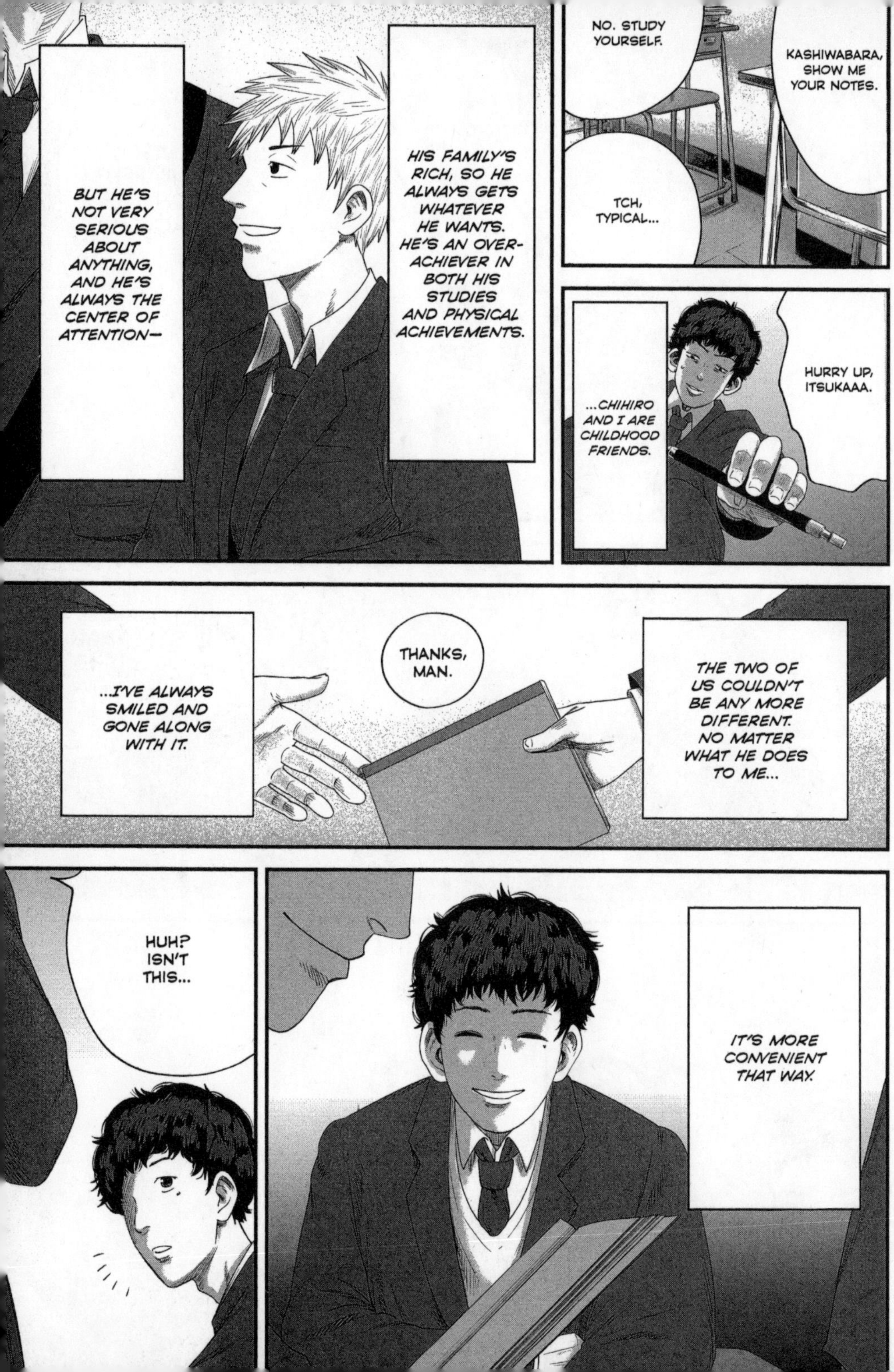
KASHIWABARA, SHOW ME YOUR NOTES.
NO. STUDY YOURSELF.
TCH, TYPICAL...
HURRY UP, ITSUKAAA.
...CHIHIRO AND I ARE CHILDHOOD FRIENDS.
HIS FAMILY'S RICH, SO HE ALWAYS GETS WHATEVER HE WANTS. HE'S AN OVER-ACHIEVER IN BOTH HIS STUDIES AND PHYSICAL ACHIEVEMENTS.
BUT HE'S NOT VERY SERIOUS ABOUT ANYTHING, AND HE'S ALWAYS THE CENTER OF ATTENTION—
THE TWO OF US COULDN'T BE ANY MORE DIFFERENT. NO MATTER WHAT HE DOES TO ME...
THANKS, MAN.
...I'VE ALWAYS SMILED AND GONE ALONG WITH IT.
IT'S MORE CONVENIENT THAT WAY.
HUH? ISN'T THIS...

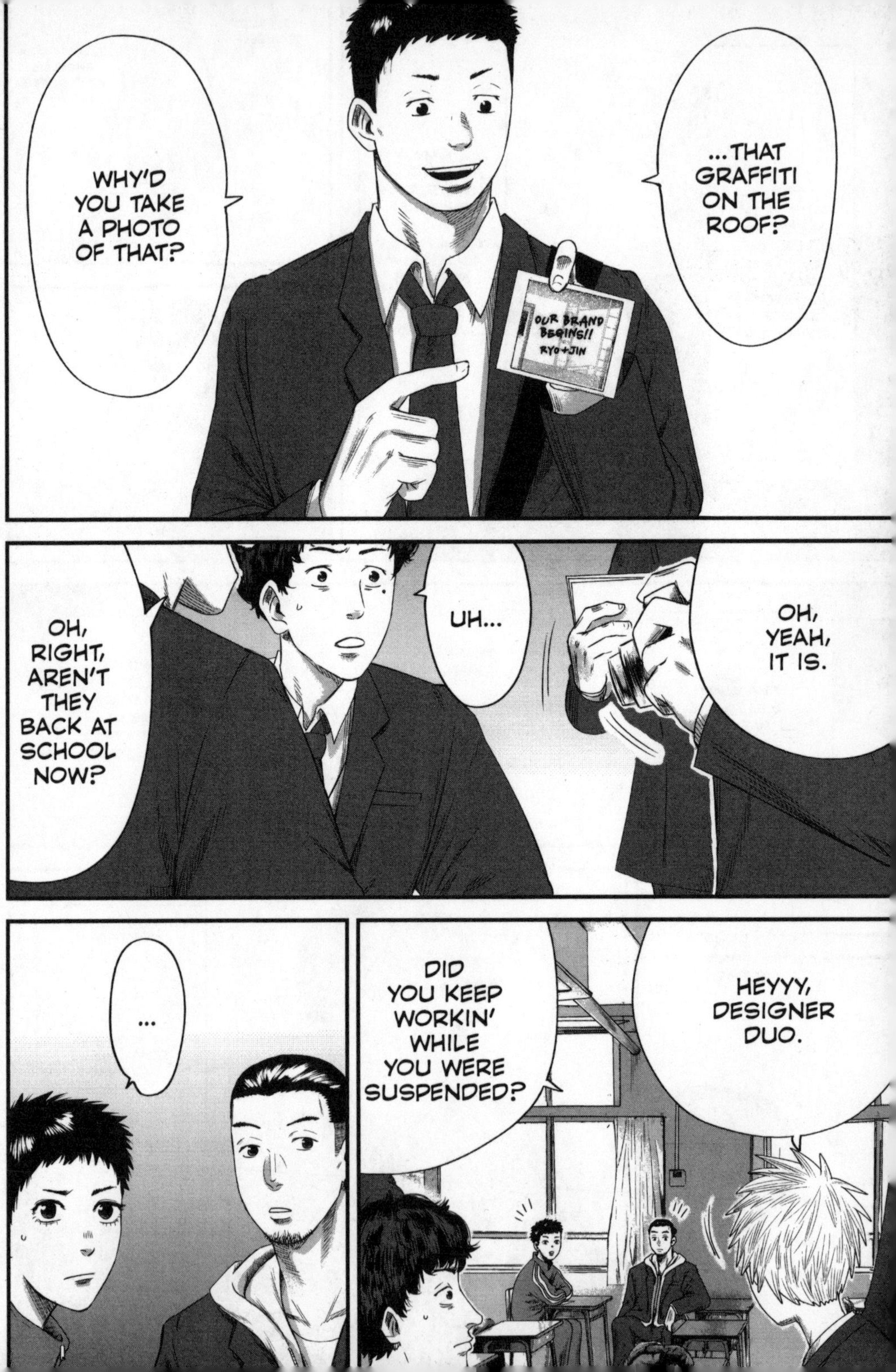
...THAT GRAFFITI ON THE ROOF?
WHY'D YOU TAKE A PHOTO OF THAT?
OUR BRAND BEGINS!! RYO+JIN
OH, YEAH, IT IS.
UH...
OH, RIGHT, AREN'T THEY BACK AT SCHOOL NOW?
HEYYY, DESIGNER DUO.
DID YOU KEEP WORKIN' WHILE YOU WERE SUSPENDED?
...

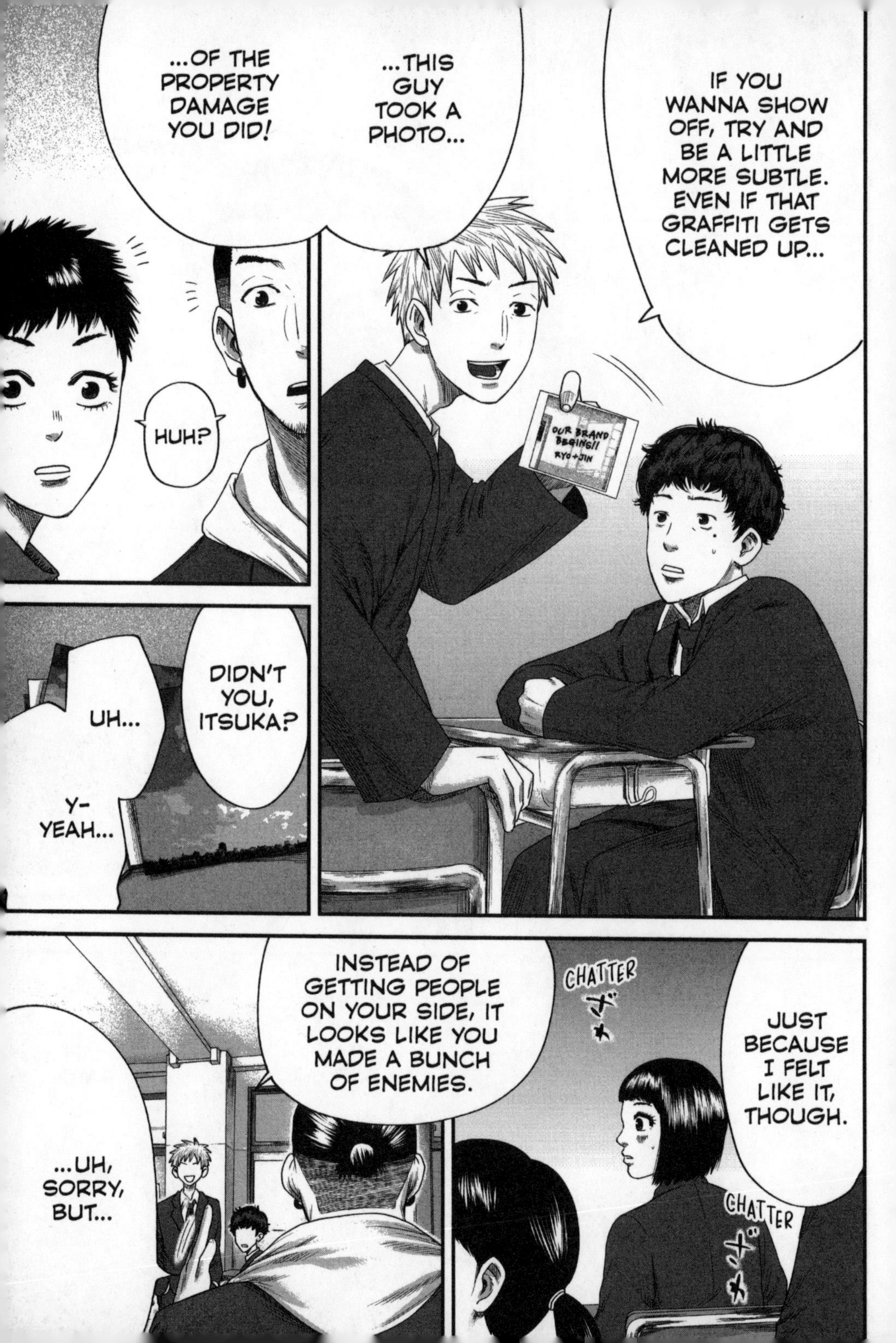
IF YOU WANNA SHOW OFF, TRY AND BE A LITTLE MORE SUBTLE. EVEN IF THAT GRAFFITI GETS CLEANED UP...
...THIS GUY TOOK A PHOTO...
...OF THE PROPERTY DAMAGE YOU DID!
OUR BRAND BEGINS!! RYO+JIN
HUH?
DIDN'T YOU, ITSUKA?
UH...
Y-YEAH...
JUST BECAUSE I FELT LIKE IT, THOUGH.
CHATTER
CHATTER
INSTEAD OF GETTING PEOPLE ON YOUR SIDE, IT LOOKS LIKE YOU MADE A BUNCH OF ENEMIES.
...UH, SORRY, BUT...

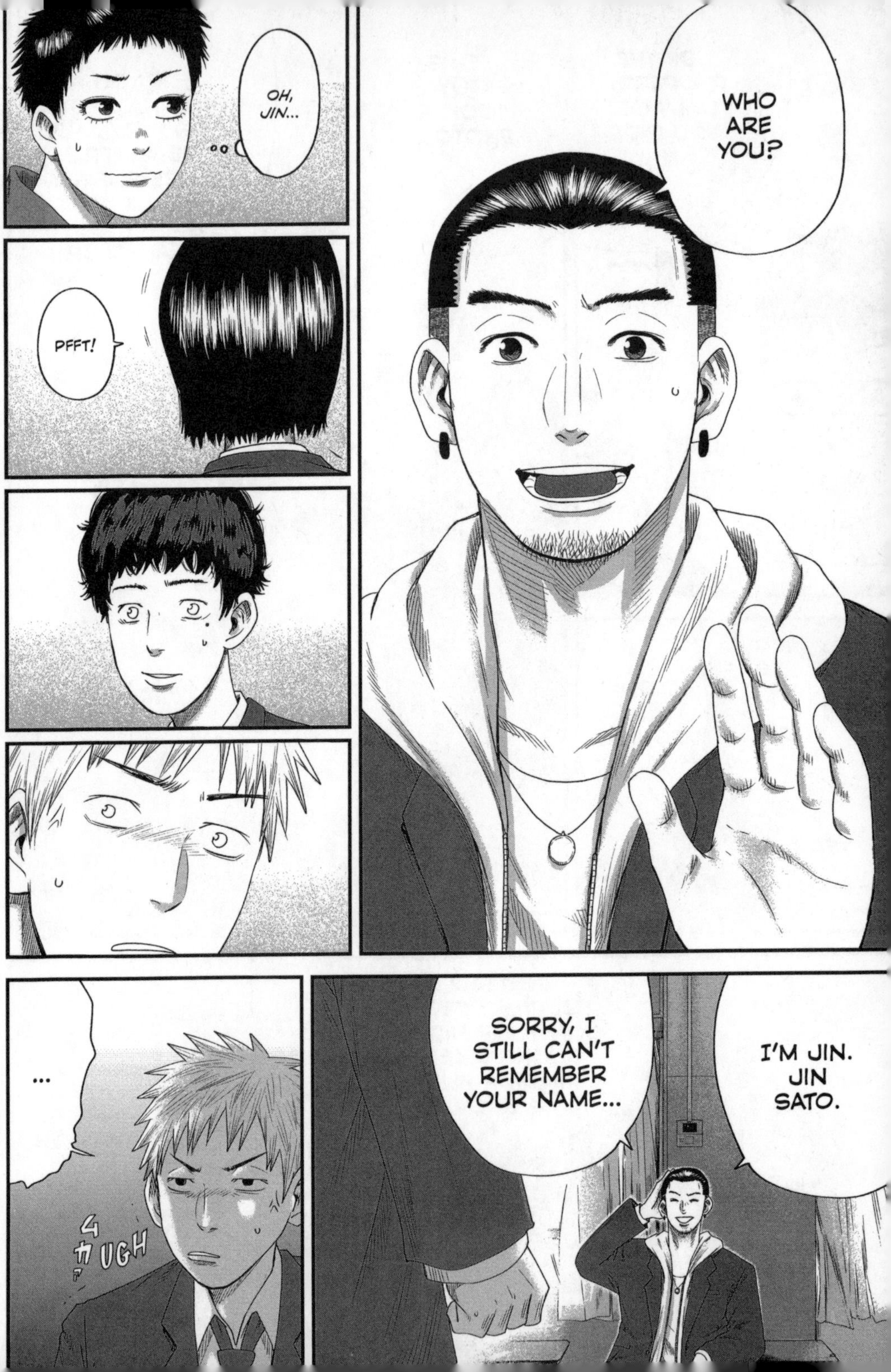
WHO ARE YOU?
OH, JIN...
PFFT!
I'M JIN. JIN SATO.
SORRY, I STILL CAN'T REMEMBER YOUR NAME...
...
UGH

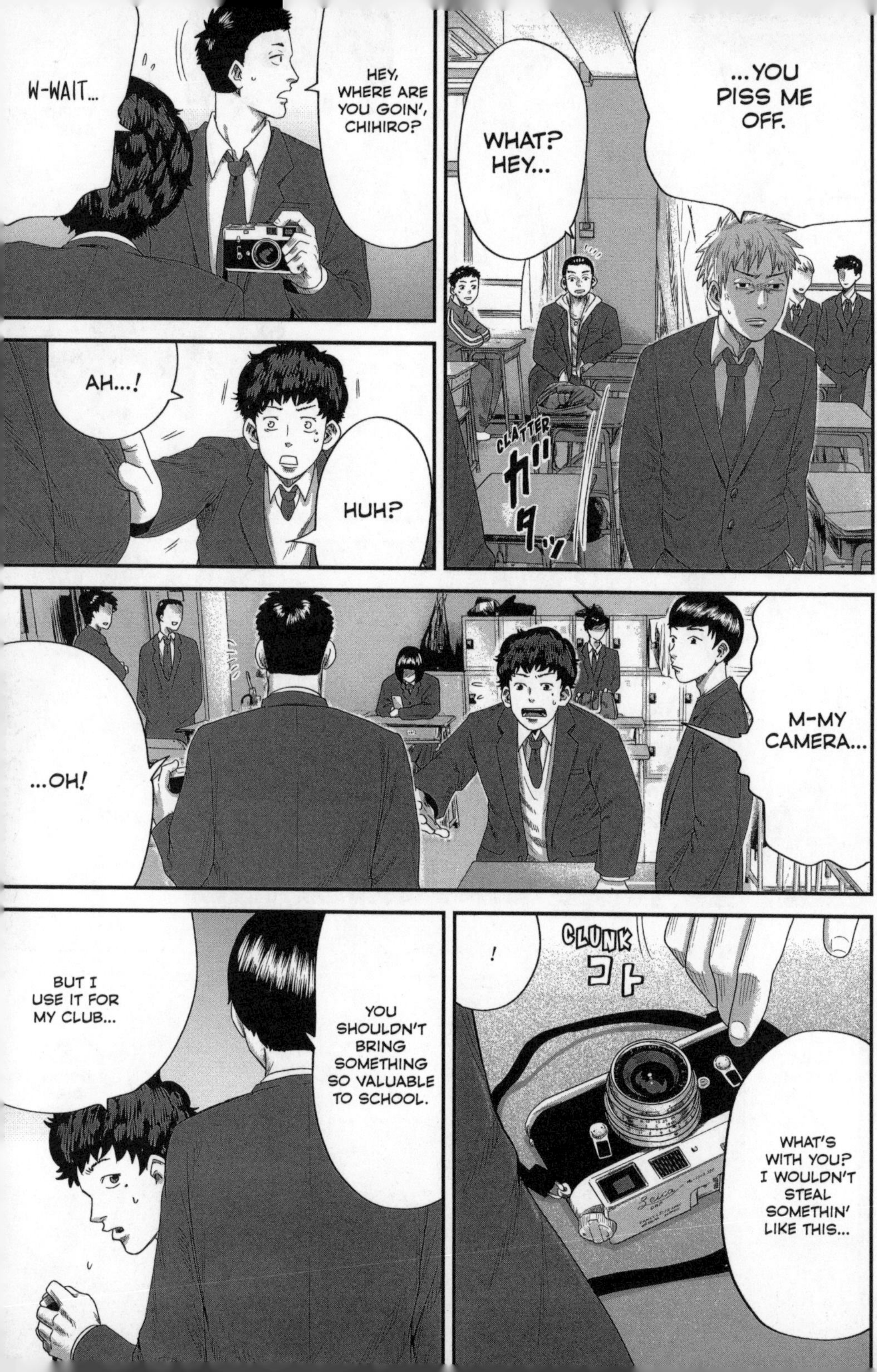
...YOU PISS ME OFF.
WHAT? HEY...
CLATTER
カタッ
HEY, WHERE ARE YOU GOIN', CHIHIRO?
W-WAIT...
HUH?
AH...!
M-MY CAMERA...
...OH!
CLUNK
コト
!
WHAT'S WITH YOU? I WOULDN'T STEAL SOMETHIN' LIKE THIS...
YOU SHOULDN'T BRING SOMETHING SO VALUABLE TO SCHOOL.
BUT I USE IT FOR MY CLUB...

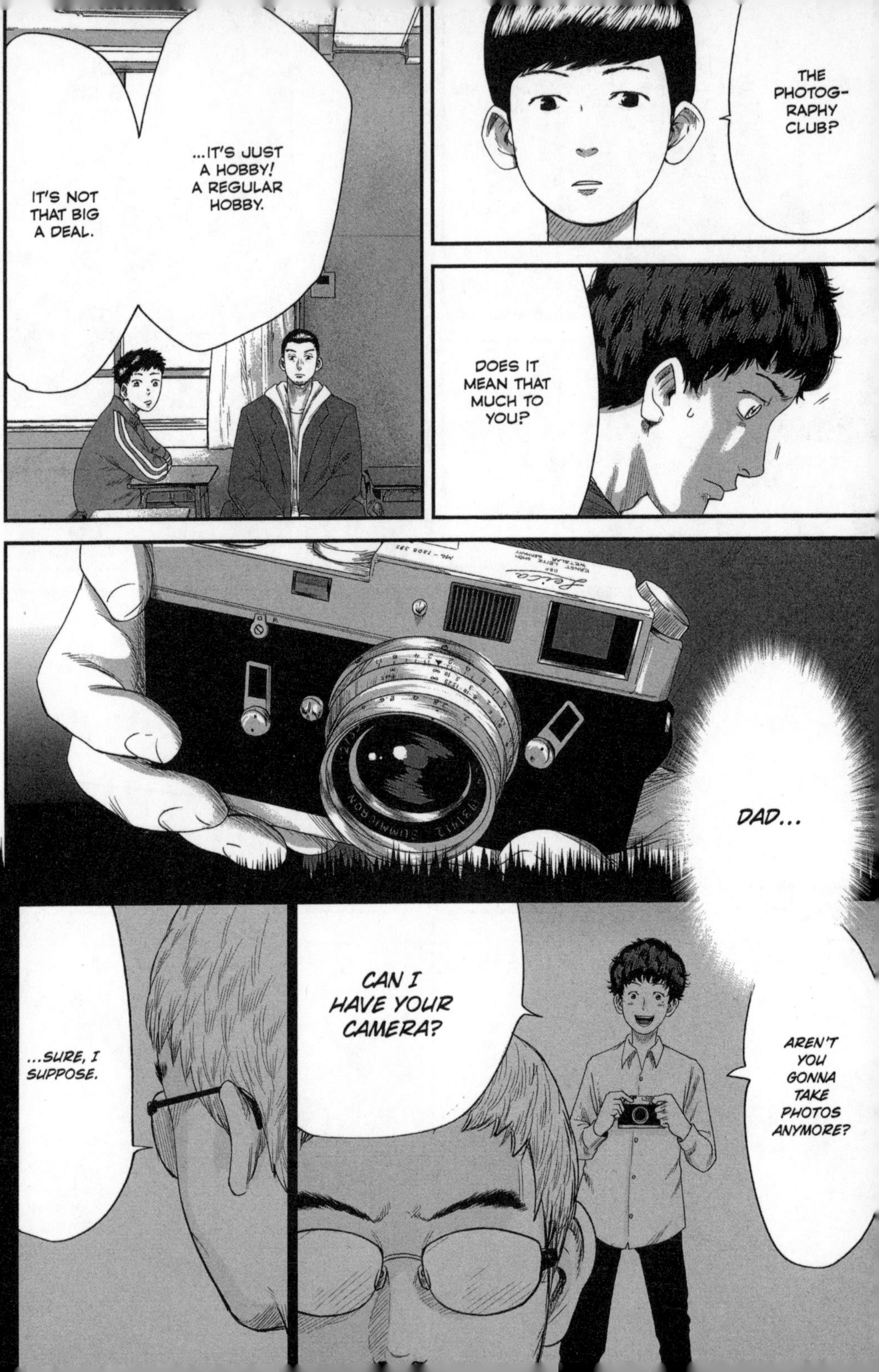
THE PHOTOG-RAPHY CLUB?
DOES IT MEAN THAT MUCH TO YOU?
...IT'S JUST A HOBBY! A REGULAR HOBBY.
IT'S NOT THAT BIG A DEAL.
DAD...
AREN'T YOU GONNA TAKE PHOTOS ANYMORE?
CAN I HAVE YOUR CAMERA?
...SURE, I SUPPOSE.

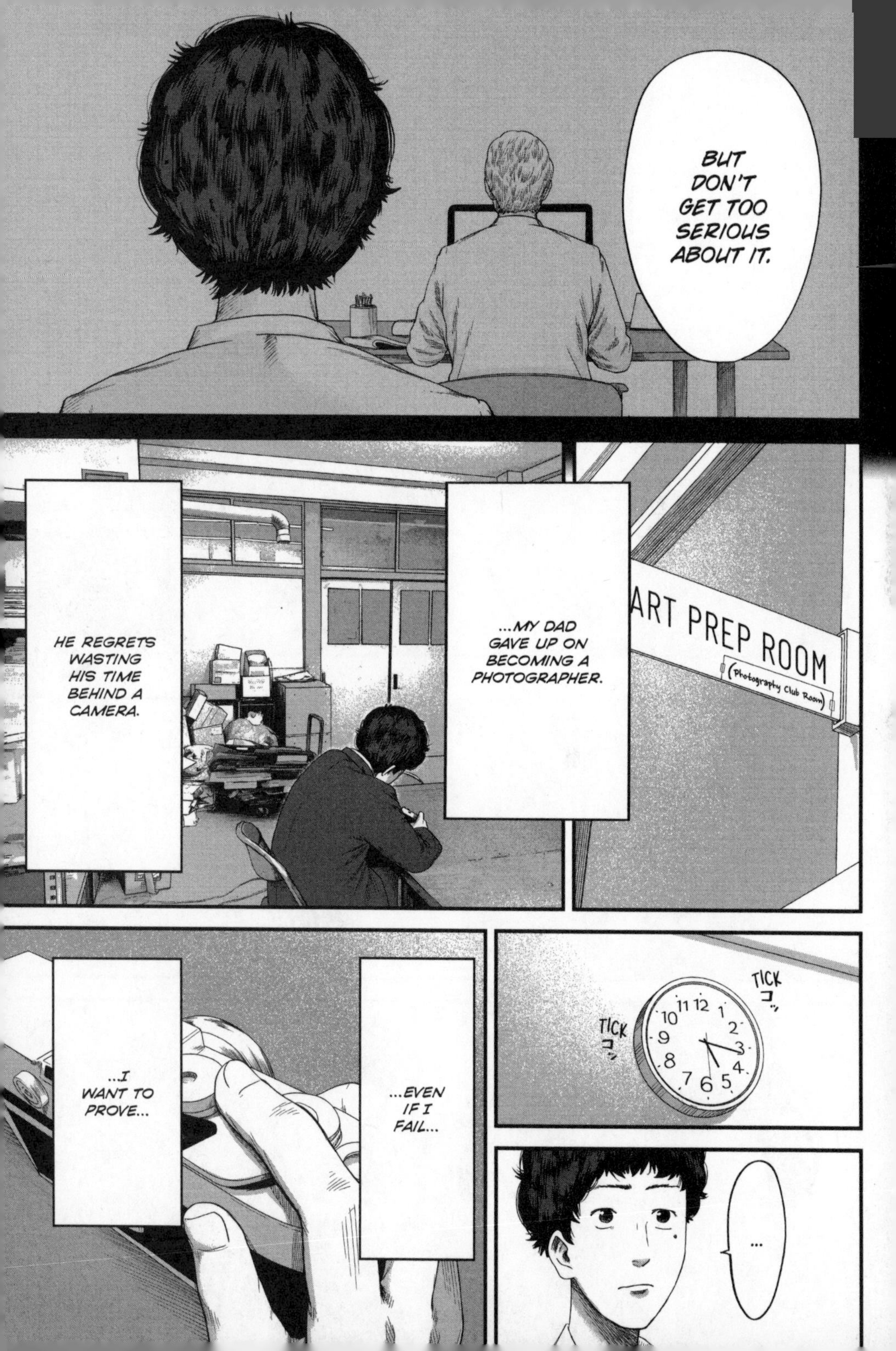
BUT DON'T GET TOO SERIOUS ABOUT IT.
ART PREP ROOM
(Photography Club Room)
...MY DAD GAVE UP ON BECOMING A PHOTOGRAPHER.
HE REGRETS WASTING HIS TIME BEHIND A CAMERA.
TICK コッ
TICK コッ
...
...EVEN IF I FAIL...
...I WANT TO PROVE...

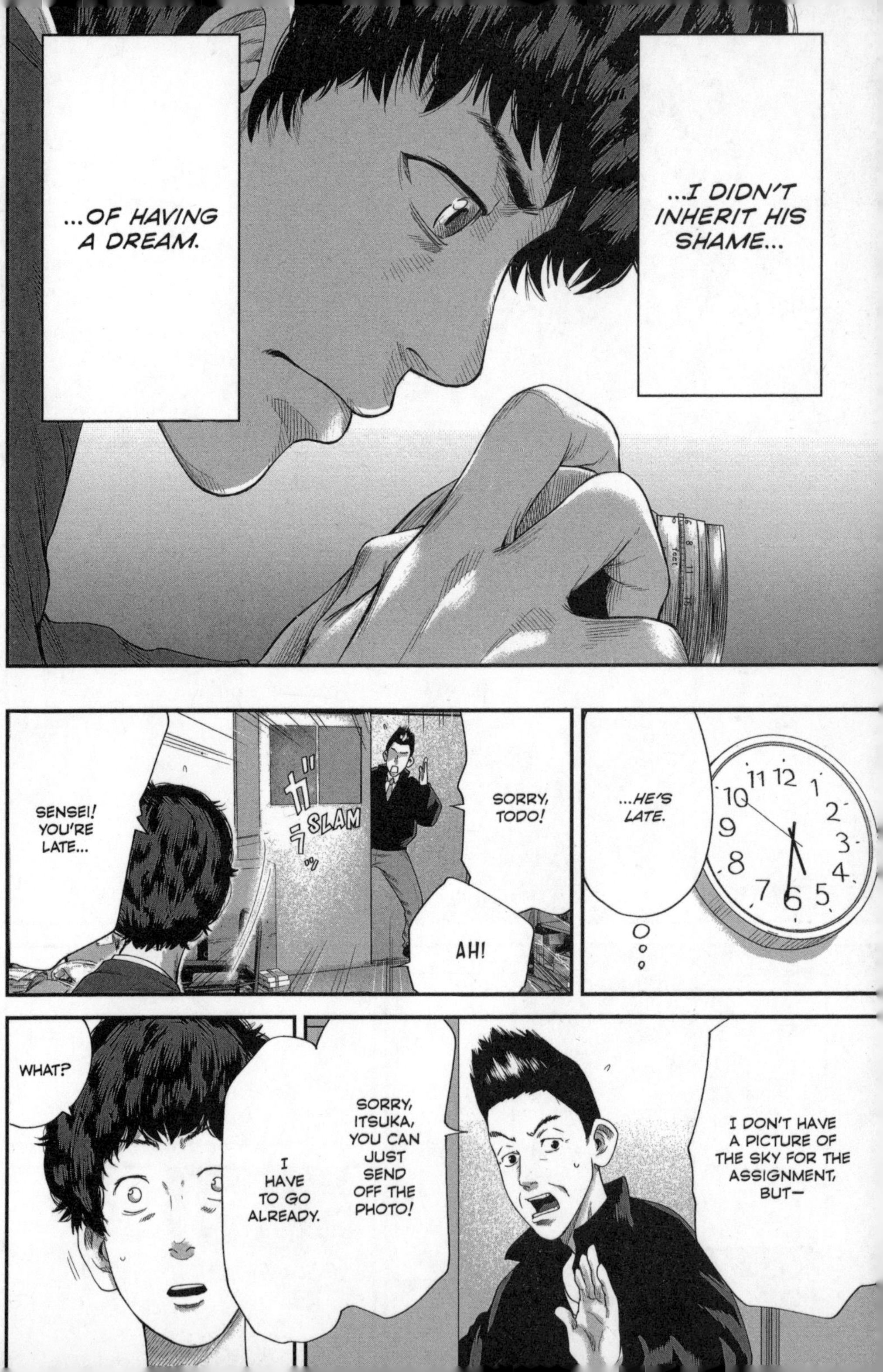
...I DIDN'T INHERIT HIS SHAME...
...OF HAVING A DREAM.
...HE'S LATE.
SORRY, TODO!
SENSEI! YOU'RE LATE...
SLAM
AH!
I DON'T HAVE A PICTURE OF THE SKY FOR THE ASSIGNMENT, BUT—
SORRY, ITSUKA, YOU CAN JUST SEND OFF THE PHOTO!
I HAVE TO GO ALREADY.
WHAT?

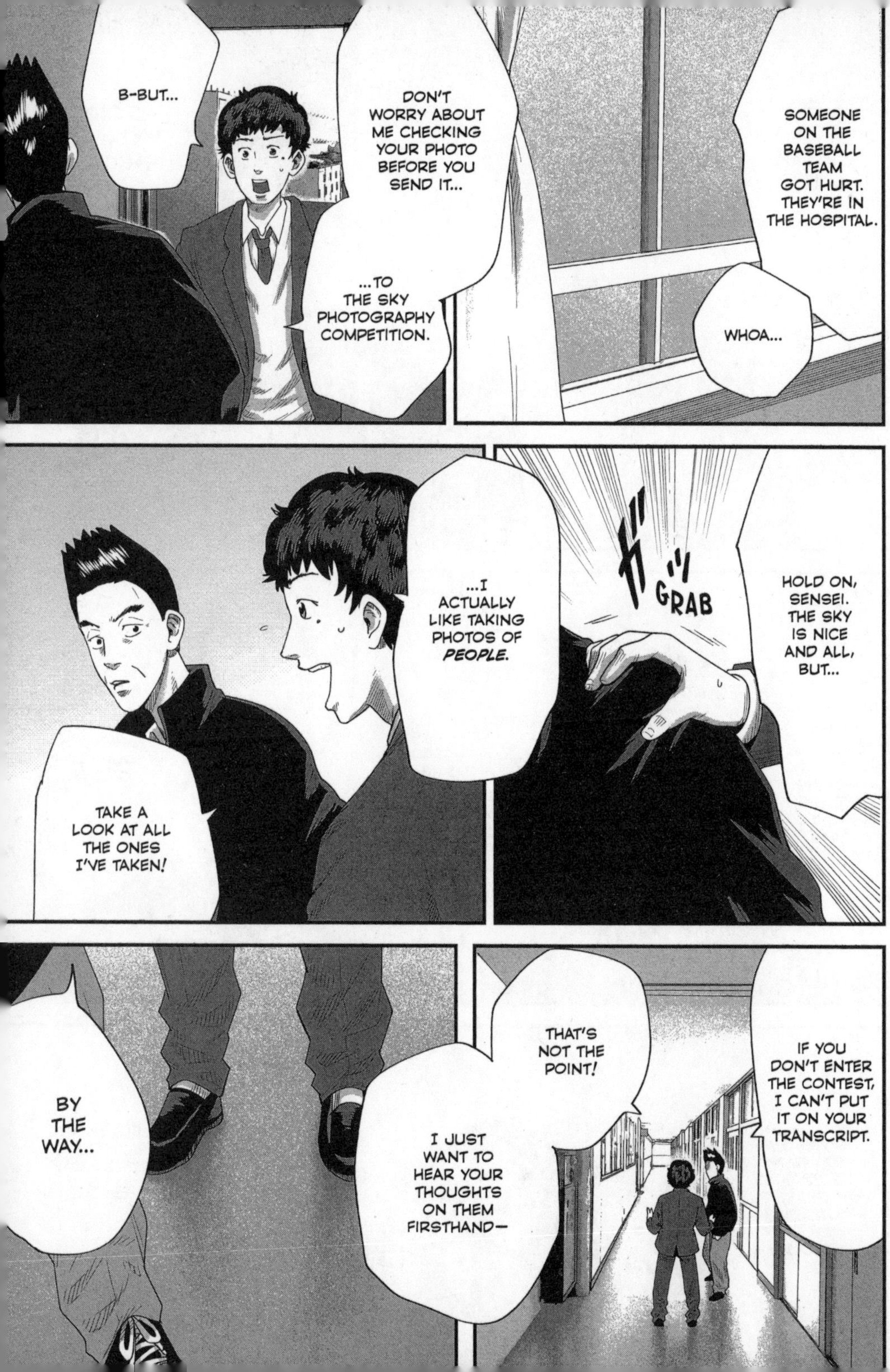
SOMEONE ON THE BASEBALL TEAM GOT HURT. THEY'RE IN THE HOSPITAL.
WHOA...
DON'T WORRY ABOUT ME CHECKING YOUR PHOTO BEFORE YOU SEND IT...
B-BUT...
...TO THE SKY PHOTOGRAPHY COMPETITION.
HOLD ON, SENSEI. THE SKY IS NICE AND ALL, BUT...
GRAB
...I ACTUALLY LIKE TAKING PHOTOS OF *PEOPLE*.
TAKE A LOOK AT ALL THE ONES I'VE TAKEN!
IF YOU DON'T ENTER THE CONTEST, I CAN'T PUT IT ON YOUR TRANSCRIPT.
THAT'S NOT THE POINT!
I JUST WANT TO HEAR YOUR THOUGHTS ON THEM FIRSTHAND—
BY THE WAY...

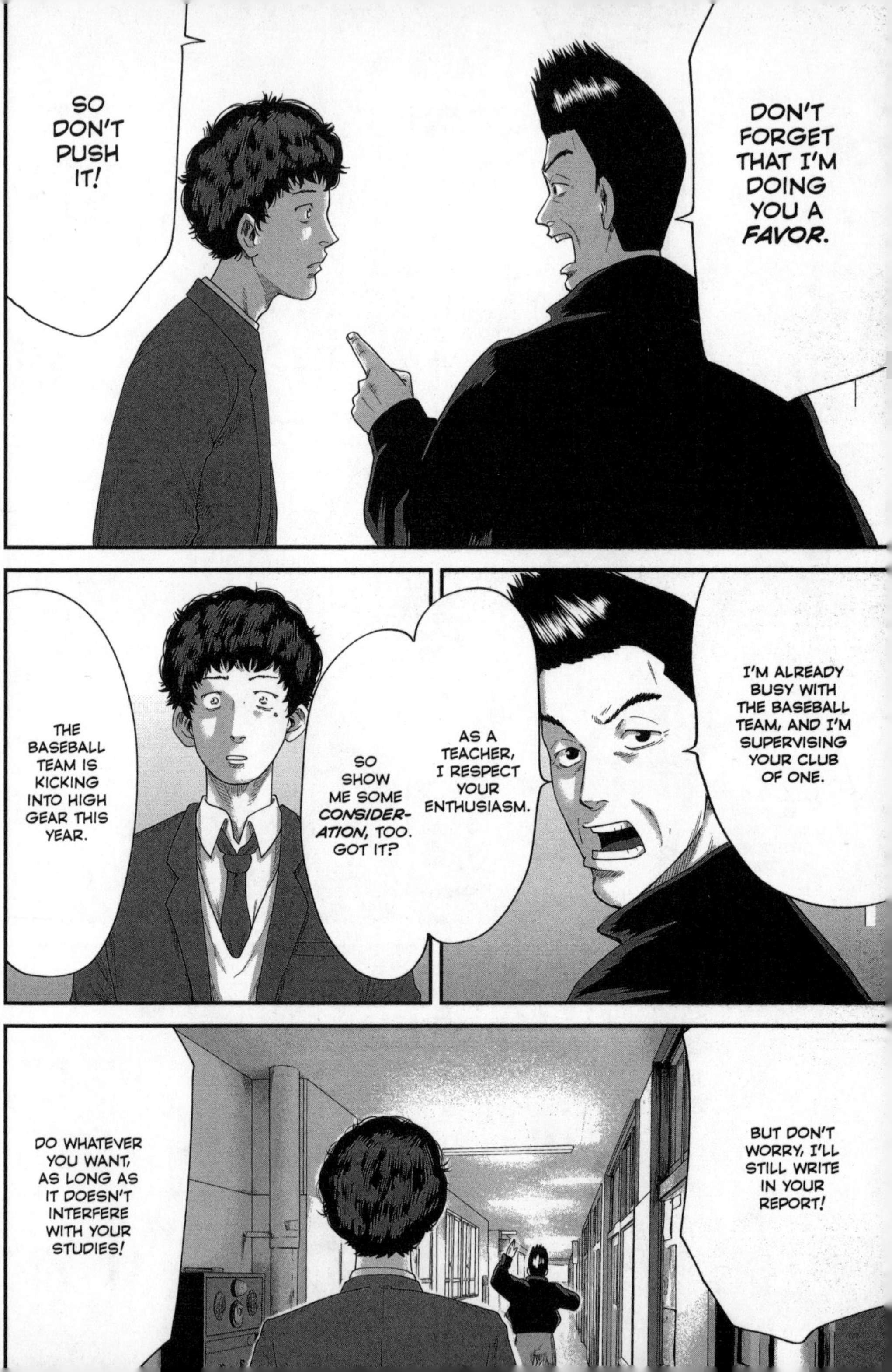
DON'T FORGET THAT I'M DOING YOU A *FAVOR*.
SO DON'T PUSH IT!
I'M ALREADY BUSY WITH THE BASEBALL TEAM, AND I'M SUPERVISING YOUR CLUB OF ONE.
AS A TEACHER, I RESPECT YOUR ENTHUSIASM.
SO SHOW ME SOME *CONSIDERATION*, TOO. GOT IT?
THE BASEBALL TEAM IS KICKING INTO HIGH GEAR THIS YEAR.
BUT DON'T WORRY, I'LL STILL WRITE IN YOUR REPORT!
DO WHATEVER YOU WANT, AS LONG AS IT DOESN'T INTERFERE WITH YOUR STUDIES!

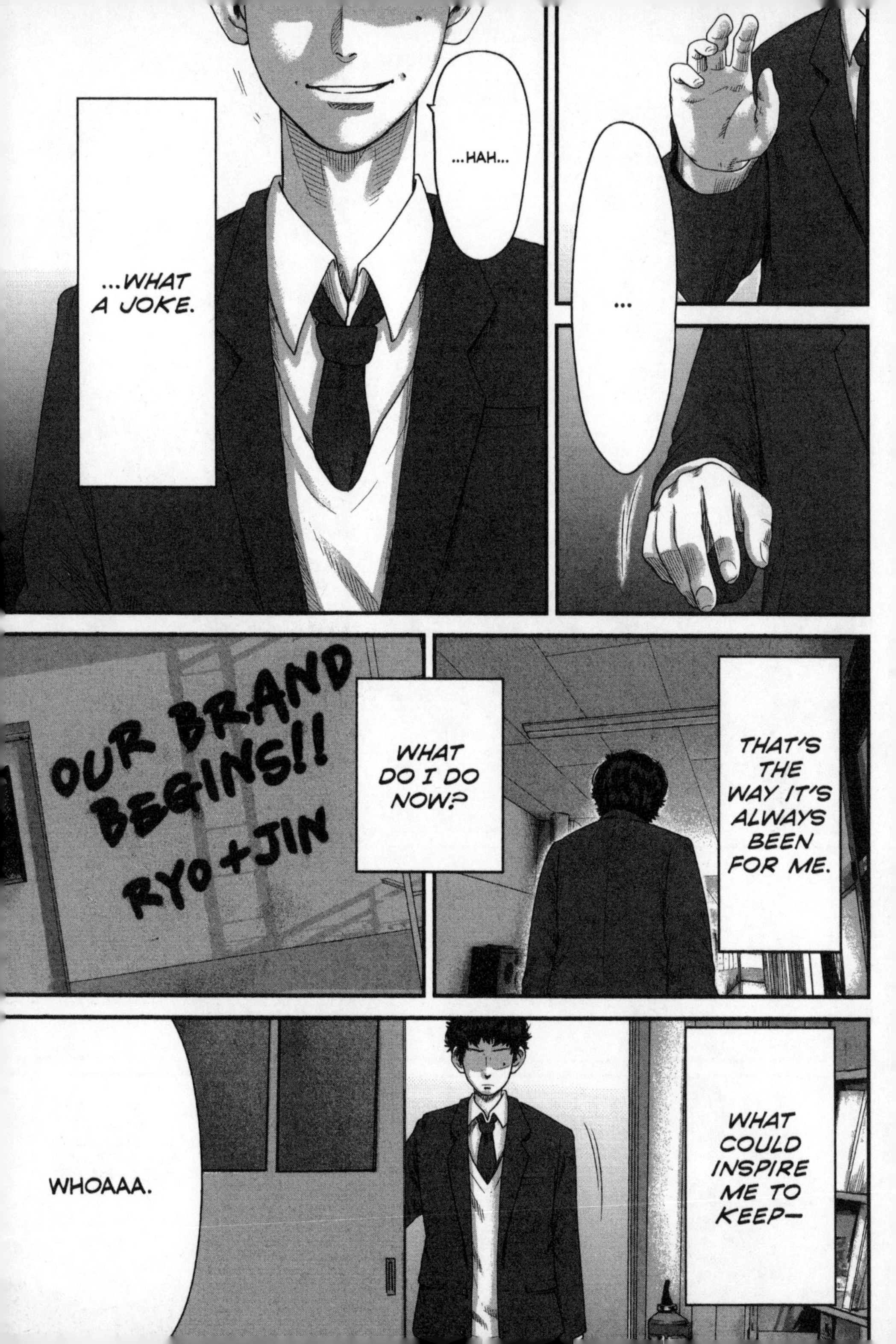
...
...HAH...
...WHAT A JOKE.
THAT'S THE WAY IT'S ALWAYS BEEN FOR ME.
WHAT DO I DO NOW?
OUR BRAND BEGINS!! RYO+JIN
WHAT COULD INSPIRE ME TO KEEP—
WHOAAA.

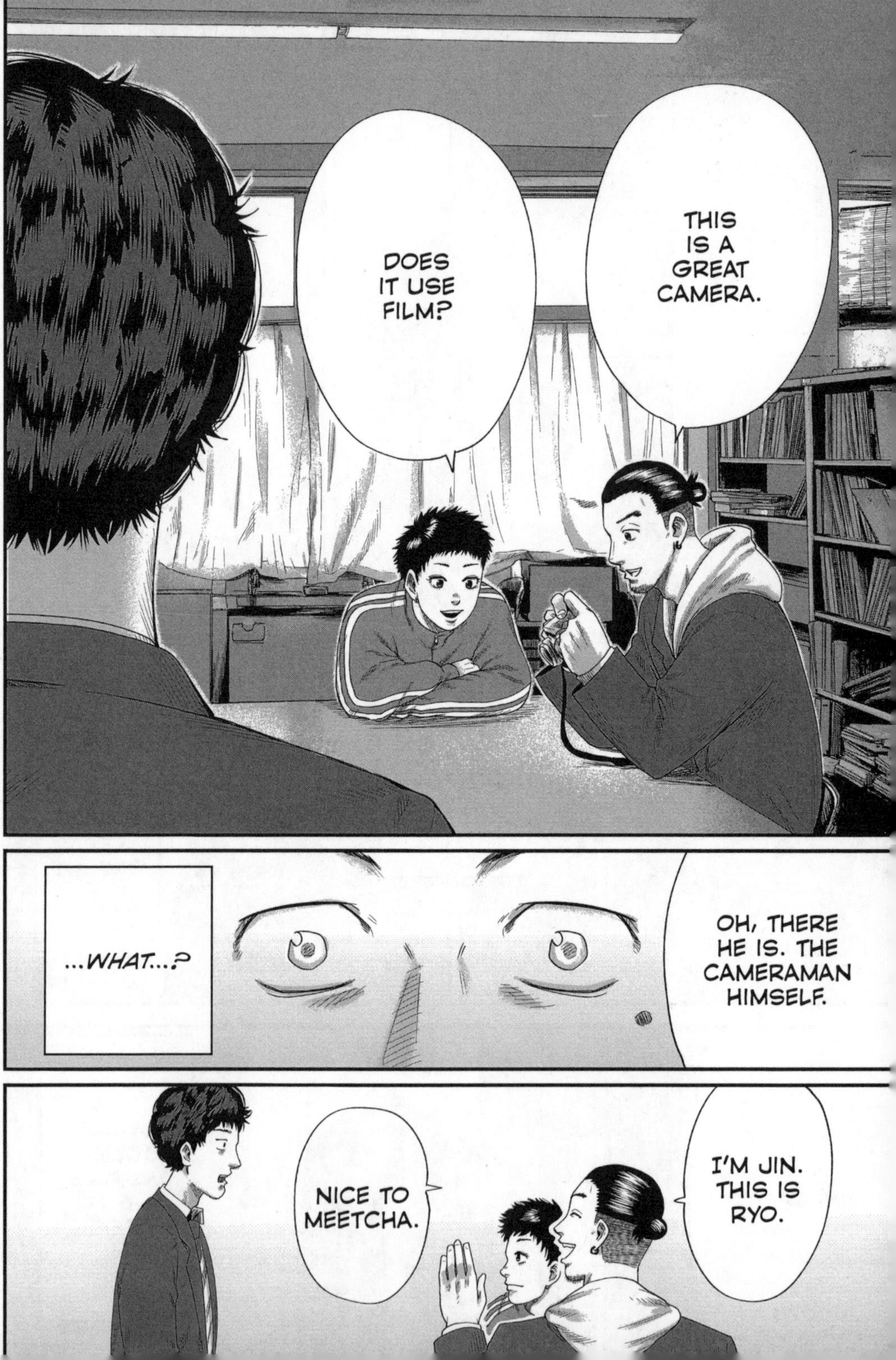
THIS IS A GREAT CAMERA.
DOES IT USE FILM?
OH, THERE HE IS. THE CAMERAMAN HIMSELF.
...WHAT...?
I'M JIN. THIS IS RYO.
NICE TO MEETCHA.

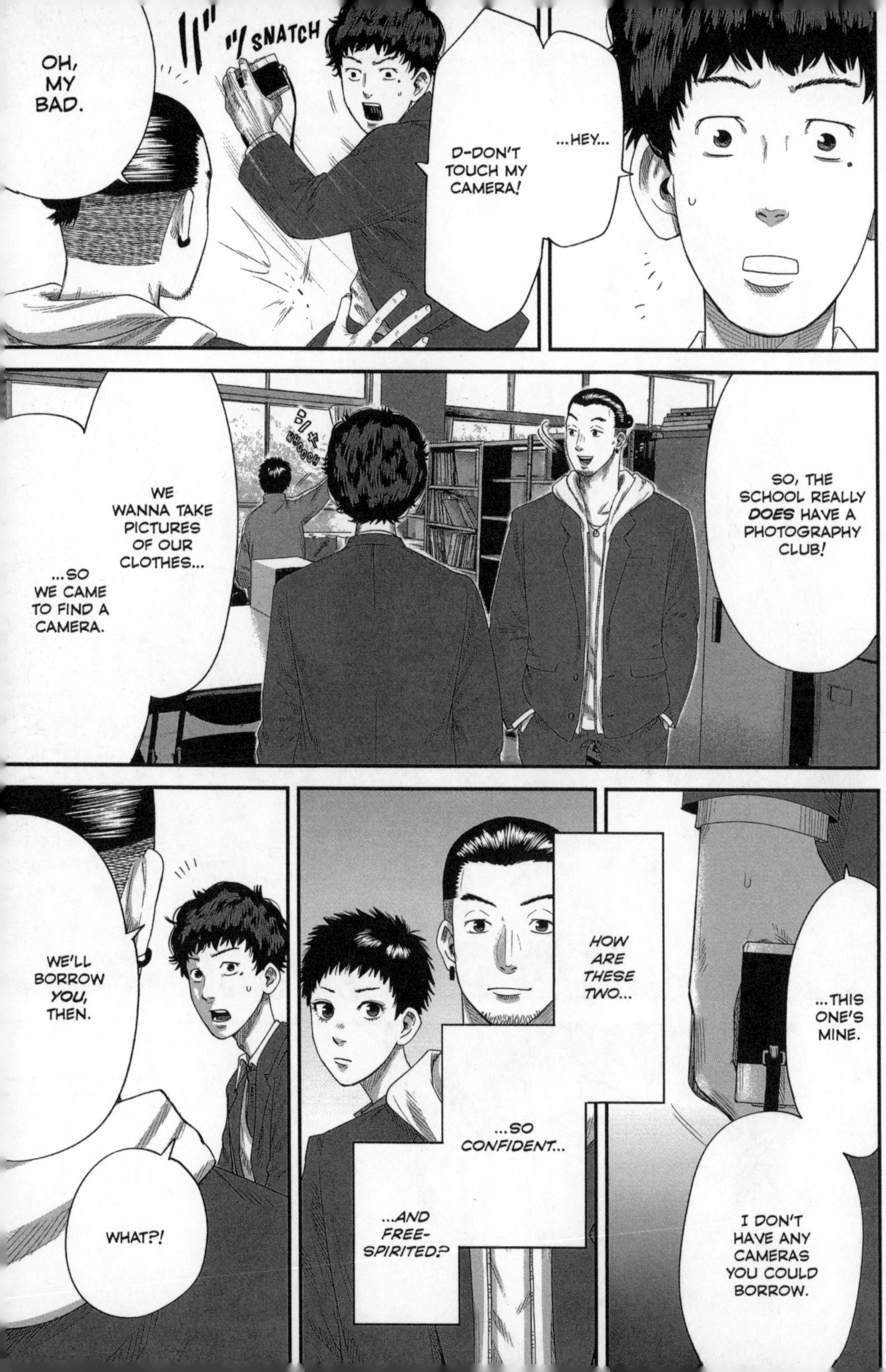
...HEY...
SNATCH
D-DON'T TOUCH MY CAMERA!
OH, MY BAD.
SO, THE SCHOOL REALLY *DOES* HAVE A PHOTOGRAPHY CLUB!
WHOOSH
WE WANNA TAKE PICTURES OF OUR CLOTHES...
...SO WE CAME TO FIND A CAMERA.
...THIS ONE'S MINE.
I DON'T HAVE ANY CAMERAS YOU COULD BORROW.
HOW ARE THESE TWO...
...SO CONFIDENT...
...AND FREE-SPIRITED?
WE'LL BORROW *YOU*, THEN.
WHAT?!

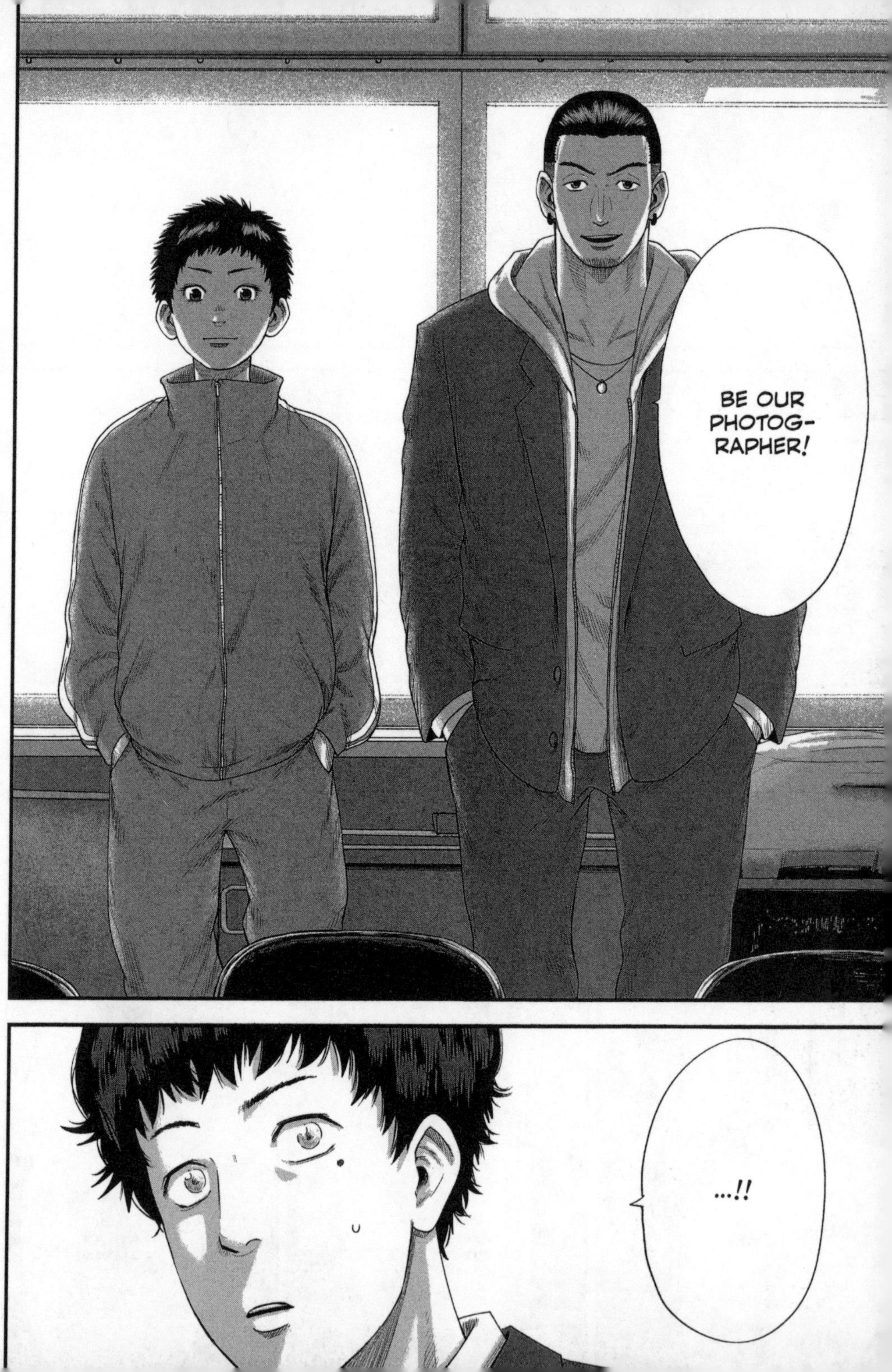
BE OUR PHOTOG-RAPHER!
...!!

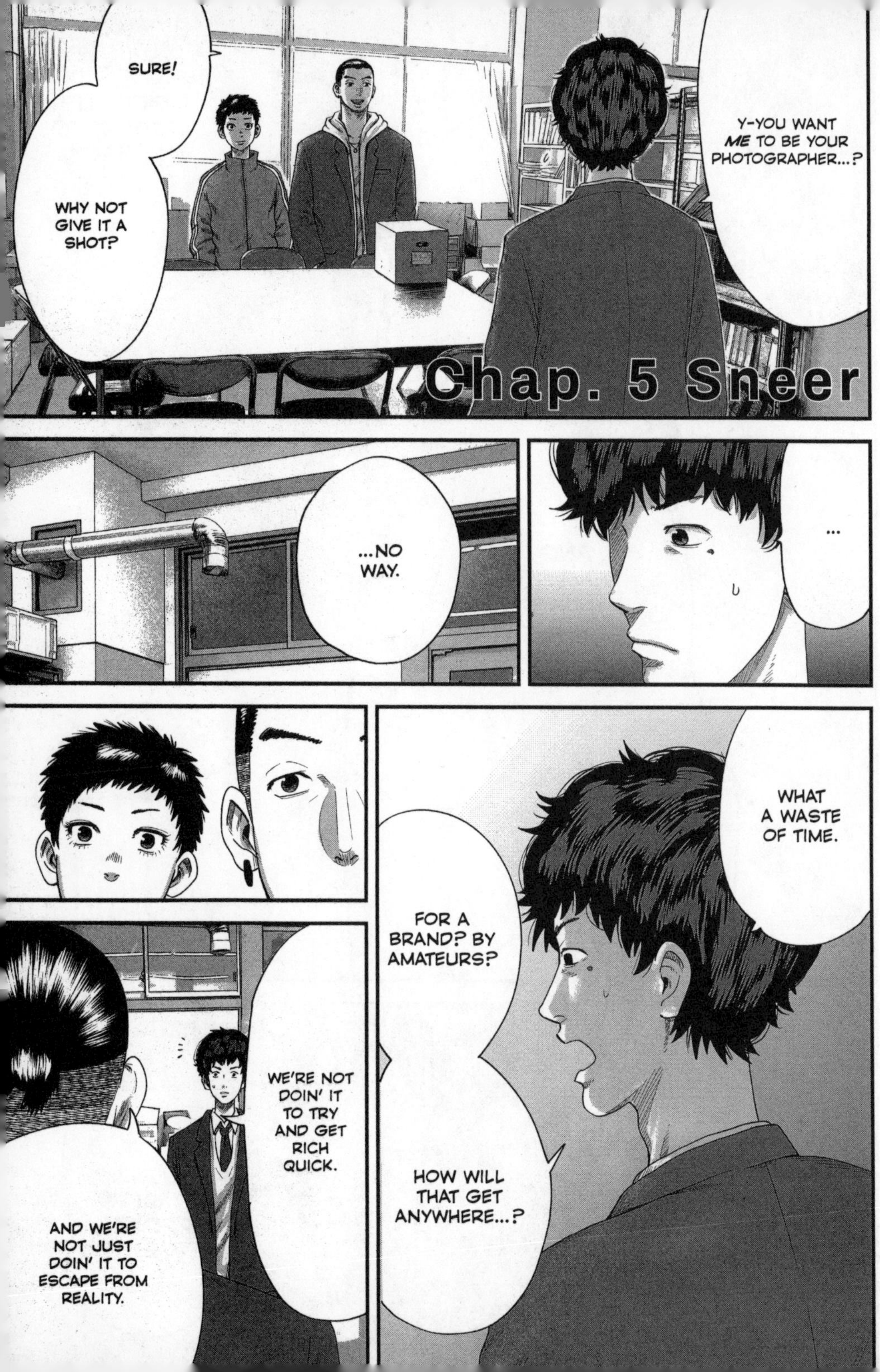
Y-YOU WANT *ME* TO BE YOUR PHOTOGRAPHER...?
SURE!
WHY NOT GIVE IT A SHOT?
Chap. 5 Sneer
...
...NO WAY.
WHAT A WASTE OF TIME.
FOR A BRAND? BY AMATEURS?
HOW WILL THAT GET ANYWHERE...?
WE'RE NOT DOIN' IT TO TRY AND GET RICH QUICK.
AND WE'RE NOT JUST DOIN' IT TO ESCAPE FROM REALITY.

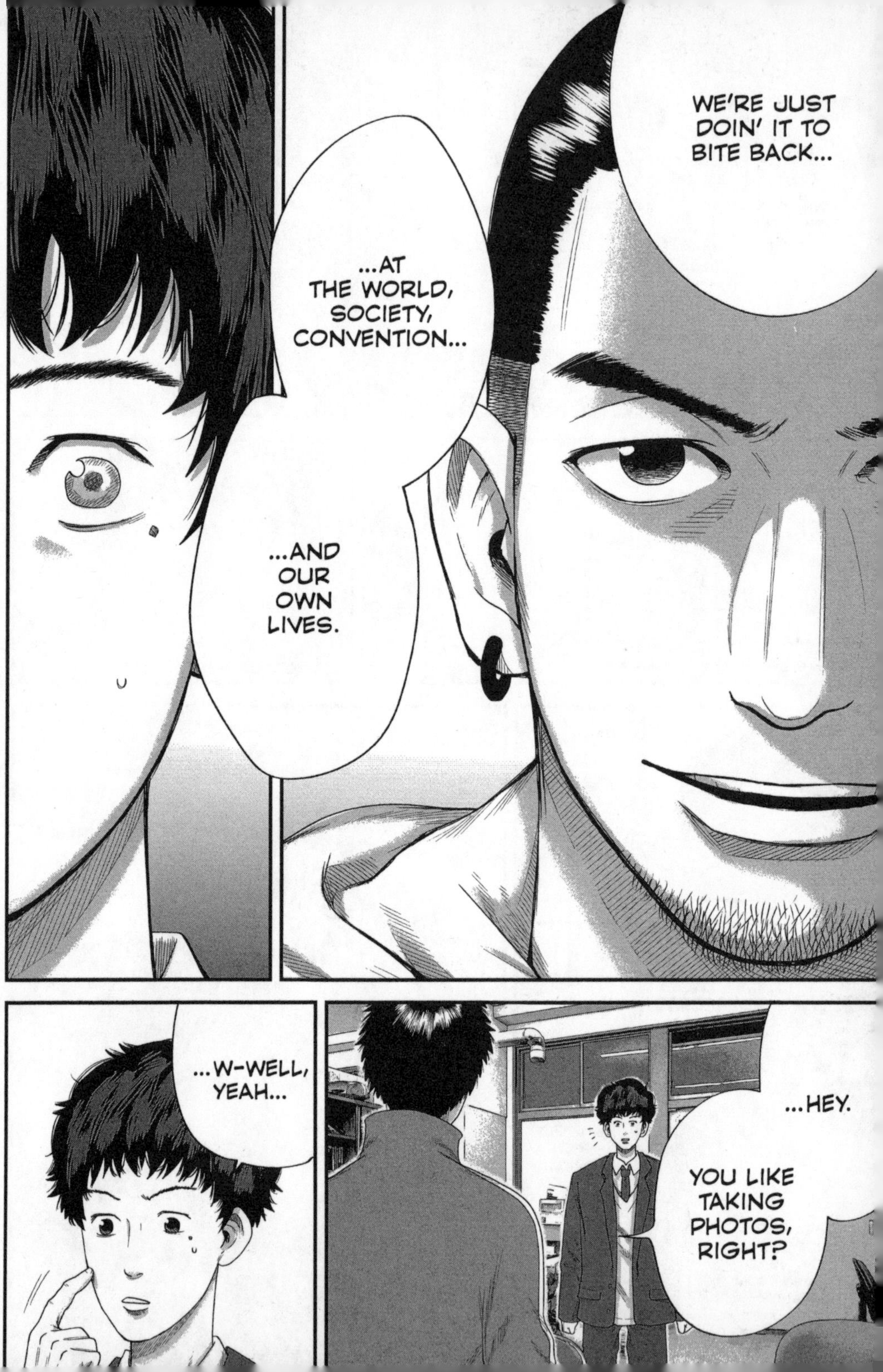
WE'RE JUST DOIN' IT TO BITE BACK...
...AT THE WORLD, SOCIETY, CONVENTION...
...AND OUR OWN LIVES.
...HEY.
YOU LIKE TAKING PHOTOS, RIGHT?
...W-WELL, YEAH...

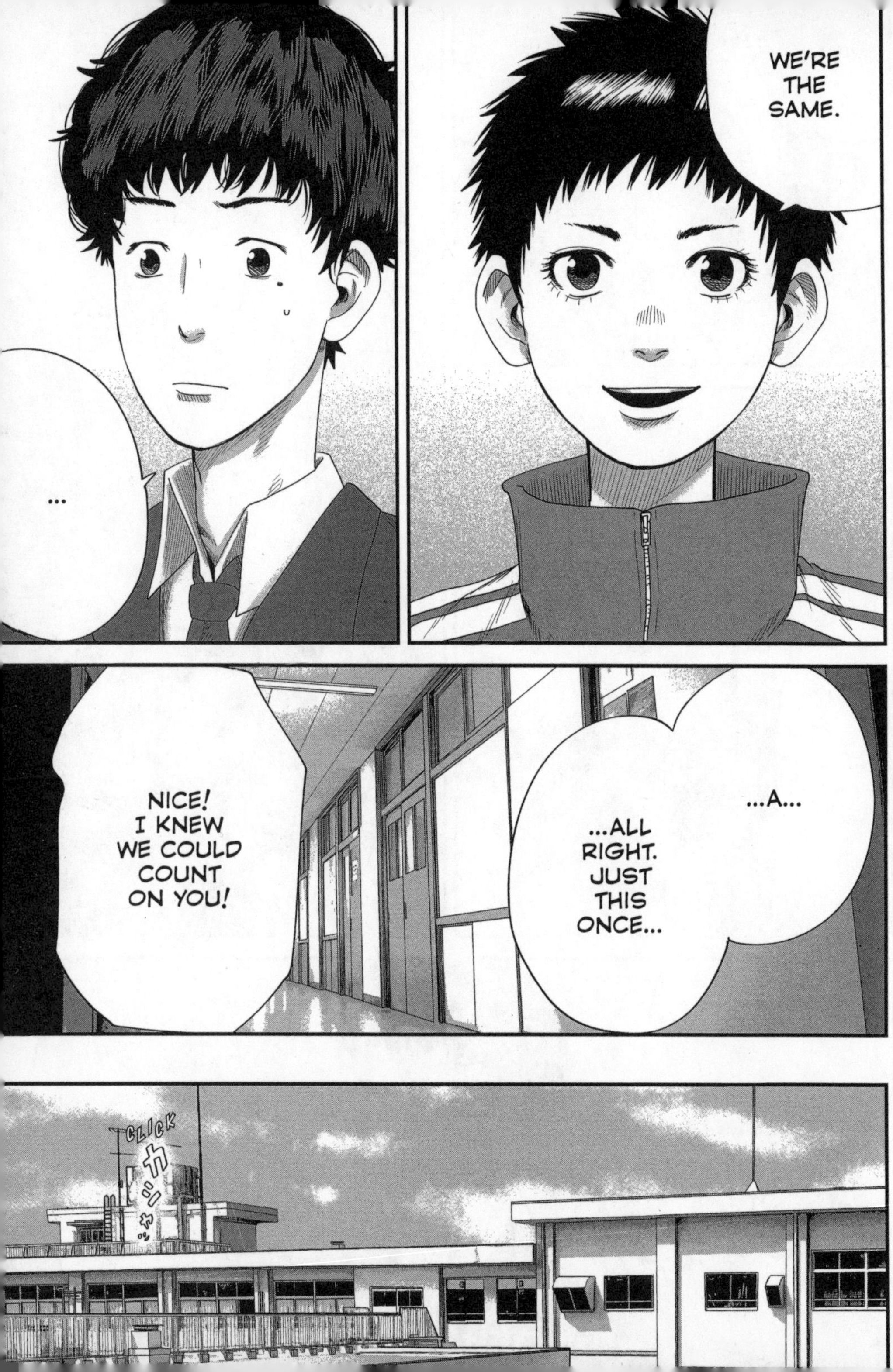
WE'RE THE SAME.
...
...A...
...ALL RIGHT. JUST THIS ONCE...
NICE! I KNEW WE COULD COUNT ON YOU!
CLICK

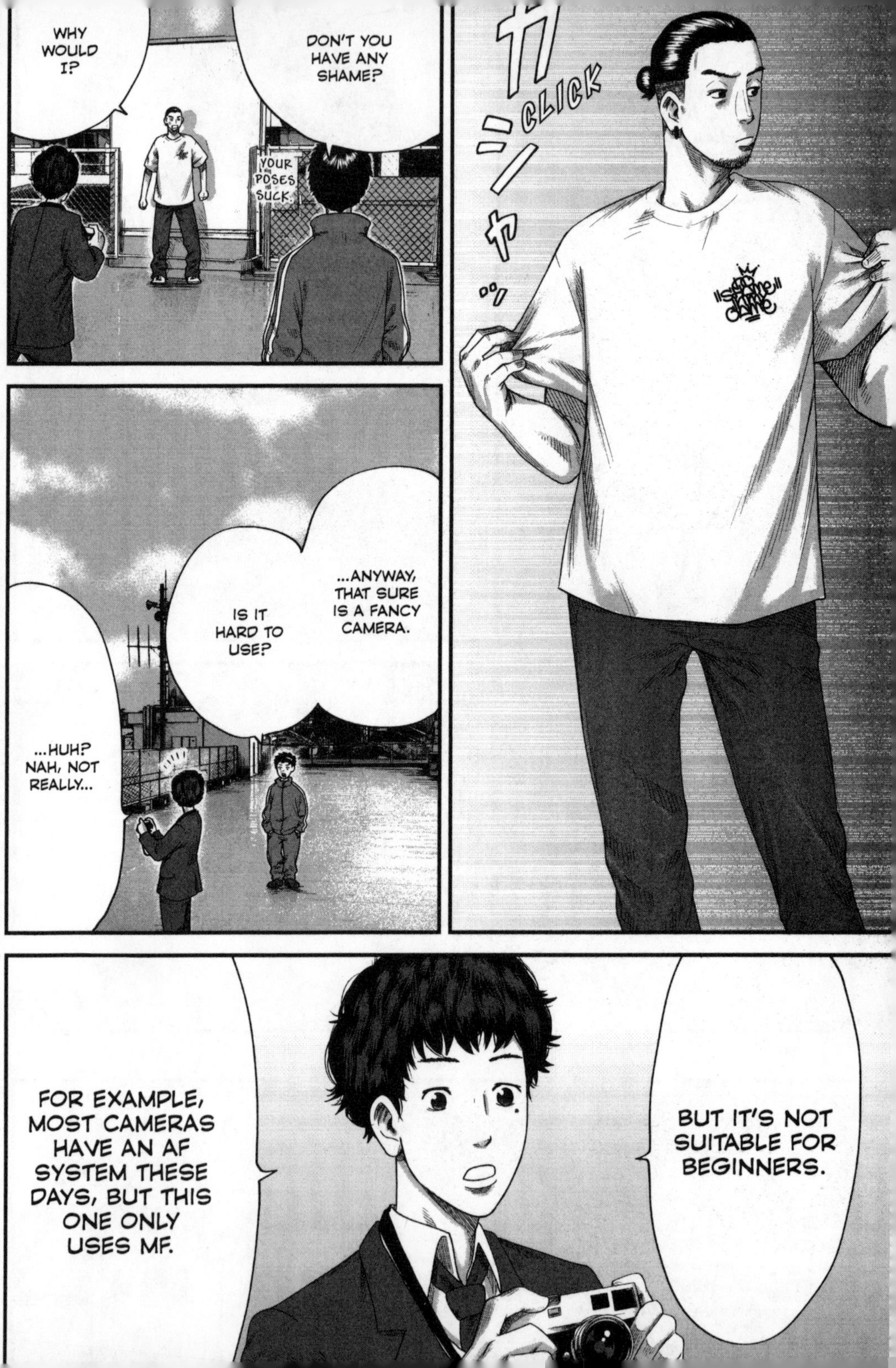
CLICK
DON'T YOU HAVE ANY SHAME?
WHY WOULD I?
YOUR POSES SUCK
...ANYWAY, THAT SURE IS A FANCY CAMERA.
IS IT HARD TO USE?
...HUH? NAH, NOT REALLY...
BUT IT'S NOT SUITABLE FOR BEGINNERS.
FOR EXAMPLE, MOST CAMERAS HAVE AN AF SYSTEM THESE DAYS, BUT THIS ONE ONLY USES MF.

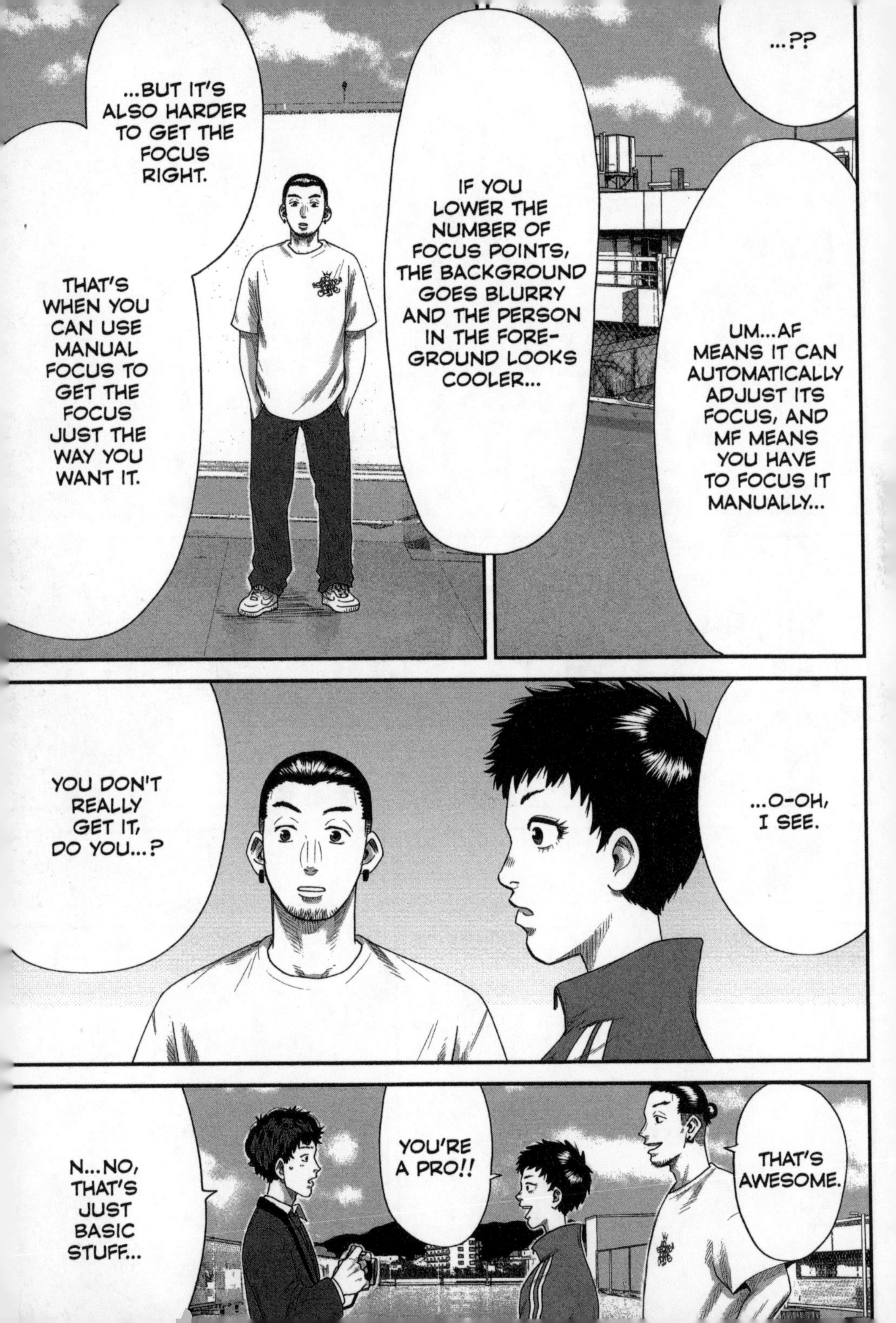
...??
UM...AF MEANS IT CAN AUTOMATICALLY ADJUST ITS FOCUS, AND MF MEANS YOU HAVE TO FOCUS IT MANUALLY...
IF YOU LOWER THE NUMBER OF FOCUS POINTS, THE BACKGROUND GOES BLURRY AND THE PERSON IN THE FORE-GROUND LOOKS COOLER...
...BUT IT'S ALSO HARDER TO GET THE FOCUS RIGHT.
THAT'S WHEN YOU CAN USE MANUAL FOCUS TO GET THE FOCUS JUST THE WAY YOU WANT IT.
...O-OH, I SEE.
YOU DON'T REALLY GET IT, DO YOU...?
THAT'S AWESOME.
YOU'RE A PRO!!
N...NO, THAT'S JUST BASIC STUFF...

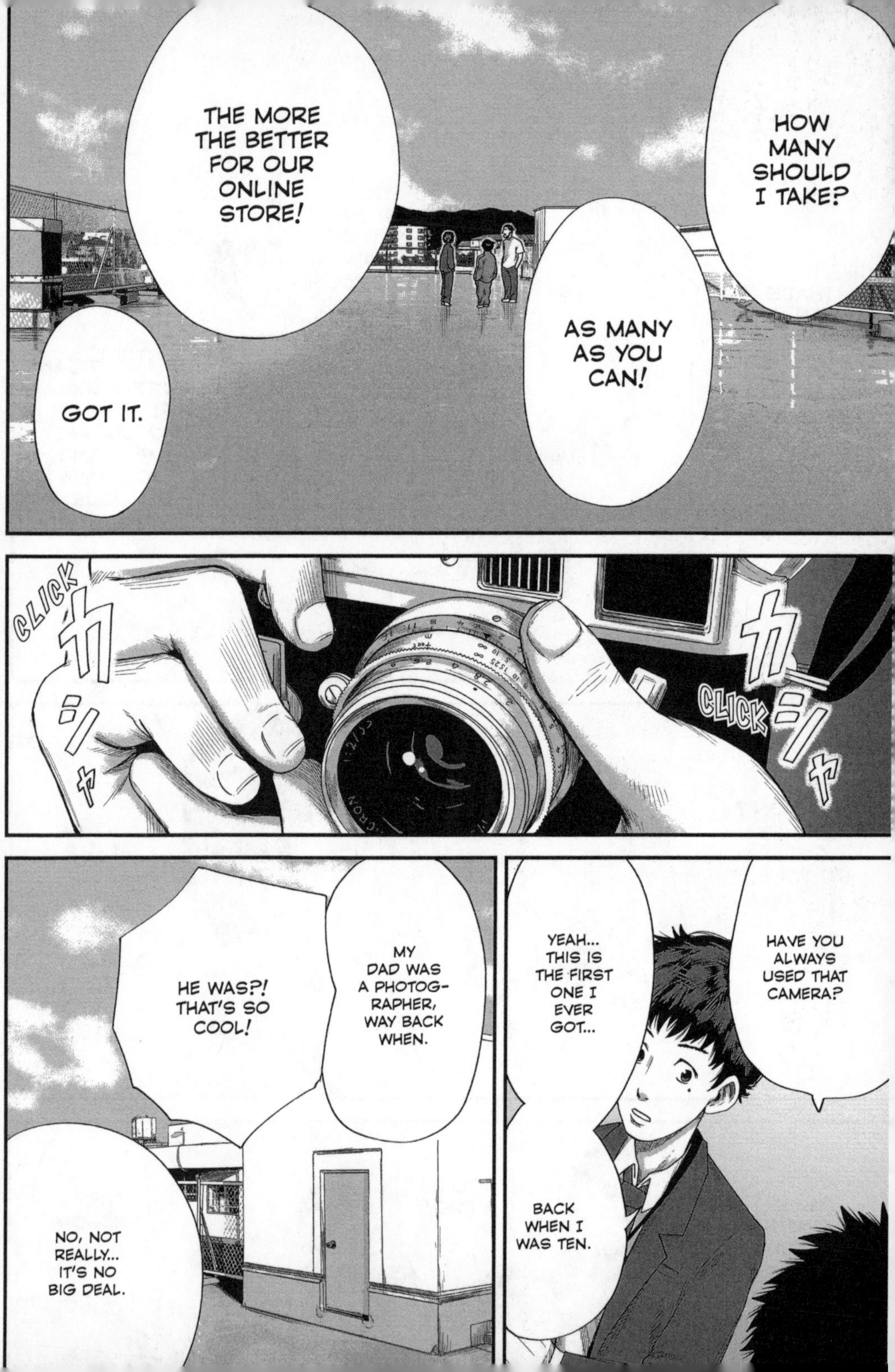
HOW MANY SHOULD I TAKE?
AS MANY AS YOU CAN!
THE MORE THE BETTER FOR OUR ONLINE STORE!
GOT IT.
CLICK
カシャ
CLICK
カシャ
HAVE YOU ALWAYS USED THAT CAMERA?
YEAH... THIS IS THE FIRST ONE I EVER GOT...
BACK WHEN I WAS TEN.
MY DAD WAS A PHOTOG-RAPHER, WAY BACK WHEN.
HE WAS?! THAT'S SO COOL!
NO, NOT REALLY... IT'S NO BIG DEAL.

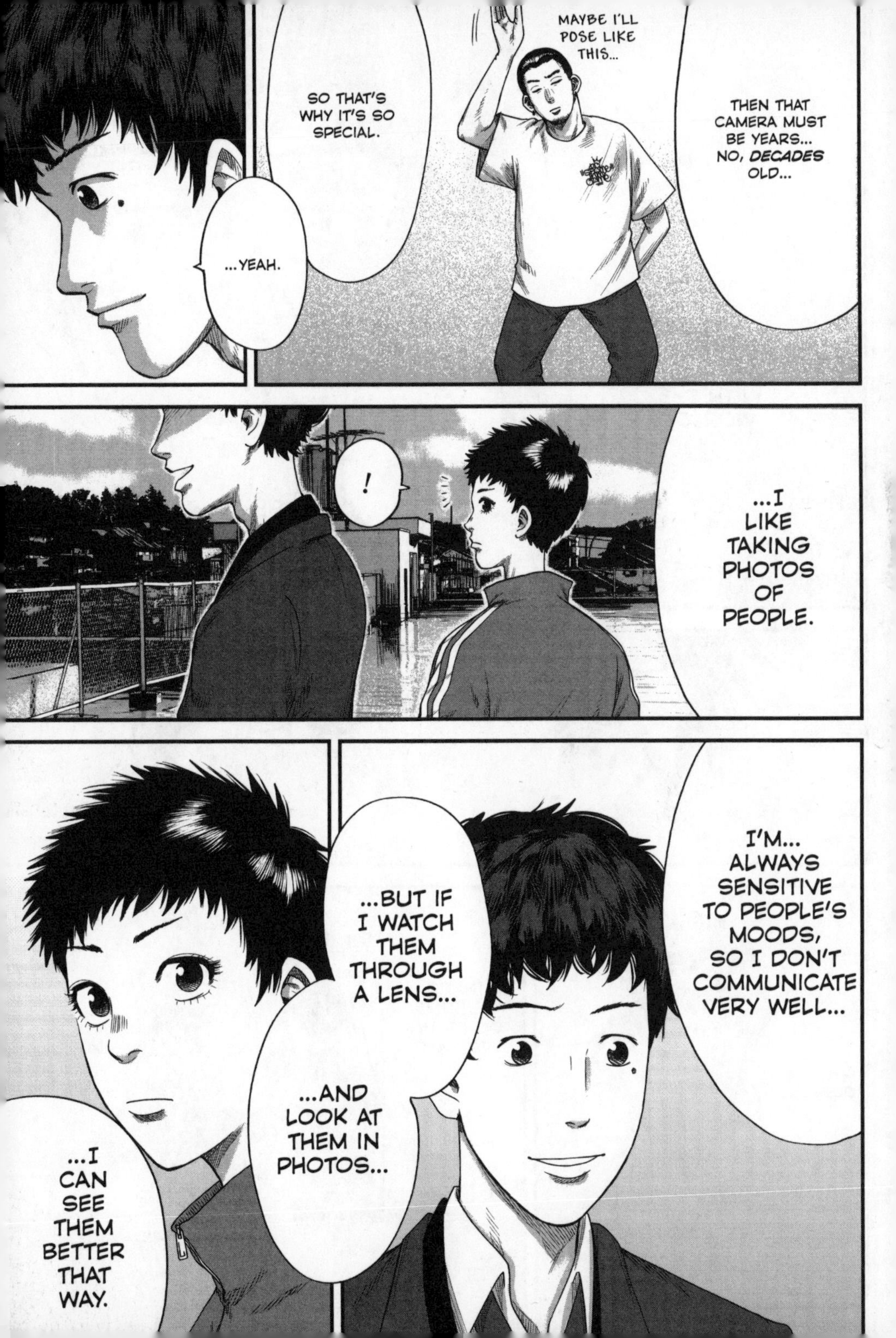
THEN THAT CAMERA MUST BE YEARS... NO, *DECADES* OLD...
MAYBE I'LL POSE LIKE THIS...
SO THAT'S WHY IT'S SO SPECIAL.
...YEAH.
...I LIKE TAKING PHOTOS OF PEOPLE.
!
I'M... ALWAYS SENSITIVE TO PEOPLE'S MOODS, SO I DON'T COMMUNICATE VERY WELL...
...BUT IF I WATCH THEM THROUGH A LENS...
...AND LOOK AT THEM IN PHOTOS...
...I CAN SEE THEM BETTER THAT WAY.

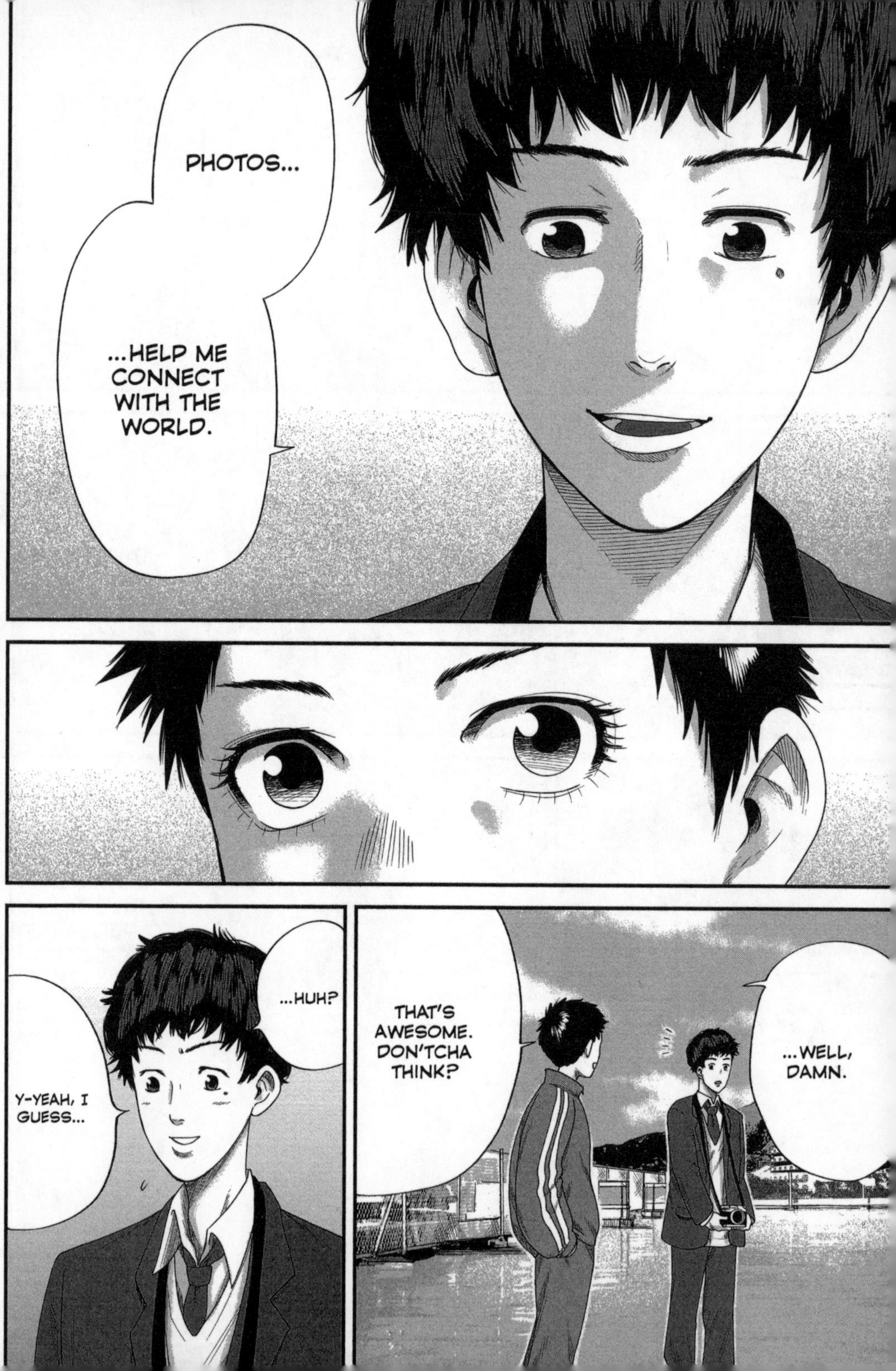
PHOTOS...
...HELP ME CONNECT WITH THE WORLD.
...WELL, DAMN.
THAT'S AWESOME. DON'TCHA THINK?
...HUH?
Y-YEAH, I GUESS...

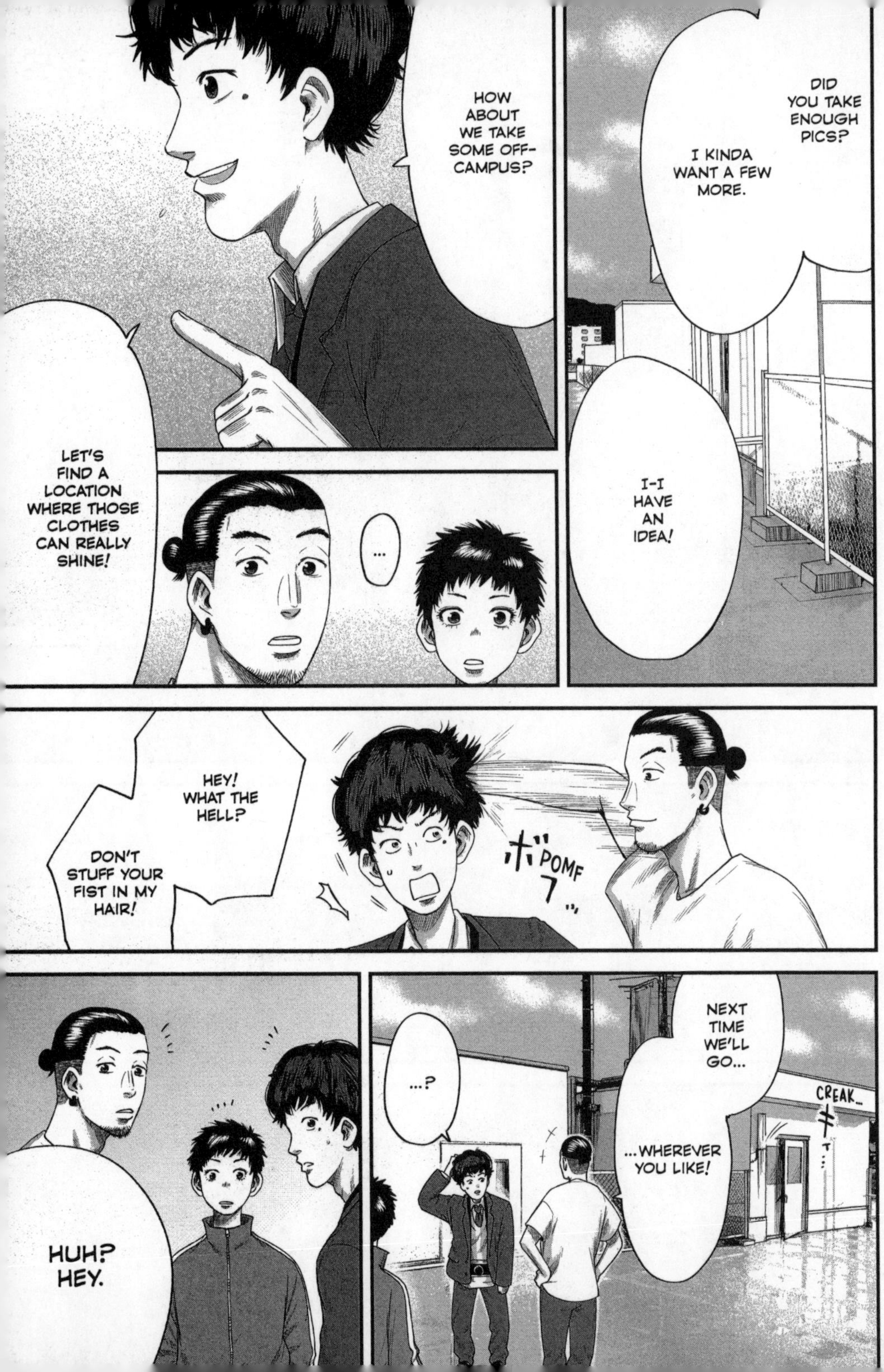
DID YOU TAKE ENOUGH PICS?
I KINDA WANT A FEW MORE.
I-I HAVE AN IDEA!
HOW ABOUT WE TAKE SOME OFF-CAMPUS?
LET'S FIND A LOCATION WHERE THOSE CLOTHES CAN REALLY SHINE!
...
HEY! WHAT THE HELL?
DON'T STUFF YOUR FIST IN MY HAIR!
ボフ POMF
NEXT TIME WE'LL GO...
CREAK...
...WHEREVER YOU LIKE!
...?
HUH? HEY.

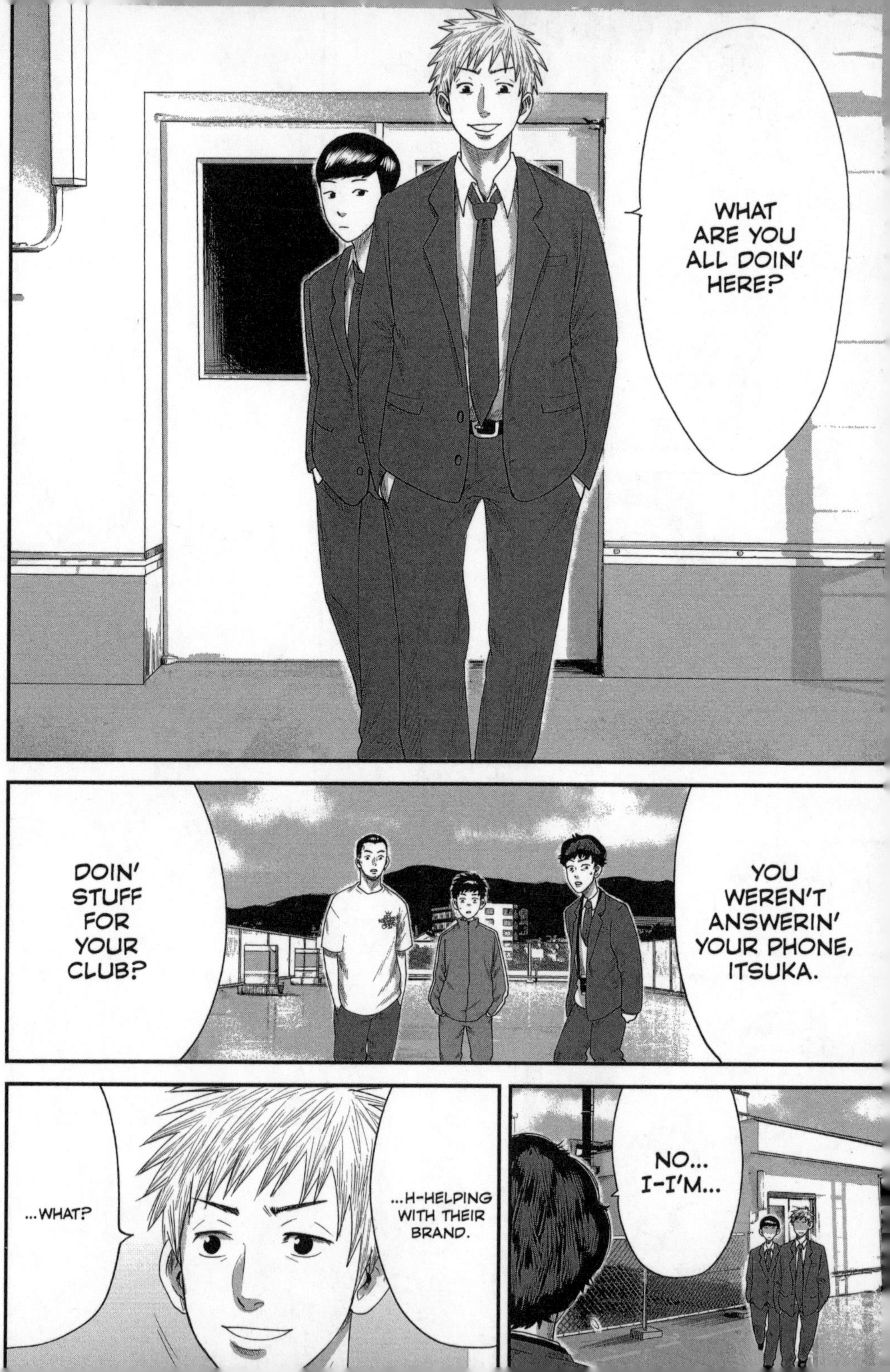
WHAT ARE YOU ALL DOIN' HERE?
YOU WEREN'T ANSWERIN' YOUR PHONE, ITSUKA.
DOIN' STUFF FOR YOUR CLUB?
NO... I-I'M...
...H-HELPING WITH THEIR BRAND.
...WHAT?

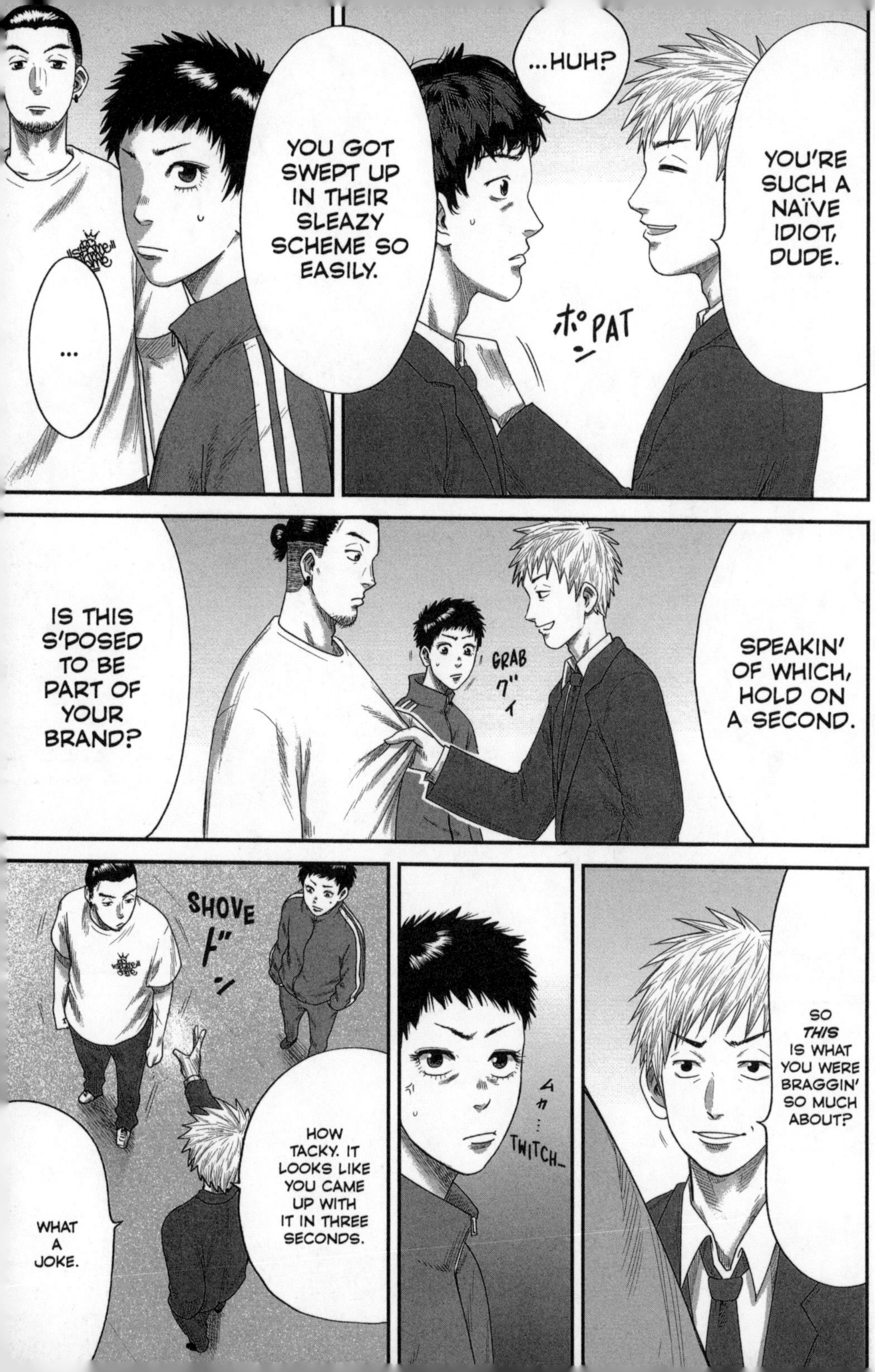
YOU'RE SUCH A NAÏVE IDIOT, DUDE.
ポン PAT
...HUH?
YOU GOT SWEPT UP IN THEIR SLEAZY SCHEME SO EASILY.
...
SPEAKIN' OF WHICH, HOLD ON A SECOND.
GRAB グイ
IS THIS S'POSED TO BE PART OF YOUR BRAND?
SO *THIS* IS WHAT YOU WERE BRAGGIN' SO MUCH ABOUT?
ムカ… TWITCH
SHOVE ドン
HOW TACKY. IT LOOKS LIKE YOU CAME UP WITH IT IN THREE SECONDS.
WHAT A JOKE.

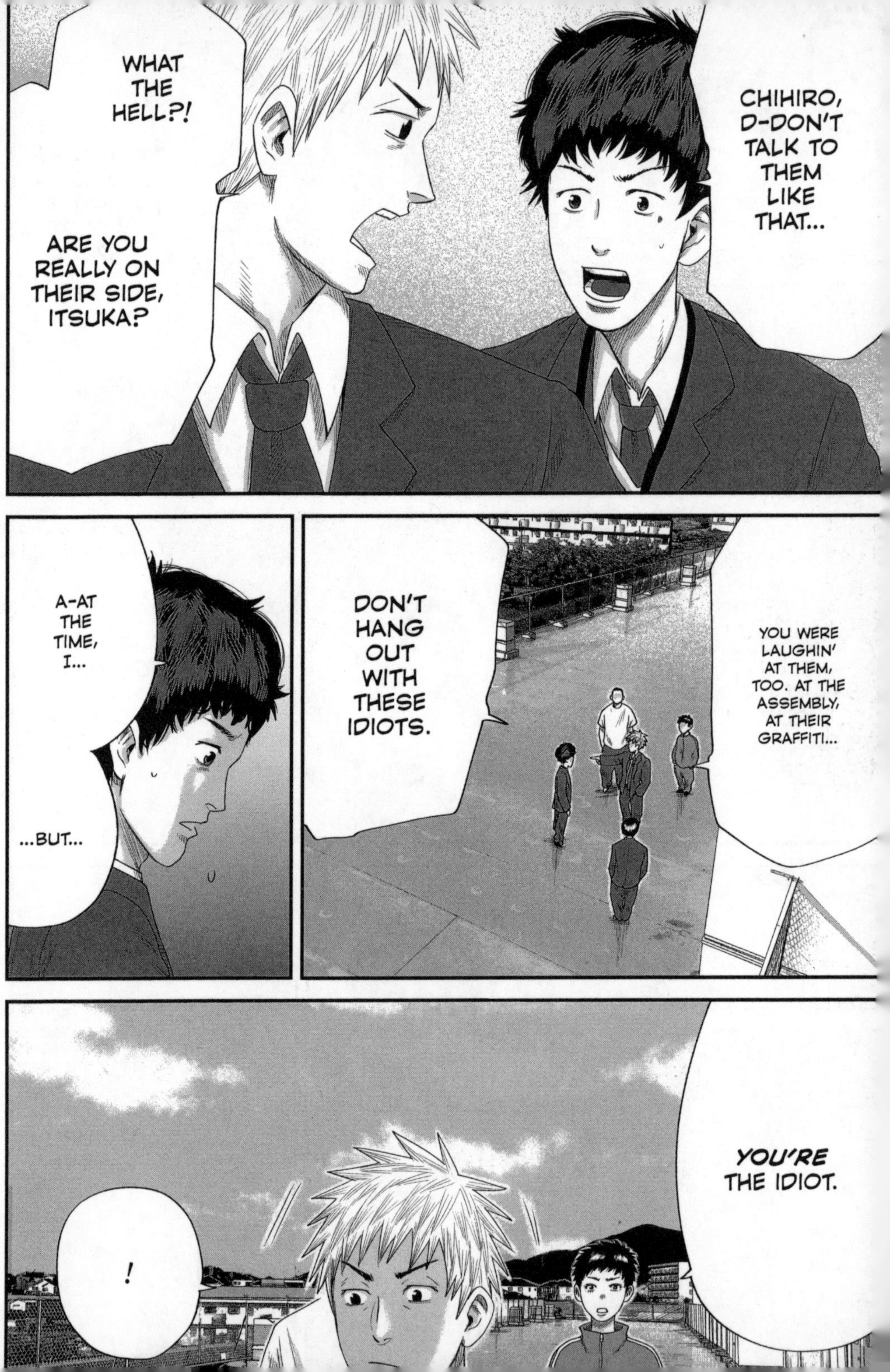
CHIHIRO, D-DON'T TALK TO THEM LIKE THAT...
WHAT THE HELL?!
ARE YOU REALLY ON THEIR SIDE, ITSUKA?
YOU WERE LAUGHIN' AT THEM, TOO. AT THE ASSEMBLY, AT THEIR GRAFFITI...
DON'T HANG OUT WITH THESE IDIOTS.
A-AT THE TIME, I...
...BUT...
YOU'RE THE IDIOT.
!

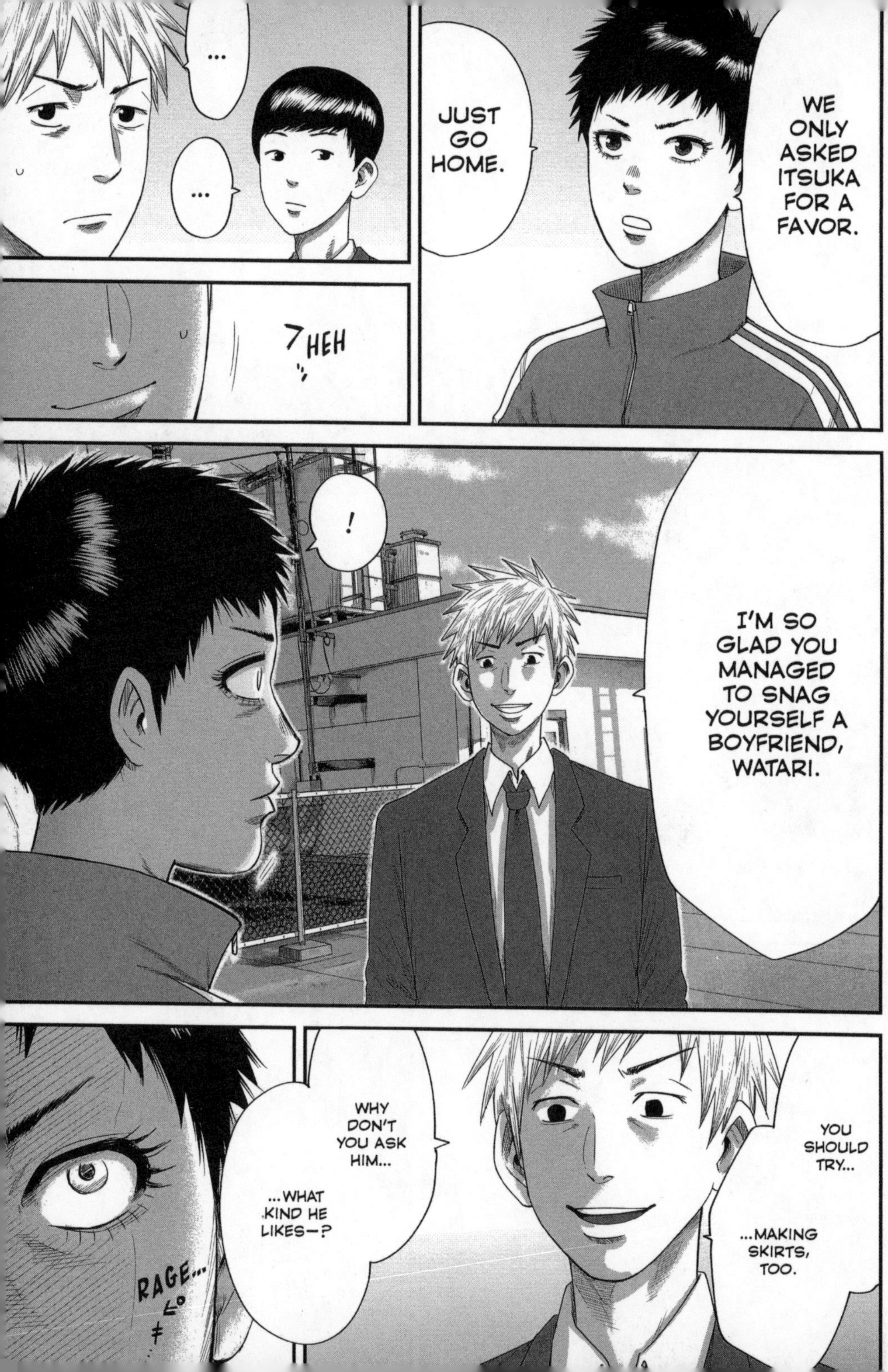
WE ONLY ASKED ITSUKA FOR A FAVOR.
JUST GO HOME.
...
...
HEH
I'M SO GLAD YOU MANAGED TO SNAG YOURSELF A BOYFRIEND, WATARI.
!
YOU SHOULD TRY...
...MAKING SKIRTS, TOO.
WHY DON'T YOU ASK HIM...
...WHAT KIND HE LIKES—?
RAGE...

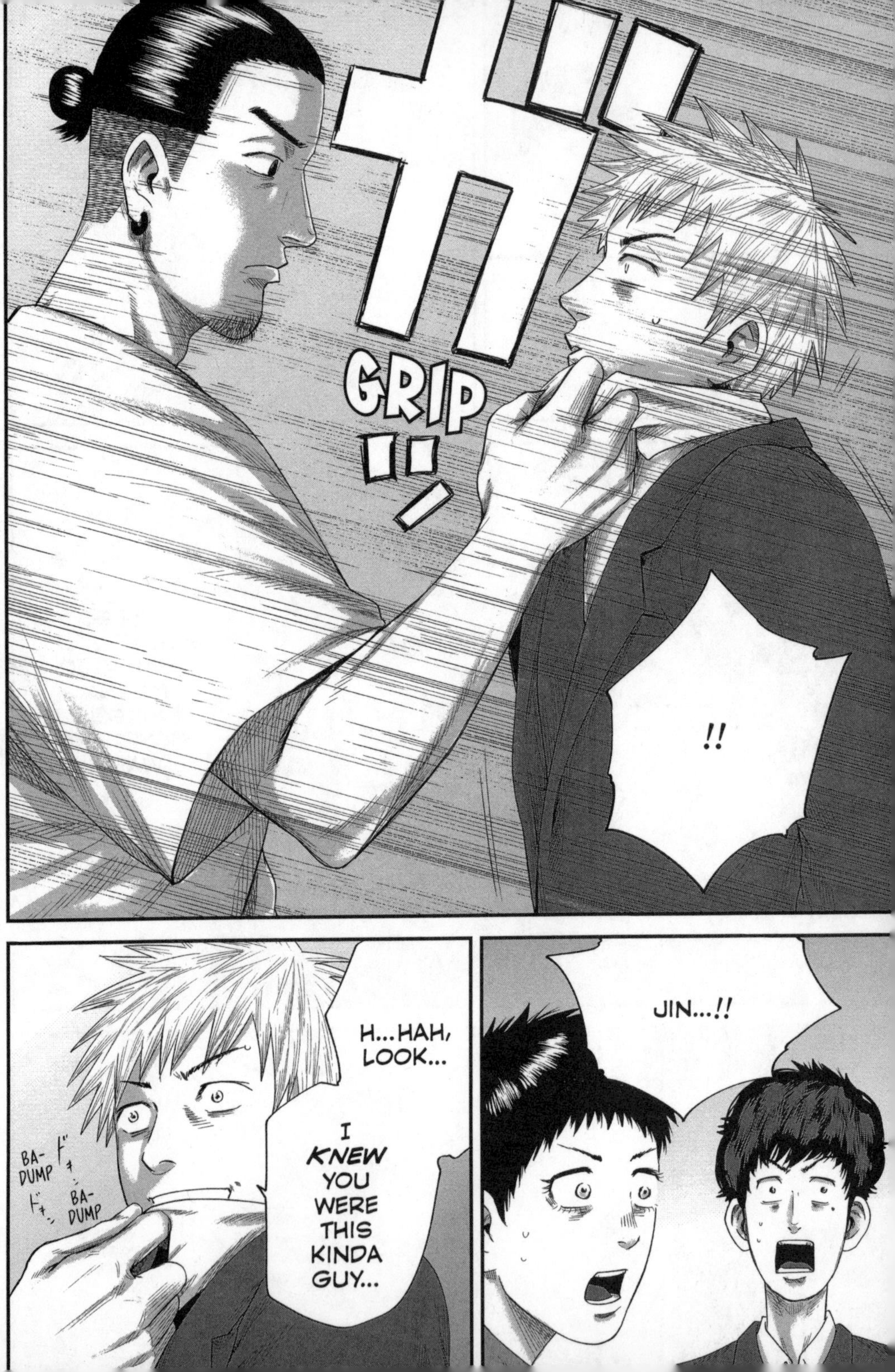
GRIP
!!
JIN...!!
H...HAH, LOOK...
I KNEW YOU WERE THIS KINDA GUY...
BA-DUMP
BA-DUMP

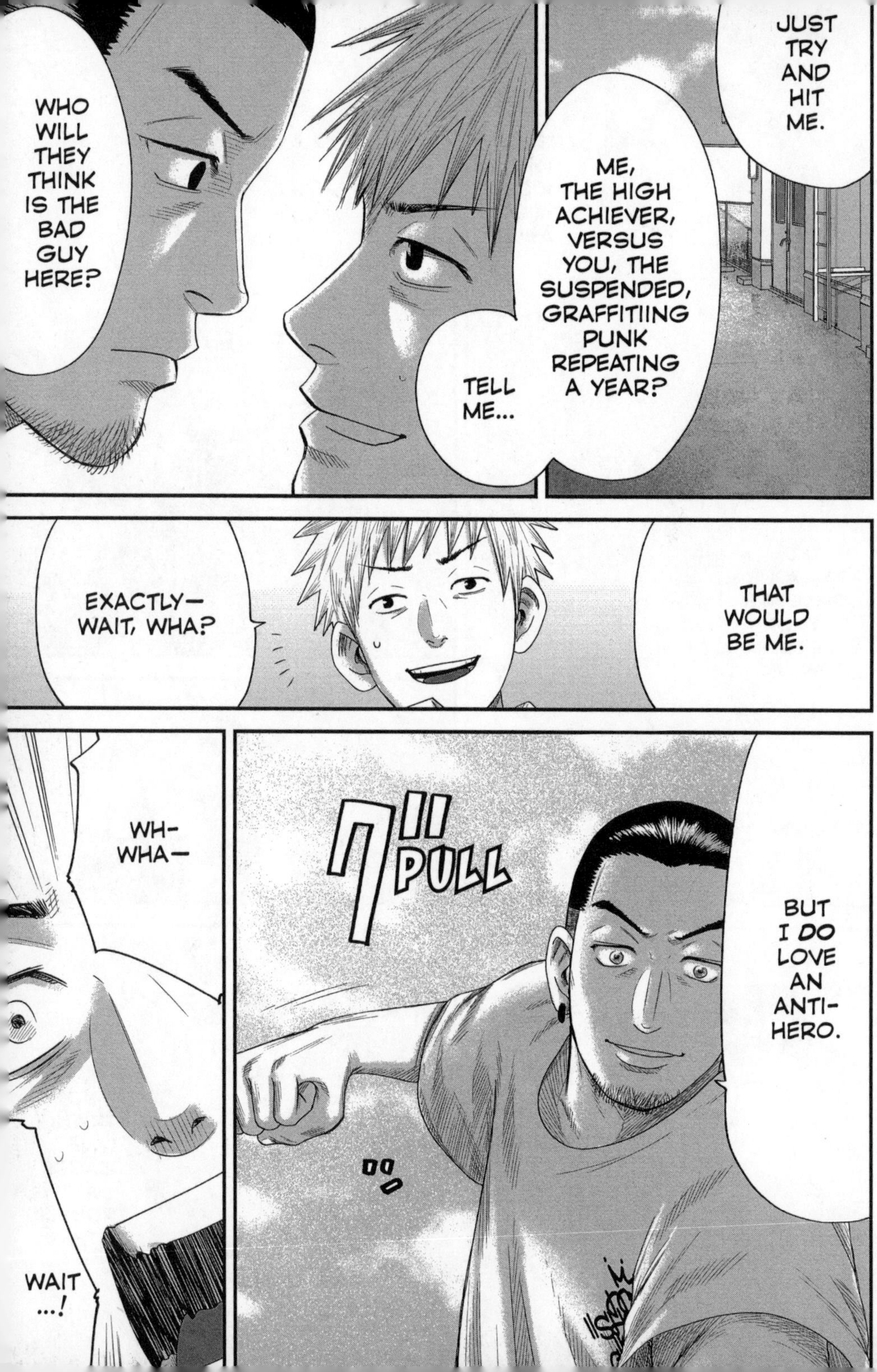
JUST TRY AND HIT ME.
ME, THE HIGH ACHIEVER, VERSUS YOU, THE SUSPENDED, GRAFFITIING PUNK REPEATING A YEAR?
TELL ME...
WHO WILL THEY THINK IS THE BAD GUY HERE?
THAT WOULD BE ME.
EXACTLY— WAIT, WHA?
BUT I *DO* LOVE AN ANTI-HERO.
PULL
WH- WHA—
WAIT ...!

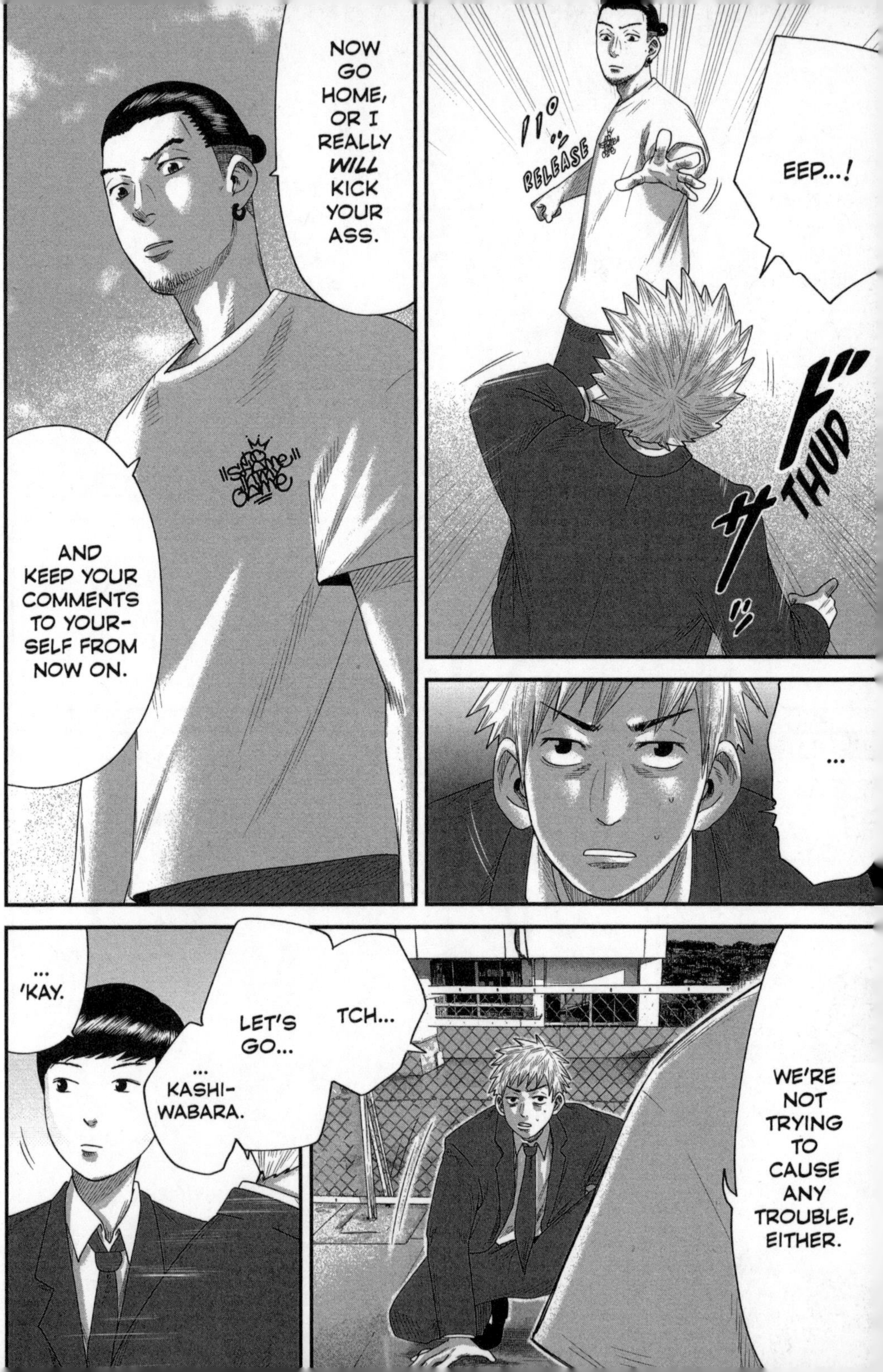
EEP...!
RELEASE
THUD
...
NOW GO HOME, OR I REALLY *WILL* KICK YOUR ASS.
AND KEEP YOUR COMMENTS TO YOUR-SELF FROM NOW ON.
WE'RE NOT TRYING TO CAUSE ANY TROUBLE, EITHER.
TCH...
LET'S GO... ...KASHI-WABARA.
...'KAY.

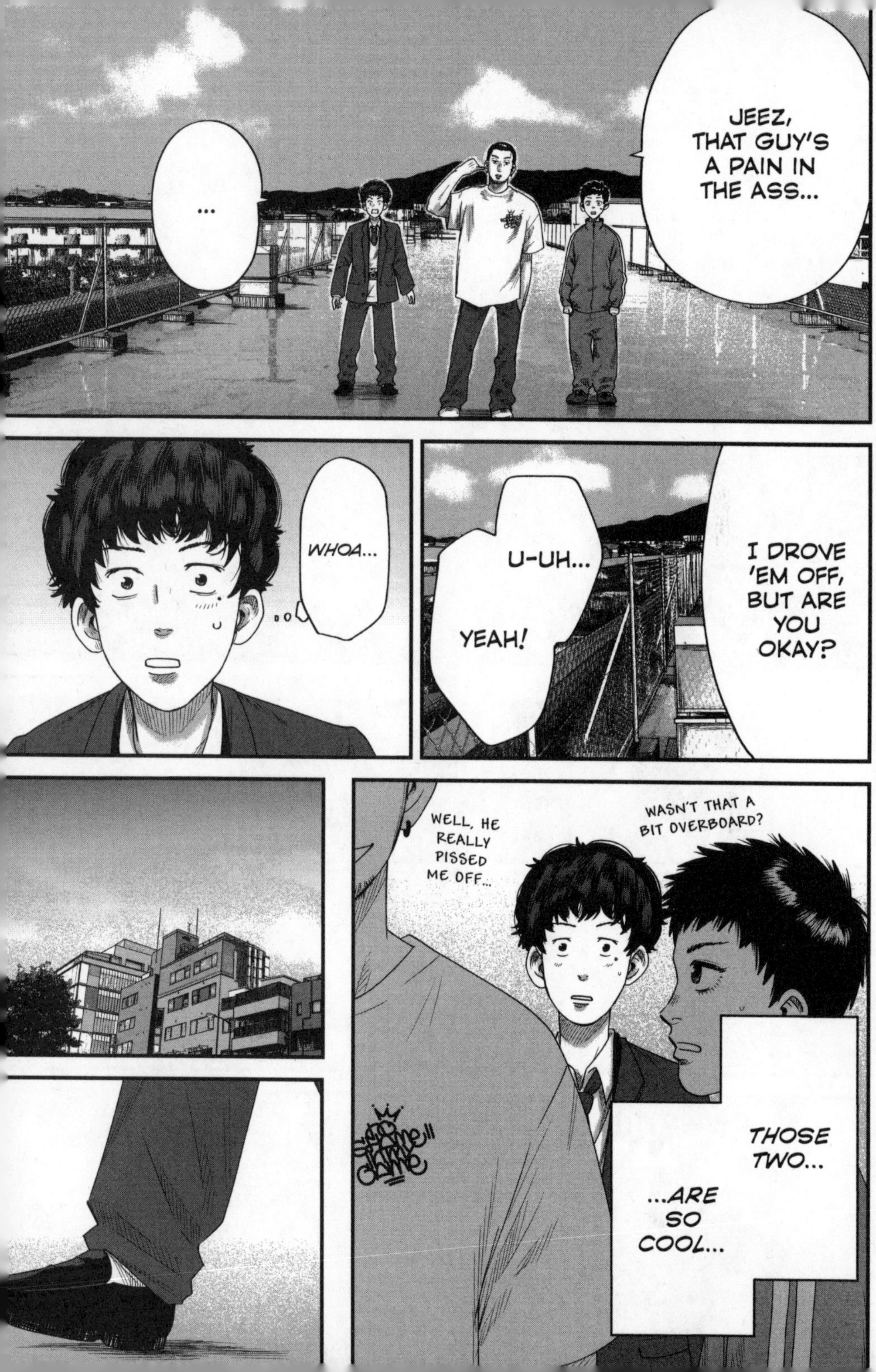
JEEZ, THAT GUY'S A PAIN IN THE ASS...
...
I DROVE 'EM OFF, BUT ARE YOU OKAY?
U-UH... YEAH!
WHOA...
WASN'T THAT A BIT OVERBOARD?
WELL, HE REALLY PISSED ME OFF...
THOSE TWO...
...ARE SO COOL...

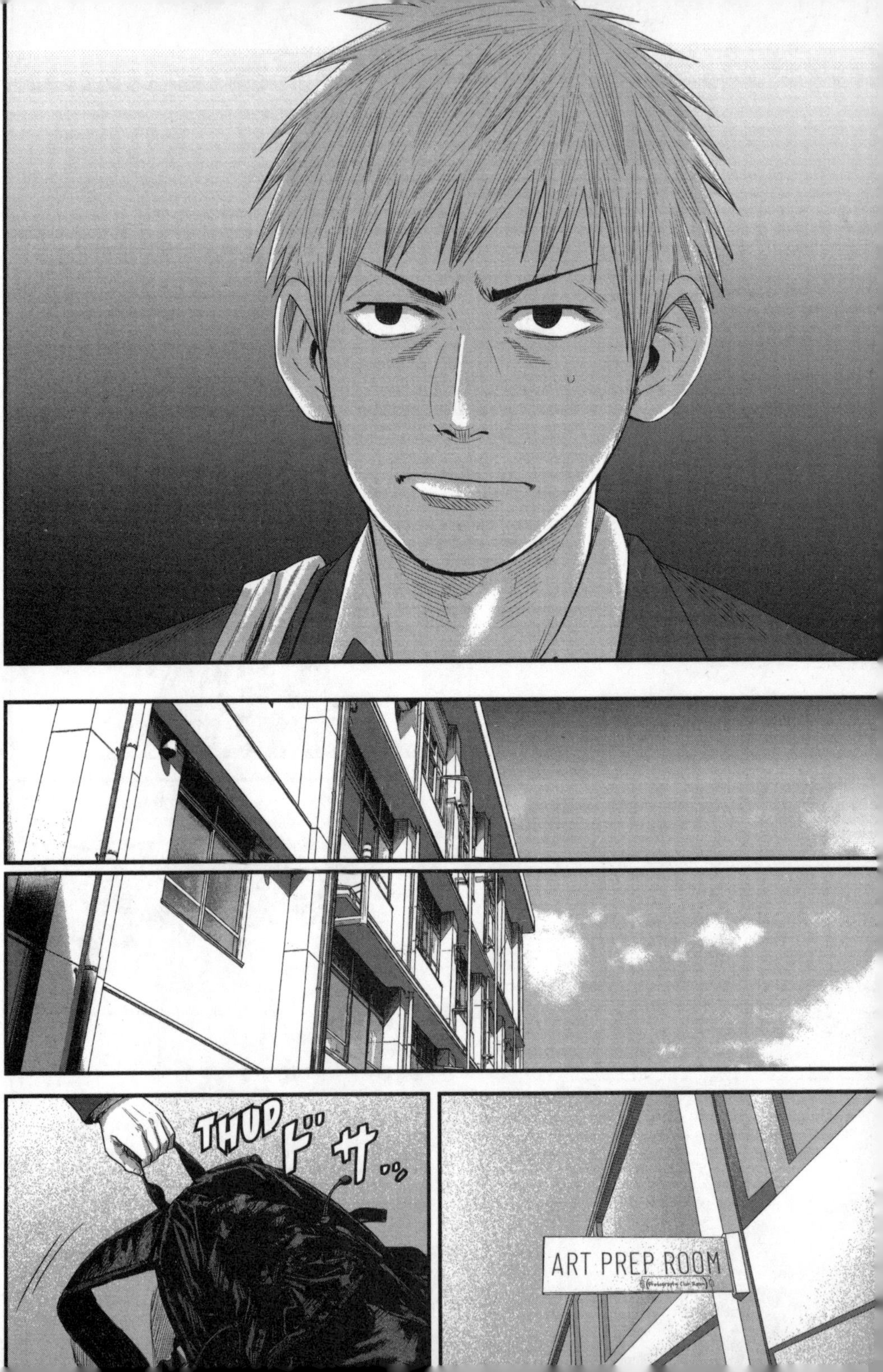
ART PREP ROOM
(Photography Club Room)
THUD
ドサッ

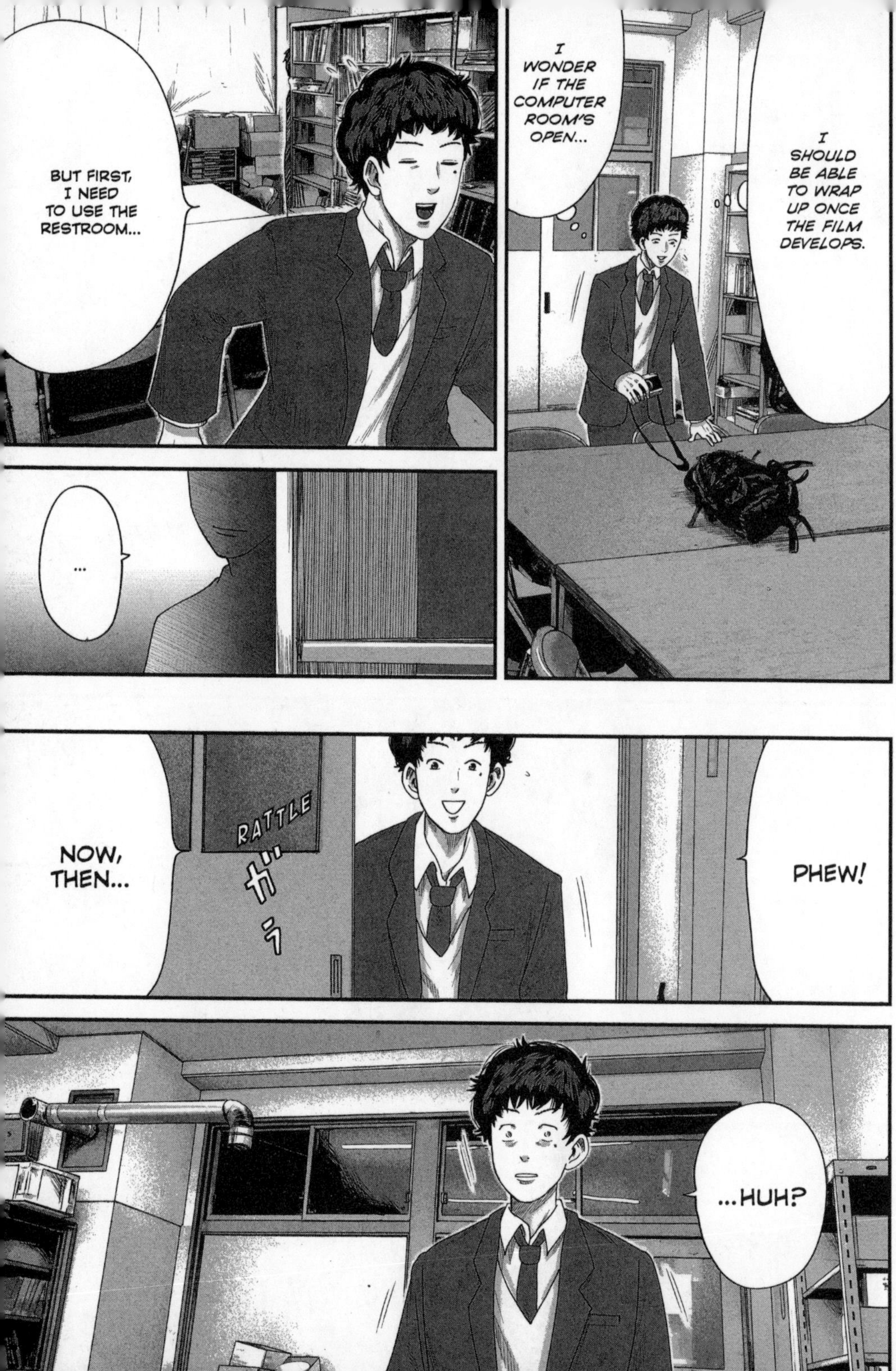
I SHOULD BE ABLE TO WRAP UP ONCE THE FILM DEVELOPS.
I WONDER IF THE COMPUTER ROOM'S OPEN...
BUT FIRST, I NEED TO USE THE RESTROOM...
...
PHEW!
RATTLE
ガラ
NOW, THEN...
...HUH?

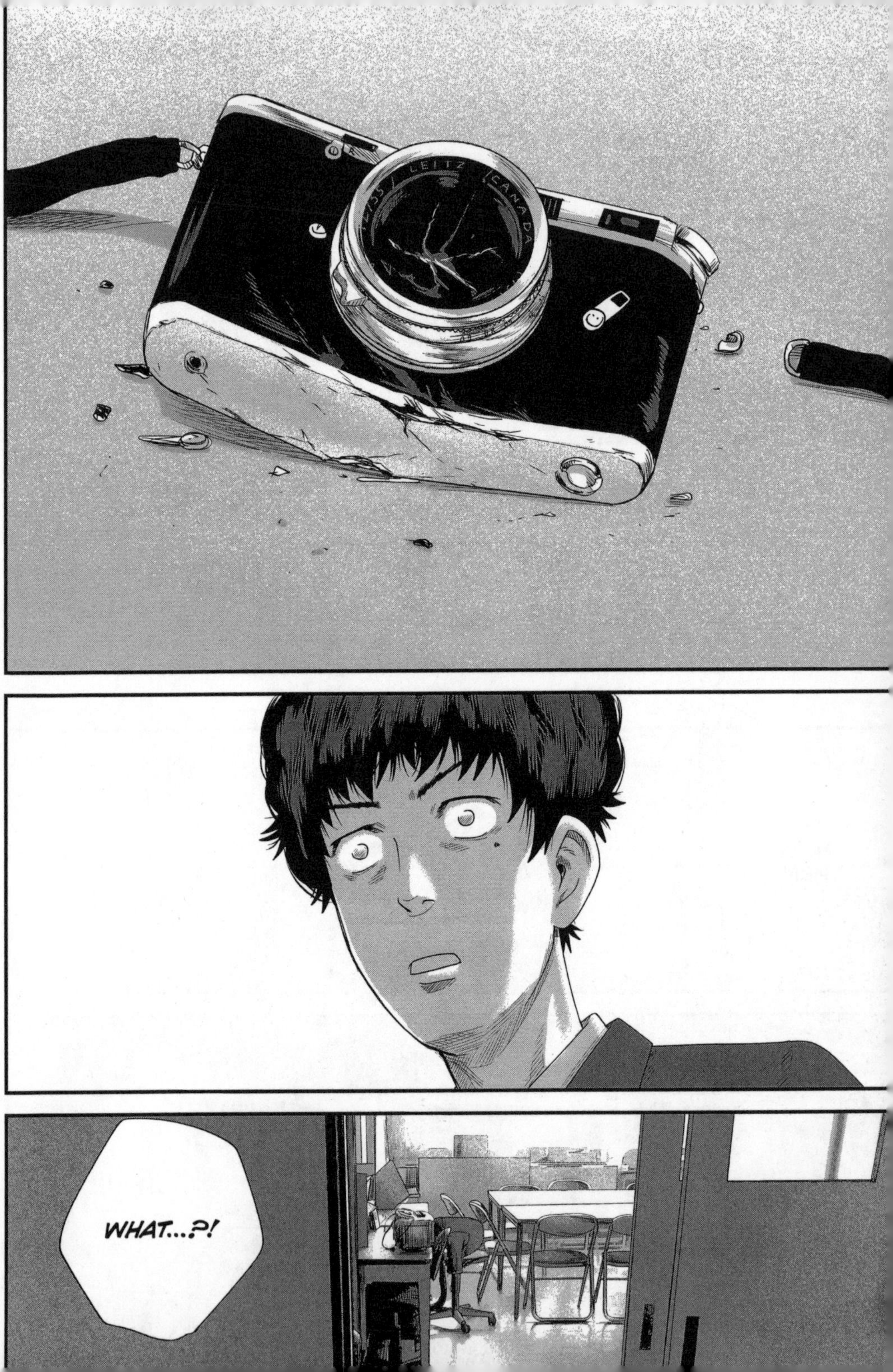
LEITZ CANADA
WHAT...?!

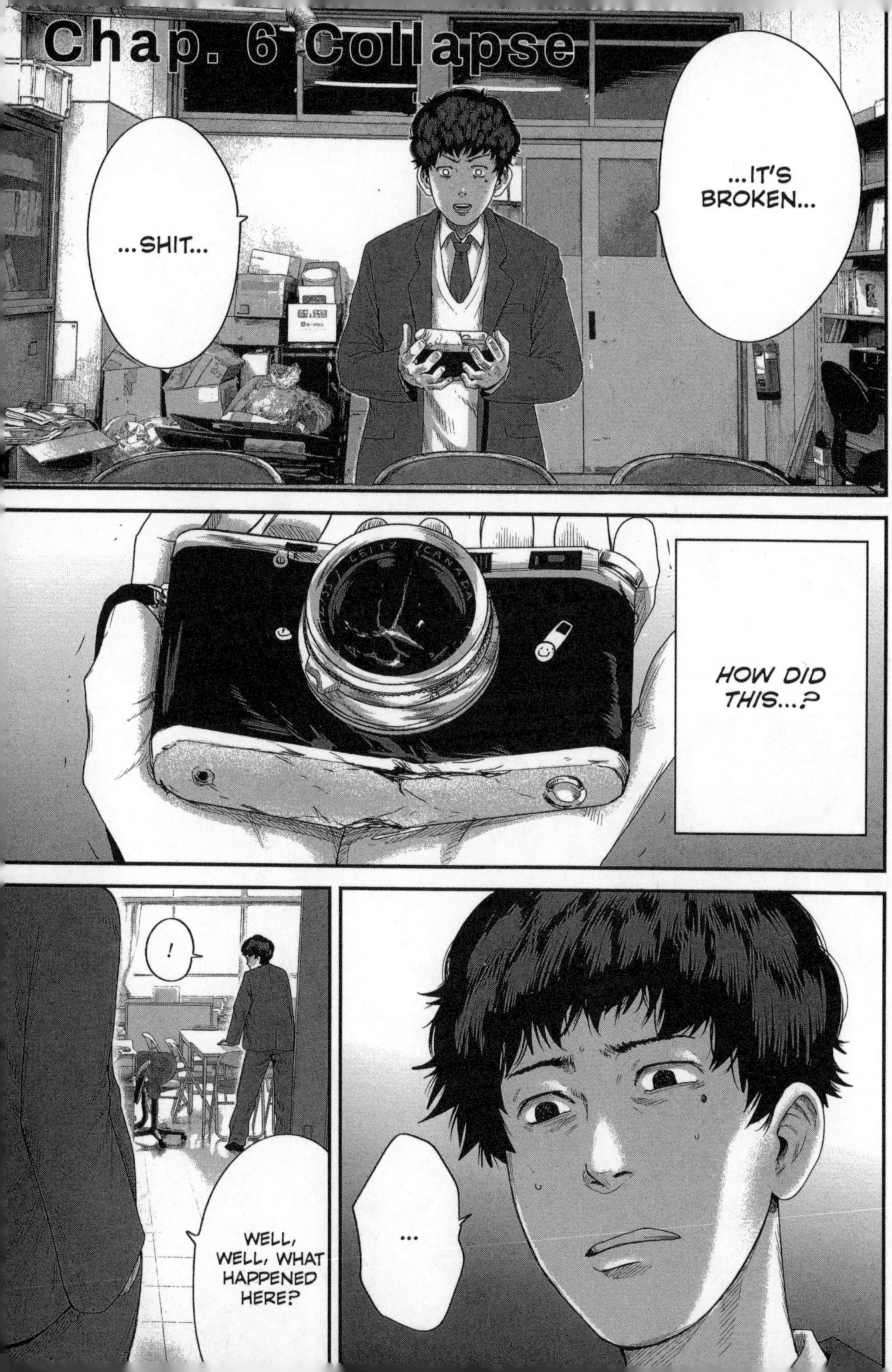
Chap. 6 Collapse
...IT'S BROKEN...
...SHIT...
HOW DID THIS...?
...
!
WELL, WELL, WHAT HAPPENED HERE?

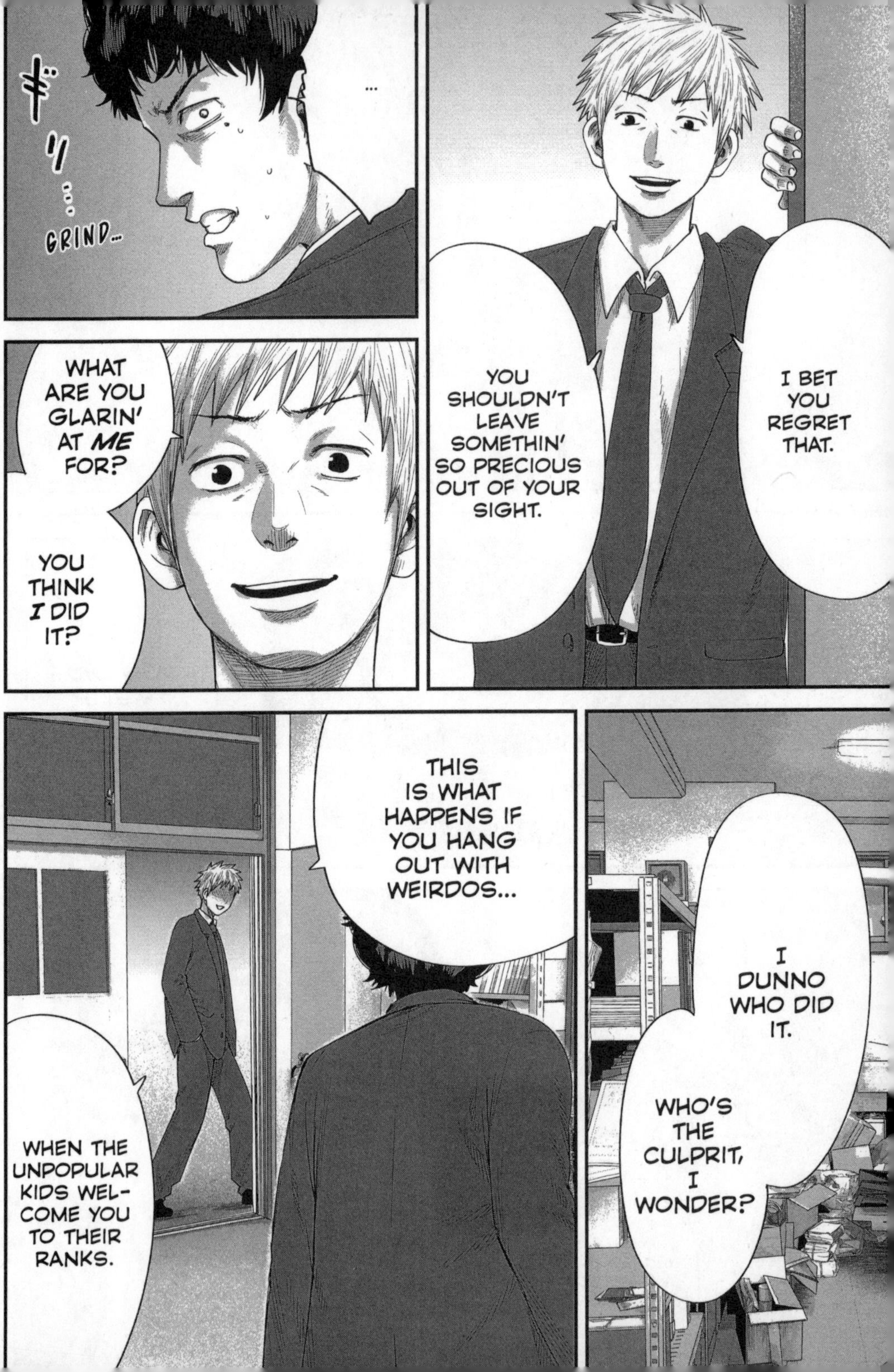
I BET YOU REGRET THAT.
YOU SHOULDN'T LEAVE SOMETHIN' SO PRECIOUS OUT OF YOUR SIGHT.
...
GRIND...
WHAT ARE YOU GLARIN' AT *ME* FOR?
YOU THINK *I* DID IT?
I DUNNO WHO DID IT.
WHO'S THE CULPRIT, I WONDER?
THIS IS WHAT HAPPENS IF YOU HANG OUT WITH WEIRDOS...
WHEN THE UNPOPULAR KIDS WEL-COME YOU TO THEIR RANKS.

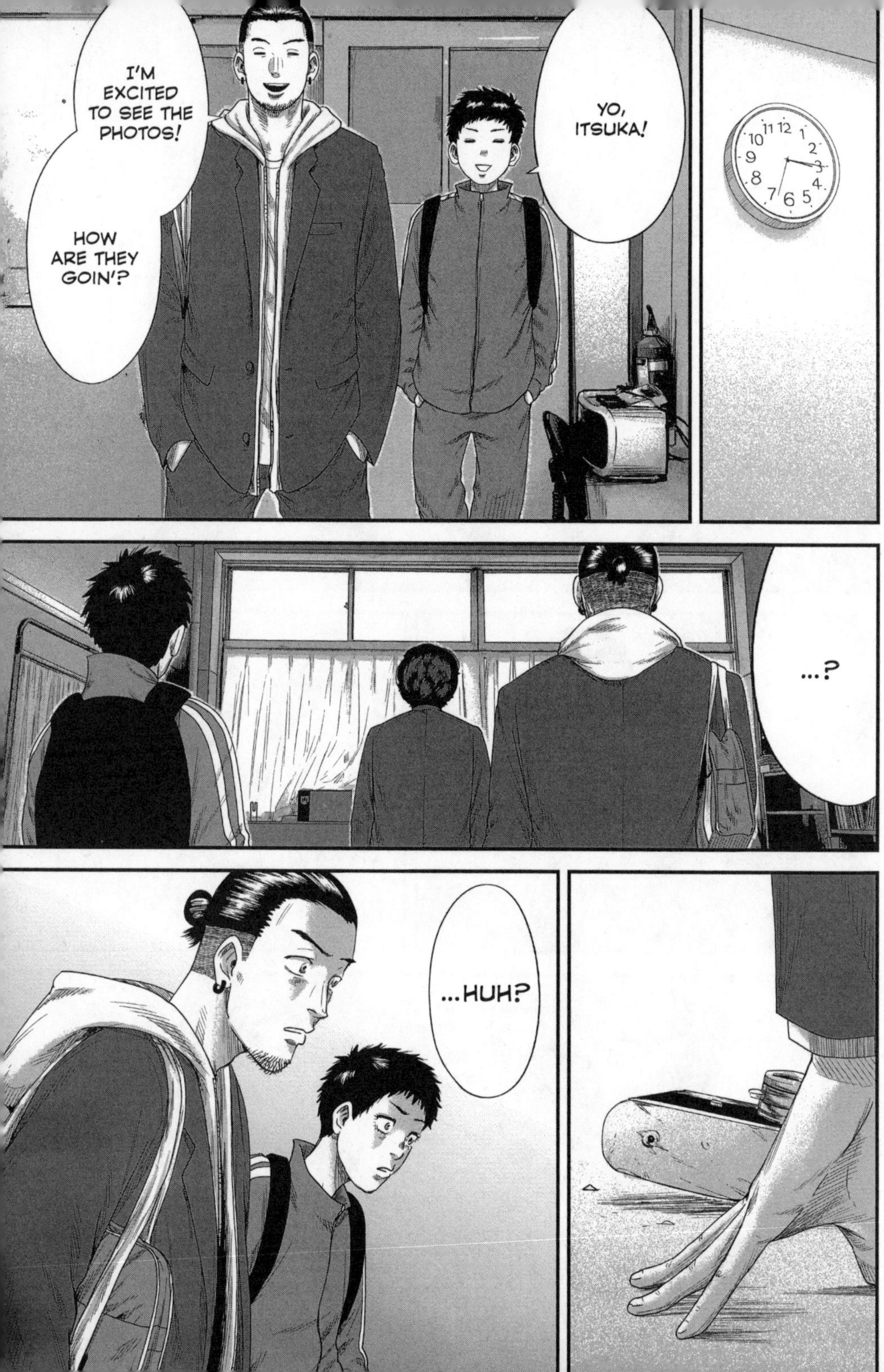
YO, ITSUKA!
I'M EXCITED TO SEE THE PHOTOS!
HOW ARE THEY GOIN'?
...?
...HUH?

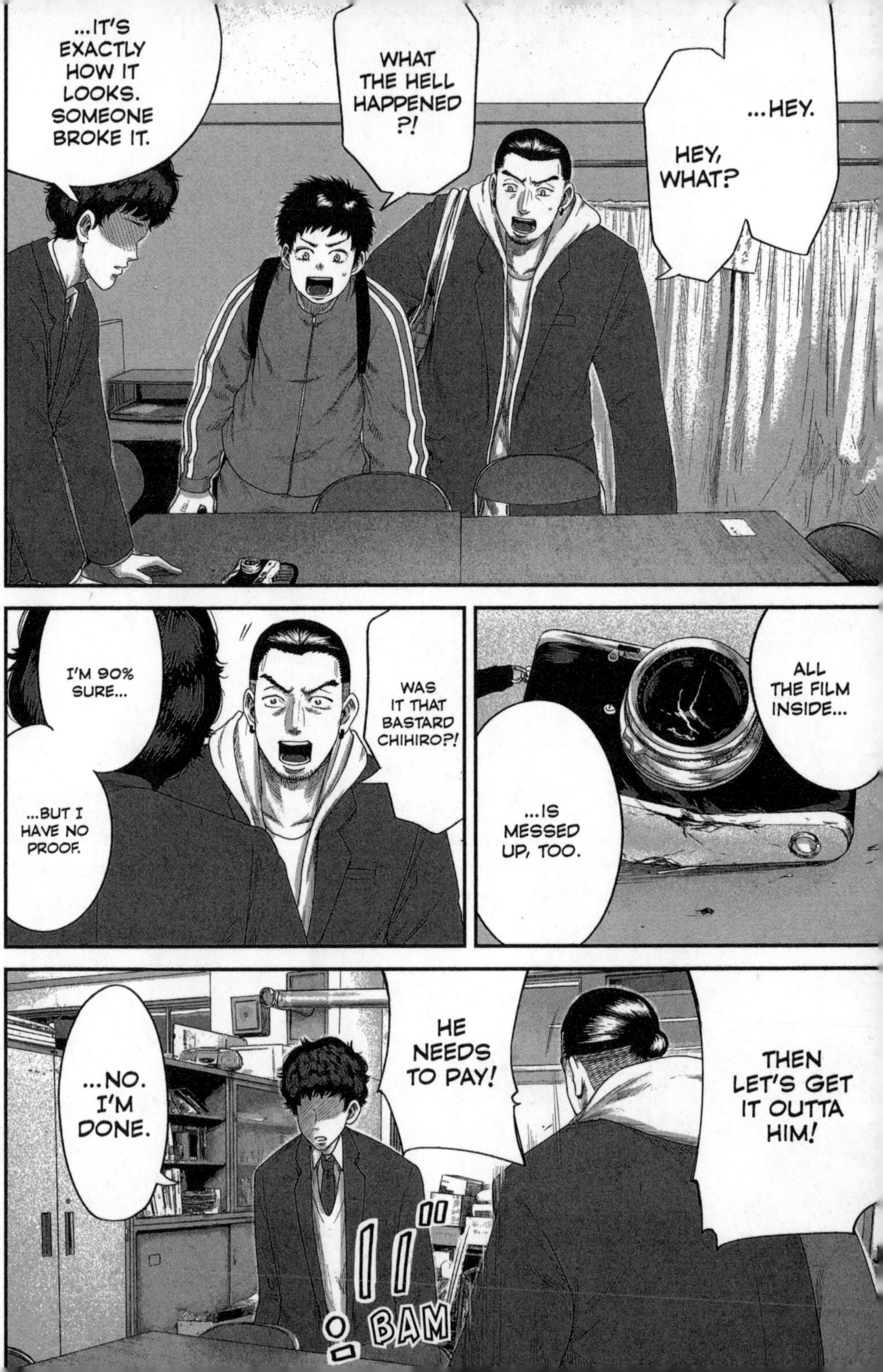
...HEY.
HEY, WHAT?
WHAT THE HELL HAPPENED?!
...IT'S EXACTLY HOW IT LOOKS. SOMEONE BROKE IT.
ALL THE FILM INSIDE...
...IS MESSED UP, TOO.
WAS IT THAT BASTARD CHIHIRO?!
I'M 90% SURE...
...BUT I HAVE NO PROOF.
THEN LET'S GET IT OUTTA HIM!
HE NEEDS TO PAY!
...NO. I'M DONE.
BAM

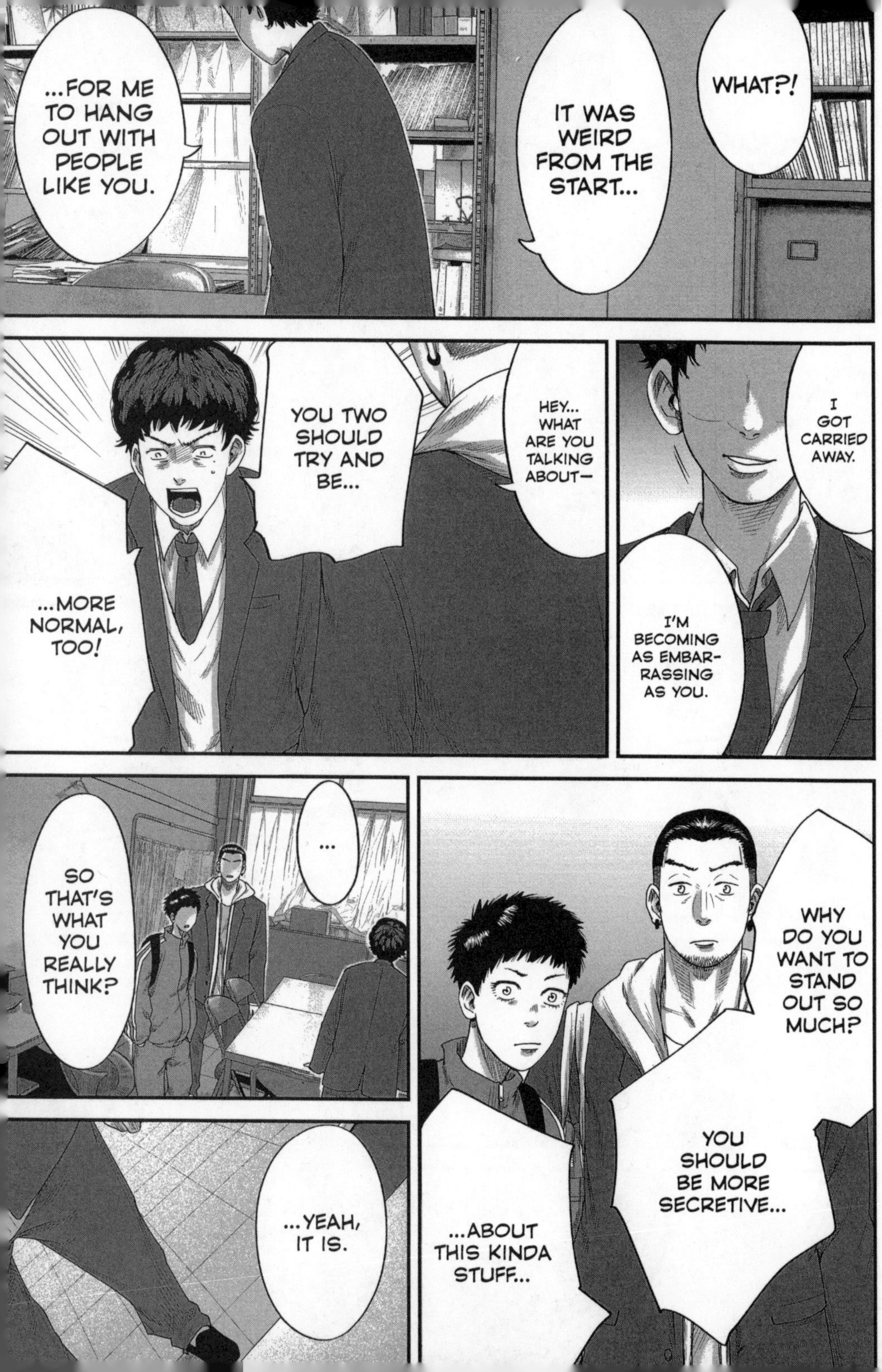
WHAT?!
IT WAS WEIRD FROM THE START...
...FOR ME TO HANG OUT WITH PEOPLE LIKE YOU.
I GOT CARRIED AWAY.
I'M BECOMING AS EMBARRASSING AS YOU.
HEY... WHAT ARE YOU TALKING ABOUT—
YOU TWO SHOULD TRY AND BE...
...MORE NORMAL, TOO!
WHY DO YOU WANT TO STAND OUT SO MUCH?
YOU SHOULD BE MORE SECRETIVE...
...ABOUT THIS KINDA STUFF...
...
SO THAT'S WHAT YOU REALLY THINK?
...YEAH, IT IS.

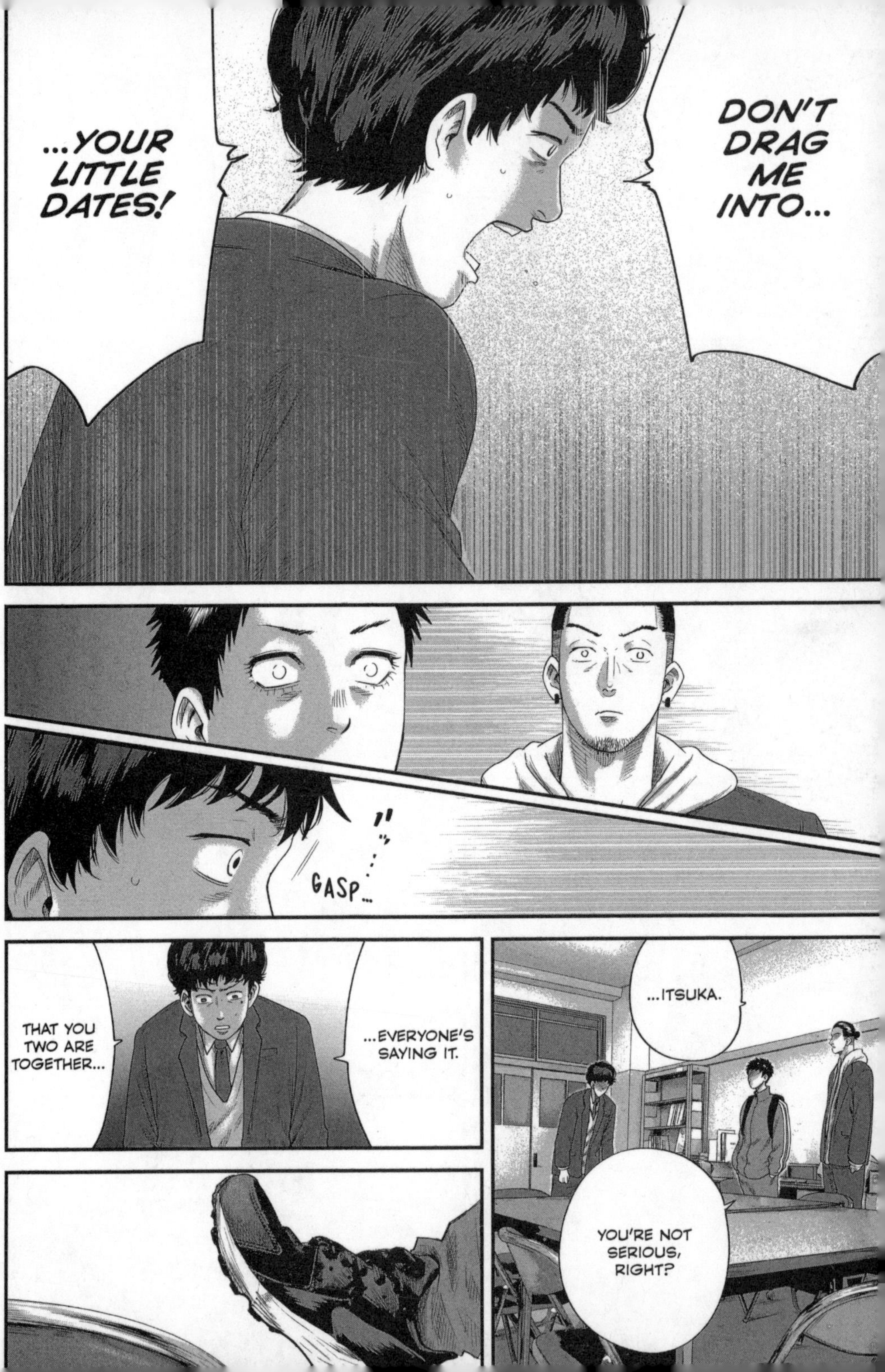
DON'T DRAG ME INTO...
...YOUR LITTLE DATES!
GASP...
...ITSUKA.
YOU'RE NOT SERIOUS, RIGHT?
...EVERYONE'S SAYING IT.
THAT YOU TWO ARE TOGETHER...

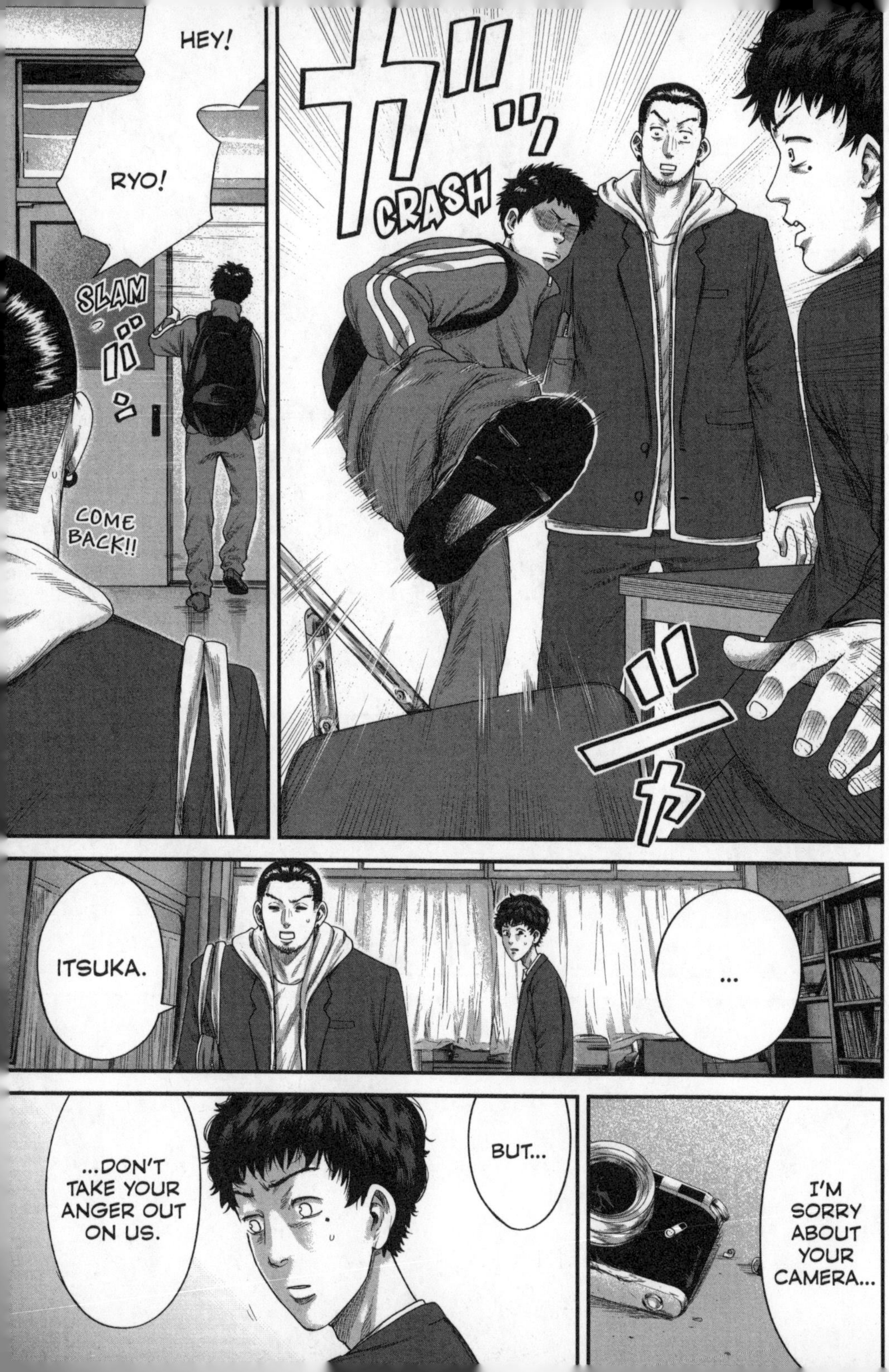
CRASH
HEY!
RYO!
SLAM
COME BACK!!
...
ITSUKA.
I'M SORRY ABOUT YOUR CAMERA...
BUT...
...DON'T TAKE YOUR ANGER OUT ON US.

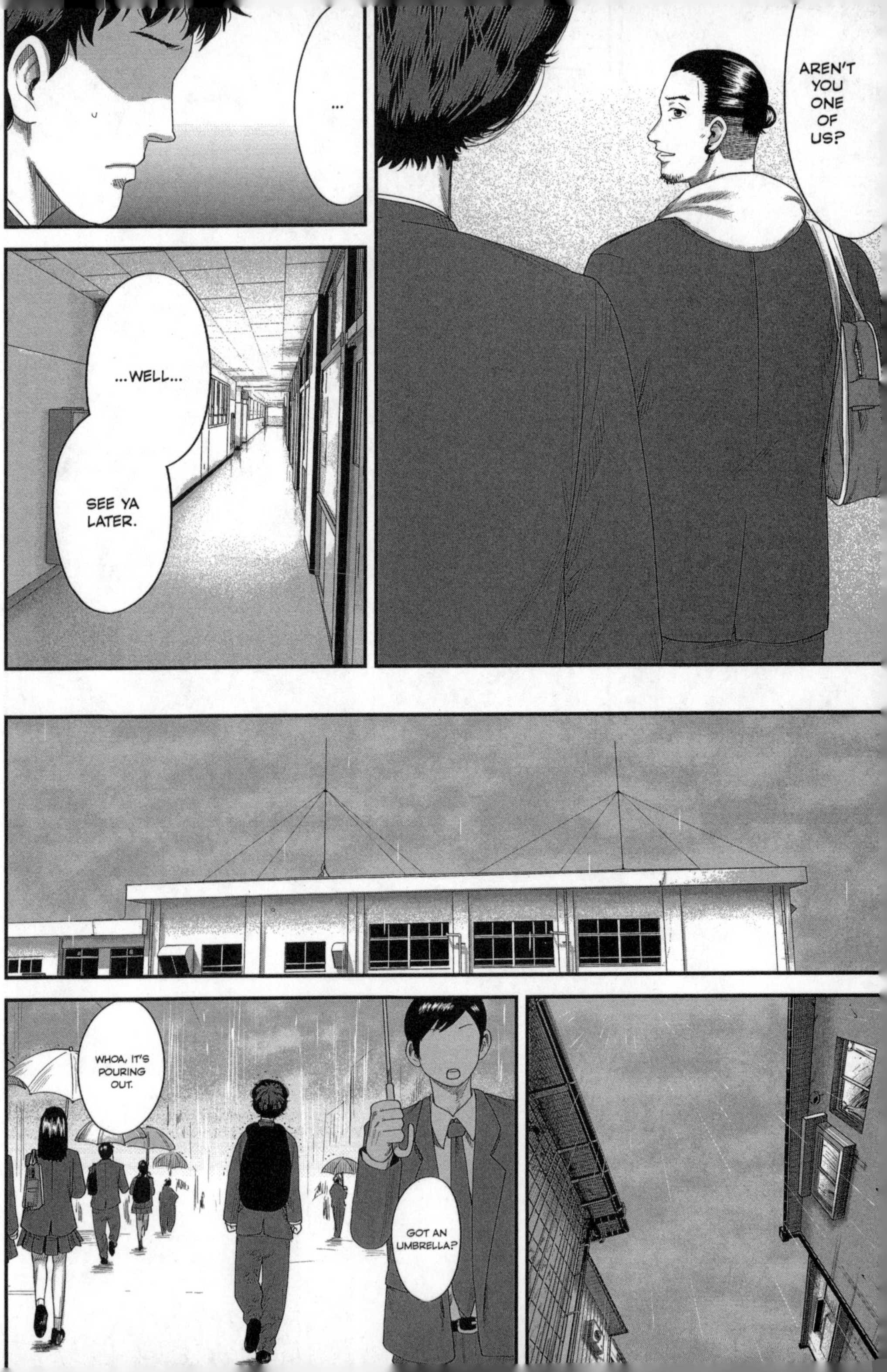
AREN'T YOU ONE OF US?
...
...WELL...
SEE YA LATER.
WHOA, IT'S POURING OUT.
GOT AN UMBRELLA?

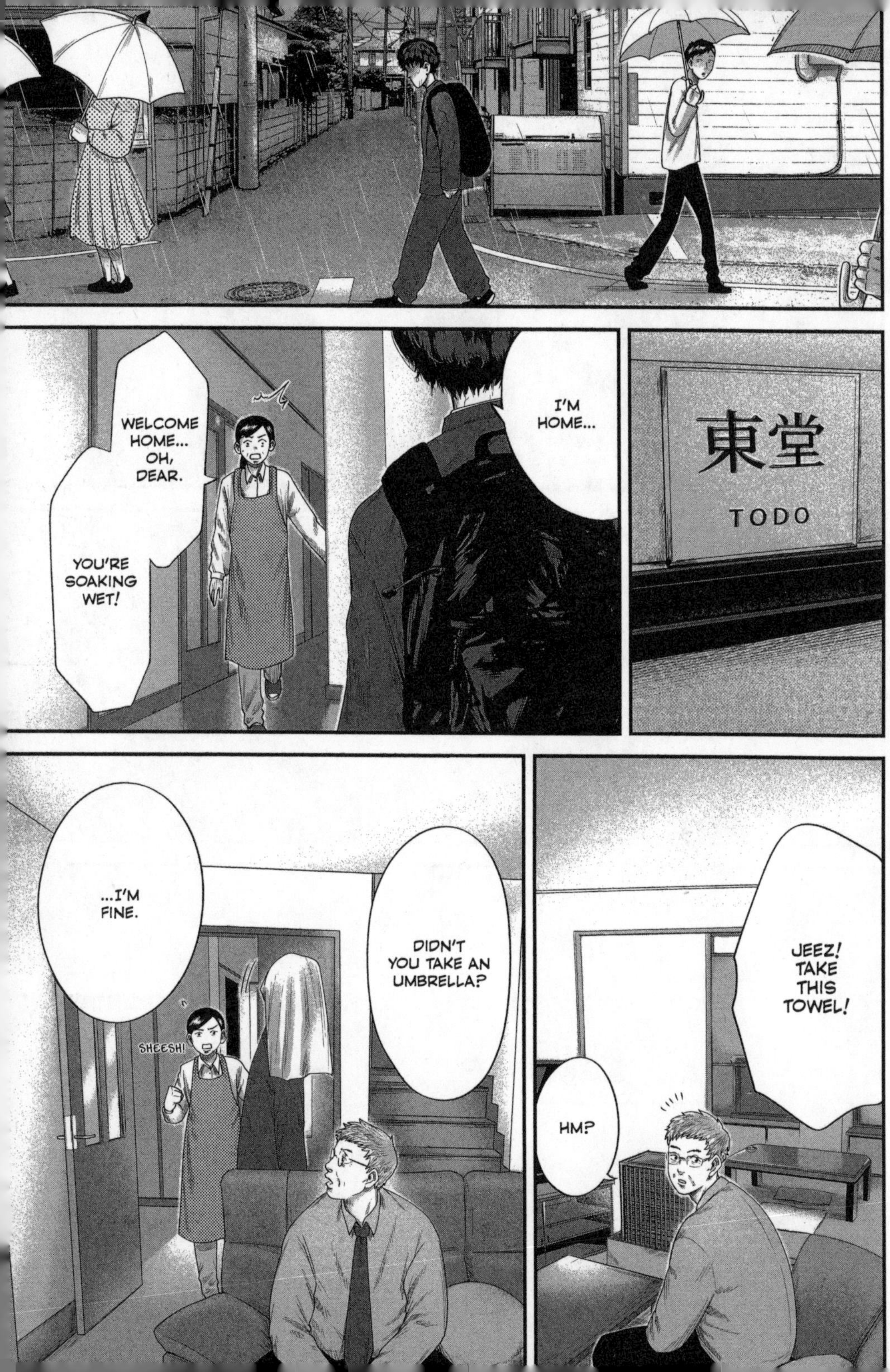
東堂
TODO
I'M HOME...
WELCOME HOME... OH, DEAR.
YOU'RE SOAKING WET!
JEEZ! TAKE THIS TOWEL!
HM?
DIDN'T YOU TAKE AN UMBRELLA?
...I'M FINE.
SHEESH!

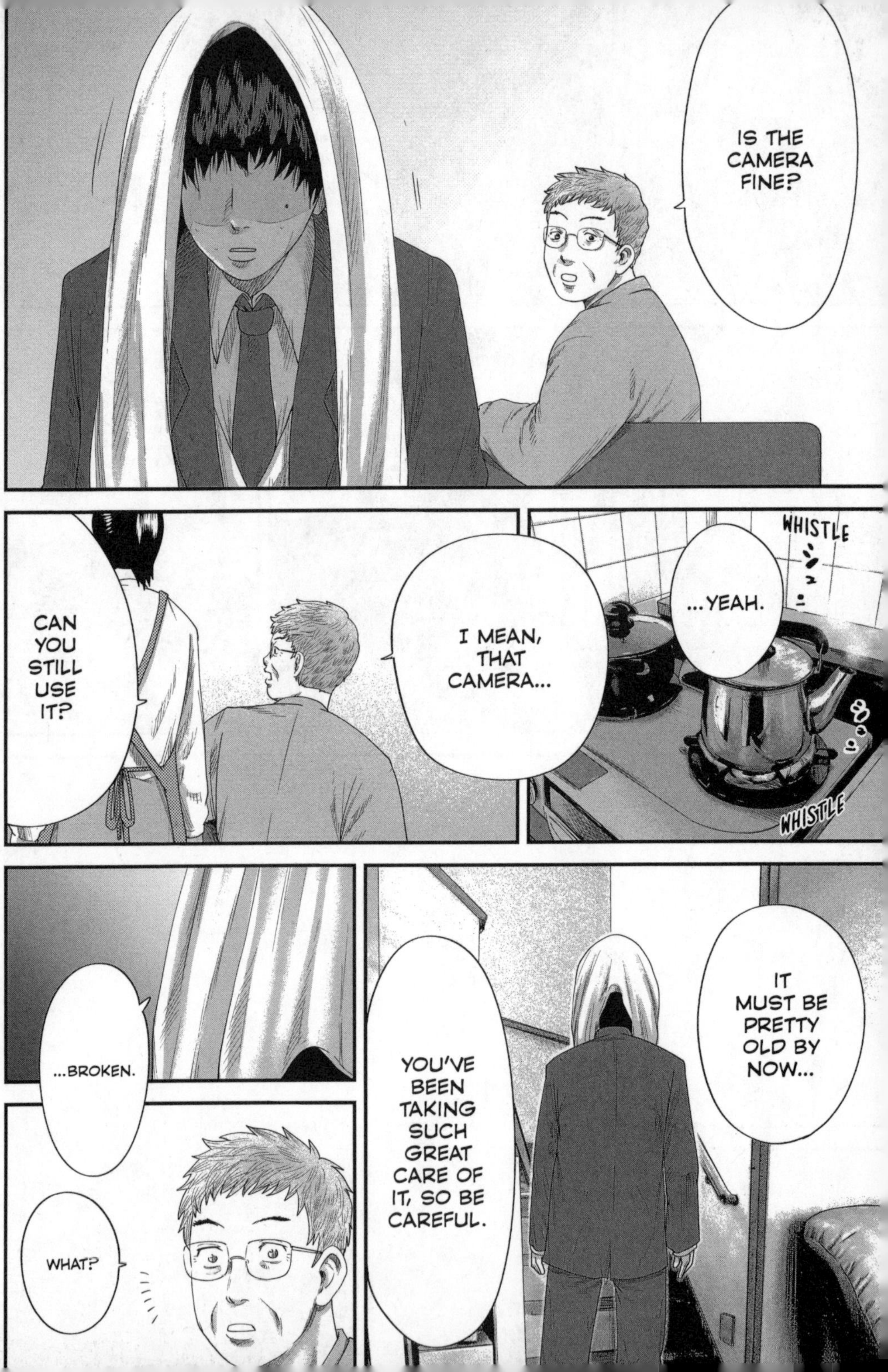
IS THE CAMERA FINE?
WHISTLE
...YEAH.
WHISTLE
I MEAN, THAT CAMERA...
CAN YOU STILL USE IT?
IT MUST BE PRETTY OLD BY NOW...
YOU'VE BEEN TAKING SUCH GREAT CARE OF IT, SO BE CAREFUL.
...BROKEN.
WHAT?

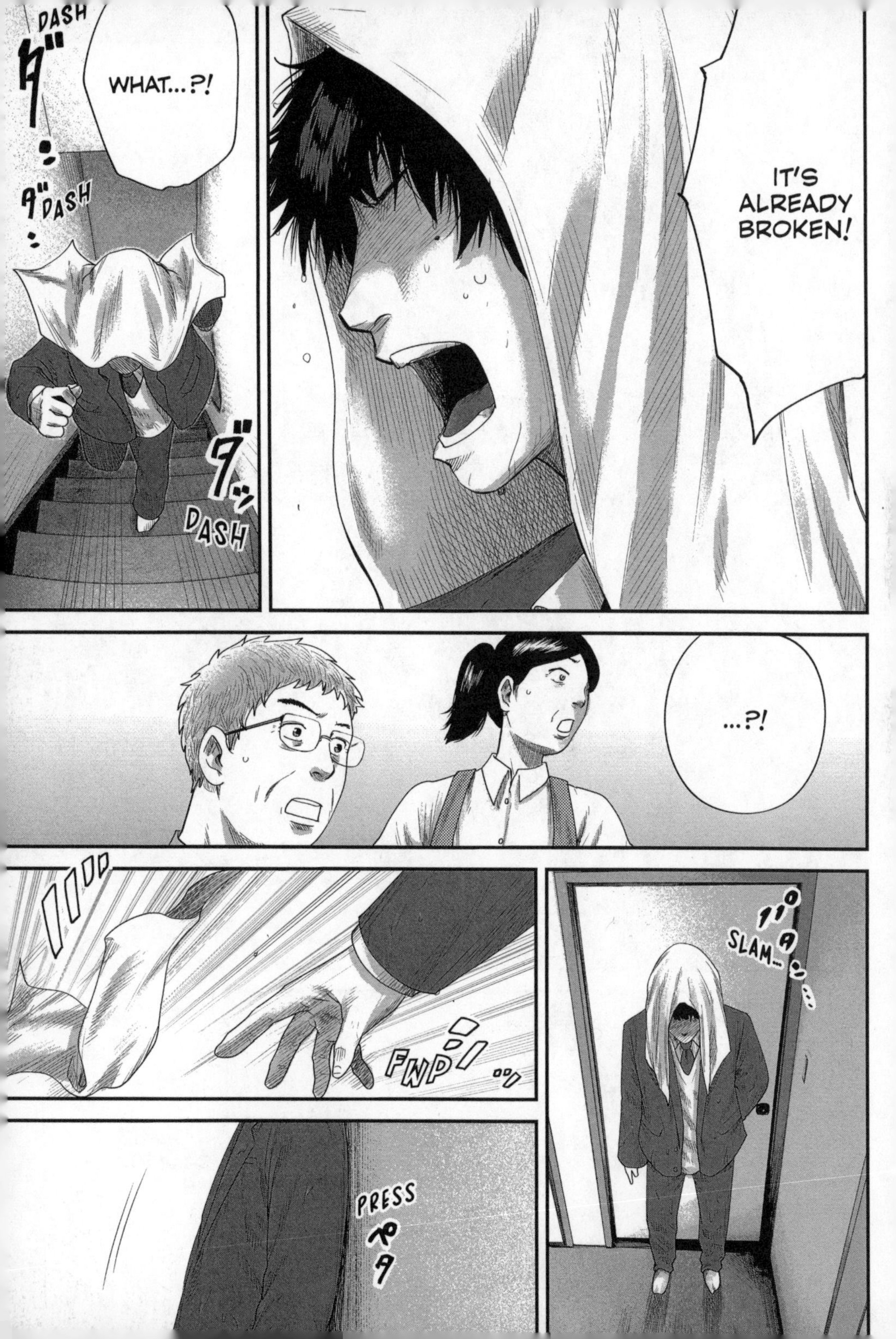
IT'S ALREADY BROKEN!
DASH
WHAT...?!
DASH
DASH
...?!
SLAM...
FWP
PRESS

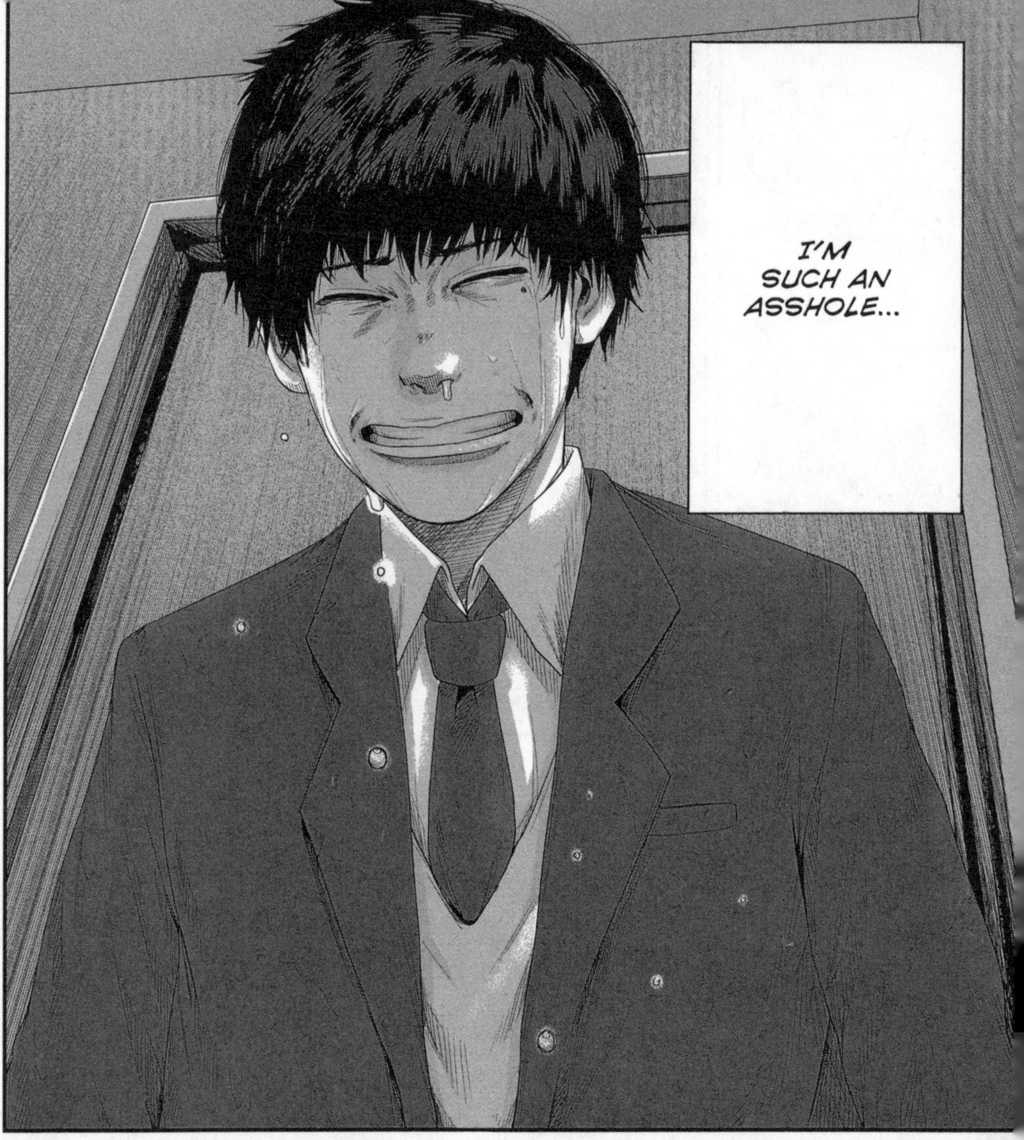
I'M SUCH AN ASSHOLE...
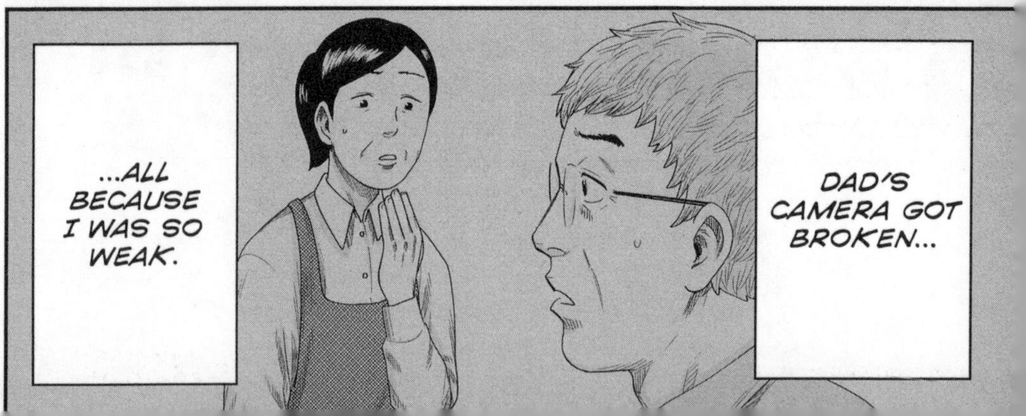
DAD'S CAMERA GOT BROKEN...
...ALL BECAUSE I WAS SO WEAK.

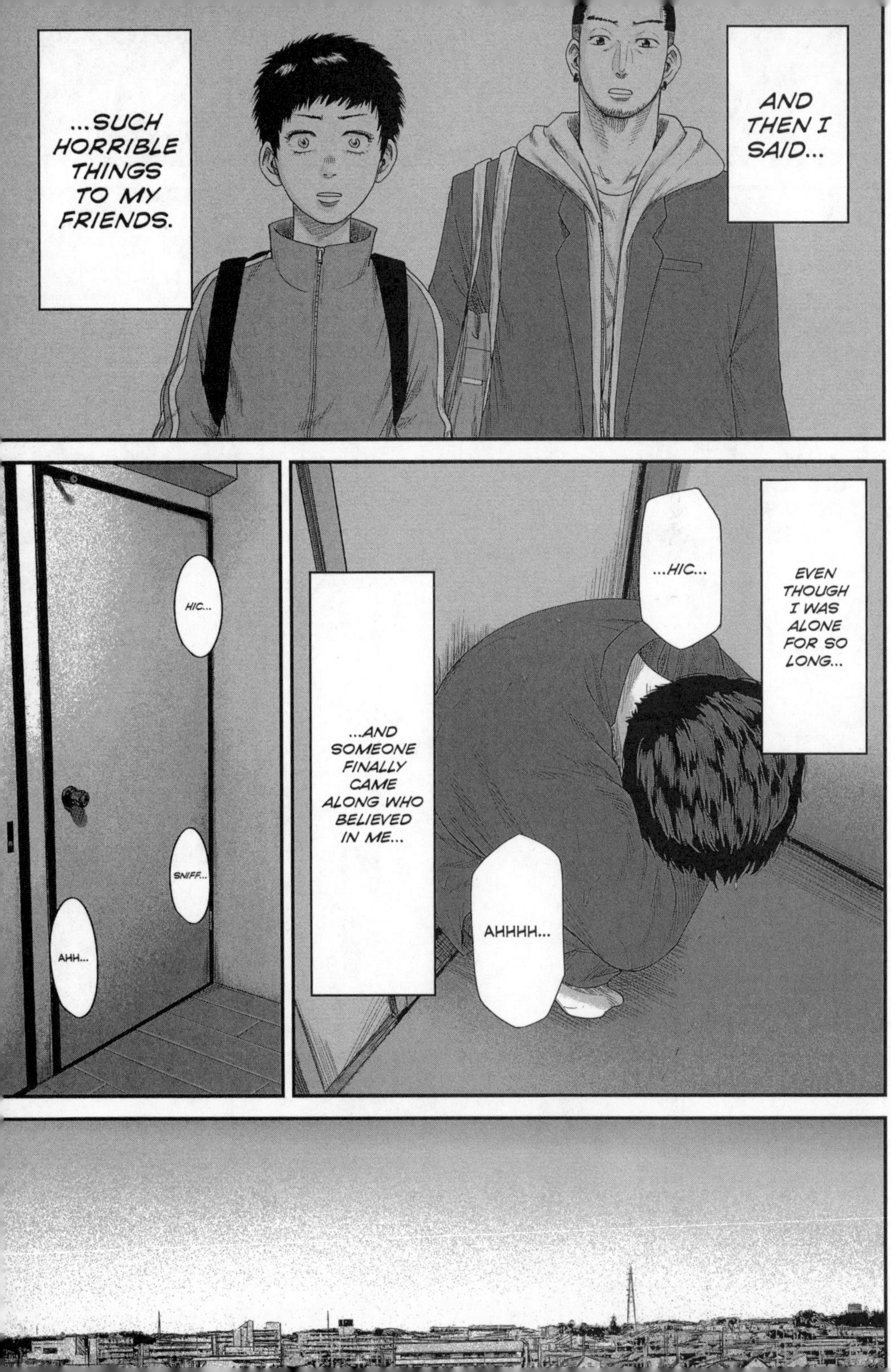
AND THEN I SAID...
...SUCH HORRIBLE THINGS TO MY FRIENDS.
EVEN THOUGH I WAS ALONE FOR SO LONG...
...HIC...
...AND SOMEONE FINALLY CAME ALONG WHO BELIEVED IN ME...
AHHHH...
HIC...
SNIFF...
AHH...

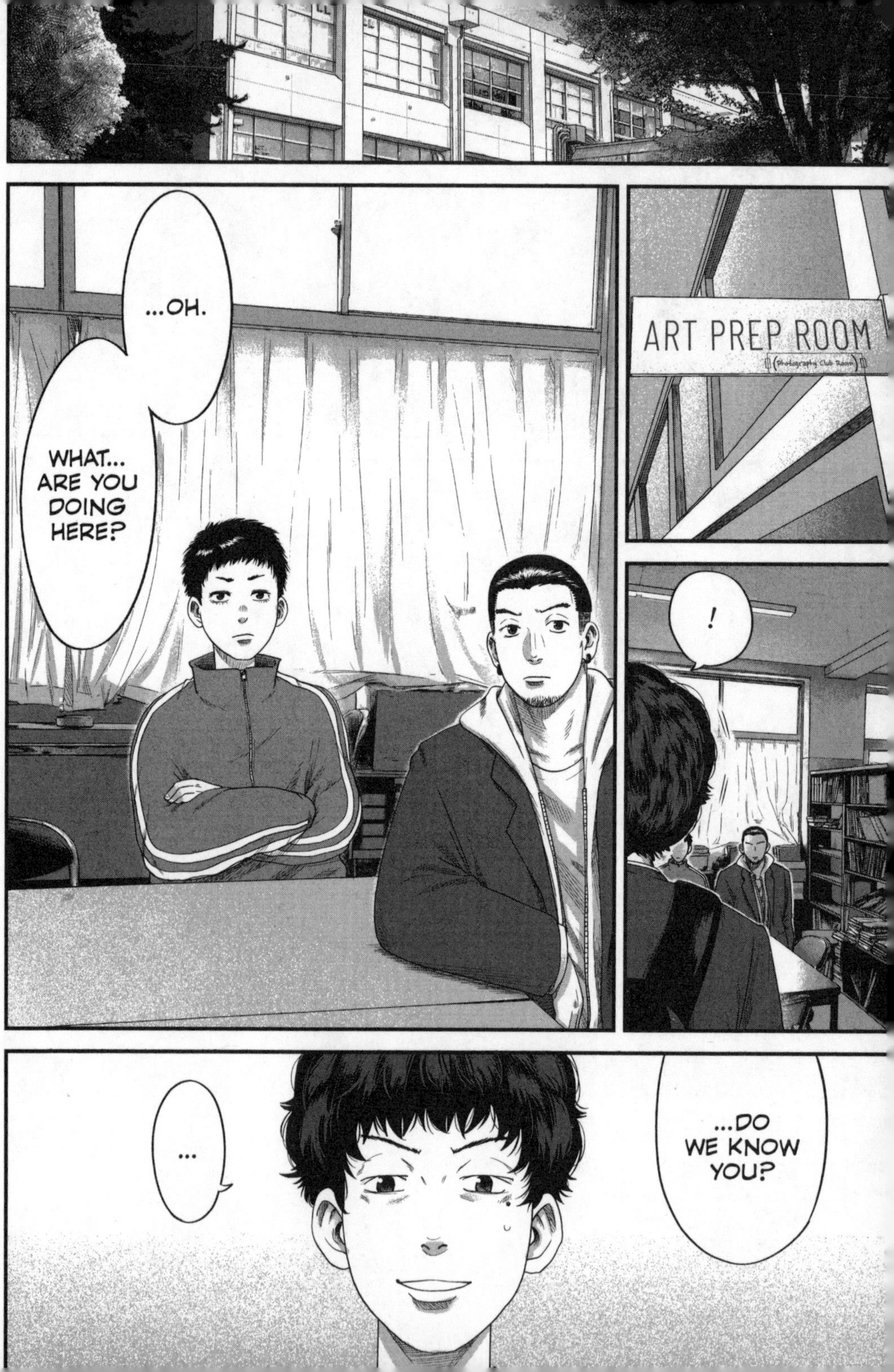
ART PREP ROOM
(Photography Club Room)
!
...OH.
WHAT... ARE YOU DOING HERE?
...DO WE KNOW YOU?
...

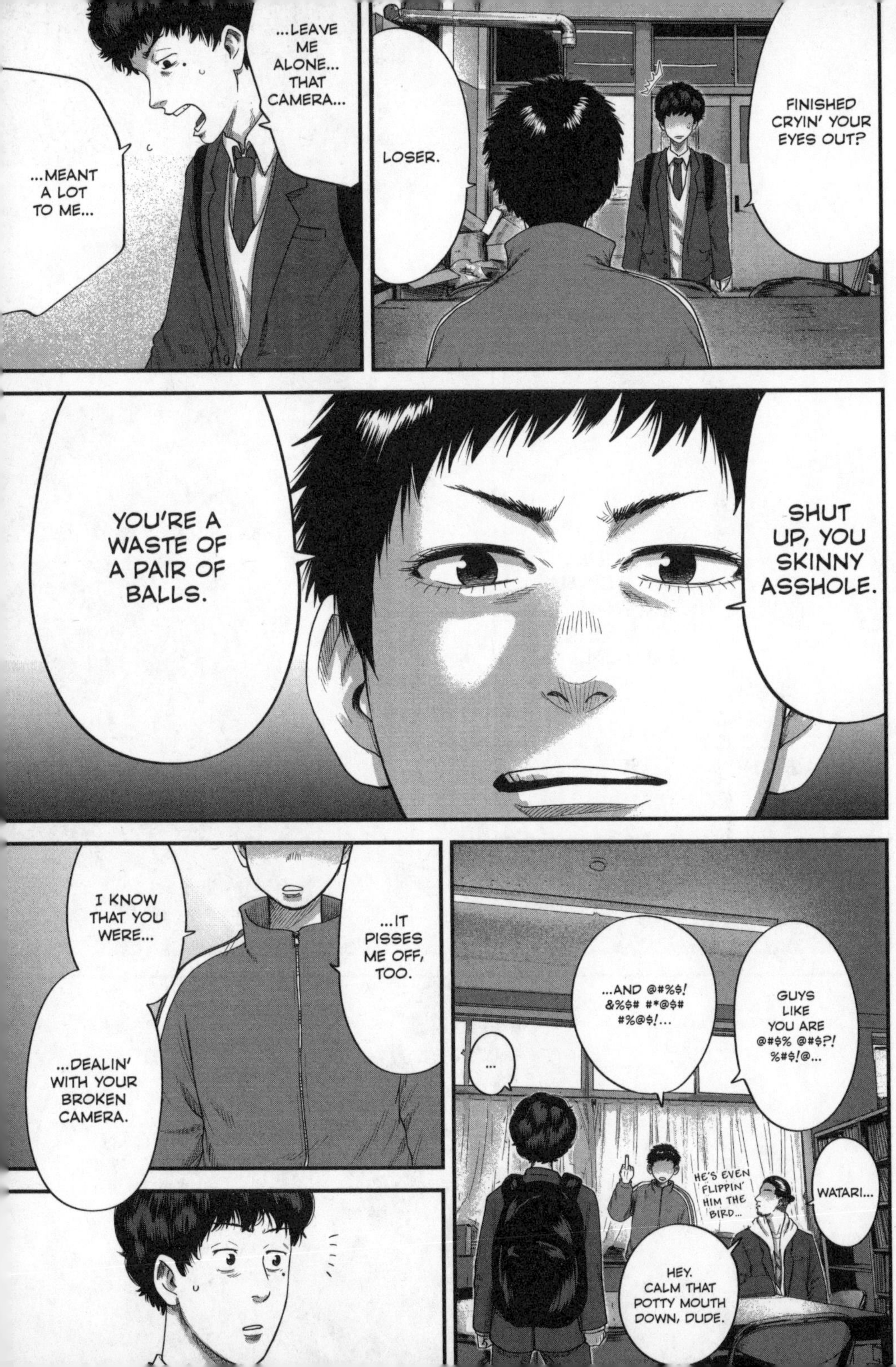
FINISHED CRYIN' YOUR EYES OUT?
LOSER.
...LEAVE ME ALONE... THAT CAMERA...
...MEANT A LOT TO ME...
SHUT UP, YOU SKINNY ASSHOLE.
YOU'RE A WASTE OF A PAIR OF BALLS.
GUYS LIKE YOU ARE @#$% @#$?! %#$!@...
...AND @#%$! &%$# #*@$# #%@$!...
...
WATARI...
HE'S EVEN FLIPPIN' HIM THE BIRD...
HEY. CALM THAT POTTY MOUTH DOWN, DUDE.
...IT PISSES ME OFF, TOO.
I KNOW THAT YOU WERE...
...DEALIN' WITH YOUR BROKEN CAMERA.

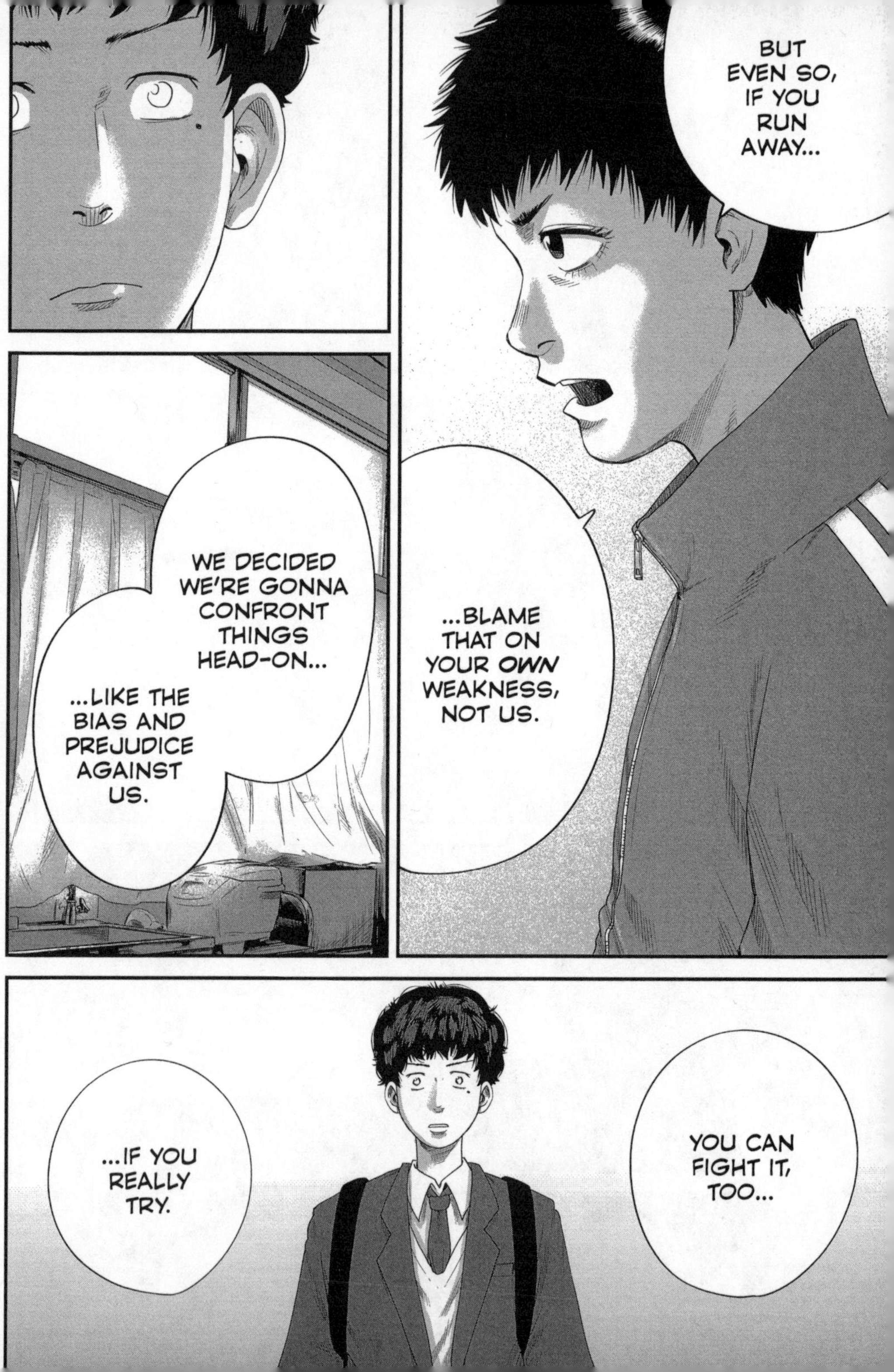
BUT EVEN SO, IF YOU RUN AWAY...
...BLAME THAT ON YOUR *OWN* WEAKNESS, NOT US.
WE DECIDED WE'RE GONNA CONFRONT THINGS HEAD-ON...
...LIKE THE BIAS AND PREJUDICE AGAINST US.
YOU CAN FIGHT IT, TOO...
...IF YOU REALLY TRY.

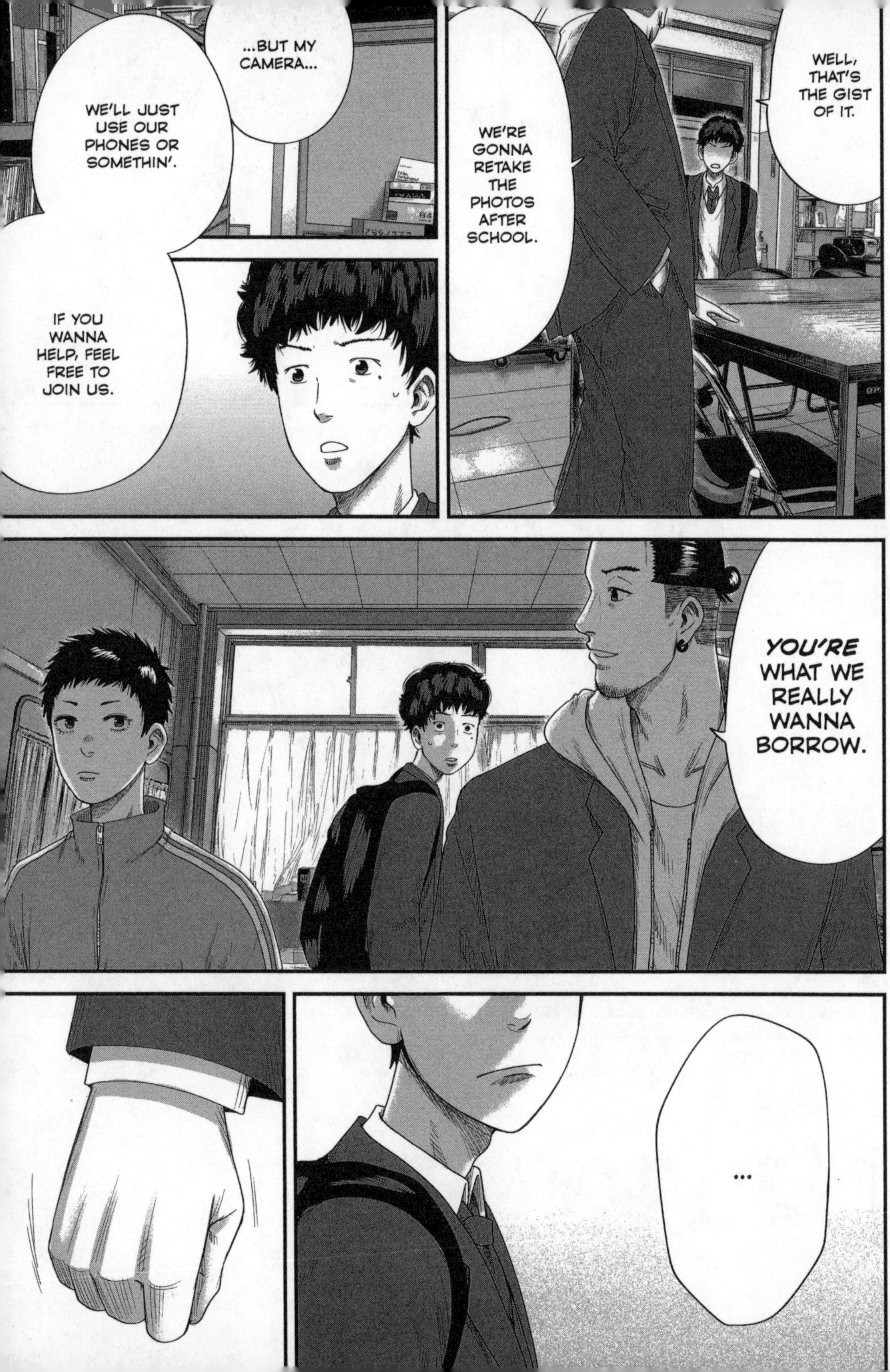
WELL, THAT'S THE GIST OF IT.
WE'RE GONNA RETAKE THE PHOTOS AFTER SCHOOL.
...BUT MY CAMERA...
WE'LL JUST USE OUR PHONES OR SOMETHIN'.
IF YOU WANNA HELP, FEEL FREE TO JOIN US.
YOU'RE WHAT WE REALLY WANNA BORROW.
...

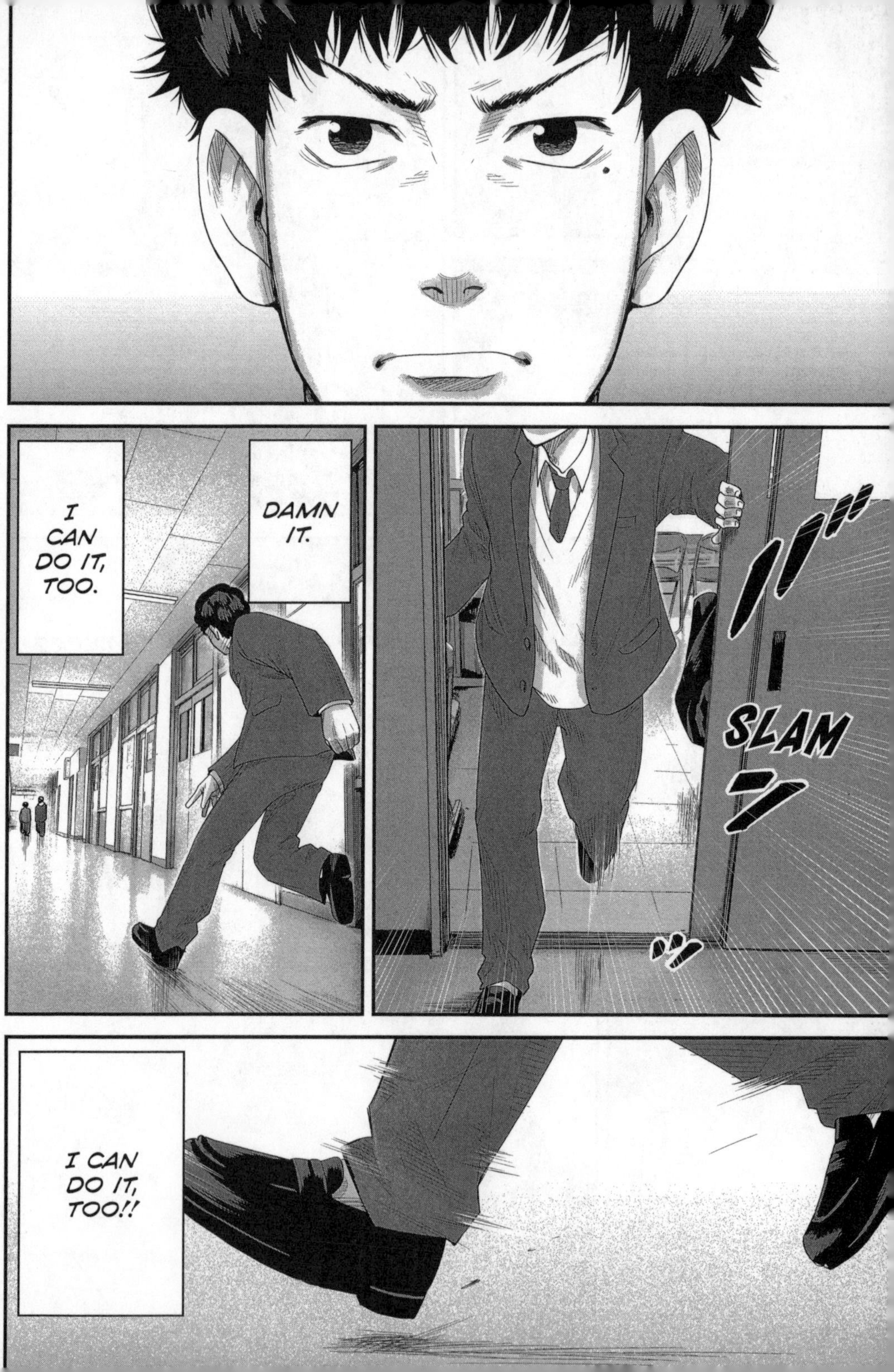
SLAM
DAMN IT.
I CAN DO IT, TOO.
I CAN DO IT, TOO!!

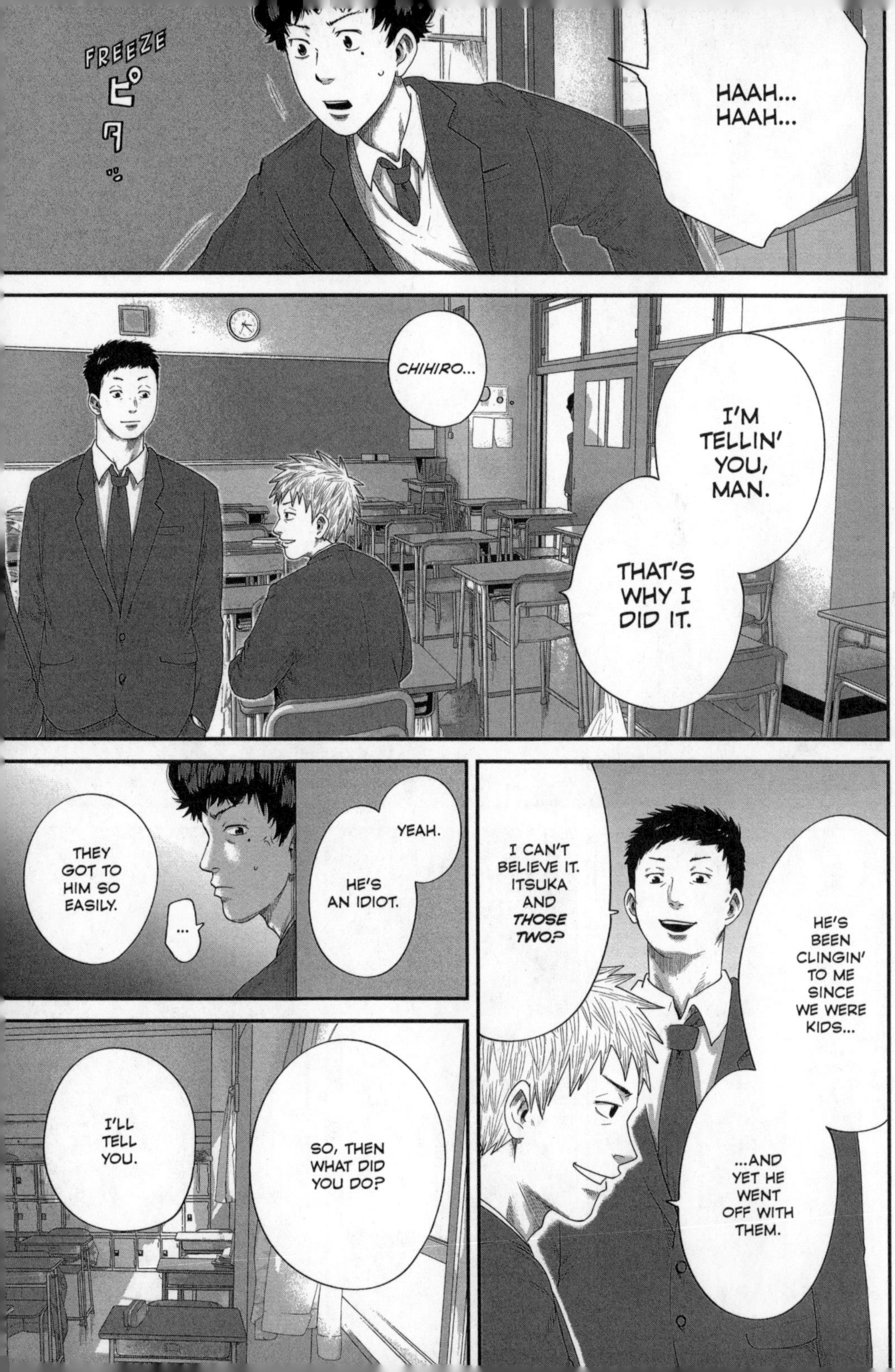
HAAH... HAAH...
FREEZE
ピタ
I'M TELLIN' YOU, MAN.
THAT'S WHY I DID IT.
CHIHIRO...
I CAN'T BELIEVE IT. ITSUKA AND *THOSE TWO?*
HE'S BEEN CLINGIN' TO ME SINCE WE WERE KIDS...
...AND YET HE WENT OFF WITH THEM.
YEAH.
HE'S AN IDIOT.
THEY GOT TO HIM SO EASILY.
...
SO, THEN WHAT DID YOU DO?
I'LL TELL YOU.

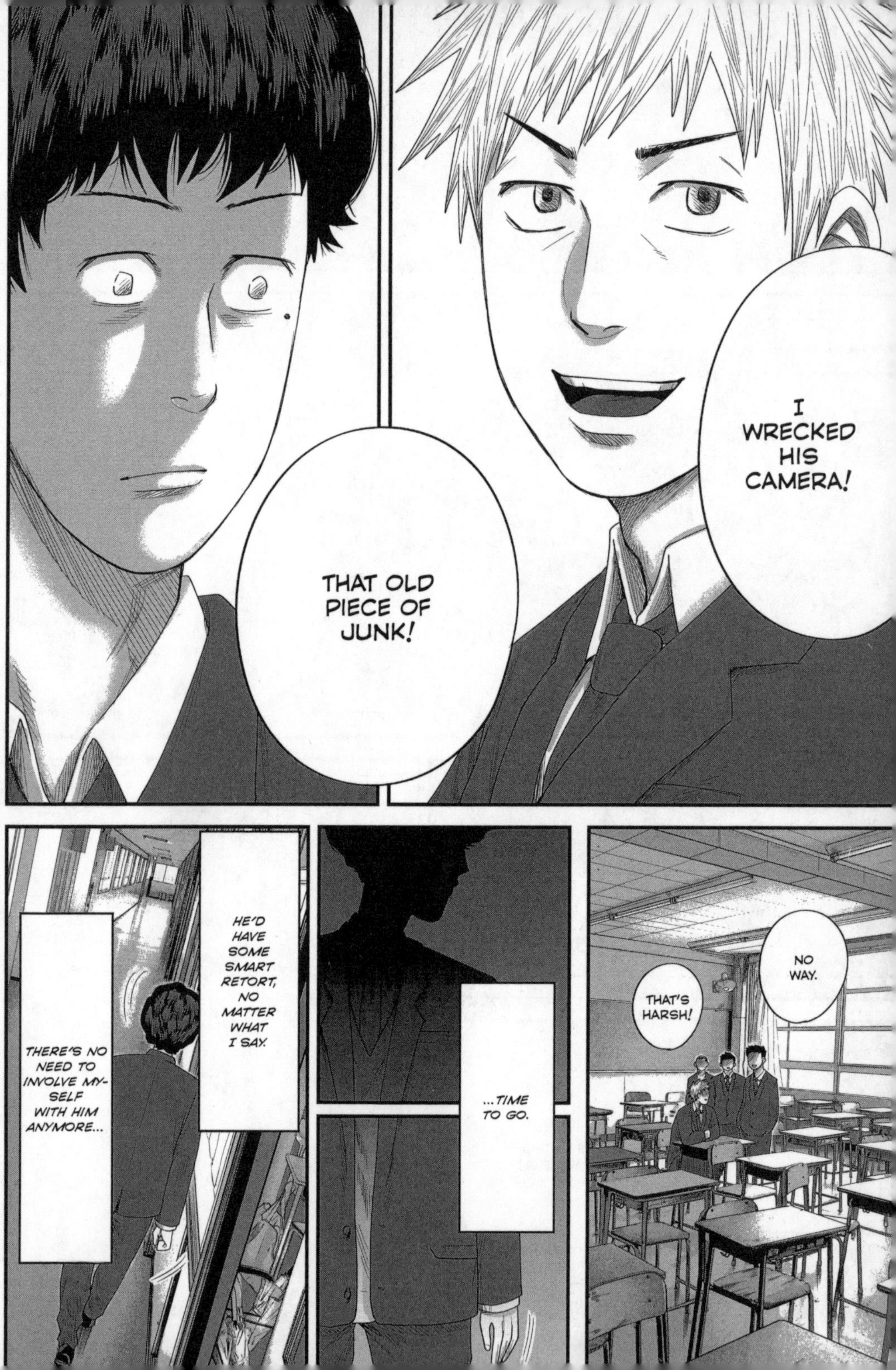
I WRECKED HIS CAMERA!
THAT OLD PIECE OF JUNK!
NO WAY.
THAT'S HARSH!
...TIME TO GO.
HE'D HAVE SOME SMART RETORT, NO MATTER WHAT I SAY.
THERE'S NO NEED TO INVOLVE MY-SELF WITH HIM ANYMORE...

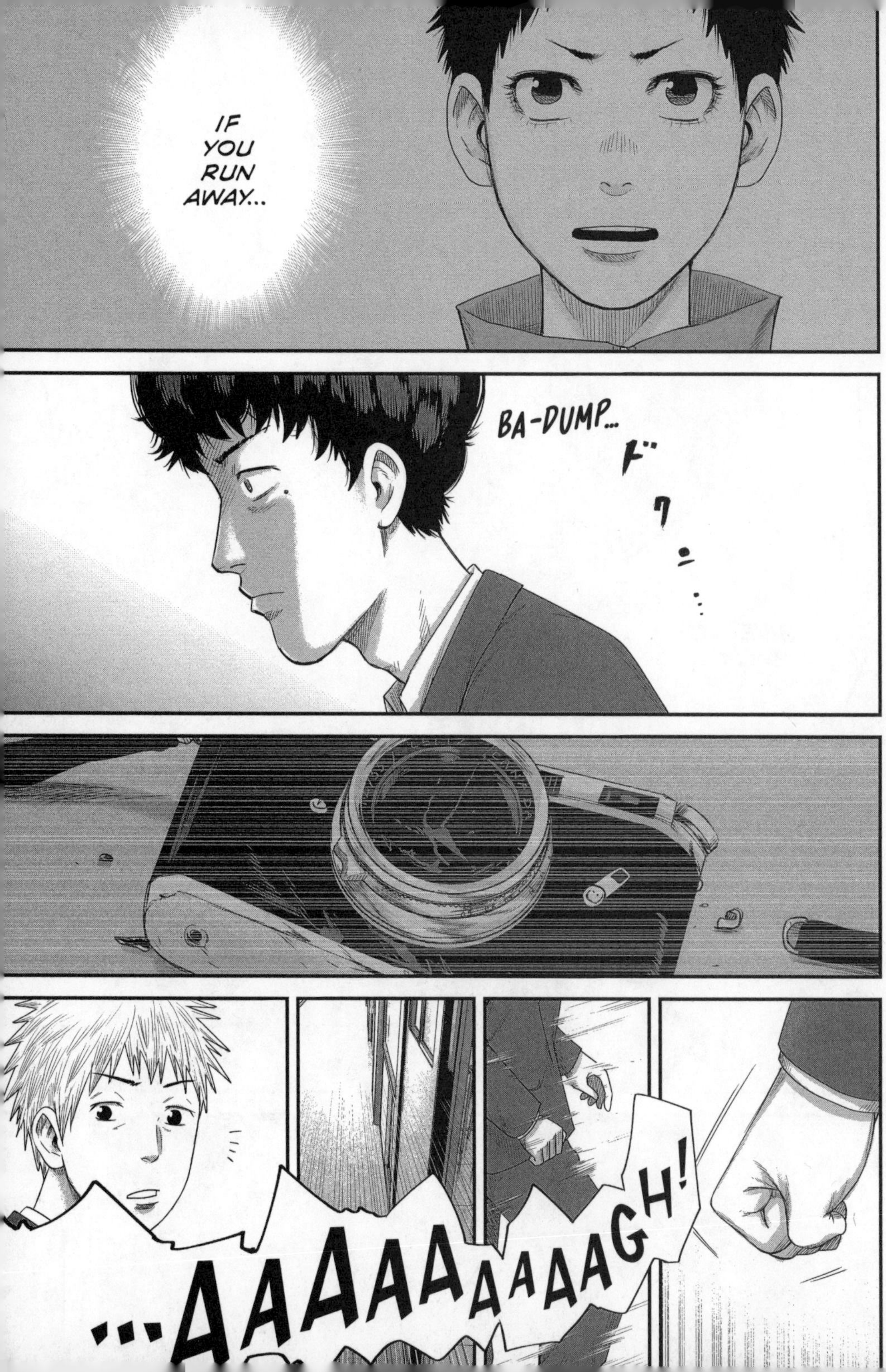

IF YOU RUN AWAY...
BA-DUMP...
ドクン…
...AAAAAAAAAGH!

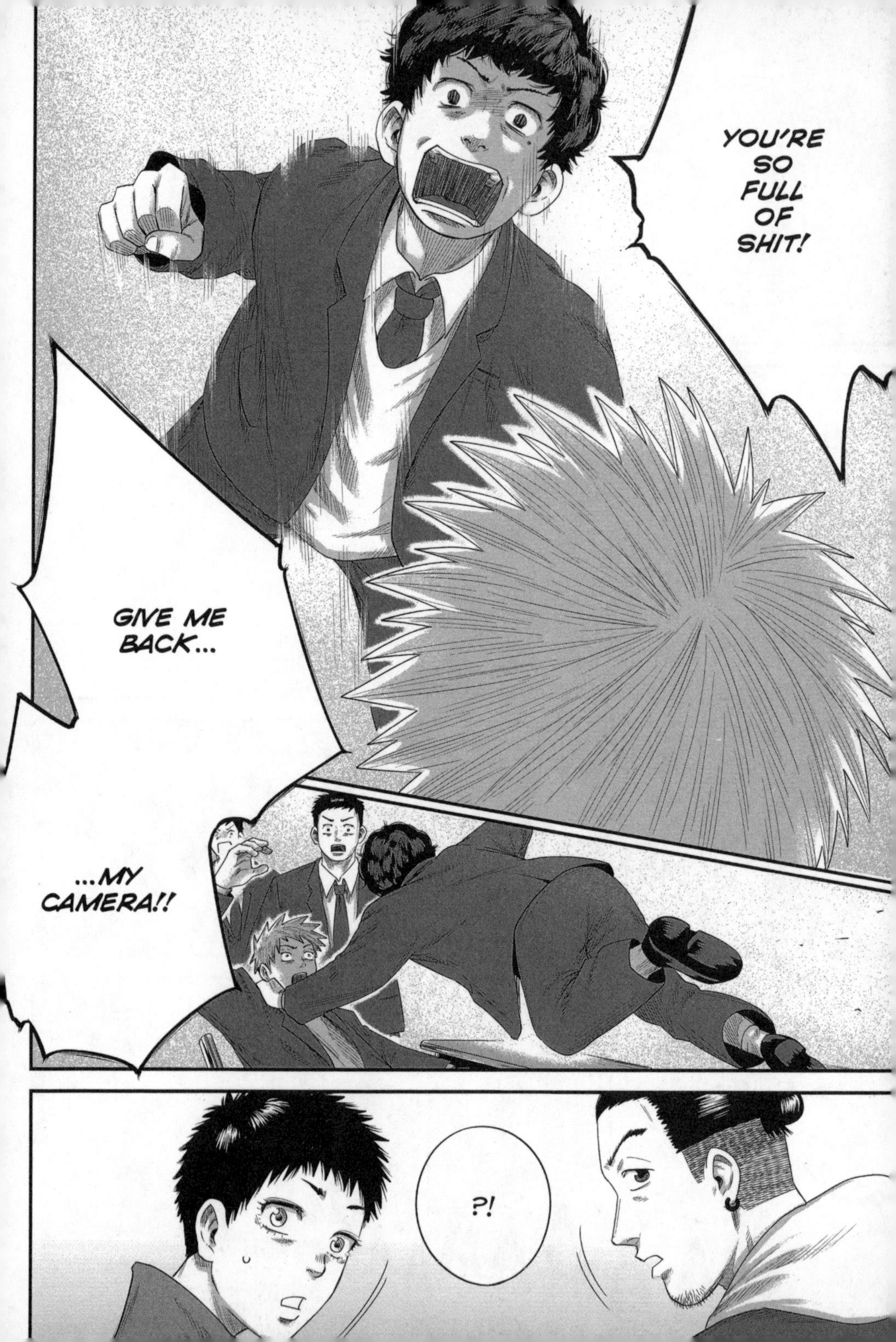
YOU'RE SO FULL OF SHIT!
GIVE ME BACK...
...MY CAMERA!!
?!

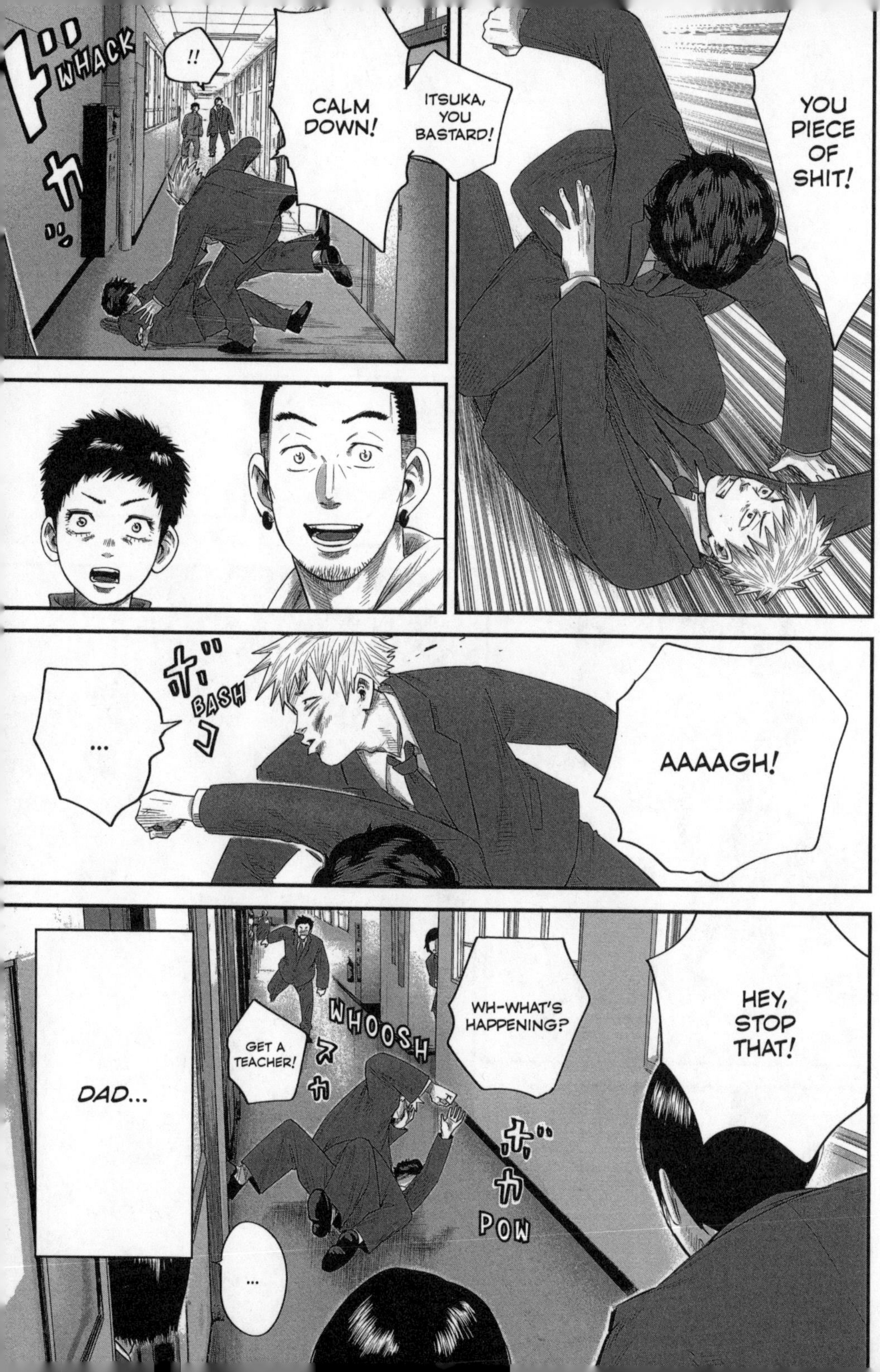
YOU PIECE OF SHIT!
ITSUKA, YOU BASTARD!
CALM DOWN!
WHACK
!!
AAAAGH!
BASH
...
HEY, STOP THAT!
WH-WHAT'S HAPPENING?
WHOOSH
GET A TEACHER!
POW
...
DAD...

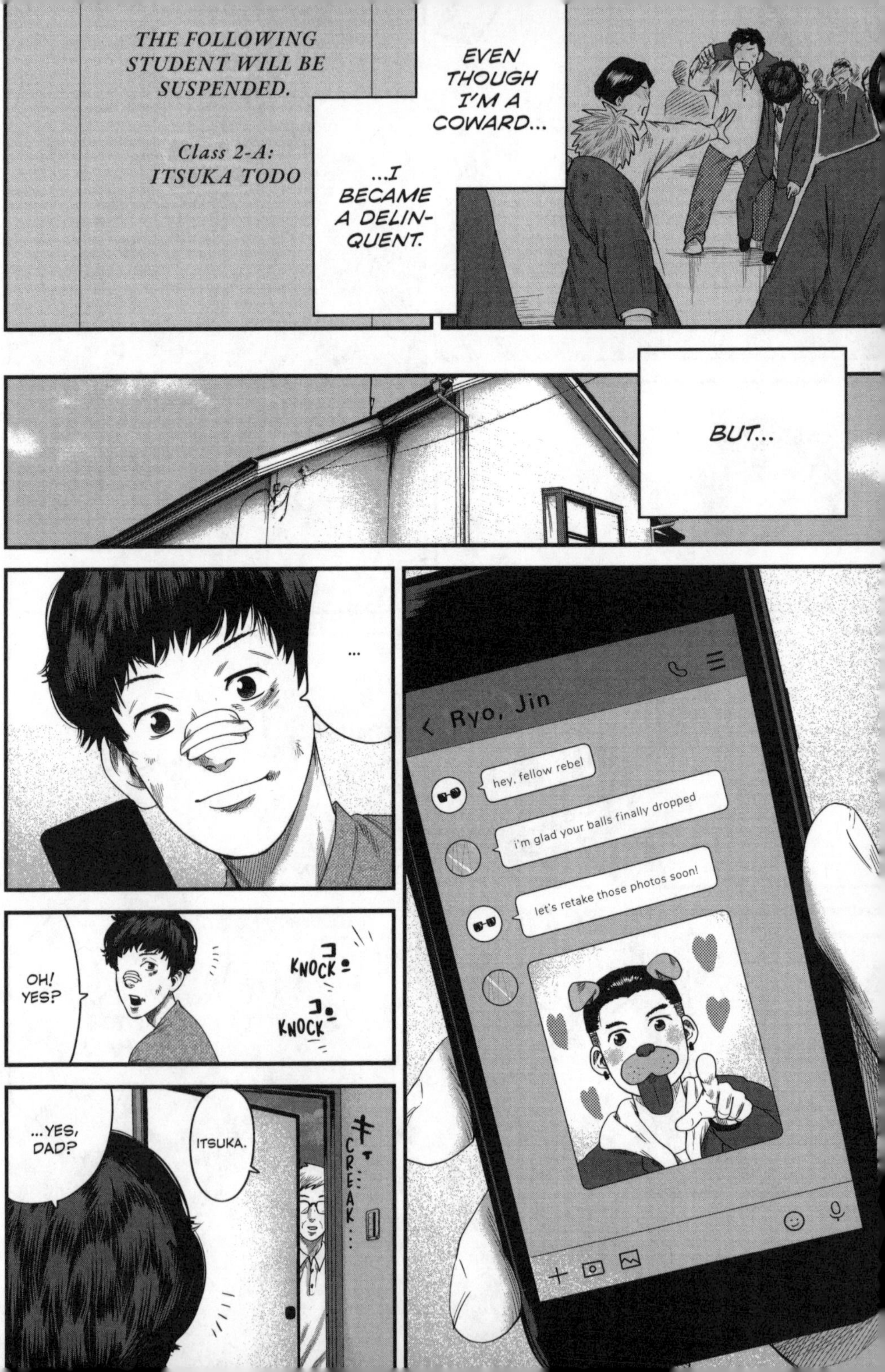
EVEN THOUGH I'M A COWARD...
...I BECAME A DELIN-QUENT.
THE FOLLOWING STUDENT WILL BE SUSPENDED.
Class 2-A: ITSUKA TODO
BUT...
Ryo, Jin
hey, fellow rebel
i'm glad your balls finally dropped
let's retake those photos soon!
...
KNOCK
KNOCK
OH! YES?
CREAK...
ITSUKA.
...YES, DAD?

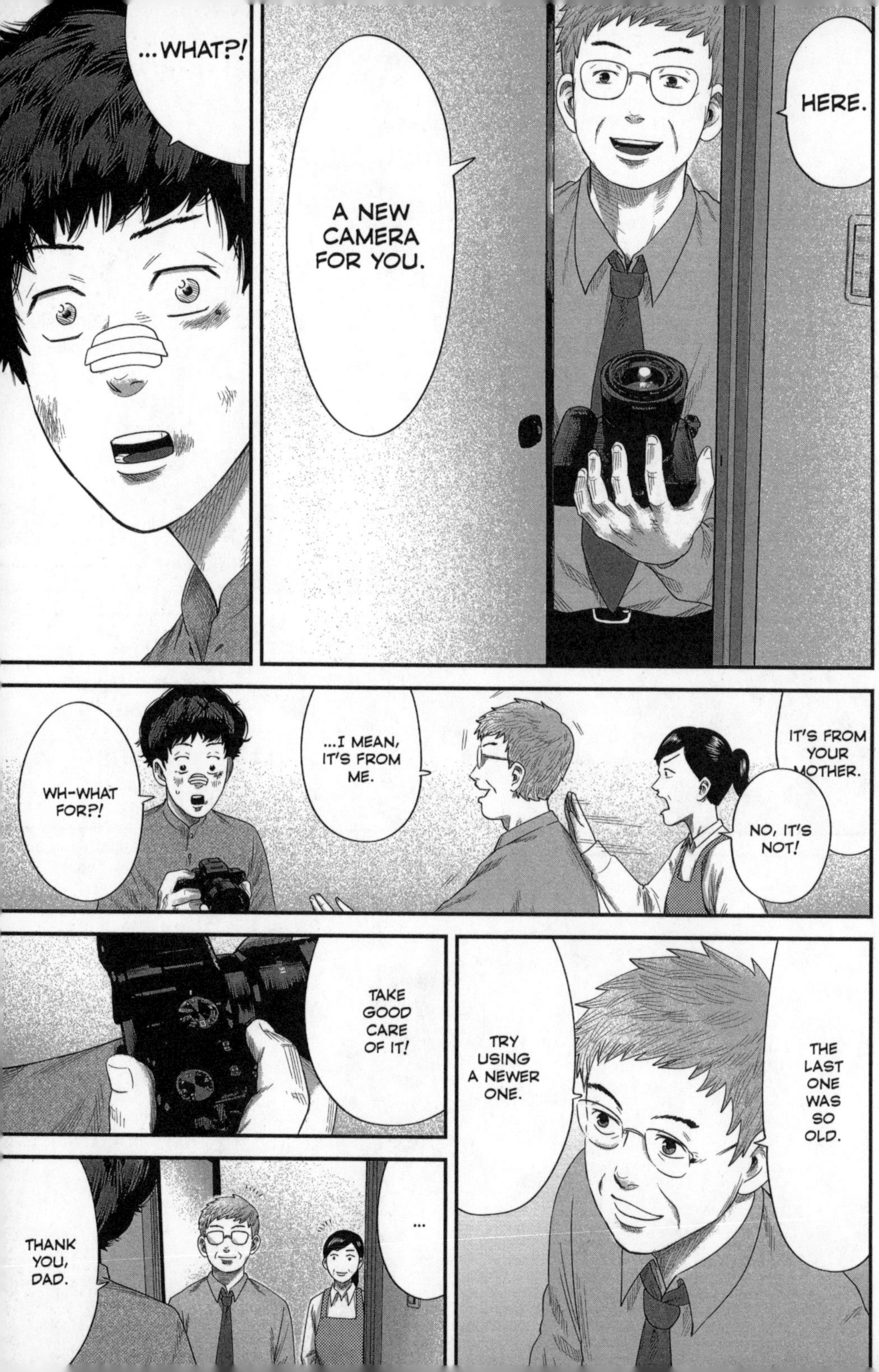
HERE.
A NEW CAMERA FOR YOU.
...WHAT?!
IT'S FROM YOUR MOTHER.
NO, IT'S NOT!
...I MEAN, IT'S FROM ME.
WH-WHAT FOR?!
THE LAST ONE WAS SO OLD.
TRY USING A NEWER ONE.
TAKE GOOD CARE OF IT!
...
THANK YOU, DAD.

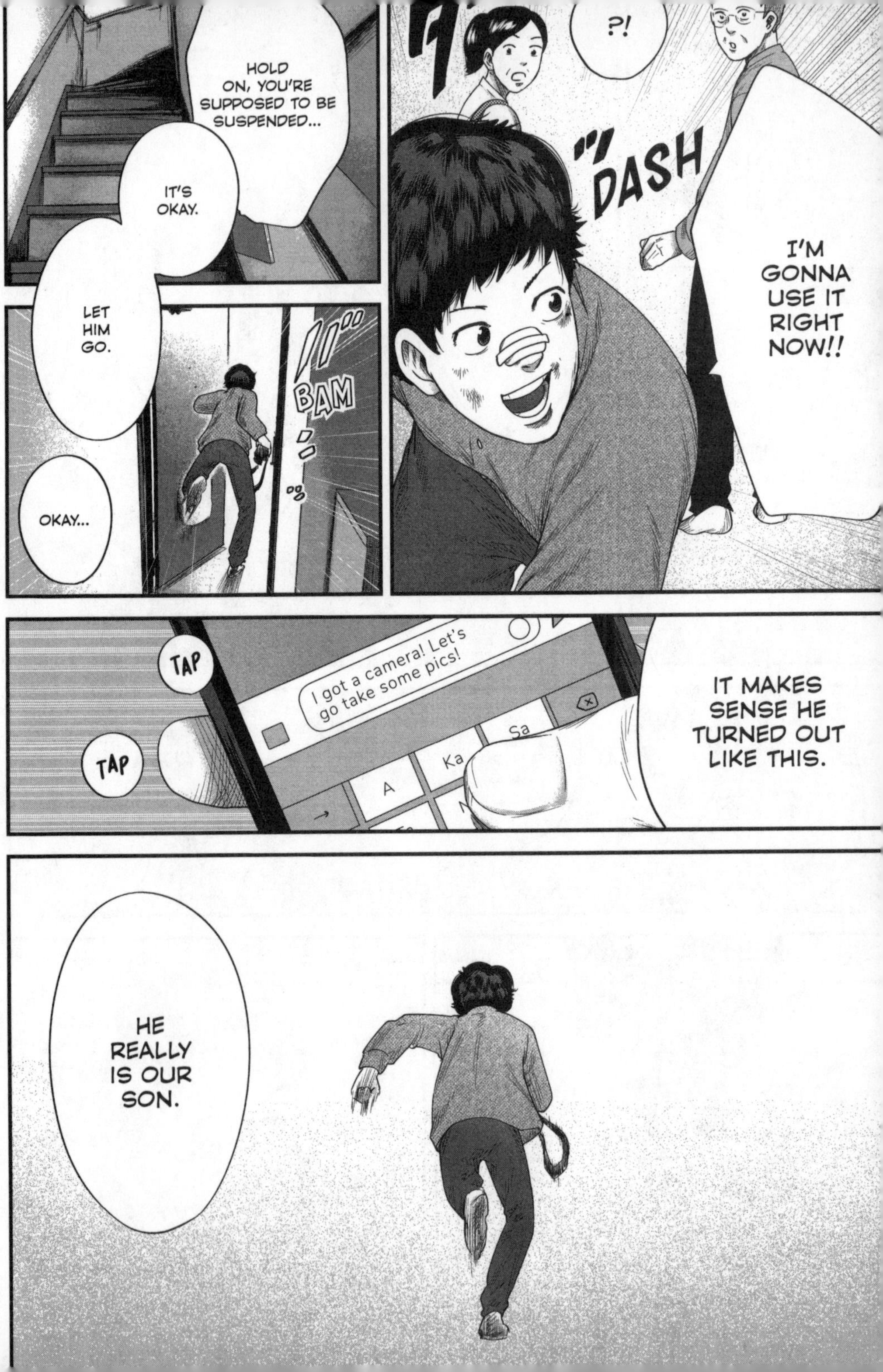
?!
DASH
I'M GONNA USE IT RIGHT NOW!!
HOLD ON, YOU'RE SUPPOSED TO BE SUSPENDED...
IT'S OKAY.
LET HIM GO.
BAM
OKAY...
IT MAKES SENSE HE TURNED OUT LIKE THIS.
I got a camera! Let's go take some pics!
Sa
Ka
A
TAP
TAP
HE REALLY IS OUR SON.

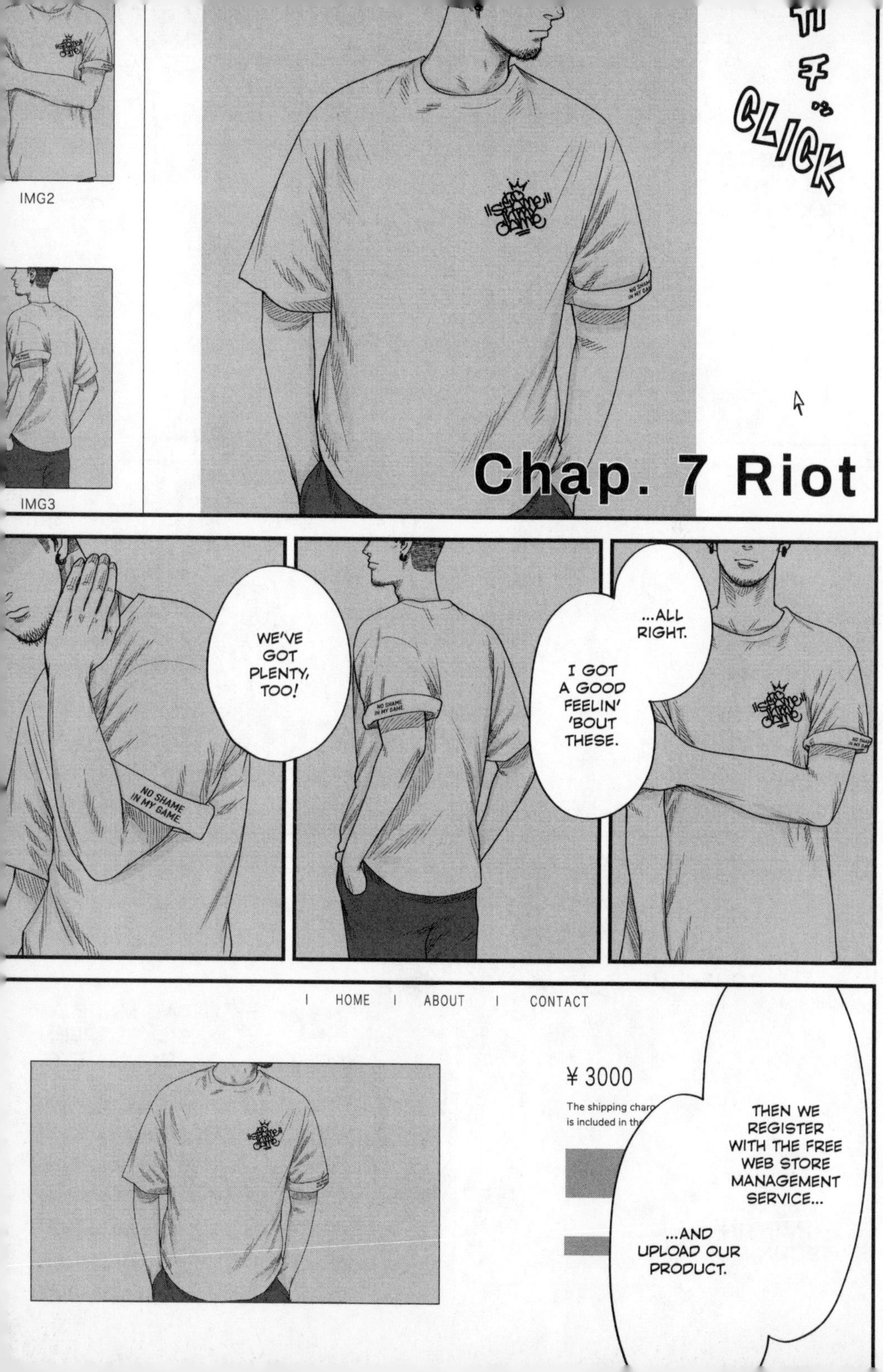
CLICK
Chap. 7 Riot
IMG2
IMG3
...ALL RIGHT.
I GOT A GOOD FEELIN' 'BOUT THESE.
NO SHAME IN MY GAME.
WE'VE GOT PLENTY, TOO!
NO SHAME IN MY GAME.
| HOME | ABOUT | CONTACT
¥ 3000
THEN WE REGISTER WITH THE FREE WEB STORE MANAGEMENT SERVICE...
...AND UPLOAD OUR PRODUCT.

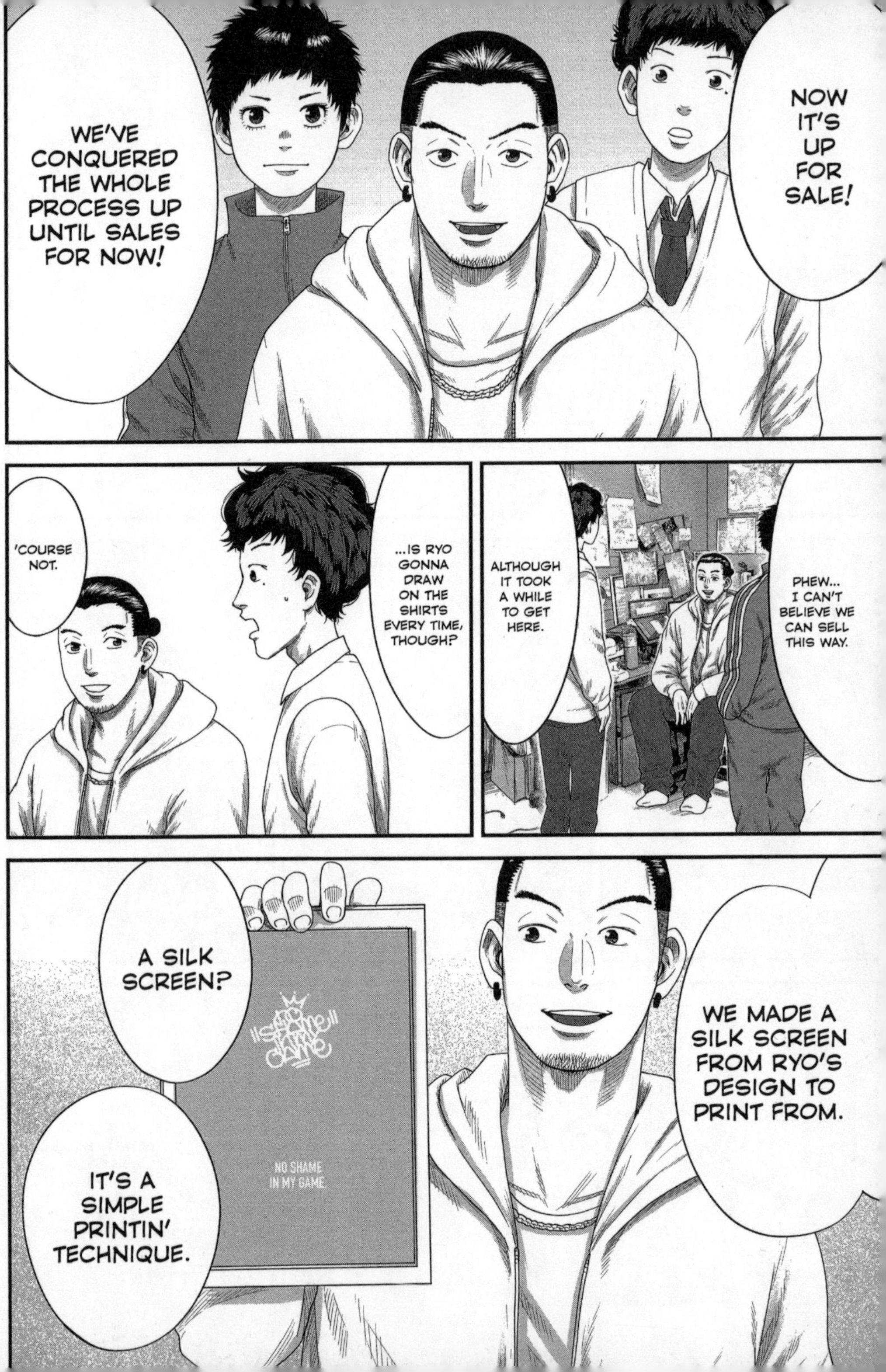
NOW IT'S UP FOR SALE!
WE'VE CONQUERED THE WHOLE PROCESS UP UNTIL SALES FOR NOW!
PHEW... I CAN'T BELIEVE WE CAN SELL THIS WAY.
ALTHOUGH IT TOOK A WHILE TO GET HERE.
...IS RYO GONNA DRAW ON THE SHIRTS EVERY TIME, THOUGH?
'COURSE NOT.
WE MADE A SILK SCREEN FROM RYO'S DESIGN TO PRINT FROM.
A SILK SCREEN?
NO SHAME IN MY GAME.
IT'S A SIMPLE PRINTIN' TECHNIQUE.

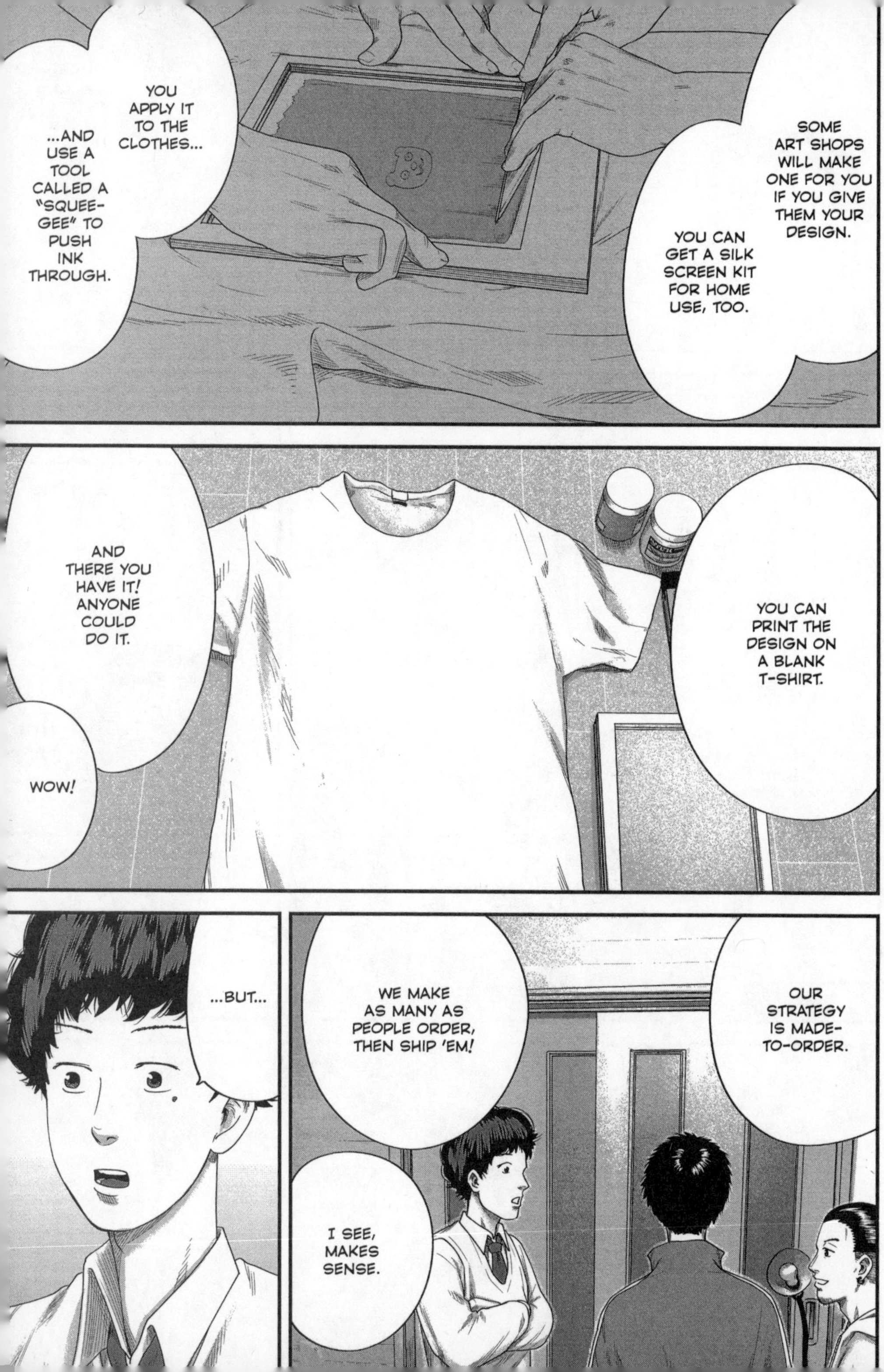

SOME ART SHOPS WILL MAKE ONE FOR YOU IF YOU GIVE THEM YOUR DESIGN.
YOU CAN GET A SILK SCREEN KIT FOR HOME USE, TOO.
YOU APPLY IT TO THE CLOTHES...
...AND USE A TOOL CALLED A "SQUEE-GEE" TO PUSH INK THROUGH.
YOU CAN PRINT THE DESIGN ON A BLANK T-SHIRT.
AND THERE YOU HAVE IT! ANYONE COULD DO IT.
WOW!
OUR STRATEGY IS MADE-TO-ORDER.
WE MAKE AS MANY AS PEOPLE ORDER, THEN SHIP 'EM!
I SEE, MAKES SENSE.
...BUT...

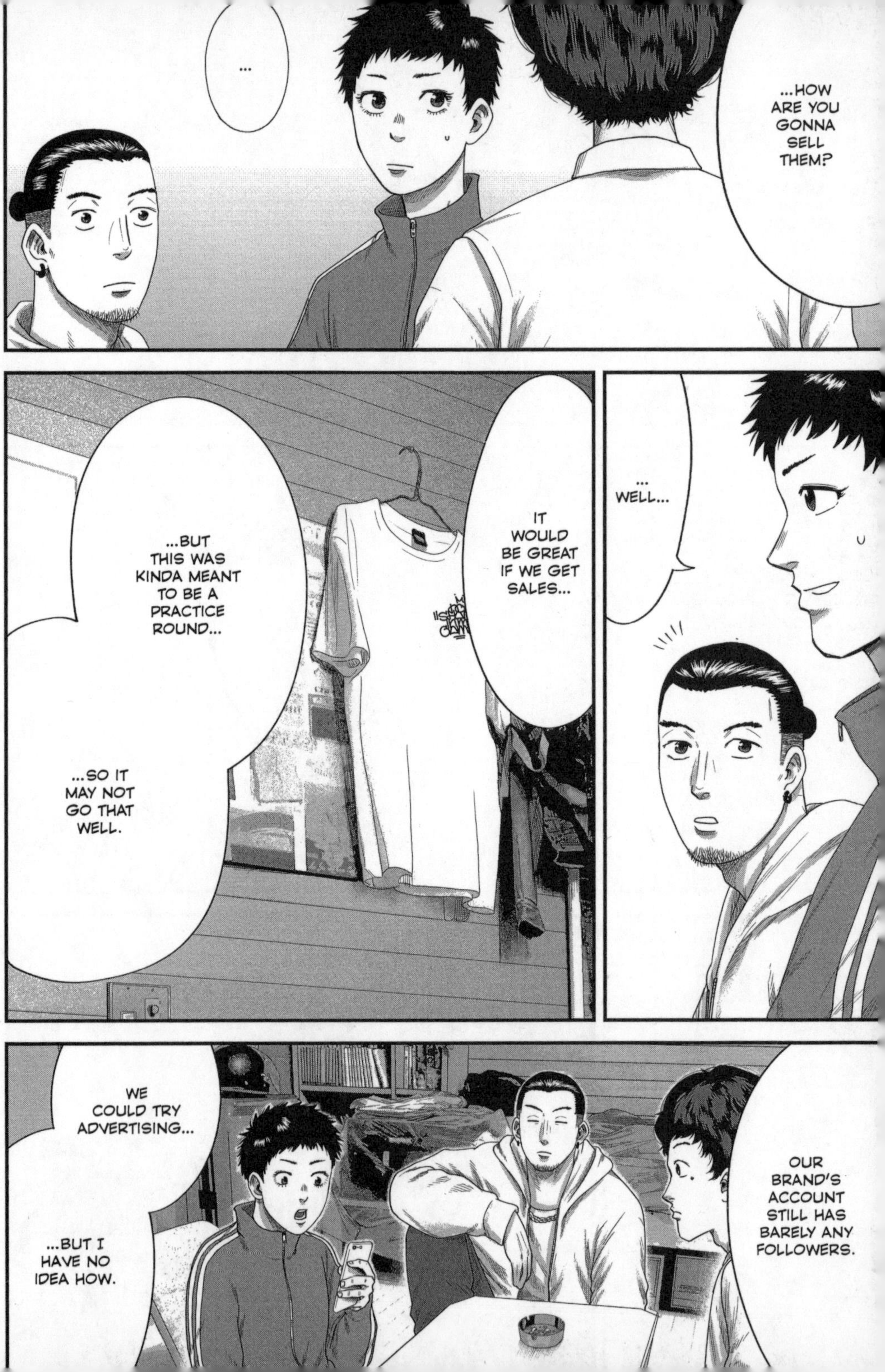
...HOW ARE YOU GONNA SELL THEM?
...
... WELL...
IT WOULD BE GREAT IF WE GET SALES...
...BUT THIS WAS KINDA MEANT TO BE A PRACTICE ROUND...
...SO IT MAY NOT GO THAT WELL.
OUR BRAND'S ACCOUNT STILL HAS BARELY ANY FOLLOWERS.
WE COULD TRY ADVERTISING...
...BUT I HAVE NO IDEA HOW.

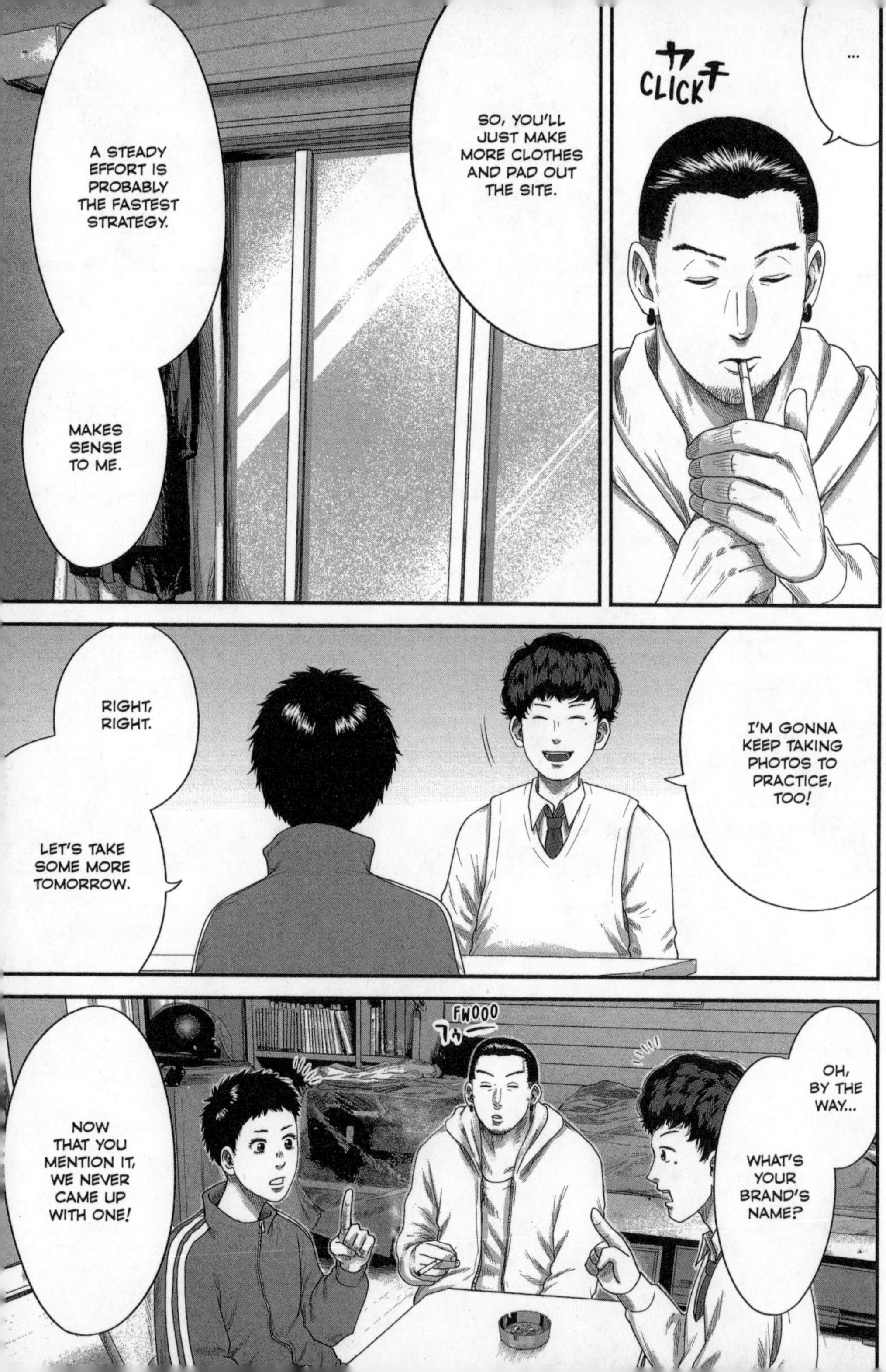
...
CLICK
SO, YOU'LL JUST MAKE MORE CLOTHES AND PAD OUT THE SITE.
A STEADY EFFORT IS PROBABLY THE FASTEST STRATEGY.
MAKES SENSE TO ME.
I'M GONNA KEEP TAKING PHOTOS TO PRACTICE, TOO!
RIGHT, RIGHT.
LET'S TAKE SOME MORE TOMORROW.
OH, BY THE WAY...
WHAT'S YOUR BRAND'S NAME?
FWOOO
NOW THAT YOU MENTION IT, WE NEVER CAME UP WITH ONE!

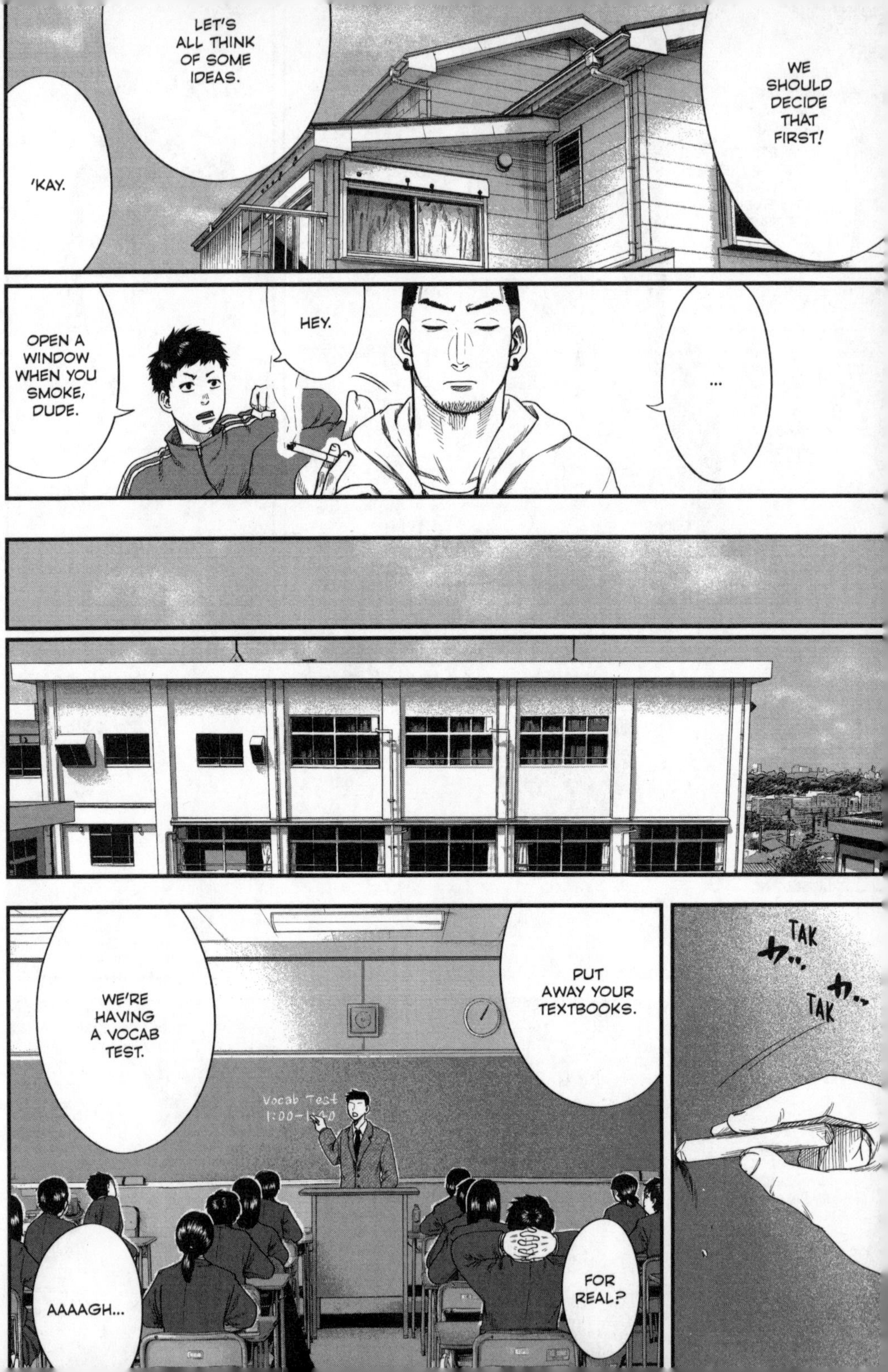
WE SHOULD DECIDE THAT FIRST!
LET'S ALL THINK OF SOME IDEAS.
'KAY.
...
HEY.
OPEN A WINDOW WHEN YOU SMOKE, DUDE.
TAK
TAK
PUT AWAY YOUR TEXTBOOKS.
WE'RE HAVING A VOCAB TEST.
Vocab Test
FOR REAL?
AAAAGH...

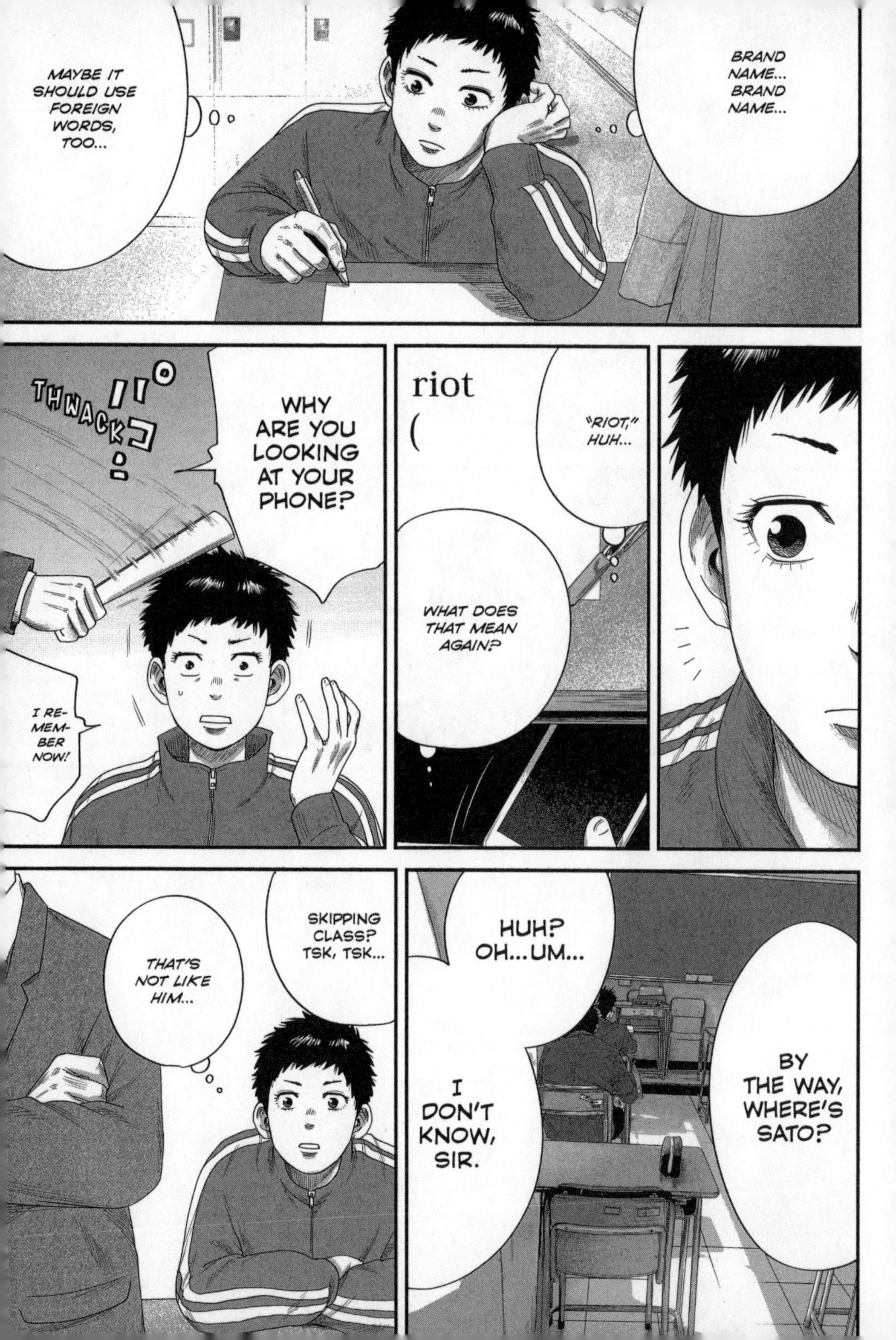
BRAND NAME... BRAND NAME...
MAYBE IT SHOULD USE FOREIGN WORDS, TOO...
riot
(
"RIOT," HUH...
WHAT DOES THAT MEAN AGAIN?
WHY ARE YOU LOOKING AT YOUR PHONE?
THWACK
I RE-MEM-BER NOW!
BY THE WAY, WHERE'S SATO?
HUH? OH...UM...
I DON'T KNOW, SIR.
SKIPPING CLASS? TSK, TSK...
THAT'S NOT LIKE HIM...

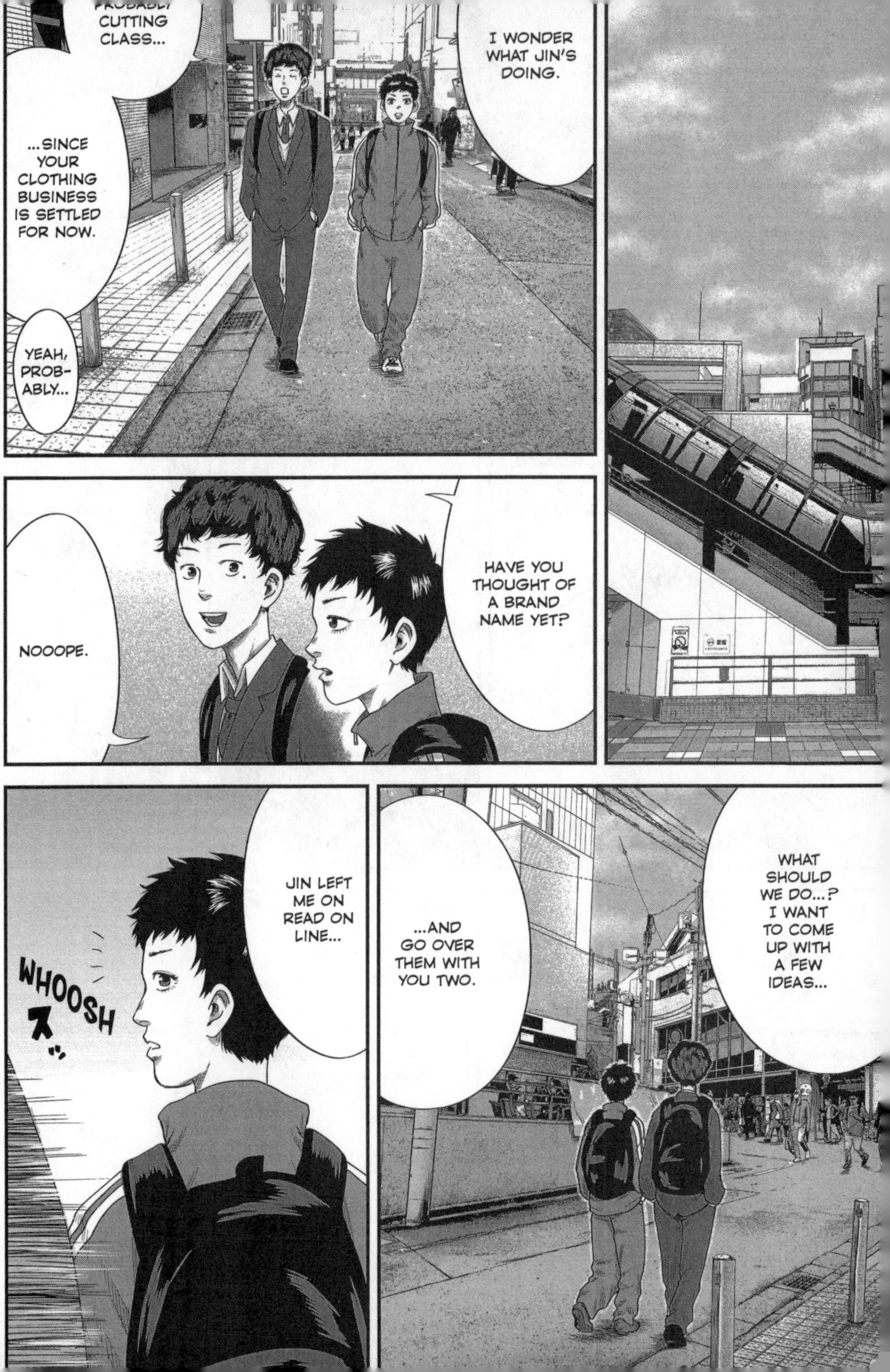
I WONDER WHAT JIN'S DOING.
CUTTING CLASS...
...SINCE YOUR CLOTHING BUSINESS IS SETTLED FOR NOW.
YEAH, PROBABLY...
HAVE YOU THOUGHT OF A BRAND NAME YET?
NOOOPE.
WHAT SHOULD WE DO...? I WANT TO COME UP WITH A FEW IDEAS...
...AND GO OVER THEM WITH YOU TWO.
JIN LEFT ME ON READ ON LINE...
WHOOSH

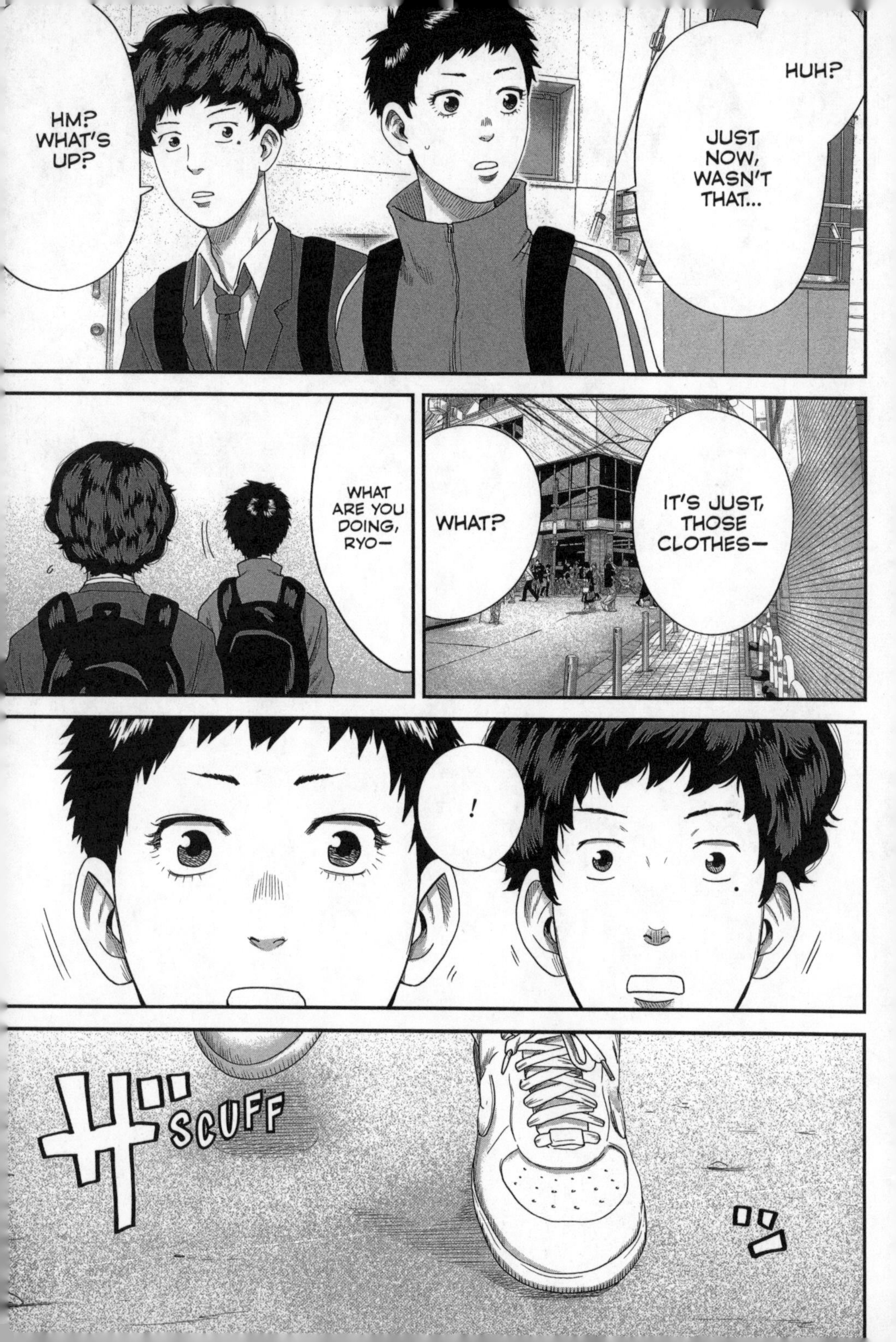
HUH?
JUST NOW, WASN'T THAT...
HM? WHAT'S UP?
IT'S JUST, THOSE CLOTHES—
WHAT?
WHAT ARE YOU DOING, RYO—
!
SCUFF

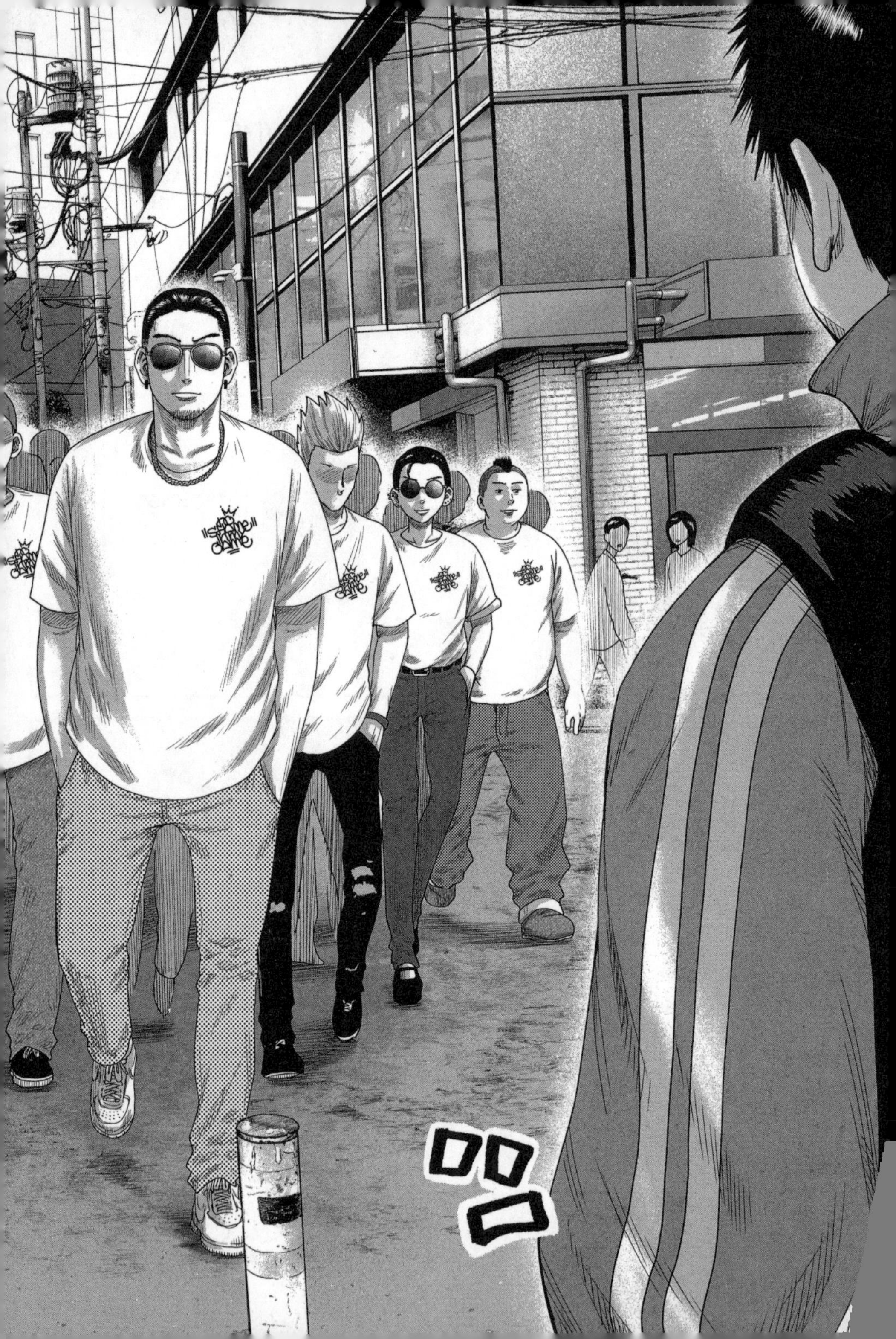

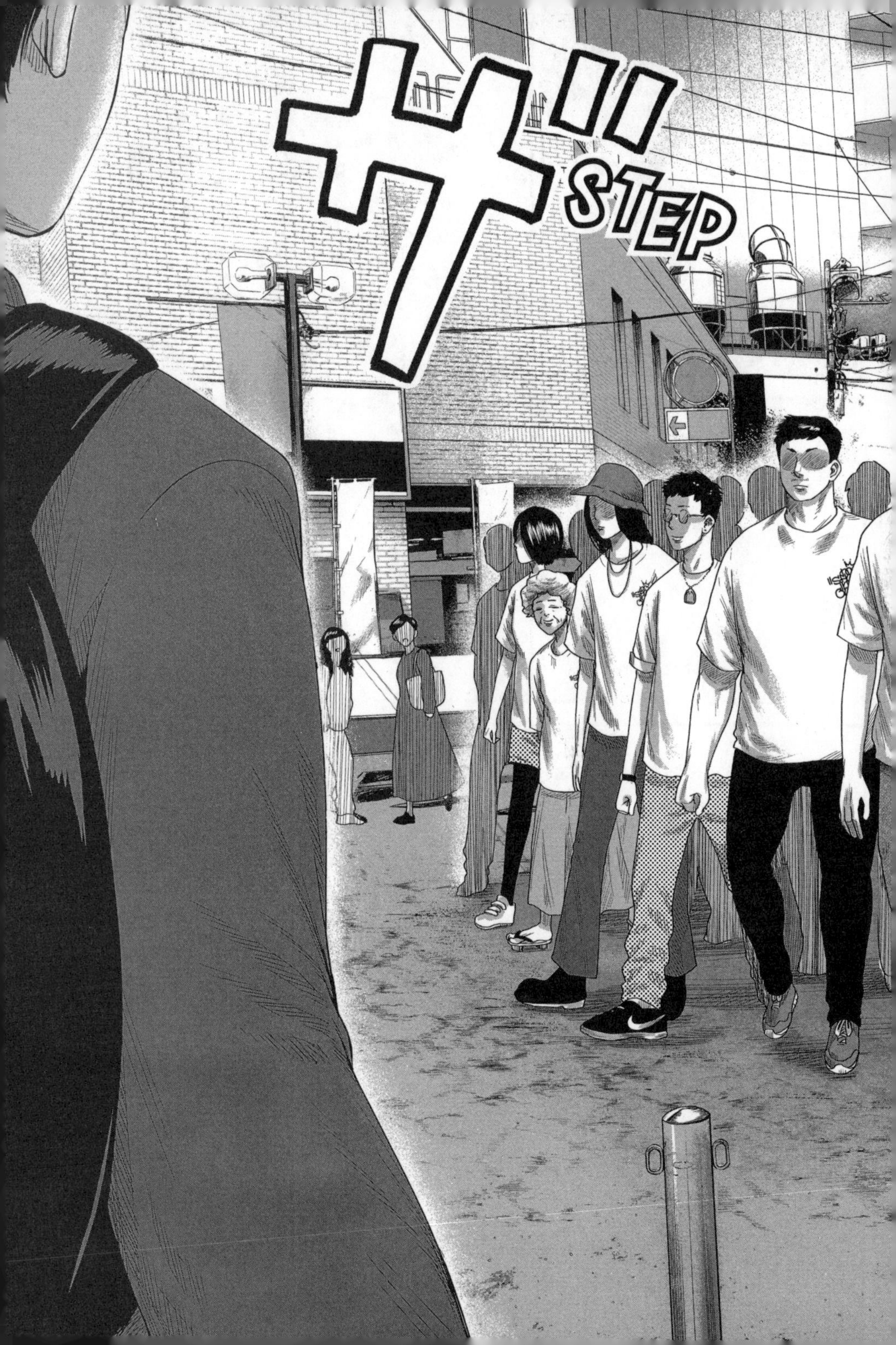
ザ
STEP

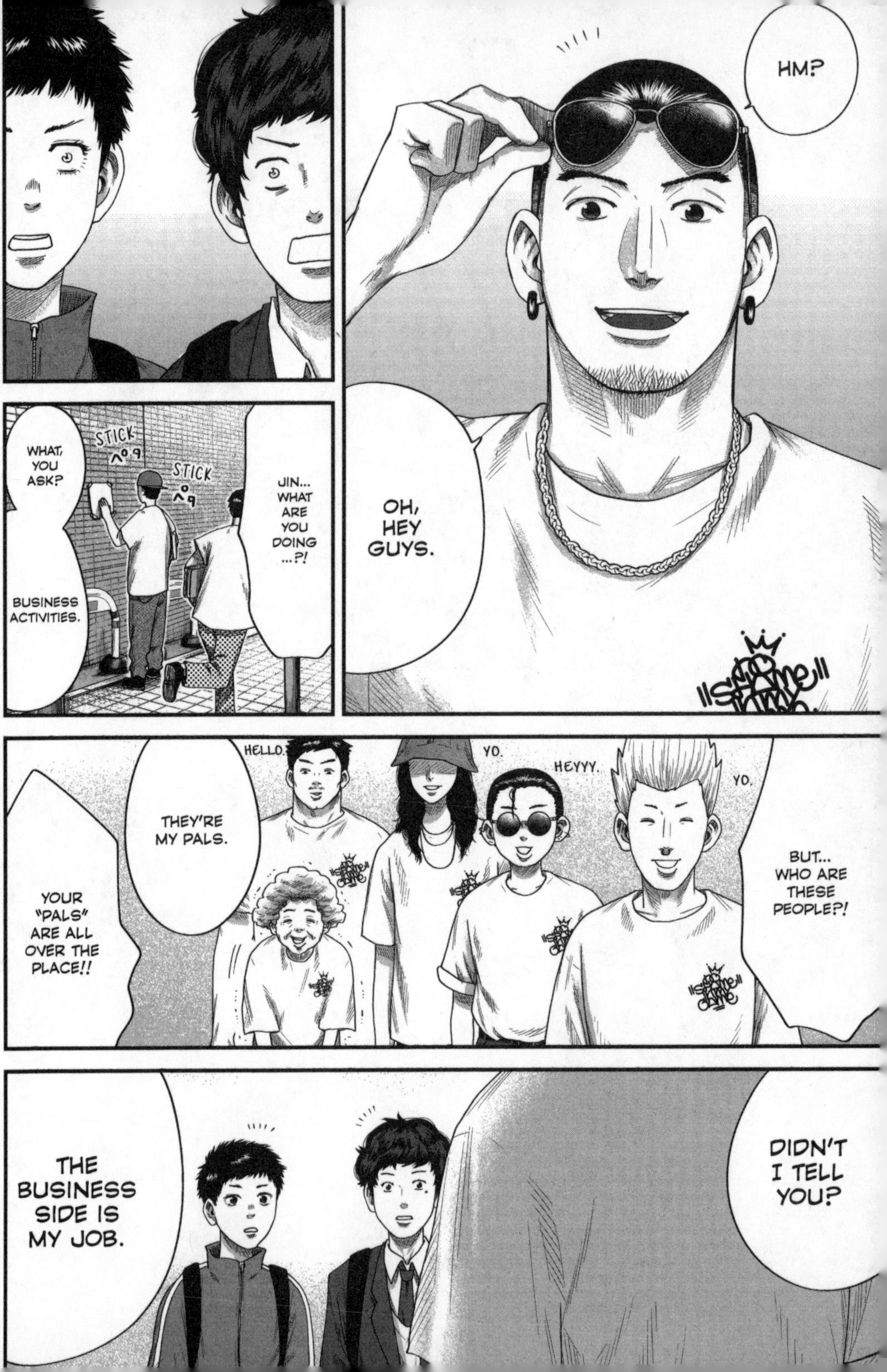
HM?
OH, HEY GUYS.
JIN... WHAT ARE YOU DOING ...?!
STICK
STICK
WHAT, YOU ASK?
BUSINESS ACTIVITIES.
BUT... WHO ARE THESE PEOPLE?!
YO.
HEYYY.
YO.
HELLO.
THEY'RE MY PALS.
YOUR "PALS" ARE ALL OVER THE PLACE!!
DIDN'T I TELL YOU?
THE BUSINESS SIDE IS MY JOB.

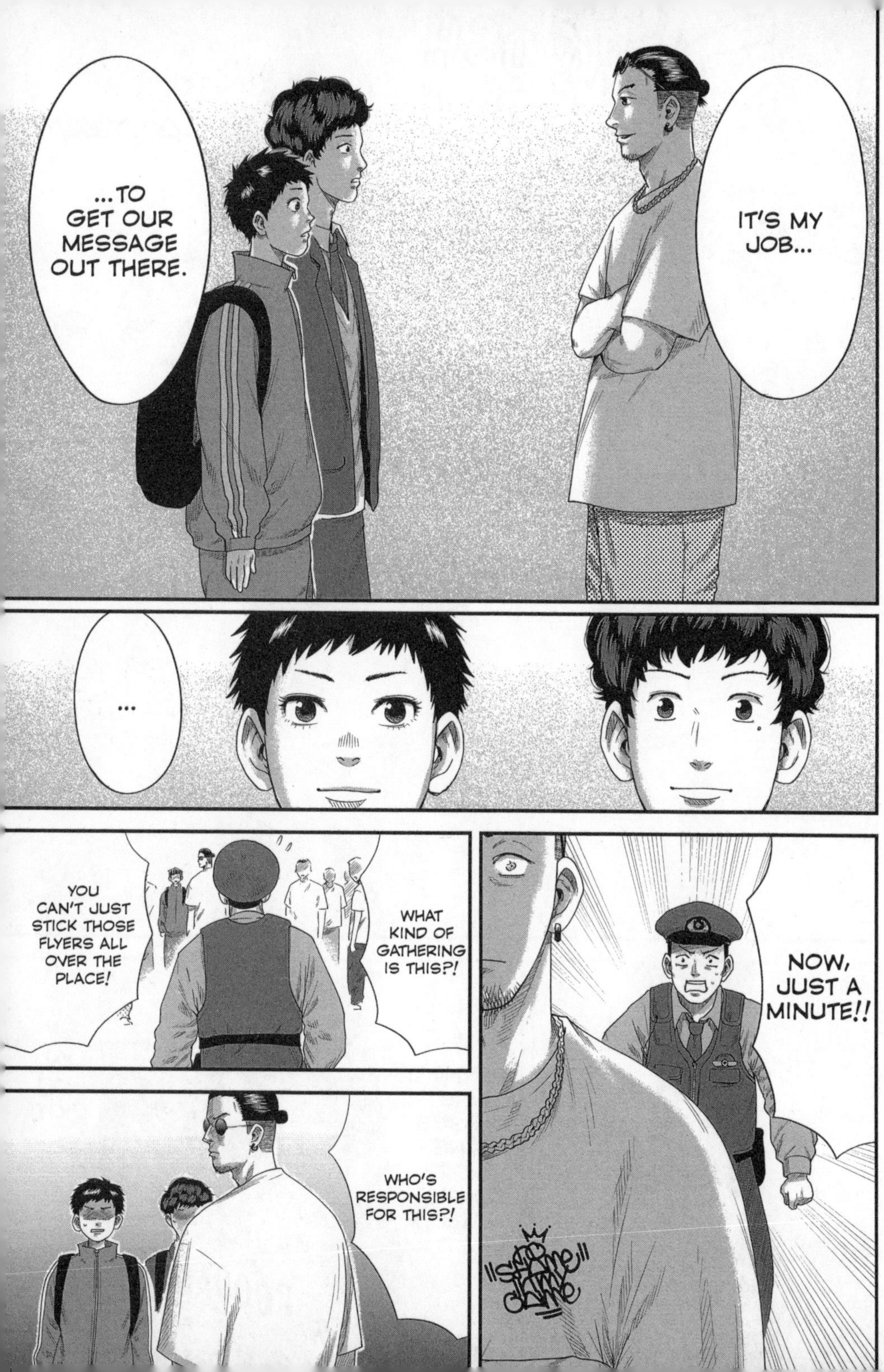
IT'S MY JOB...
...TO GET OUR MESSAGE OUT THERE.
...
NOW, JUST A MINUTE!!
WHAT KIND OF GATHERING IS THIS?!
YOU CAN'T JUST STICK THOSE FLYERS ALL OVER THE PLACE!
WHO'S RESPONSIBLE FOR THIS?!

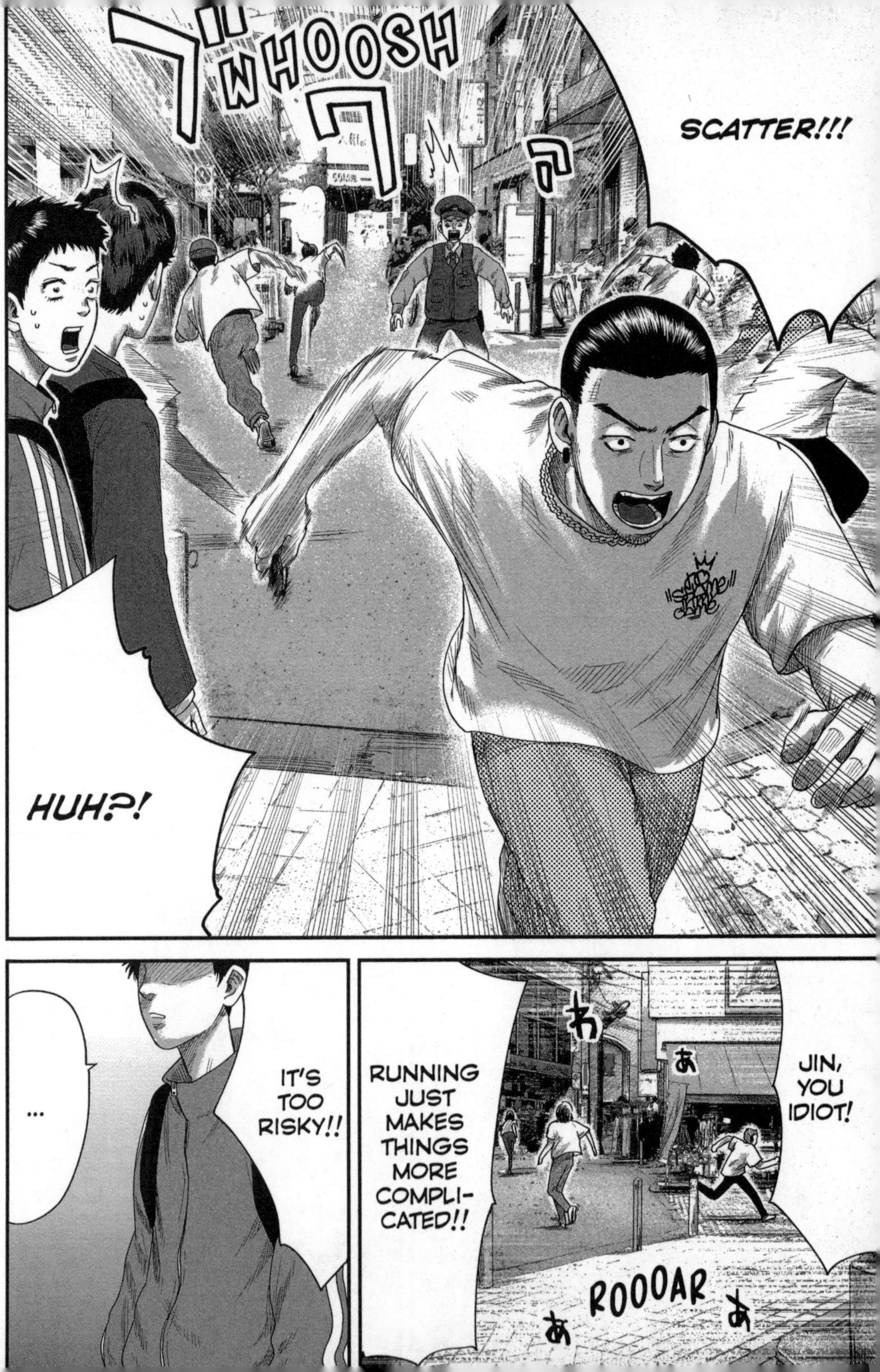

SCATTER!!!
WHOOSH
HUH?!
JIN, YOU IDIOT!
RUNNING JUST MAKES THINGS MORE COMPLI-CATED!!
ROOOAR
IT'S TOO RISKY!!
...

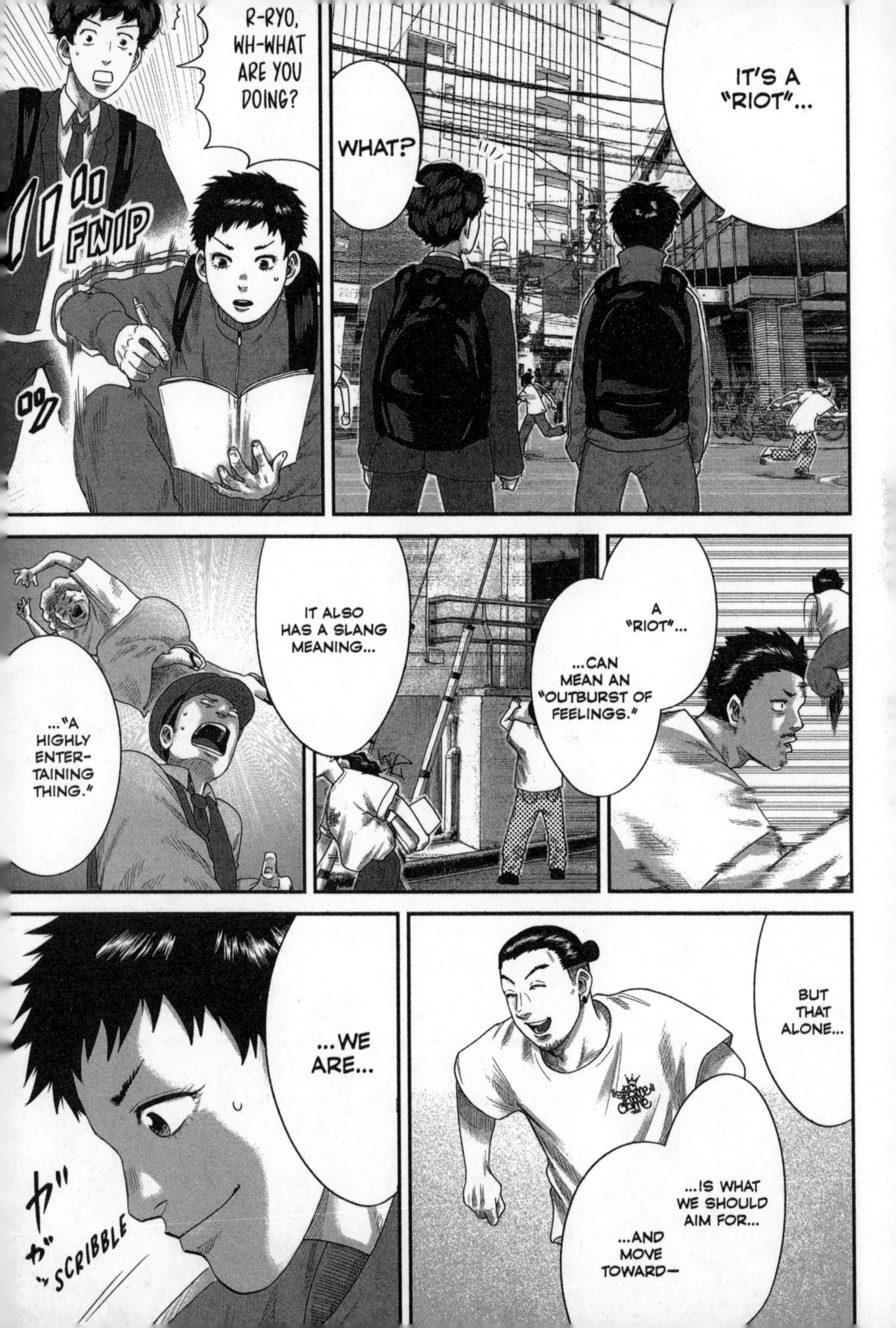
IT'S A "RIOT"...
WHAT?
R-RYO, WH-WHAT ARE YOU DOING?
FWIP
A "RIOT"...
...CAN MEAN AN "OUTBURST OF FEELINGS."
IT ALSO HAS A SLANG MEANING...
..."A HIGHLY ENTER-TAINING THING."
BUT THAT ALONE...
...IS WHAT WE SHOULD AIM FOR...
...AND MOVE TOWARD—
...WE ARE...
SCRIBBLE

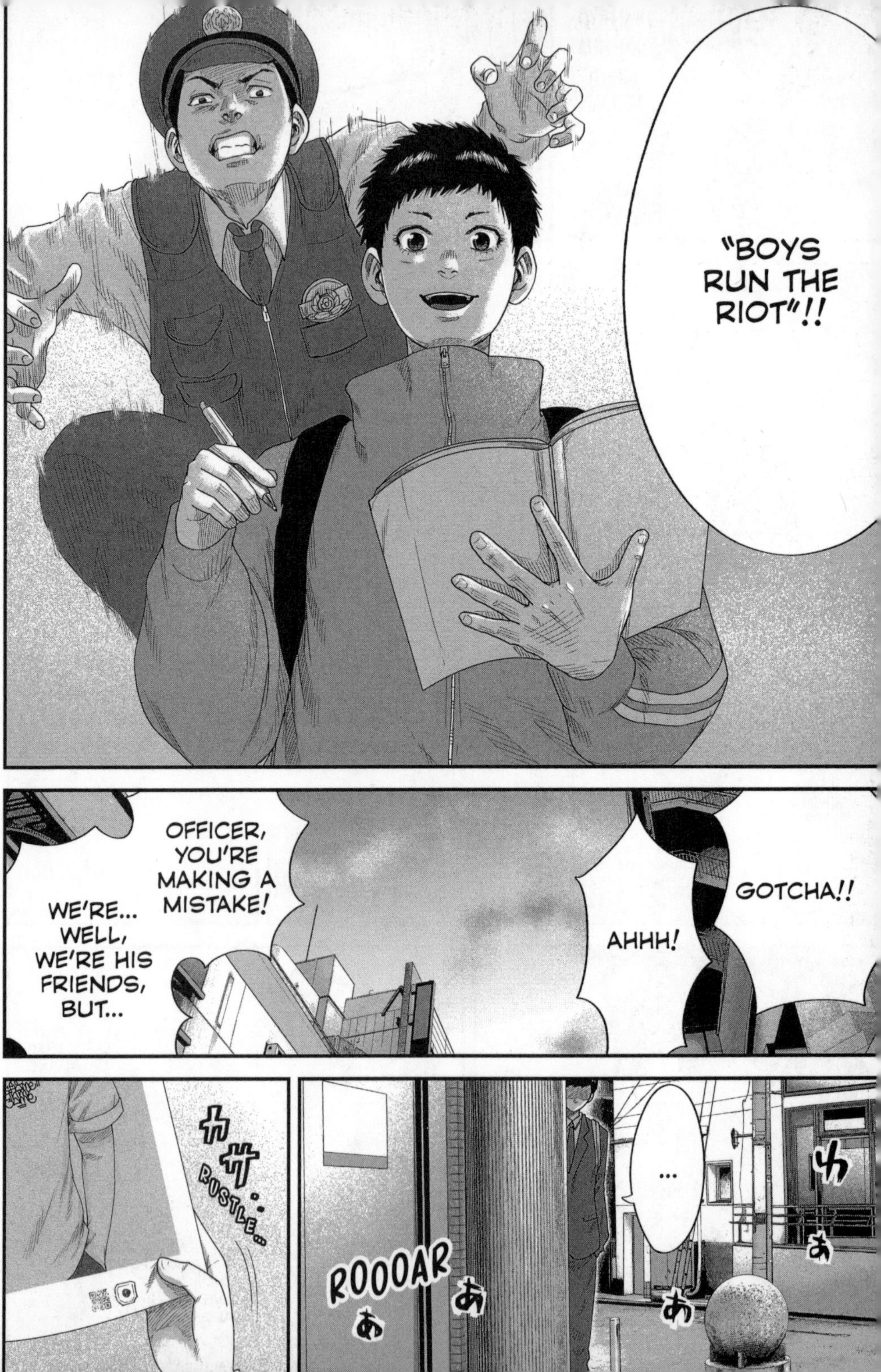
"BOYS RUN THE RIOT"!!
GOTCHA!!
AHHH!
OFFICER, YOU'RE MAKING A MISTAKE!
WE'RE... WELL, WE'RE HIS FRIENDS, BUT...
ゆ
あ
あ
...
ROOOAR
あ
あ
カサ
RUSTLE...

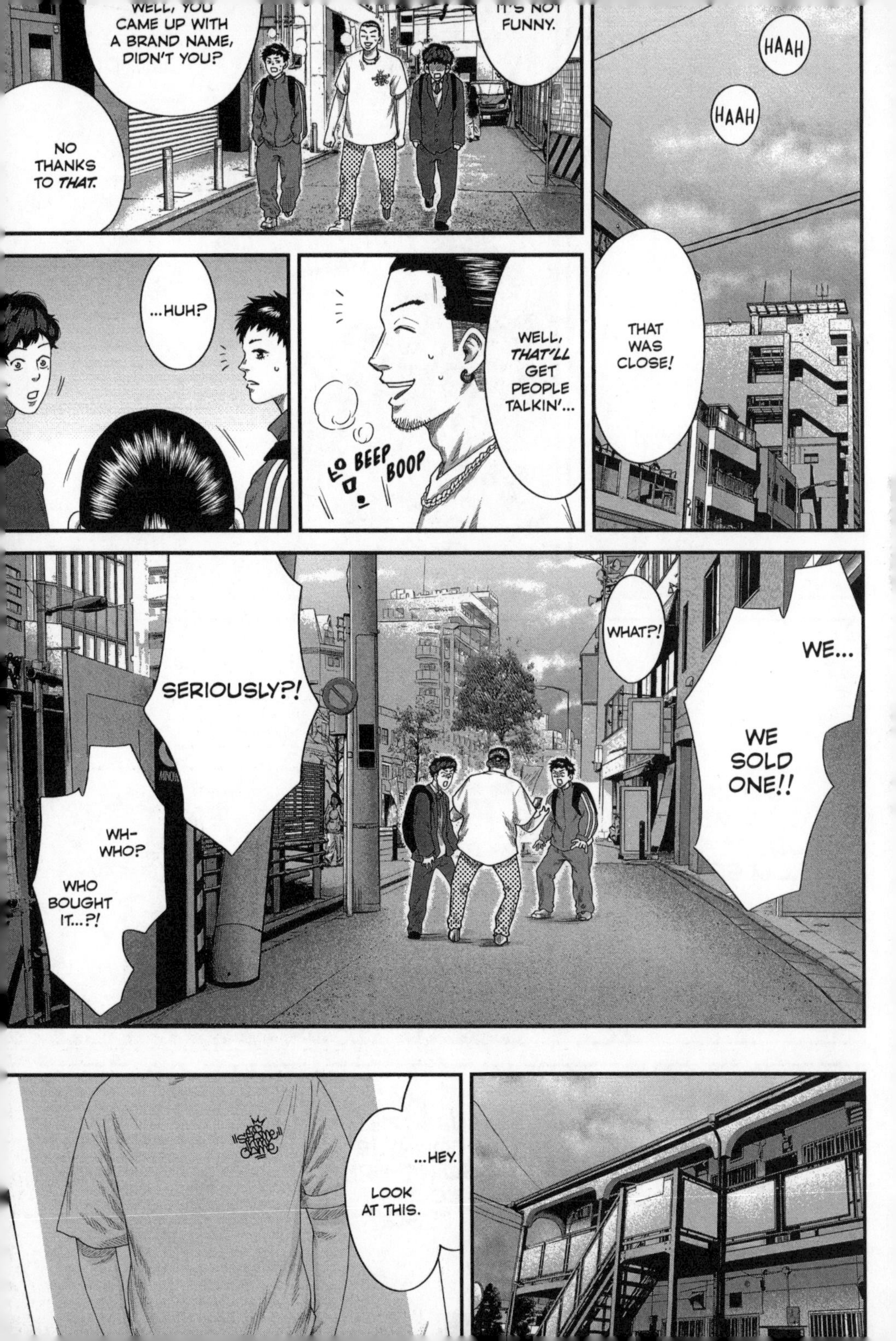
HAAH
HAAH
THAT WAS CLOSE!
IT'S NOT FUNNY.
WELL, YOU CAME UP WITH A BRAND NAME, DIDN'T YOU?
NO THANKS TO *THAT.*
WELL, *THAT'LL* GET PEOPLE TALKIN'...
BEEP BOOP
...HUH?
WE...
WE SOLD ONE!!
WHAT?!
SERIOUSLY?!
WH- WHO?
WHO BOUGHT IT...?!
...HEY.
LOOK AT THIS.

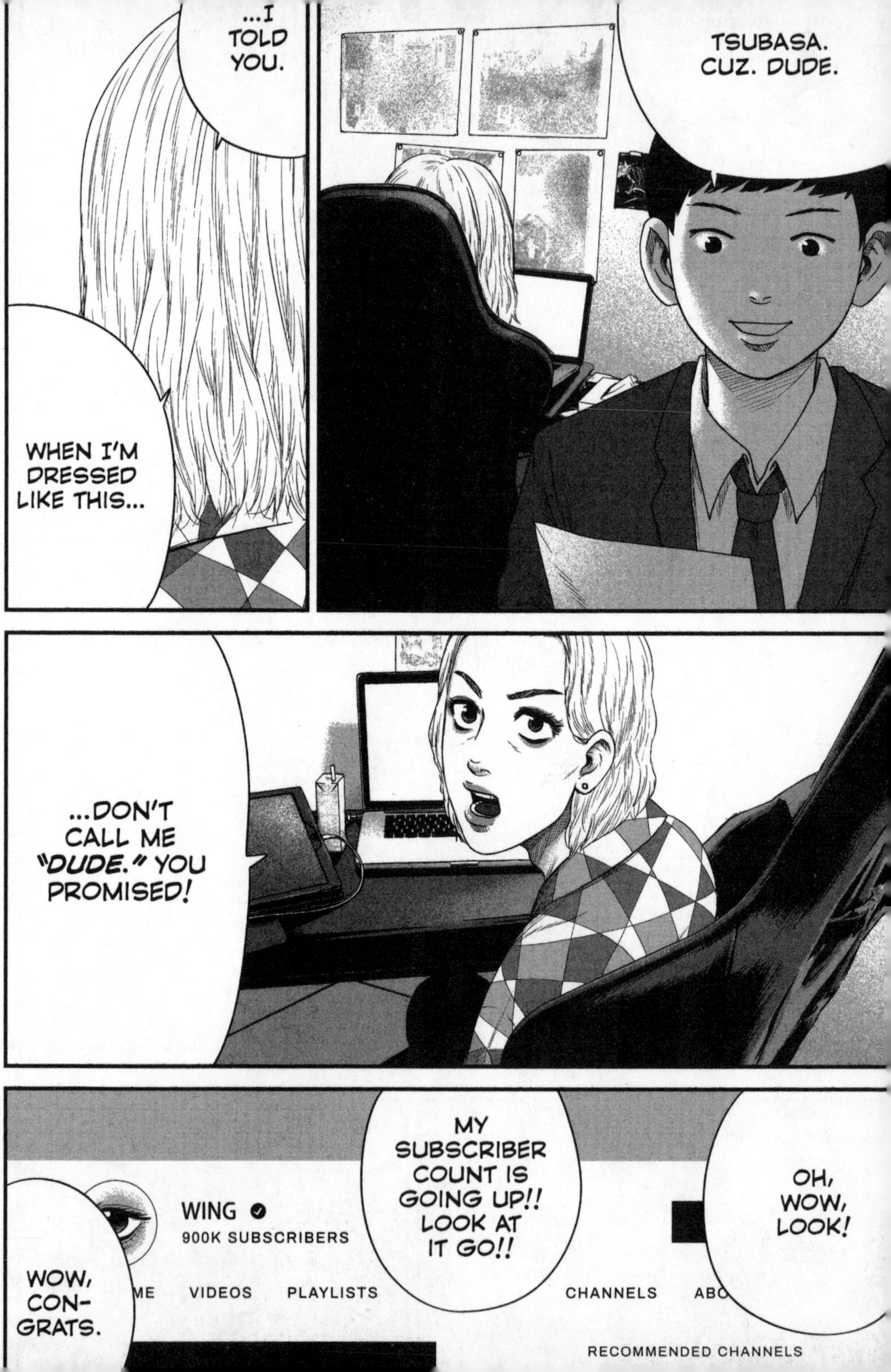
TSUBASA. CUZ. DUDE.
...I TOLD YOU.
WHEN I'M DRESSED LIKE THIS...
...DON'T CALL ME "DUDE." YOU PROMISED!
OH, WOW, LOOK!
MY SUBSCRIBER COUNT IS GOING UP!! LOOK AT IT GO!!
WING
900K SUBSCRIBERS
VIDEOS
PLAYLISTS
CHANNELS
RECOMMENDED CHANNELS
WOW, CON-GRATS.

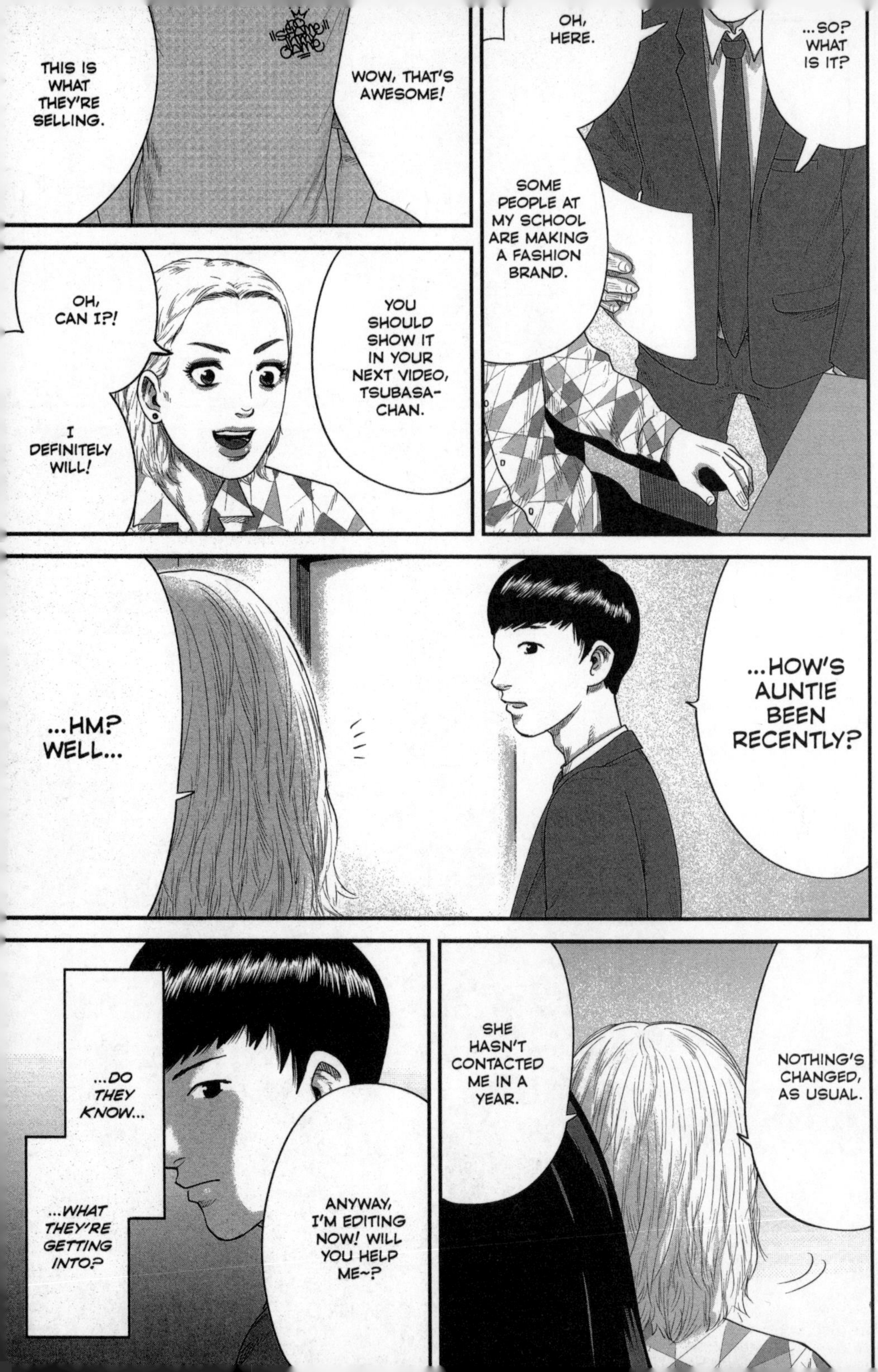
...SO? WHAT IS IT?
OH, HERE.
SOME PEOPLE AT MY SCHOOL ARE MAKING A FASHION BRAND.
WOW, THAT'S AWESOME!
THIS IS WHAT THEY'RE SELLING.
YOU SHOULD SHOW IT IN YOUR NEXT VIDEO, TSUBASA-CHAN.
OH, CAN I?!
I DEFINITELY WILL!
...HOW'S AUNTIE BEEN RECENTLY?
...HM? WELL...
NOTHING'S CHANGED, AS USUAL.
SHE HASN'T CONTACTED ME IN A YEAR.
...DO THEY KNOW...
...WHAT THEY'RE GETTING INTO?
ANYWAY, I'M EDITING NOW! WILL YOU HELP ME~?

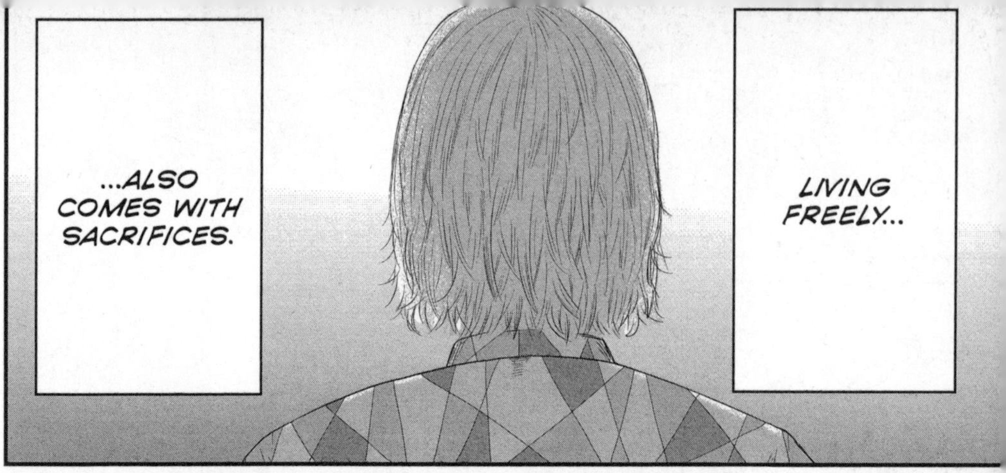
LIVING FREELY...
...ALSO COMES WITH SACRIFICES.

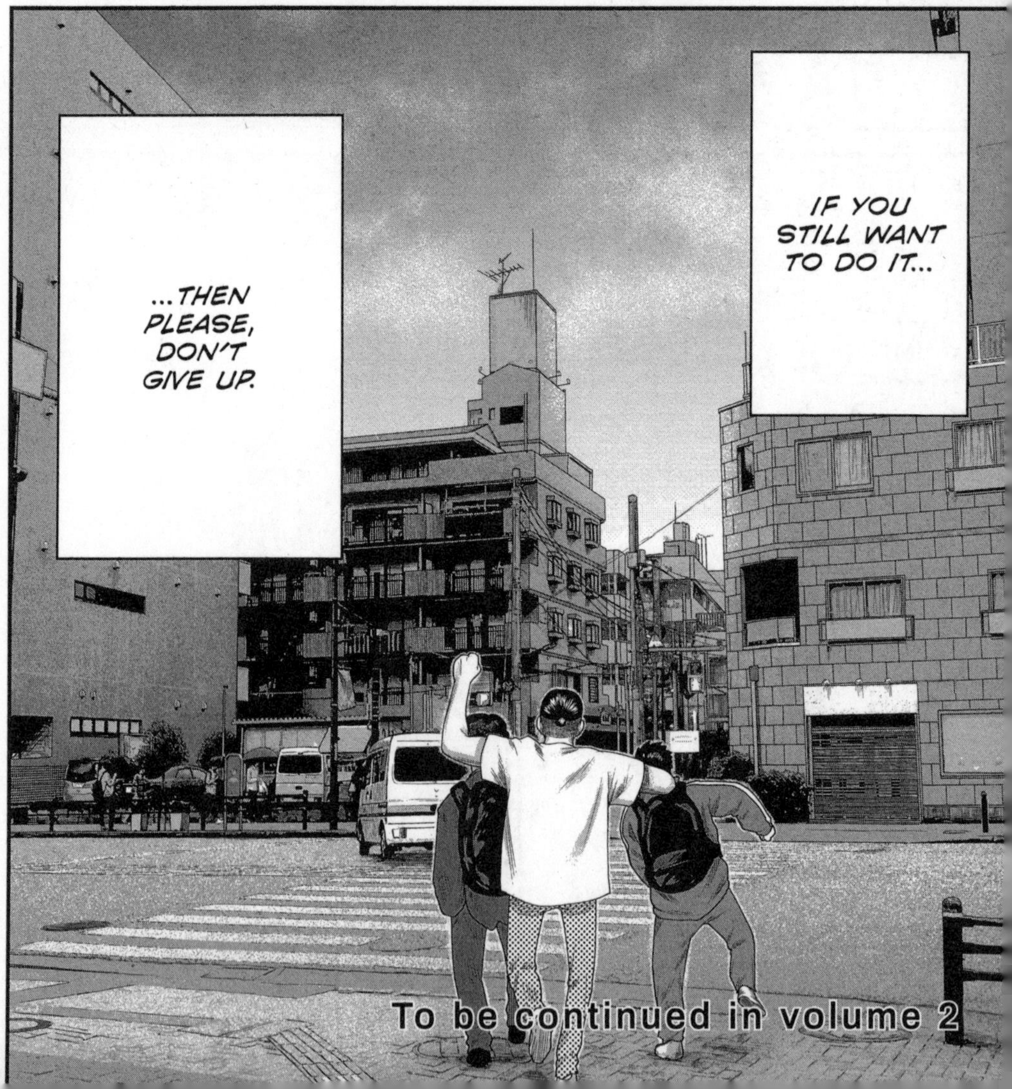
IF YOU STILL WANT TO DO IT...
...THEN PLEASE, DON'T GIVE UP.
To be continued in volume 2

SPECIAL THANKS

FEATURED WORK

Artist | Shintaro Wein
https://www.shintarowein.com

Graphic Designer | AK! (A.K.I.)
Art Director | SAYAKA (Twitter / Instagram: @SAYAKACHAN)

DATA COLLABORATION

kahoko (TikTok ID: @kaho7911)

Narumi Kitagawa

Salix. Kousuke Kuroyanagi

JETLINK (Instagram: @jetlinkmovie)

Talking Tshirts – Shun Inanuma
Talking Tshirts – Mineo

SUGARHILL – Rikuya Hayashi

DARGO (Instagram: @dargo_japan)
/ DARGO studio and store: 2-1-14, Tainoshima, Minami-ku, Kumamoto city, Kumamoto

HARDCORE CHOCOLATE – MUNE

HEADGOONIE – Miki Ooyagi (Twitter/Instagram: @headgoonie)

SPECIAL VOLUME DESIGN

fake graphics – Akito Sumiyoshi

STAFF

Igarashi
Ryuusei Terada
Taiga Miyahara
Pankue
Misaki Yoshimura

EDITORS

Hidemi Shiraki
Haruhito Uwai
Special Volume Editors
Tomohiro Ebitani
The Young Magazine editorial team

I'd like to express my gratitude to my family,
friends, teachers, seniors, and to
everyone who has supported me.

INTERVIEW WITH *BOYS RUN THE RIOT* AUTHOR
KEITO GAKU

Kodansha Comics: Congratulations on the English release of *Boys Run the Riot*! How did you react when you found out the series was going to be released in English?

Keito Gaku: I wasn't expecting it at all, so it was a huge surprise. Most of all, I feel very grateful.

KC: It's easy to assume that *Boys Run the Riot* pulls from a number of personal experiences, but were there any other inspirations for the characters or story of this manga?

KG: I drew a lot of inspiration from people I've met in my past and the people around me. Whenever I didn't know something, particularly when it came to people involved in fashion, I reached out to designers and people who run fashion brands for some insight. I applied what I learned from a lot of them to my work.

KC: You drew new cover illustrations for the English volumes of *Boys Run the Riot*. Can you talk about what the process was like to draw the new illustrations?

KG: The U.S. editorial staff came up with some design ideas and rough ideas for the illustrations, which they then shared with me, and this helped it go smoothly. They also gave me plenty of time before the deadline, so I could take my time drawing it. I was really happy that I could draw characters who hadn't been shown in color before in the series.

KC: I'm sure for many readers, both in Japan and abroad, *Boys Run the Riot* may be the first manga they ever read written by and featuring a transgender main character. Before you started working on *Boys Run the Riot*, were there any manga series that you read that featured transgender characters where, as you were reading, you thought "Oh, that's me!"?

KG: I've not read many manga works about transgender people. And out of the ones I have, they tend to be about transgender women, so I don't think there are many stories that I could personally relate to. However, I think that I was probably moved in some way by stories with protagonists who face oppression and really struggle to live as themselves, regardless of gender.

KC: While *Boys Run the Riot* was being serialized, did you receive a lot of fan letters from LGBTQ+ and transgender readers that related to Ryo or any of the other characters?

KG: People have sent me feedback on my work through social media, but I haven't received any physical letters.

KC: Prior to *Boys Run the Riot*, you made your manga debut with the one-shot *Light*, which won the 77th Tetsuya Chiba Prize. While the one-shot was also about a transgender high school student, fashion didn't play as large a role in the story as it does in *Boys Run the Riot*. What led you to add that element to *Boys Run the Riot* and make it such an important part of Ryo's character?

KG: The aim of this manga was to depict the feelings of Ryo, the transgender main character, and to portray his growth in a coming-of-age tale, so I needed some other point of growth for him than just his transition. Fashion is deeply related to identity and gender, so it was easy to tell the story of Ryo's struggles with fashion as the theme. On top of that, I thought that the fashion world was something that even a high schooler could try and take on if they had the passion for it.

KC: Graffiti art also plays a role in the world of *Boys Run the Riot*. What is it about this style of art that serves as an outlet for Ryo?

KG: I put graffiti in the story as a way for Ryo to express his individuality within the fashion world. Although it is graffiti, it is a way of painting pictures, which is familiar to me as an artist. It was easier for me to imagine entering the world of fashion by bringing the story closer to what I'm familiar with.

KC: One of the most poignant scenes in Chapter 1 is when Ryo is struggling with how to vocalize his gender identity to the world, and he says, "It's ok if the only one who knows the real me is me," a sentiment which many transgender individuals can likely relate to or have felt themselves. Are there any scenes in *Boys Run the Riot* inspired by your own personal experience?

KG: The fact that Ryo hates his uniform and always comes to school in a jersey comes

from my own experience. A lot of Ryo's inner conflict about his body and mind are also things I have felt and thought a lot about before. Throughout the series, Ryo and his friends grapple with monetizing their lived experiences as LGBTQ+ people, which is something that I also went through while making this series. It kind of felt like I was working these things out alongside Ryo and his friends as I drew their story.

KC: Do you have a favorite scene (or scenes) from volume 1 of *Boys Run the Riot*?

KG: I like the final scene [in Chapter 1] with the graffiti art. I was able to create a scene that exceeded my own expectations, which was thanks in no small part to the artist who provided me the artwork for that scene.

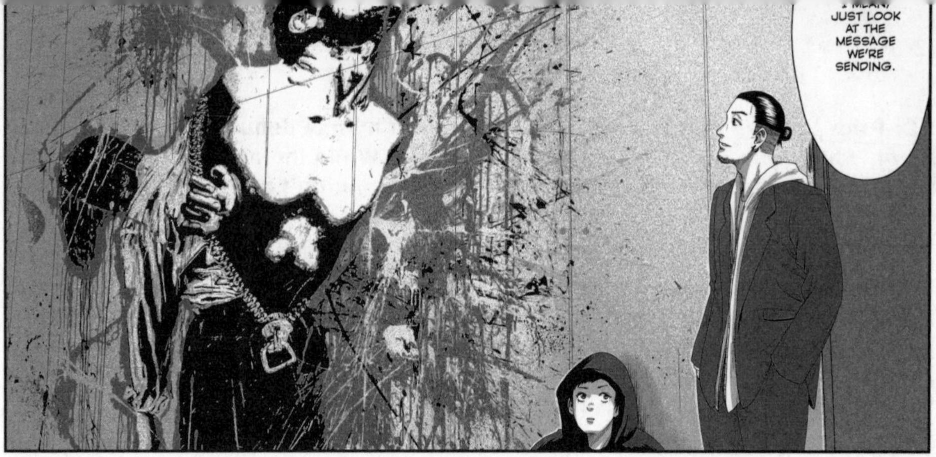
JUST LOOK AT THE MESSAGE WE'RE SENDING.

KC: With his willingness to want to learn more about and understand Ryo, Jin is a great example of someone who is not only a good friend, but a good ally. Do you have any advice for family members or friends of transgender and LGBTQ+ individuals on how they can support and better understand their transgender family members, friends, or peers?

KG: Everyone has different kinds of relationships with their family and friends, so I don't think there's one absolute rule for how people should treat transgender people.

I often hear trans people say that they simply don't want to be asked unpleasant questions about what their body looks like or what their sex life is like, but I think that most people wouldn't like being asked such questions, transgender or not.

Personally, I don't want my friends and family to have to be too cautious about how they treat me, but that doesn't mean I want them to brazenly ask me whatever questions they like. I just want to be treated equally, without them fixating on my gender.

KC: Manga artists are often known to be private about their personal lives, especially LGBTQ+ manga artists when asked about their gender identity and sexuality. You're done quite a lot of interviews in Japan about *Boys Run the Riot*, and how being a transgender man influences the kind of manga you want to create. Have you experienced any challenges or difficulties as a result of being so outspoken and honest about your identity?

KG: I actually haven't experienced many so far. However, I usually don't come out as trans unless it's necessary, but now when I meet new people and start talking about my job, I almost always end up having to come out as trans, which is a bit annoying. I don't know yet if it would, but I'm also interested to see how coming out as trans might affect my future work when I draw manga about any other themes.

KC: What do you hope transgender or LGBTQ+ readers can learn from reading *Boys Run the Riot* and from your personal experience as an out transgender manga artist?

KG: This manga was created from my own experiences, and I think that it was because of that that I was able to debut as the manga artist I wanted to be.

I think I was able to use those experiences to my advantage in my work. I know it's easier said than done to internalize this way of thinking, but I hope that I can show people through my work that you can live while using your experiences, instead of being trapped by them.

KC: At the end of volume 1, the reader is briefly introduced to Kashiwabara's cousin, Tsubasa, who's genderqueer. Tsubasa mentions that they haven't been in contact with their mother for a year, and Kashiwabara later states that "Living freely also comes with sacrifices." Do you have any advice to transgender and LGBTQ+ individuals who may be struggling to come out, or have faced adversity from their friends or family after having come out?

KG: Personally, I also still have a lot of problems with figuring out how to interact with family, friends, and relatives. As for my parents, I was half-forced to create a situation where they had to accept me, so I don't think I'm in any position to give advice on these matters.

However, I think that the person you're coming out to also needs time to process it, just as you probably took years to process it yourself before coming out. You might be worried about rejection or hurting people, and although it might be irresponsible to say this, I really feel that time heals all wounds. If you have the courage to tell them, then all you can do after that is show them that you're putting your all into living happily as your authentic self and doing your best to be positive and face the future.

KC: What do you hope to convey to young transgender boys and men with *Boys Run the Riot*?

KG: I know you must be worried about a lot of things, particularly if you're a teenager, but I hope that you can find a reason to keep going and something to pour your heart and soul into, like Ryo does with fashion. With this manga, I wanted to show how amazing it is to find something like that.

However, for the people who hide their transgender identity and blend into society, they could be very anxious having this manga in their workplace and might even think that it's unnecessary. If you're one of those people, I'm sorry. If we ever meet, let's go get a drink somewhere.

KC: Finally, do you have any last words for the U.S. fans of *Boys Run the Riot* who will be picking up the English edition?

KG: I've wanted to visit the U.S. the most out of any country for a very long time, but I never would have imagined that my own work would end up there before I did. I'm even more curious to see how this manga will be received there than in Japan, so I can't wait to hear what people think. I look forward to working with you on *Boys Run the Riot*.

TRANSLATION NOTES

BINDING, page 5
In panels 2 and 3, we see Ryo binding his chest, a practice common among transgender and nonbinary individuals to reduce the appearance of a person's chest to traditionally appear more masculine. Transgender people might bind their chests in order to relieve their gender dysphoria (see following page). When binding, please remember to do so responsibly: remember to take breaks, and to never bind using elastic bandages or tape, wear a binder that is too small for your body, or bind for more than eight hours. If you experience any pain while binding, take off your binder immediately.

-CHAN, page 8
In Japanese, people will often address one another using honorifics as a form respect or endearment (similar to using Mr., Ms., or Mx. in English). Depending on the honorific one uses when speaking to someone, it can give insight into the nature of the relationship between the two characters, as well as how close the characters are. Here, Chika calls Ryo Ryo-*chan,* with the honorific *-chan* being used to express endearment and signify that the two are close friends. *-chan* often implies as sense of childish cuteness and is mostly used towards girls, but can also be used to address little children, pets, and anything considered cute.

GYARU, page 9
Gyaru, though initially borrowed from the English term "girl" and "gal", has since become a subculture of Japanese street fashion. *Gyaru* typically bleach and dye their hair lighter, wear a lot of make-up and gaudy accessories, and often tan their skin. *Gyaru* are considered to be cheerful, sociable, and trendy, but, because of their appearance, are also sometimes thought of as vain, shallow, or airheaded.

-KUN, page 9
An honorific often attached to the names of boys or younger men. As with most honorifics, though, there's some nuance to the exact use of *-kun*, and it can also be used in cases of superiors addressing or referring to juniors or subordinates, such as a teacher addressing a student, or a boss mentioning an employee.

"OH, ME TOO."; "I-I MEAN... IF I *HAD* TO CHOOSE A GIRL, LIKE *ME*..." pages 9 and 10
In Japanese, Ryo first refers to himself using the first-person pronoun *ore*, a pronoun most often exclusively used by men, and which gives the connotation of masculinity or roughness. Ryo's classmates are surprised by his use of *ore* to refer to himself for this reason. Seeing his classmates' reaction, Ryo then switches to the personal pronoun *uchi,* which is commonly used by girls.

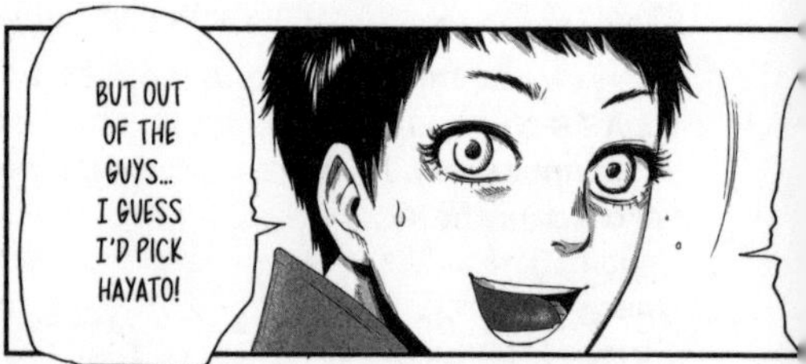
BUT OUT OF THE GUYS... I GUESS I'D PICK HAYATO!

-SAN, page 10
One of the most commonly heard Japanese honorifics, *-san* is used to convey general politeness, and is equivalent to referring to someone as Mr., Ms., Mx., etc.

GENDER IDENTITY DISORDER, page 19
In the United States, the term "gender identity disorder" has not been used in medical settings since 2013, being referred to exclusively as "gender dysphoria" to remove the stigma of the term "disorder." In Japan, as of 2020, gender dysphoria continues to be categorized as a medical disorder called "gender identity disorder," as it is in this book that Ryo picks up.

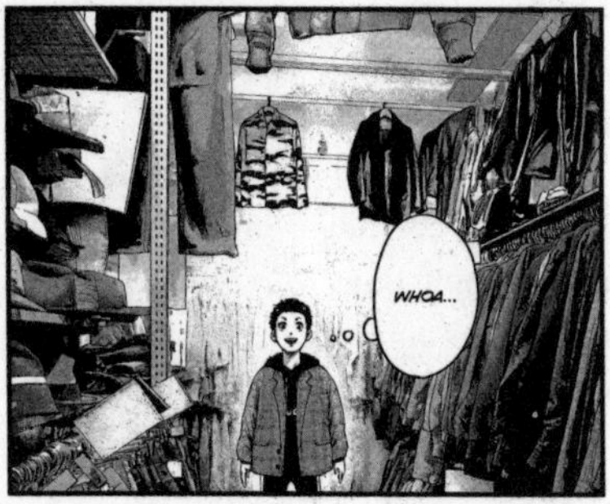
WHOA...

POP-UP STORE, page 27
As the name implies, a pop-up store is a temporary retail space that will often remain open for only a few days to a few weeks before closing down. Pop-up stores may sometimes serve as a store's soft opening to test their popularity before deciding to open up a permanent location, or may be timed to open during a specific holiday season or in conjunction with an event. Pop-up stores have grown in popularity in recent years, and are most often found in the apparel, toy, and food and beverage industries.

"WANNA CHAT AT A CHEAP RESTAURANT?", page 82
Ryo is specifically referring to a family restaurant here, shortened to *famiresu* in Japanese. Family restaurants in Japan are often chains catering to people of all ages, and are also popular with students due to their very low-cost meals.

-SENSEI, page 106
Literally translated as "person born before another" or "one who comes before", the honorific *-sensei* is often used to either address someone directly or after a person's name, and means "teacher." The term *sensei* can be used to refer not just to school teachers, but also to anyone who is regarded as an instructor or master of a subject, such as a doctor, novelist, manga artist, etc.

TRANSCRIPT, page 149
At Japanese high schools, students are not just graded on their classes, but their attitude towards school life and extra-curricular activities as well. In addition to their grades, any record of a student's involvement in any school sports or clubs, and the details of their involvement, would also likely be mentioned on their transcript as well. This transcript is shown to future schools that the student applies to.

CLASS 2-A, page 198
In Japanese schools, students are assigned to a homeroom where they spend most of the school day, and it's the teachers, not the students, who move from room to room between periods. These homerooms are designated with a combination of a number, representing the class year, and a letter. So 2-A, for example, would be second-year, class A. (The individual classes are sometimes known in Japanese as *kumi,* or "groups.")

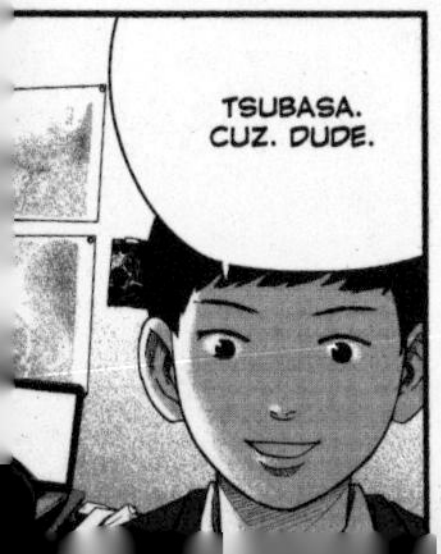
TSUBASA. CUZ. DUDE.

"CUZ. DUDE.", page 218
In the original Japanese, Kashiwabara addresses Tsubasa as *Tsubasa nii-chan*, with *nii-chan* being a word of affection and respect towards an older brother, or an older-brother figure. In this instance, the kanji characters used to write *nii-chan* are different from the usual characters used for "older brother," and literally translate to "elder male cousin."

ACKNOWLEDGMENTS

I first discovered manga artist Keito Gaku after reading his one-shot *Light*, about a transgender high school student coming to terms with his gender identity, after it had been awarded the 77th Tetsuya Chiba Prize. As a nonbinary, transgender manga fan who longed to discover more of those narratives in manga, I couldn't wait to read more of his work. I was ecstatic when the serialization of *Boys Run the Riot* was announced, and completely gobsmacked when I read the first volume in Japanese. As someone who was struggling to understand their gender identity, like Ryo, and who found comfort and peace only when certain clothes allowed me to express my true self to the world, I had never read a manga more poignant nor relatable. I was immediately enamored with how *Boys Run the Riot* so authentically captured such a relatable transgender experience: from the struggles and anxieties one feels when first trying to understand and put a name to their gender identity, to the euphoria one feels when they finally discover and can express oneself, as well as the relief and solace that comes with having the support of friends, family, and allies who love and accept you for who you are.

Having the opportunity to edit the English language edition of *Boys Run the Riot* has been a dream come true, and the publication of this important, poignant series in the U.S. would not have been possible without the support and hard work of so many people. Thank you to author Keito Gaku, who so generously not only drew brand-new cover illustrations for the English edition of *Boys Run the Riot*, but also (virtually) sat down with us for a Kodansha Comics-exclusive English language interview; to Kodansha USA staff Kiichiro Sugawara, Maya Rosewood, Yae Sahashi, Tomo Tran, and Ivan Salazar for their support and championship of this series, from license to publication; to Ben Applegate, Noelle Webster, Haruko Hashimoto, and the rest of my colleagues at Penguin Random House and Kodansha Comics, for their support, encouragement, and the creative freedom they gave me to arrange to have an all-transgender localization team behind the English-language release of this amazing, one-of-a-kind transgender manga from a transgender artist; to Leo McDonagh, for not only his fantastic translation, but whose excitement and passion for this series was palpable in every line he translated; to Ashley Caswell, for their amazing lettering work bringing the *Boys Run the Riot* reading experience into English; to Shinichiro Tanaka, for his assistance coordinating the interview translation with Gaku-sensei into Japanese; to Stephen Pakula, Angela Zurlo, and Emi Lotto at Penguin Random House for helping me bring the packaging and cover finish ideas I had for this series to life; to Phil Balsman, for his extraordinary cover design, and for going the extra mile from the very beginning to give this series the unique, important, and special design it deserved; and to everyone else who supported this series and the English localization of this first volume.

Whether you're transgender, or have someone in your life that is, I hope this first volume of *Boys Run the Riot* resonated with you, and reminded you that you're not alone.

Thank you for reading, and we hope you continue to support the English release of *Boys Run the Riot*!

Tiff Joshua TJ Ferentini
Editor, Kodansha Comics

BOYS RUN

ボーイズ・ラン・ザ・ライオット

THE RIOT

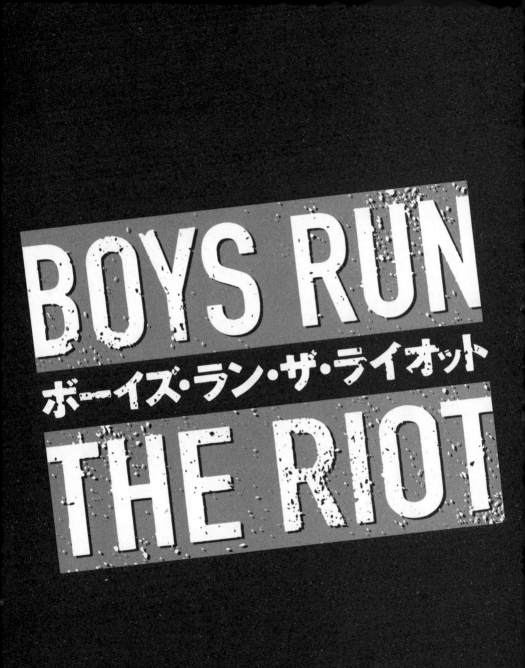

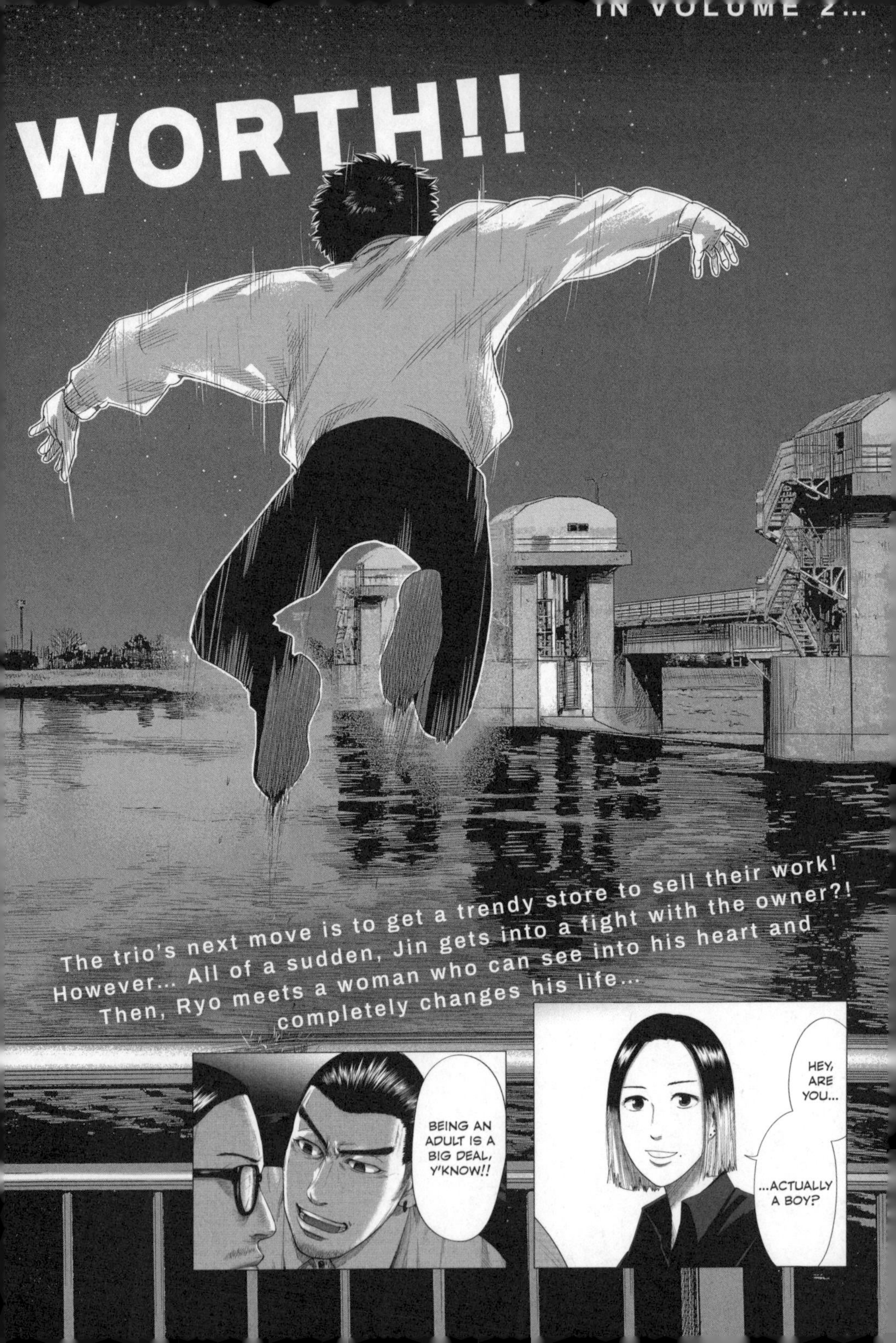
IN VOLUME 2...
WORTH!!
The trio's next move is to get a trendy store to sell their work! However... All of a sudden, Jin gets into a fight with the owner?! Then, Ryo meets a woman who can see into his heart and completely changes his life...
HEY, ARE YOU...
...ACTUALLY A BOY?
BEING AN ADULT IS A BIG DEAL, Y'KNOW!!

WE'RE GONNA PROVE OUR
BOY MEETS NEW WORLD!!
BOYS RUN THE RIOT VOLUME 2
COMING SOON!!

The slow-burn queer romance that'll sweep you off your feet!

10 DANCE

Inouesatoh presents

"A FANTASTIC DEBUT VOLUME... ONE OF MY FAVORITE BOOKS OF THE YEAR..."
— AiPT!

"10 DANCE IS A MUST-READ FOR ANYONE WHO'S ENJOYED MANGA AND ANIME ABOUT COMPETITIVE DANCE (ON OR OFF THE ICE!)."
—Anime UK News

Shinya Sugiki, the dashing lord of Standard Ballroom, and Shinya Suzuki, passionate king of Latin Dance: The two share more than just a first name and a love of the sport. They each want to become champion of the 10-Dance Competition, which means they'll need to learn the other's specialty dances, and who better to learn from than the best? But old rivalries die hard, and things get further complicated when they realize there might be more between them than an uneasy partnership...

KC
KODANSHA COMICS

A BL romance between a good boy who didn't know he was waiting for a hero, and a bad boy who comes to his rescue!

Masahiro Setagawa doesn't believe in heroes, but wishes he could: He's found himself in a gang of small-time street bullies, and with no prospects for a real future. But when high school teacher (and scourge of the streets) Kousuke Ohshiba comes to his rescue, he finds he may need to start believing after all... in heroes, and in his budding feelings, too.

Hitorijime My Hero

Memeco Arii

KC
KODANSHA
COMICS

CARDCAPTOR SAKURA
COLLECTOR'S EDITION
C L A M P

Ten-year-old Sakura
Kinomoto lives a pretty
normal life with her
older brother, Tōya, and
widowed father, Fujitaka—
until the day she discovers
a strange book in her
father's library, and her
life takes a magical turn...

- A deluxe large-format
  hardcover edition
  of CLAMP's shojo
  manga classic
- All-new foil-
  stamped cover art
  on each volume
- Comes with exclusive
  collectible art card

17 years after the original *Cardcaptor Sakura* manga ended, CLAMP returns with more magical adventures from a beloved manga classic!

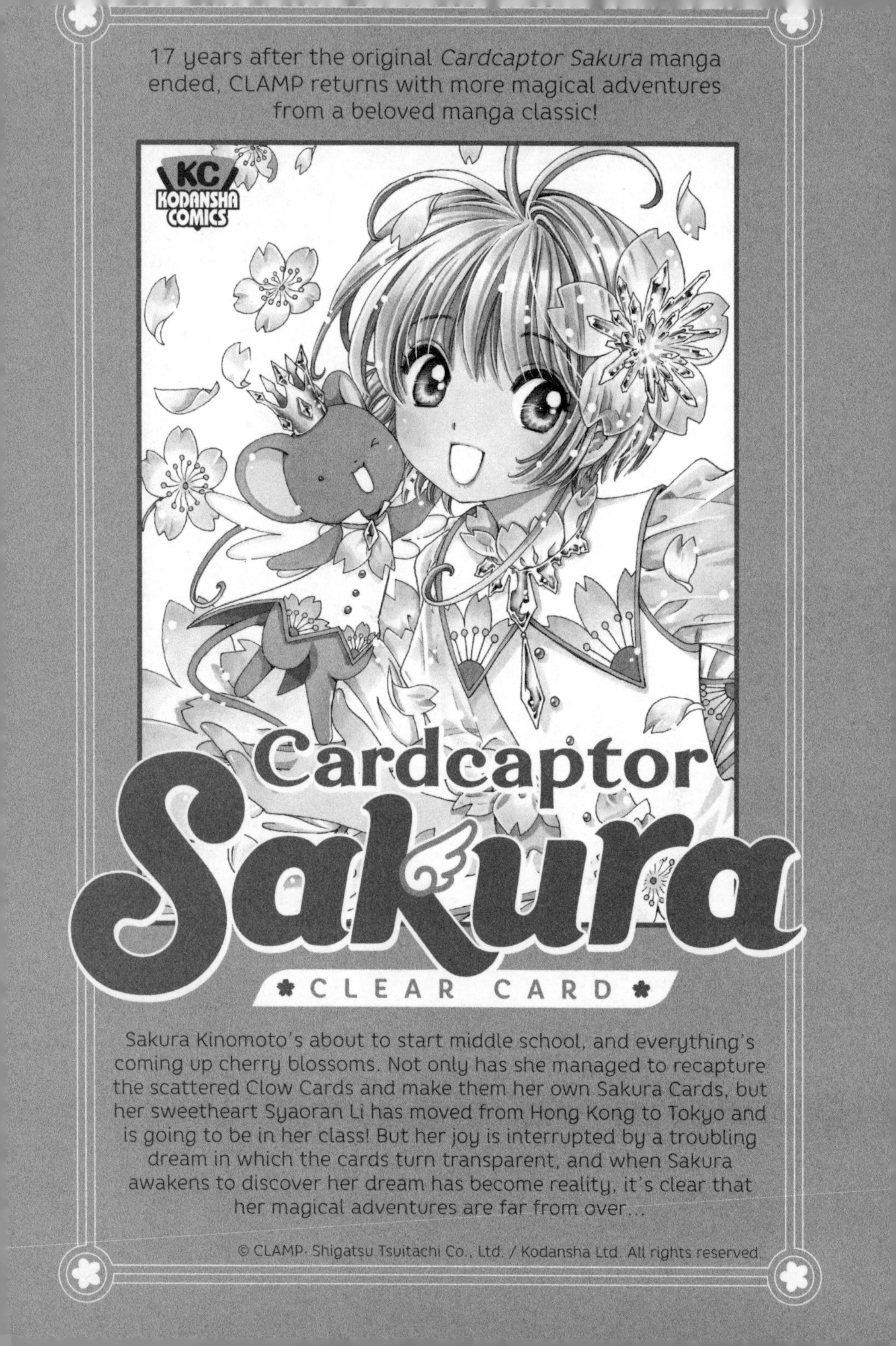
KC
KODANSHA COMICS
Cardcaptor
Sakura
CLEAR CARD

Sakura Kinomoto's about to start middle school, and everything's coming up cherry blossoms. Not only has she managed to recapture the scattered Clow Cards and make them her own Sakura Cards, but her sweetheart Syaoran Li has moved from Hong Kong to Tokyo and is going to be in her class! But her joy is interrupted by a troubling dream in which the cards turn transparent, and when Sakura awakens to discover her dream has become reality, it's clear that her magical adventures are far from over...

CLAMP

1 Chobits

20TH ANNIVERSARY EDITION

"A wonderfully entertaining story that would be a great installment in anybody's manga collection."
— Anime News Network

"CLAMP is an all-female manga-creating team whose feminine touch shows in this entertaining, sci-fi soap opera."
— Publishers Weekly

Poor college student Hideki is down on his luck. All he wants is a good job, a girlfriend, and his very own "persocom"—the latest and greatest in humanoid computer technology. Hideki's luck changes one night when he finds Chi—a persocom thrown out in a pile of trash. But Hideki soon discovers that there's much more to his cute new persocom than meets the eye.

KC
KODANSHA
COMICS

MAGIC KNIGHT RAYEARTH

25TH ANNIVERSARY EDITION

CLAMP

A BELOVED CLASSIC MAKES ITS STUNNING RETURN IN THIS GORGEOUS, LIMITED EDITION BOX SET!

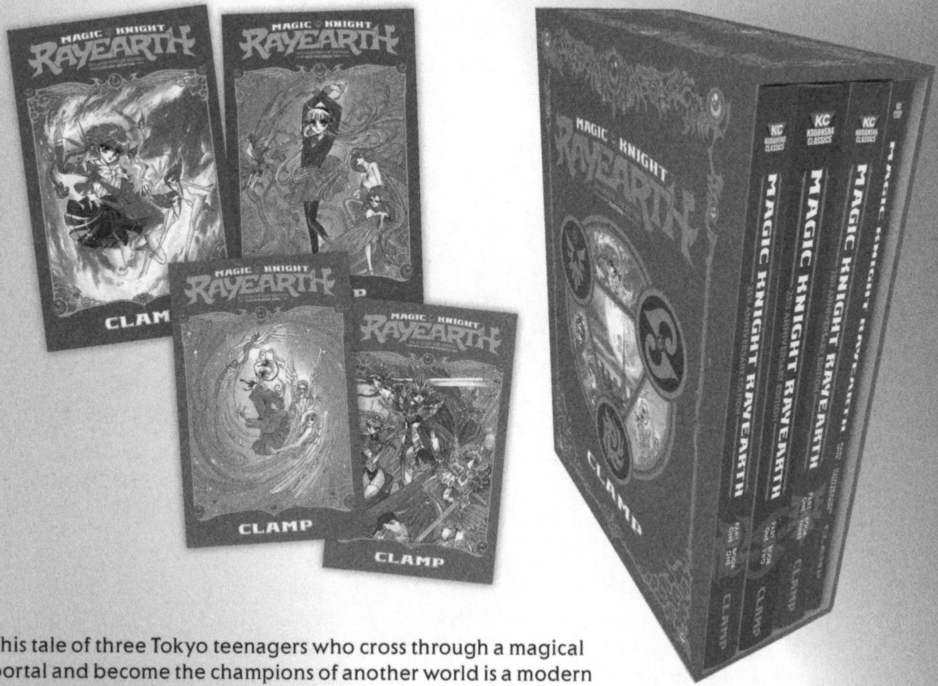

This tale of three Tokyo teenagers who cross through a magical portal and become the champions of another world is a modern manga classic. The box set includes three volumes of manga covering the entire first series of *Magic Knight Rayearth*, plus the series's super-rare full-color art book companion, all printed at a larger size than ever before on premium paper, featuring a newly-revised translation and lettering, and exquisite foil-stamped covers.

A strictly limited edition, this will be gone in a flash!

The beloved characters from *Cardcaptor Sakura* return in a brand new, reimagined fantasy adventure!

"[*Tsubasa*] takes readers on a fantastic ride that only gets more exhilarating with each successive chapter." —Anime News Network

In the Kingdom of Clow, an archaeological dig unleashes an incredible power, causing Princess Sakura to lose her memories. To save her, her childhood friend Syaoran must follow the orders of the Dimension Witch and travel alongside Kurogane, an unrivaled warrior; Fai, a powerful magician; and Mokona, a curiously strange creature, to retrieve Sakura's dispersed memories!

THE WORLD OF CLAMP!

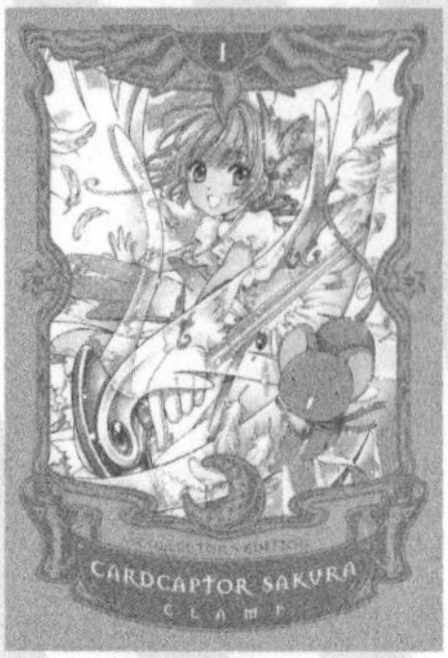
1
CARDCAPTOR SAKURA
CLAMP

Cardcaptor Sakura
Collector's Edition

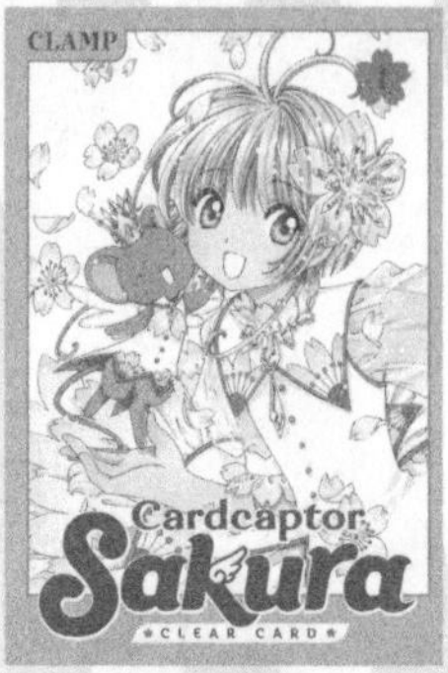
CLAMP
Cardcaptor
Sakura
CLEAR CARD

Cardcaptor Sakura:
Clear Card

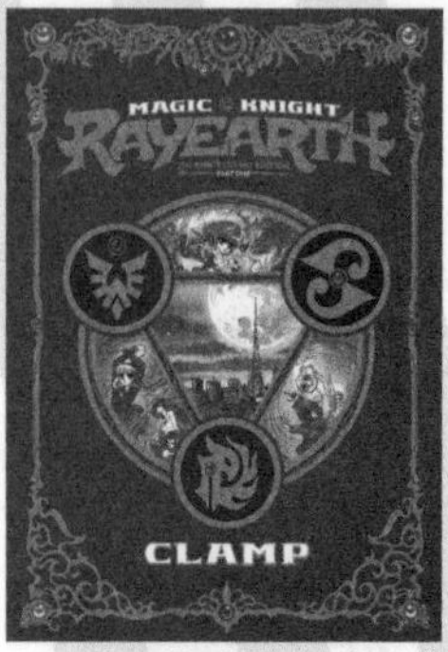
MAGIC KNIGHT
RAYEARTH
CLAMP

Magic Knight Rayearth
25th Anniversary Box Set

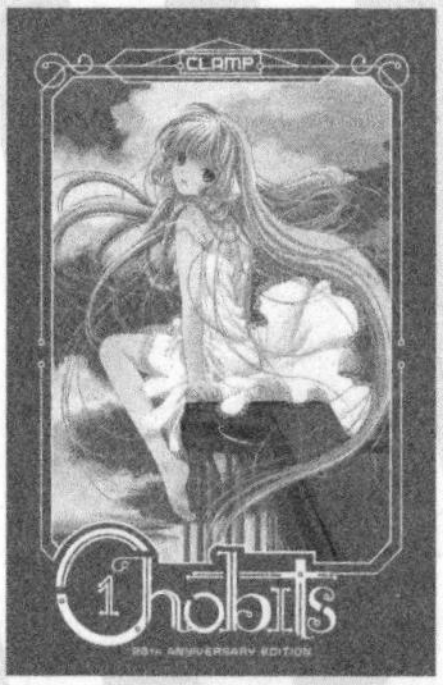
CLAMP
Chobits

Chobits

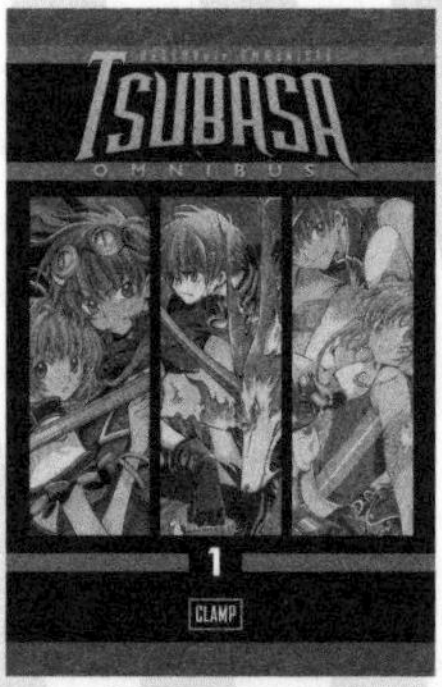
TSUBASA
OMNIBUS
1
CLAMP

TSUBASA Omnibus

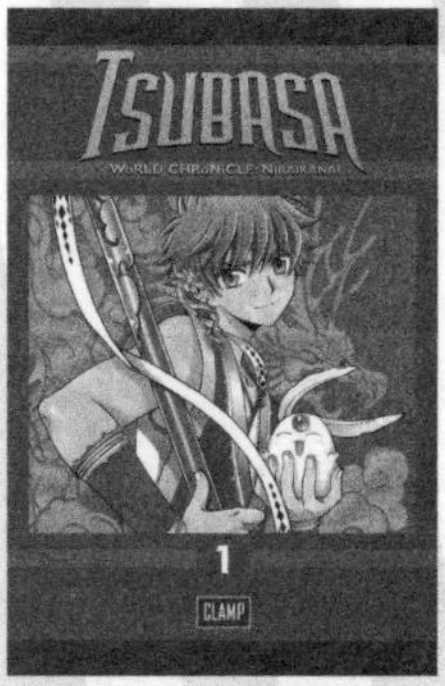
TSUBASA
1
CLAMP

TSUBASA WoRLD CHRoNiCLE

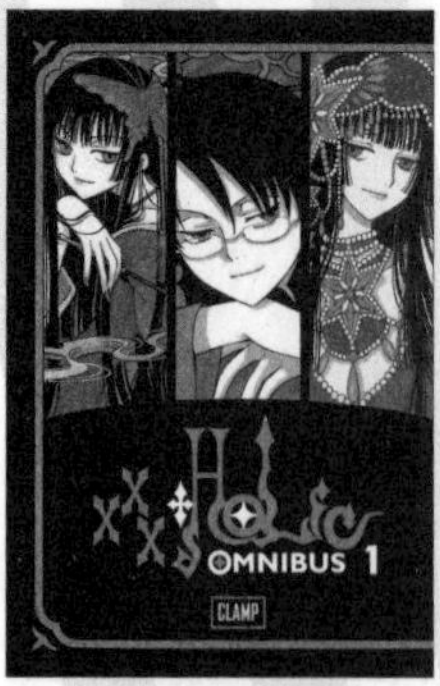
xxxHOLiC
OMNIBUS 1
CLAMP

xxxHOLiC Omnibus

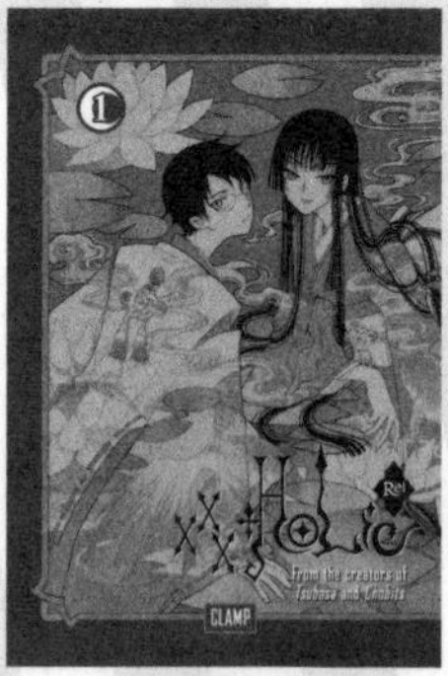
1
xxxHOLiC
CLAMP

xxxHOLiC Rei

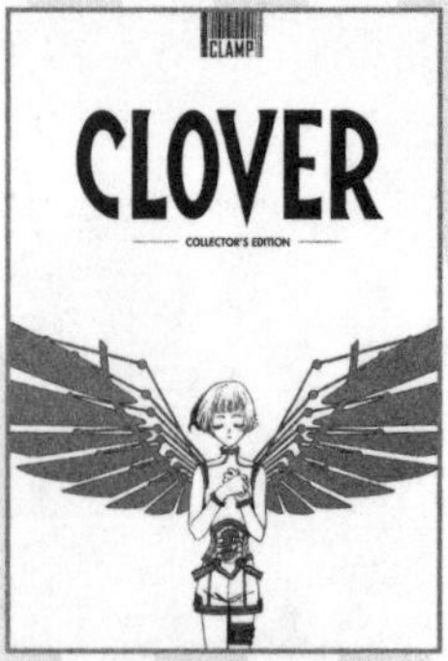
CLAMP
CLOVER
COLLECTOR'S EDITION

CLOVER Collector's Edition

Kodansha Comics welcomes you to explore the expansive world of CLAMP, the all-female artist collective that has produced some of the most acclaimed manga of the century. Our growing catalog includes icons like *Cardcaptor Sakura* and *Magic Knight Rayearth*, each crafted with CLAMP's one-of-a-kind style and characters!

Young characters and steampunk setting, like *Howl's Moving Castle* and *Battle Angel Alita*

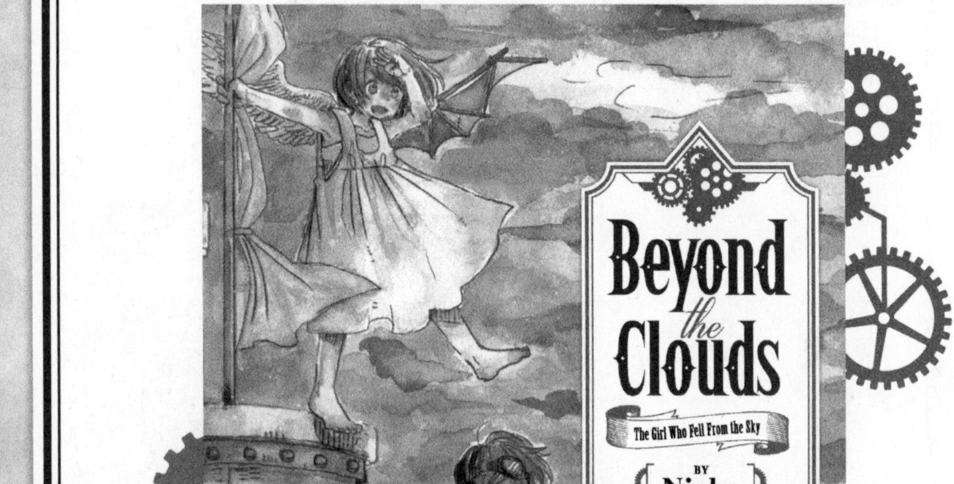
Beyond the Clouds
The Girl Who Fell From the Sky
BY Nicke
VOLUME 01
KC KODANSHA COMICS

Beyond the Clouds © 2018 Nicke / Ki-oon

A boy with a talent for machines and a mysterious girl whose wings he's fixed will take you beyond the clouds! In the tradition of the high-flying, resonant adventure stories of Studio Ghibli comes a gorgeous tale about the longing of young hearts for adventure and friendship!

A SMART, NEW ROMANTIC COMEDY FOR FANS OF *SHORTCAKE CAKE* AND *TERRACE HOUSE!*

A romance manga starring high school girl Meeko, who learns to live on her own in a boarding house whose living room is home to the odd (but handsome) Matsunaga-san. She begins to adjust to her new life away from her parents, but Meeko soon learns that no matter how far away from home she is, she's still a young girl at heart — especially when she finds herself falling for Matsunaga-san.

Knight of the ICE

Yayoi Ogawa

Knight of the Ice ©Yayoi Ogawa/Kodansha Ltd.

SKATING THRILLS AND ICY CHILLS WITH THIS NEW TINGLY ROMANCE SERIES!

A rom-com on ice, perfect for fans of *Princess Jellyfish* and *Wotakoi*. Kokoro is the talk of the figure-skating world, winning trophies and hearts. But little do they know... he's actually a huge nerd! From the beloved creator of *You're My Pet* (*Tramps Like Us*).

Chitose is a serious young woman, working for the health magazine *SASSO*. Or at least, she would be, if she wasn't constantly getting distracted by her childhood friend, international figure skating star Kokoro Kijinami! In the public eye and on the ice, Kokoro is a gallant, flawless knight, but behind his glittery costumes and breathtaking spins lies a secret: He's actually a hopelessly romantic otaku, who can only land his quad jumps when Chitose is on hand to recite a spell from his favorite magical girl anime!

A Kodansha Comics Trade Paperback Original
Boys Run the Riot 1 copyright © 2020 Keito Gaku
English translation copyright © 2021 Keito Gaku

All rights reserved.

Published in the United States by Kodansha Comics, an imprint of Kodansha USA Publishing, LLC, New York.

Publication rights for this English edition arranged through Kodansha Ltd., Tokyo.

First published in Japan in 2020 by Kodansha Ltd., Tokyo as *Boys Run the Riot*, volume 1.

ISBN 978-1-64651-248-5

Printed in the United States of America.

www.kodansha.us

9 8 7 6 5 4 3 2 1
Translation: Leo McDonagh
Lettering: Ashley Caswell
Editing: Tiff Joshua TJ Ferentini
Kodansha Comics edition cover design by Phil Balsman

Publisher: Kiichiro Sugawara

Director of publishing services: Ben Applegate
Associate director of operations: Stephen Pakula
Publishing services managing editors: Alanna Ruse, Madison Salters
Assistant production managers: Emi Lotto, Angela Zurlo
Logo and character art ©Kodansha USA Publishing, LLC